The Language of the Skies

CANADIAN PUBLIC ADMINISTRATION
SERIES

COLLECTION ADMINISTRATION PUBLIQUE
CANADIENNE

J. E. Hodgetts, *General Editor/Directeur général*
Roch Bolduc, *Directeur associé/Associate Editor*

The Institute of Public Administration of Canada
L'Institut d'administration publique du Canada

This series is sponsored by the Institute of Public
Administration of Canada as part of its constitutional
commitment to encourage research on contemporary
issues in Canadian public administration and public
policy, and to foster wider knowledge and understanding amongst practitioners and the concerned citizen.
There is no fixed number of volumes planned for the
series, but under the supervision of the Research
Committee of the Institute, the General Editor,
and the Associate Editor, efforts will be made to
ensure that significant areas will receive appropriate
attention.

L'Institut d'administration publique du Canada
commandite cette collection dans le cadre de ses
engagements statutaires. Il se doit de promouvoir la
recherche sur des problèmes d'actualité portant sur
l'administration publique et la détermination des poli-
tiques publiques ainsi que d'encourager les praticiens
et les citoyens intéressés à les mieux connaître et à les
mieux comprendre. Il n'a pas été prévu de nombre de
volumes donné pour la collection mais, sous la direction du Comité de recherche de l'Institut, du Directeur
général, et du Directeur associé, l'on s'efforce d'ac-
corder l'attention voulue aux questions importantes.

Canada and Immigration:
Public Policy and Public Concern
Freda Hawkins

The Biography of an Institution:
The Civil Service Commission of Canada, 1908–1967
J. E. Hodgetts, William McCloskey, Reginald
Whitaker, V. Seymour Wilson

An edition in French has been published under the
title *Histoire d'une institution: La Commission de la*
Fonction publique du Canada, 1908–1967,
by Les Presses de l'Université Laval

Old Age Pensions and Policy-Making in Canada
Kenneth Bryden

Provincial Governments as Employers:
A Survey of Public Personnel Administration
in Canada's Provinces
J. E. Hodgetts and O. P. Dwivedi

Transport in Transition:
The Reorganization of the Federal Transport Portfolio
John W. Langford

Initiative and Response:
The Adaptation of Canadian Federalism to
Regional Economic Development
Anthony G. S. Careless

Canada's Salesman to the World:
The Department of Trade and Commerce, 1892–1939
O. Mary Hill

Health Insurance and Canadian Public Policy:
The Seven Decisions that Created the Canadian
Health Insurance System
Malcolm G. Taylor

Conflict over the Columbia:
The Canadian Background to an Historic Treaty
Neil A. Swainson

L'Economiste et la chose publique
Jean-Luc Migué
(Published by Les Presses de l'Université du Québec)

Federalism, Bureaucracy, and Public Policy:
The Politics of Highway Transport Regulation
Richard J. Schultz

Federal-Provincial Collaboration:
The Canada–New Brunswick General Development Agreement
Donald J. Savoie

Judicial Administration in Canada
Perry S. Millar and Carl Baar

The Language of the Skies:
The Bilingual Air Traffic Control Conflict in Canada
Sandford F. Borins

An edition in French has been published under the title
*Le français dans les airs: le conflit du bilinguisme
dans le contrôle de la circulation aérienne au Canada*
by Les Editions Chenelière et Stanké

The Language
of the Skies

The Bilingual Air Traffic
Control Conflict in Canada

SANDFORD F. BORINS

The Institute of Public Administration of Canada
L'Institut d'administration publique du Canada

McGill-Queen's University Press
Kingston and Montreal

© The Institute of Public Administration of Canada /
L'Institut d'administration publique du Canada 1983

ISBN 0-7735-0402-8 (cloth)
ISBN 0-7735-0403-6 (paper)

Legal deposit 2nd quarter 1983
Bibliothèque nationale du Québec

Printed in Canada
Paperback edition reprinted 1983

Lines from "Trans-Canada" by F. R. Scott are reprinted with permission of The Canadian Publishers, McClelland and Stewart Limited, Toronto.

Lines from "The Second Coming" are reprinted with permission of Michael and Anne Yeats, Macmillan London Limited, and Macmillan Publishing Co., Inc., from *Collected Poems* of William Butler Yeats. Copyright 1924 by Macmillan Publishing Co., Inc., renewed 1952 by Bertha Georgie Yeats.

The cartoon by Aislin, "It's Old Charley Swiftfeathers Again," is reprinted with permission of the *Toronto Star*.

The woodcut by M. C. Escher, "Day and Night," is reproduced with permission of Visual Artists and Galleries Association, Inc. ©BEELDRECHT, Amsterdam / V.A.G.A., New York, Collection Haags Gemeentemusem—The Hague, 1981.

Canadian Cataloguing in Publication Data

Borins, Sandford F., 1949–
   The language of the skies
   (Canadian public administration series = Collection
   Administration publique canadienne)
   Co-published by the Institute of Public Administration of Canada.
   Includes index.
   ISBN 0-7735-0402-8 (bound). – ISBN 0-7735-0403-6
   (pbk.)
   1. Air traffic control, Bilingual – Quebec (Province).
   2. Air traffic control, Bilingual → Political
   aspects – Canada. 3. Language policy – Canada.
   4. Canada – English-French relations. I. Institute
   of Public Administration of Canada. I. Title.
   II. Series: Canadian public administration series.

TL725.3.T7B67   363.1'2472'09714   C82-095300-8

39,001

To my parents,
Sidney and Beverley Borins

Contents

CONTENTS

Illustrations

Preface

The election of the Parti Québécois in November 1976 occasioned a rethinking of the premises of Canadian nationhood, whether in fact it was possible to devise a set of institutions which would allow French and English Canadians to coexist within the same state. In the academic world, those who had long studied relations between English and French Canada or federal-provincial relations quickly responded with analyses of the current situation and recommendations for change. There were many others, myself included, who had always felt that French-English relations were an important subject, but who had never found the time to give it detailed study.

As I considered re-ordering my priorities, the controversy over bilingual air traffic control soon came to mind as an event which seemed to epitomize the tense and often hostile atmosphere of French-English relations which had preceded the election of the Parti Québécois. I had several vivid memories of its angriest moment — the pilots' strike in June 1976. I recalled hearing English Canadians who were generally liberal in their attitudes and sympathetic with the Quiet Revolution, affirming, as though from wide personal experience, that English *was* the international language of aviation. I felt a great sense of frustration because the elementary facts in the dispute (such as the number of countries with bilingual air traffic control and comparative accident records in countries with bilingual and unilingual air traffic control) were unavailable. Still worse, ignorance of the facts was no constraint on the expression of dogmatic opinion. After recalling these feelings and reading a few back issues of newspapers, I began to view this issue as a paradigm of how Canada could (or perhaps would) split up. By understanding what went wrong in this case, we might learn something about the conditions necessary to keep English and French Canada together. This book is the result of my attempt to unravel and piece together the facts and emotions that, together, fuelled the air traffic control crisis.

Acknowledgements

The process of writing this book has occupied much of my time for the last three years. Along the way, many institutions and individuals have provided support and encouragement, for which I am deeply grateful. Initial financial support for the writing of a case study, to be used for teaching purposes, came from the Public Policy Curricular Materials Development Program, which is administered jointly by the Rand Graduate Institute and the Duke University Institute of Policy Sciences and Public Affairs and funded by the Sloan Foundation. In order to expand the case study into a full-fledged book, I received a grant from the Institute for Research on Public Policy. Additional funds for research and writing were provided by the J. L. Kellogg Graduate School of Management, Northwestern University, the Faculty of Administrative Studies, York University and the University of Toronto / York University Joint Program in Transportation. Finally, this book has been published with the help of grants from the Faculty of Administrative Studies, York University, the University of Toronto / York University Joint Program in Transportation, and the Social Science Federation of Canada, using funds provided by the Social Sciences and Humanities Research Council of Canada. Publication has also been assisted by the Canada Council under its block grant program.

The assistance of the Institute of Public Administration of Canada, of whose Canadian Public Administration series this book is a volume, has been invaluable. Professor J. E. Hodgetts, general editor of the series, conducted a speedy but thorough editorial review, and Maurice Demers, assistant executive director of the Institute, played the role of a veritable impresario in orchestrating collaboration between author, funding agencies, and publisher. David Norton, editor of McGill-Queen's University Press, has smoothed and expedited the publication process and my manuscript editor, Joan Harcourt, has made many suggestions that have improved the manuscript.

My research assistants have been outstanding. Irène Lépine, then a graduate student in sociology at McGill University, conducted many of the first wave of interviews during the summer of 1978 and attended the hearings of the Commission of Inquiry in 1979. The research project itself became a cooperative effort between an anglophone and a francophone, and we had to deal with the differences in perspective we inherited from our cultures. Thus, we carried on an intense, yet constructive, dialogue about the interpretation of conflicting evidence and the implications of our findings. Irène's M.A. thesis, "The Air Traffic Controllers Dispute: 1976" (McGill University, August 1980), most convincingly applies the relative deprivation and resource mobilization theories of social change to the bilingual air traffic control issue. I commend it to the reader, and I hope that a published article based on it will be available soon. Albert Pace has been a most cheerful and diligent research assistant and editorial adviser over the last two years. Gwen Baker provided useful comparative information about air traffic control practices in the United States. John Houle was helpful in finding documents in the catacombs of Ottawa. Irene Borins attended the 1980 convention of the International Federation of Air Traffic Controllers Associations in Toronto and capably provided an international perspective. Michael Borins diligently searched back issues of Hansard for every comment any MP made about the topic. David Gillies and Stephen Weinstein helped with indexing and proofreading.

A critical moment in writing a book comes when an author, who solitarily has struggled for many months, shows the penultimate draft to a small circle of respected friends and colleagues, hoping both for critical comments, so as to improve the nearly completed work, and for their approval, so as to summon up the will to complete it. In both regards I have been most fortunate. Raymond Breton and William Stanbury, both associated with the Institute for Research on Public Policy, provided detailed and exceedingly helpful comments. The book was also read in its entirety by Carole Uhlaner, G. Bruce Doern, Richard Johnston, Norman Spector, Malcolm Taylor, Morton Weinfeld, Arlene Zuckernick, Ken McRoberts, and the students in my public management seminar at York. I am deeply appreciative of their insight and many useful suggestions.

In addition, many of those who played minor roles in the air traffic crisis read sections concerning themselves in order to ensure accuracy, and all the major players (Otto Lang, Sylvain Cloutier, Walter McLeish, Jim Livingston, Ken Maley, Jean-Luc Patenaude, Pierre Beaudry, Keith Spicer, Paul Stager) read the entire manuscript. Their comments began a dialogue which was tantamount to another round of interviews and thus were extremely helpful.

The initial case study was typed by Julia Taylor and Anne Pyshos; tape recordings of interviews were transcribed by Manon Cassidy; and the final draft typed by Linda Clemow, Maureen McCann, Gisela Birmingham, and Carol Hume. I thank them all for their capable work. Julia Taylor and Linda Clemow took a particularly strong interest in the story they were typing and served as de facto editorial assistants on many occasions: their interest was a great boost to my morale.

Finally, my thanks go out to the many people whom I interviewed in the course of writing this book. Many gave me a great deal of time, and were surprisingly candid. Without their willingness to cooperate, this book truly would not have been possible. Thus, my final hope is that all the participants find the product an honest reconstruction of a critical period in their lives and in our nation's history.

Introduction

Laws and constitutions can prepare a soil in which mutual respect and trust can grow. Whether, in fact, they do grow depends on ourselves, whether French-speaking Canadians and English-speaking Canadians can become civilized enough to be friends despite their differences.

J. A. Corry, *The Power of the Law*

The history of relations between French and English Canadians has been one of long periods of uneasy though quiescent coexistence broken by occasional confrontations. These crises have often resulted from some external opportunity or change in the status quo to which the two groups responded in completely different ways. Examples of such incidents are the opening of the west, which led to the Manitoba schools crisis, and the two world wars, both of which provoked conscription crises.

This book is about one of the most recent such crises, that between English and French Canadians over bilingual air traffic control. It arose in the mid-1970s when francophone pilots and controllers in Quebec attempted to use French, in addition to English, in aviation in the province of Quebec. They mobilized to form a pressure group, l'Association des Gens de l'Air du Québec, and gained the support of the federal government, but met with the determined opposition of the anglophone aviation community. The issue first surfaced in the collective bargaining process between the anglophone-dominated air traffic controllers' union and the federal government. It became a full-blown crisis in mid-June 1976 when airline pilots went on strike to support the controllers: the English-Canadian public overwhelmingly supported the anglophone aviators, and the French-Canadian public, with equal unanimity, supported the francophone pilots and controllers. The strike was resolved by an agreement between the minister of transport and the pilots' and con-

1

trollers' unions, an agreement the French Canadians felt to be a humiliating defeat. The turning point in the struggle came in the months following the agreement, as the anglophone aviators lost public support in English-Canada, while support for the francophones grew in Quebec. The problem then went to a commission of inquiry, which, after three years of thorough study, ultimately concluded that bilingual air traffic control could be implemented safely. The Clark government accepted the commission's conclusion in August 1979, and in 1980 implemented its recommendations, thereby making air traffic services available in French as well as English in Quebec.

There are many ways to study French-English relations. Some writers have concentrated on the periods of uneasy coexistence, in particular by exploring the changes in demography, attitudes, and elite composition which might point the way to the next confrontation. I have chosen to look in detail at one such confrontation, to examine the entire set of forces which caused it and to assess its implication for French-English relations in the future. We should realize that these crises play an almost disproportionately large role in the formulation of the myths which both English and French Canadians hold, and which therefore influence future events. One objective of this book, therefore, is to record the events accurately, while the principal actors' memories are fresh and the files are available, so that a realistic view of what actually took place will enter into our national memory.

An interesting by-product of the exercise to separate fact from assumption that emerges from this story bears heavily on one of our national myths, namely the Canadian self-image as a complacent, phlegmatic, and unperturbable people. It is as though, to paraphrase Napoleon's comment about the British, we Canadians are a nation of bureaucrats. The irony of this tale is that its key actors are quintessential Canadians—almost all bureaucrats—but that their professional behaviour clearly displays such "unusual" traits as passion, anger, individualism, and, in many instances, risk-taking and courage. Our national history often reads as dull and unexciting, precisely because we have emphasized the dull and unexciting in our national character. By dealing with this rather passionate episode, I hope to suggest that there is another side to our national character, one which deserves deeper study.

There are five main themes which run through this story. The first concerns the pattern of conflict between linguistic groups. Economic self-interest, the struggle between French and English Canadians for a few hundred lucrative jobs at the Montreal air traffic control centre, is one strand. Interweaved with it, however, are the professional ethics of pilots and air traffic controllers. For both groups, the touchstone of professional ethics is the pursuit of safety, just as for doctors it is the saving of life, or for economists the preservation and improvement of the functioning of the market. Economic self-interest and professional ethics motivated both the anglophone and francophone pilots and controllers, and neither factor can be reduced to a justification for the other. The struggle for economic advantage has complications of its own. For the last several decades, English Canadians have gradually, and relatively peacefully, been ceding control of Quebec's regional economy to French Canadians. Why was this instance so atypical, so marked with hostility and threats of violence?

The second theme is the ambiguous role played by the federal government in the controversy. According to the pluralist vision of society, there is a continuing struggle between interest groups for social advantage. Government's role here is that of mediator and scorekeeper, to ensure that the struggle does not spill over into open warfare, to total up the strengths of the various groups and to declare the winners and losers. A rival theory sees government in a more active role, serving either as an expression of the interests of certain classes or as a vehicle for the ideas of political leaders, shaping society's evolution in definite directions. This story shows government adopting both roles; at times we see the minister of transport and his senior officials attempting to mediate a dispute within the aviation community, and at other times we see them favouring the francophone stance. On the lower bureaucratic levels we encounter a similar equivocation, except that here it is between the mediating role and partisanship on the anglophone side. As we will see, this ambiguity of roles sent conflicting signals to the outside world, and made it difficult for the federal government to formulate a clear strategy.

The third major theme in this story is the influence of personality on history. To say that personality has an influence is to say that if different individuals with different character traits had held key leadership positions, the results would have been different. Of course, this position is at odds with much current Canadian historical research, which ignores the personalities of leaders and focuses on demographic and social forces.[1] To show that personality has influence, it is necessary to identify the significant personality traits of the key actors and to demonstrate how those traits led to specific outcomes.

The fourth theme the book examines is the importance of public opinion. The popularity of the various actors greatly influenced their ability to communicate their positions to the public and often served as a constraint upon their actions. The book also examines particular tactics used to influence public opinion, the role of the media in shaping public opinion, and the sharp differences between English and French Canadians' views of Canada's language problem.

The ultimate theme this book explores is the viability of Canada as a nation. Given the ability of interest group leaders to mobilize hostility between anglophone and francophone, and the tendency of the media to accentuate conflict, can Canada cope with crises such as this and remain a workable federation?

This book is written for three different readers: the informed citizen, the amateur or professional member of the aviation community, and the social scientist. I hope that the informed citizen will find it an interesting behind-the-scenes recounting of an important episode in contemporary history. Furthermore this episode has in common with many of the great political issues of our day a substantial scientific and technological component. I believe that if citizens leave such issues to the experts, we are opening the door to a rule by elites, ultimately, a threat to democracy. I began this study completely untutored in the skills of the pilot or the controller. I have therefore tried, particularly in chapters one and three, to convey enough of the aviation background I subsequently acquired so that the citizen-reader can appreciate the professional concerns of the pilots and controllers.

The Canadian aviation community, defined to encompass pilots, controllers, flight crew, and managers—past, present, and in training—probably numbers close to 150,000 persons. This community is very much technically oriented, and its members probably share a disdain for the Machiavellian side of politics. However, bilingual air traffic control was an issue that affected them so directly and personally that it could not be ignored. If my interviewees were typical of their community, all of its members also have vivid recollections of certain key moments. For them, I have attempted to reconstruct the context within which these personal experiences occurred. The message I hope to give them is that the notion of being a "pure professional" or a "pure technician" is most unrealistic. No profession stands apart from society.

The third reader is the social scientist. One of the sad consequences of the intellectual division of labour in our society is that there are few, if any, scholars who call themselves social scientists, only economists, political scientists, sociologists, and the like. If one views the bilingual air traffic control controversy as encompassing a small cross-section of human behaviour, it becomes clear how multi-faceted it was. People exhibited rational, symbolic, and affective behaviour, in the varied contexts of markets, organizational hierarchies, and political institutions. To limit oneself to any one approach is to fail to see the whole. This book, then, should be of interest to many types of social scientists, because it goes beyond the usual domain of each discipline. The groups that should find it closest to their interests are sociologists and / or psychologists who study organizations or ethnicity, and students of the public sector, including policy analysts.

Since, by and large, this book concerns contemporary history, a few words should be said about my research methodology. My first sources were documentary. Because of the magnitude of the crisis, there were very thorough newspaper reports available. Furthermore, the Commission of Inquiry made public numerous classified documents. Working from both these sources, I developed a detailed outline of the story. The next step was interviewing. In the process of this research, I, and / or my research assistant, Irène Lépine, interviewed over 90 people, including long initial interviews and subsequent re-interviews with all the major actors. Classified by category, we interviewed fifteen federal politicians and political appointees, twenty-eight federal public servants, seventeen leaders of the anglophone aviation organizations, ten leaders of the francophone controllers' movement, two Quebec provincial politicians, ten journalists, six operational pilots and controllers, and six controllers and aviation officials of foreign countries.

By the time of the interviews (1978 to 1980), many of the interviewees did not recall exact dates or sequences of events. However, through the documentary research, I had acquired knowledge of both, and therefore could concentrate on individuals' perceptions of and reactions to events. Because these were of great significance to so many of the people involved, their memories were very vivid, and my task became one of associating an individual's mental image with a particular time and place. Even though their powers of recollection were not perfect, both they and I were surprised at their accuracy and depth of recall, when prodded. Many read all or part of the penultimate draft, which brought back still more memories. Finally, of the many controllers or pilots interviewed, the clarity and precision that is so crucial to their work was very much in evidence in their recollections. As many of the interviews were conducted in the summer, they were often at summer homes far off the beaten track: the directions the controllers and pilots gave me over the phone were so precise that getting lost en route was an impossibility!

In conducting these interviews, I was not looking for "just the facts." Rather, I was interested in the way these people saw their roles and conceptualized their objectives and strategies, and in the emotions they felt. I tried to get a sense of the personality and character of the people I interviewed, both from what they said about themselves and from what others said about them. Once I felt that I knew a given individual, I found it possible to deduce his behaviour in situations I initially had not asked about. One of the great rewards of this research methodology was to do the second interview (or phone call) and discover that my deductions were correct.

The condition under which these interviews were given was that they would be off-the-record. For that reason, I have omitted reference to them in the notes, and have instead used material from the public record, as much as possible. I wish to assure the reader that everything I have written based on the interviews has been checked with multiple sources to ensure veracity. In many instances, the people I interviewed substantiated their claims by making available various documents and files which have not been publicly available: in all instances, these have been referenced. Altogether, I am confident that my factual claims are valid and my interpretations reasonable.

In writing this book, I have had to come to terms with the historian's craft. One particularly difficult problem with which all historians struggle is the relationship between causality and chronology. In order to indicate patterns of causality, it is necessary to "bundle" events in various ways, with the result that the narrative tends to jump back and forth in time. This becomes particularly apparent when telling a story that has a number of tangled, interrelated subplots which are all evolving simultaneously. However, to separate the various strands in the interest of strict chronology would be too confusing. To help the reader keep unfamiliar aviation terminology and organizational acronyms in mind, I have included as appendixes glossaries of both.

Finally, I have tried to write a history that emphasizes individual choice, rather than deterministic social forces. Thus, I have taken pains to lay out for the reader the choices as seen by an individual before he made a given decision, and to show where those making collective decisions disagreed on a course of action. I have also tried to reconstruct, insofar as possible, the consequences of some of the courses of action that were not chosen. By examining the choices that were made in the light of what might have been, had different yet feasible alternatives been chosen, we can begin to draw some conclusions for future choices in similar situations. While a history may be interesting, amusing, enlightening, or even edifying, its true significance is best measured by its impact on the history that is yet to be made.

Chapter One

The Technological and Occupational Context

The plane, our planet,
Travels on roads that are not seen or laid
But sound in instruments on pilot's ears,
While underneath,
The sure wings
Are the everlasting arms of science.

F. R. Scott, "Trans Canada," 1945

THE DEVELOPMENT OF AIR TRAFFIC CONTROL INTO THE FIFTIES

This chapter sets the stage for our story by discussing the development of the air traffic control system, the nature of work involved in flying and controlling aircraft, and the role played by the pilots' and controllers' unions.

In the earliest days of aviation, navigation was very primitive. Pilots maintained a course by using a compass and spotting landmarks on the ground. They would often follow railroad tracks and occasionally drop to a low elevation to read the names on the stations. They avoided other aircraft by keeping a visual lookout: "see and be seen." Flying was possible only when visibility was good.

Aircraft must land and take off into the wind because the wind's resistance increases a plane's lift on takeoff and slows it down rapidly on landing. Early airports were built with several runways to allow pilots to land or take off into the wind for all common wind patterns. On any given day, pilots would set up a circuit around the runway in the appropriate direction. On landing, using the circuit involved flying with the wind beyond the active runway (the downwind leg), turning, and coming down to land.

Pilots joined the circuit at the beginning and followed the other planes down. Planes taking off simply waited for a break in the circuit.

When the government began to build control towers and provide air traffic controllers to coordinate aircraft in the circuit, air traffic control was initially handled by means of signal lights. While on the downwind leg, the pilot would look at the tower: a green light meant that he was allowed to land and a red light that he should fly over the runway without landing, and rejoin the circuit. A technological advance was the use of two-way radio in addition to signal lights to coordinate traffic movement: the first control tower to do this was in Cleveland in 1930. The Canadian Department of Transport, which was established in 1936, built control towers at major Canadian airports: St. Hubert, near Montreal, in 1939; Malton, Ottawa, and Vancouver in 1940; Edmonton and Winnipeg in 1941; and Dorval in 1942.

Even at this early stage, the increasing volume of traffic required additional air traffic control. In December 1935, the first air traffic control centre was established in Newark, New Jersey. The centre used two-way radio to help airline pilots flying in the New York area to keep track of one another's locations, especially under marginal weather conditions.

After World War II, commercial aviation began to develop rapidly. To enable aircraft to fly cross-country in bad weather and at night, governments built hundreds of VOR (very high frequency omnidirectional radio range) stations, which became the basis of a system of airways between major points. An airway is a three-dimensional air highway, located at a high altitude, so that there is no conflict between the commercial aircraft using it and small pleasure aircraft flying at lower altitudes. VOR stations broadcast VHF signals which radio-equipped aircraft used to stay on course. Thus, navigation became a matter of flying from VOR station to VOR station.

At this stage, there occurred a bifurcation in the development of flying, which is essential in understanding the story that follows. Some pilots, especially pleasure pilots, did not need to have the ability to fly long distances in bad weather, and did not want to spend the money to purchase sophisticated navigational equipment, such as two-way radio or a VOR system. The government permitted them to fly under visual flight rules (VFR). A pilot is permitted to fly VFR if the weather conditions are good enough that he can take the responsibility for maintaining separation from other aircraft.

Instrument flight rules (IFR) were developed for pilots whose aircraft have sophisticated communications equipment on board and who know how to use it. Only 10 percent of all pilots have IFR licences.

A necessary requirement for IFR flight is increased air traffic control because pilots are allowed to fly in situations, such as within clouds, in which they cannot maintain visual separation. This higher level of air traffic control is known as "positive control," which means that a pilot must have the appropriate controller's permission, or "clearance," to proceed on each stage of his flight.[1]

In order to coordinate IFR traffic using airways, a new level of air traffic control was established after World War II. This was called en route air traffic control, and it was the outgrowth of the early effort at Newark. En route air traffic controllers use two-way radio to communicate with aircraft and issue clearances. In order to keep track of aircraft, they initially used charts and maps. In the United States, radar was introduced for en route controllers in 1946. The radar screen gives a two-dimensional display of a given geographical area, where aircraft are indicated as blips, small points of light, on the screen. Because of its smaller volume of air traffic, Canada did not introduce radar in en route control until 1958.

To establish an en route air traffic control system, it is necessary to assign controllers to airways. This was done through the establishment of flight information regions (FIRs). All the en route, or radar, controllers for each FIR work in an area control centre, which is a large windowless control room. Canada has eight such centres: Vancouver, Edmonton, Winnipeg, Toronto, Montreal, Moncton, Gander Domestic, and Gander Oceanic (which serves aircraft flying over the western half of the north Atlantic).

The boundaries for Canadian FIRs were drawn in the early 1950s on the basis of two considerations: making FIRs consistent with major flight routes so as to minimize the number of times a pilot changes FIRs, and equalizing the number of en route controllers in each FIR. The first factor explains why Edmonton, the base for all arctic operations, was given the entire arctic. Similarly, the Moncton FIR, rather than Montreal, was given eastern Quebec because trans-Atlantic flights from the American east coast flew over the maritimes, eastern Quebec, and then Newfoundland and because a heavily travelled route in the early 1950s was from the American east coast to Quebec, due to the development of iron ore. The second factor, equalizing the number of en route controllers in each FIR, explains why the FIRs handling heavily travelled domestic airspace (Vancouver, Toronto, Montreal) were not given the northern airways.

In northern Canada, air traffic controllers are assisted by aeradio operators, who use two-way radio to provide traffic and weather information and pass along control clearances to aircraft in the region. In addition, they use charts to keep track of the location of aircraft. Unlike controllers, they provide only advisory services to traffic.

In the early and mid 1950s, coexistence between IFR pilots and amateur pilots flying VFR posed little difficulty. Since all aircraft, whether commercial or pleasure craft, used propellers, they all operated at similar speeds, which made it easy to use the circuit. Thus, on days when weather conditions were acceptable for VFR flights, IFR pilots landed under visual flight rules, providing their own separation. On days when weather permitted only IFR flights, it was even easier for IFR pilots, since the number of planes in the circuit was reduced. One factor which helped coordinate the circuit was that all planes which had radios were tuned to the tower frequency. This enabled the pilots to overhear each other's conversations with the tower and to converse with one another directly.

When weather permitted and traffic was not too heavy, commercial pilots would use VFR for an entire flight, not just for landing in the circuit. They did this because VFR permitted them to take short-cuts and because they preferred not having to take orders from controllers. The image of a pilot at that time was a romantic one: they were seen as adventurers and explorers. If pilots believed this about themselves, then they felt that taking orders from a person on the ground was demeaning, and avoided it when possible.

AIR TRAFFIC CONTROL IN THE 1960S, 1970S, AND BEYOND

The air traffic control system changed dramatically in the late fifties and early sixties for two reasons. First, the volume of traffic of all kinds increased. Second, the new jet aircraft were very different from propeller-driven planes because they flew so much faster. This made it difficult for pilots to maintain a position in the circuit because the jets had to avoid overtaking propeller-driven aircraft. Furthermore, the size of the jets made it impossible for a pilot, perched at the front, to see completely around his aircraft.

In order to cope with the new environment, there have been developments in three major aspects of the air traffic control system: expansion of positively controlled airspace, establishment of additional air traffic control positions, and improvements in air traffic control radar.

During the 1960s, new airways were created and all were extended upwards to higher altitudes. Use of airways was more strictly limited to planes under positive control. Those equipped to fly IFR were no longer switching to VFR when the weather was good. Positive control (the requirement that pilots follow directions from controllers) was also established at major airports. In 1969, positive control zones (PCZ) were established within at least a five-mile radius around and to an altitude of 2,000 feet above all major Canadian airports. In the mid-1970s, Transport Canada, henceforth referred to as MOT,[2] established terminal radar service areas (TRSA) in Montreal, Toronto, and Vancouver. The TRSA is another area of positively controlled airspace, extending outward for about a twenty-mile radius from these airports, and occupying the alti-

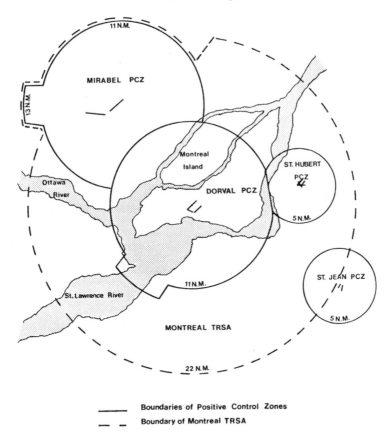

Figure 1 Montreal Airspace Organization

tudes between 2,000 and 9,500 feet. Large jets fly through the TRSA before they enter the PCZ on landing or after leaving the PCZ when taking off. Controllers use the TRSA to separate the large jets from small general aviation aircraft flying VFR. The TRSA stops at 9,500 feet, which is the altitude at which the airways begin.

Figure 1 shows the airspace organization of the Montreal region. The Montreal TRSA is situated above the positive control zones of Dorval, Mirabel, and the general aviation airports at St. Hubert and St. Jean.

The response of the air traffic control system to the increase in traffic was to create new positions, so that each controller would have a manageable workload, which is generally defined as no more than a dozen aircraft at a given time. During the period of rapid growth of commercial air travel from 1966 to 1976, the number of controllers in Canada increased from

600 to 2,100, an average annual growth rate of over 13 percent. Some of these new controllers staffed additional en route positions. Also, in 1964, MOT established terminal control units (TCU), to handle IFR aircraft within a forty-mile radius of the large airports. In addition, there are controllers in the control tower who handle VFR aircraft around the airport and all aircraft in the PCZ. Finally, there are ground controllers, also in the control tower, who direct pilots taxiing between runways and gates. This increase in the number of control positions means that any pilot will be handed from controller to controller quite frequently, especially in the vicinity of an airport. For example, an IFR pilot arriving at a major airport will be handed from the en route controller when he is within about forty miles of the airport to one of the IFR controllers in the terminal control unit. On his final approach, he is switched to the tower controller, and, as soon as he touches down, to the ground controller. To bring this about smoothly, different control units are in constant communication with one another by telephone "hotlines."

The third major development was the increased sophistication of radar. By the 1960s most air traffic control units in Canada were equipped with radar. However, there were two major difficulties with the early radar. First, the blips representing aircraft were weak and fuzzy and sometimes birds and automobiles produced radar images. Second, there was nothing on the radar scope to distinguish one aircraft from another. This problem was accentuated by the two dimensional nature of the display, which gave no indication of an aircraft's altitude. For example, if two aircraft flying at different altitudes simultaneously passed the same point on the ground, the blips representing them would merge, even though there was no collision.

To overcome the problem of weak radar images, a device called a transponder was developed. A transponder is a radar transmitter carried by an aircraft which sends a strong signal that appears on a controller's radar scope, as, for example, a triangle or two parallel horizontal lines.

Traditionally, controllers kept track of different aircraft by using flight progress strips. They wrote the relevant information about a given plane on a small strip of paper mounted on plastic. They then placed the strips on a display board, with the aircraft most recently entering a controller's airspace at the top of the board, and the aircraft on the verge of leaving it at the bottom. When the bottom strip was removed, all the others would move down a notch. One improvement in recent years is that the strips are now produced by computer. In addition to using strips to keep track of aircraft, controllers attached plastic markers (called "shrimp boats") to their radar scopes to identify the aircraft under their control, and moved the markers along the screen. Now there are radar scopes that display alongside the blips alphanumeric information, such as an identification of the plane, its speed, and its altitude. This equipment has been in operation at major airports in the United States since the early 1970s, and shortly after that in western Europe and Mexico. Canada chose not to buy a system from a foreign manufacturer but to contract with CAE Electronics, a Canadian firm which is a world leader in aircraft simulators, to develop a system of its own. After many delays, the Canadian system, called the joint enroute and terminal system (JETS), was installed at the area control centres in 1980 and 1981.

There are a number of developments in radar technology coming on stream. Collision avoidance systems will automatically warn controllers if two aircraft are on a collision course. Another development is the microwave landing system. At present, controllers are responsible for bringing aircraft into a line (referred to as "beads on a string") for landing. Microwave landing systems will use microwave communications and computers to allow aircraft to approach the airport from all angles, rather than going to the end of the line, which will reduce flying time.

A current area of controversy is the locus of the air traffic control system: whether it should be ground-based, as at present, or whether pilots should play a greater role. The latter could be achieved by putting radar displays and collision avoidance systems on aircraft, thus giving pilots more information about the traffic around them. Throughout the world, transport ministries and aviation authorities generally support ground-based control because they feel central coordination on the ground is less expensive and more efficient.

AIR TRAFFIC CONTROL AS AN OCCUPATION

All Canadian air traffic controllers are civil servants, trained and employed by MOT. To become a controller, one must have a high school education, a knowledge of English for all positions and a good knowledge of both English and French for bilingual positions, good physical and mental health, and the ability to speak clearly and to conceptualize the movement of objects through three-dimensional space. Since there are always many more applicants than places in the training program, competitions are held. Only 5 percent of the applicants survive this initial screening. Individuals with some background in aviation, avionics, or radio operation stand a better chance of being accepted. Competitions are conducted by MOT's regional administrations. Generally, these competitions are held to train tower or ground controllers.

The successful applicants then undergo a ten-month training program, consisting of an introductory course in their regions, an intensive course in air traffic control rules and procedures at the national air traffic control school in Cornwall, and, finally, individualized on-the-job training in the region.[3] Only 40 percent of the candidates who begin training receive their licences, or in controllers' jargon, "check out."

Experienced tower or ground controllers who are promoted to the more lucrative and demanding positions of radar controllers in the area control centres require several months' additional training. Occasionally, when there are severe shortages of radar controllers, trainees are recruited and directly trained for those positions. In this case, training takes two years.

Training is a continuing process for all controllers. There are five days of refresher courses required each year. Every time a controller is absent from his post for a month or more, or when he moves to a new position, he is required to "check out" with an instructor. Finally, controllers must pass a medical examination every year.

Controllers earn substantial salaries, considering the level of formal education required: the average controller's salary in 1981 was about $30,000.

The public has come to perceive air traffic controlling as a high stress job, an image which is only partially accurate.[4] What follows is a thumbnail sketch of air traffic control work, intended to distinguish its reality from its image.

To do the job well, a controller must be able to react to a rapid flow of new information, process it, and then confidently make quick decisions. The controller must be action-oriented: a speculative mind, pondering alternative courses of action, would be disastrous. Similar jobs to air traffic control are taxi dispatchers and foreign exchange or commodity traders. In all cases, information must be processed to make quick decisions which have a clear objective (safe landings, efficient operation of a cab fleet, capital gains) and whose results are evident very quickly. Because all three jobs involve rapid information processing, they could be aided, perhaps completely performed, by computer.

The key difference between controlling and the other two jobs is that the decisions made by the others involve only money, while controllers make decisions that can have life-and-death consequences. Controllers attempt to maintain a psychological distance, and to think of the job as simply "moving tin." Nevertheless, there is always an underlying awareness that human lives are involved. This realization is underscored by the fact that all controller conversations with pilots are taped and the tapes are saved for thirty days. Furthermore, whenever there appears to have been a loss of separation between aircraft (that is, a situation where two aircraft come closer than standards permit), there is an investigation by a fact-finding board organized by MOT. Fact-finding boards may recommend that controllers be required to check out again and, if they fail, that they be retrained or moved to a control position which they can handle.

Because of the importance of quick instinctive reactions in an environment where there is some underlying stress, controlling is generally a young person's occupation. Most trainees start in their late teens or early twenties, and MOT will not train anyone over the age of thirty. Few controllers remain in operational positions beyond the age of fifty. Not all tower controllers aspire to the more demanding radar jobs at the busiest airports: in fact, those locations are chronically short-staffed.

There are two other aspects of the work which controllers find troubling: the shifts and the variation in traffic level within any shift. Controllers at present work thirty-four hours a week, with shifts lasting eight hours. However, work hours vary, and controllers therefore suffer disruptions in normal family life. Within any shift, there will be great variations in traffic: hours of peak traffic, followed by periods of almost none. Skilful controllers prefer the action and excitement of the peak periods and find the slack time excruciatingly boring. Controllers are most prone to error, not when the traffic is at its heaviest, but when it begins to diminish, and they may relax too much.

Controllers switch positions and shifts sufficiently frequently that they observe a large number of their colleagues at work. Rather quickly they know who can handle a job and who is faking it. In an action-oriented job, the skilful controllers have substantial prestige among their colleagues. The less capable ones may stay on for quite a while, with the result that the more capable have to compensate for them, obviously a source of friction within a unit.[5]

With age, controllers' reflexes become slower and skills decline. Controllers in that position attempt to find jobs which they can handle: however, given their educational background, few have skills which can be employed elsewhere. Because they are protected from dismissal by their civil service status, many attempt to move into supervisory or managerial (that is, non-operational) air traffic control positions. Some of these managers lack managerial skills and receive little managerial training. As a result, operational controllers, who judge their peers on the basis of their skill in controlling have little respect, and sometimes open contempt, for their managers. In response, the managers become defensive.[6]

At present there are 2,100 controllers in Canada: this number has not increased since the mid-70s when the growth in air travel slowed dramatically. While there is not any data which could provide a detailed demographic profile, a few characteristics seem clear:

1. Controlling is an almost exclusively male occupation.
2. Except in the Quebec region, francophones are underrepresented among controllers.
3. One has the impression that controllers come from backgrounds of middle and lower-middle socio-economic status. The job requires rela-

tively little formal education, yet promises substantial economic rewards. Those who make it are ambitious and upwardly mobile. In her article about the bilingual air traffic control debate, Sandra Gwyn has caught the ambience of the group quite well:

> Like the armed services, air controllers are a club. Straight guys. Technicians. They are big on hockey tournaments, curling tournaments, on Hallowe'en parties, on chewing the fat over beer after work, and at boring their wives with incessant shoptalk.... They depend on one another, and they're ferociously proud of what they do.[7]

A few touches capture the social milieu of the Toronto area control centre, as seen by the author in 1980. The radar scopes are around the perimeter of the control room: in the centre is a large pedestal, on which stand the hockey, golf, and curling trophies. Beside the radar scopes are a number of pin-ups. Posted at the side of one is a yellowing "English is the international language of aviation" sticker, with the hand-written addendum "except in Otto Lang's airspace!"

THE ROLE OF CATCA

CATCA—the Canadian Air Traffic Control Association—is the union to which controllers belong. CATCA began as a voluntary association in 1959, and was certified as a bargaining agent for all air traffic controllers by the Public Service Staff Relations Board in November 1967.

Status as a bargaining agent means that all controllers, whether members of CATCA or not, must pay dues. In 1981 CATCA dues were 1.125 percent of salary; thus, the controller receiving an average salary of $30,000 would pay $375. With about 2,100 members at present, CATCA has an annual income of over $750,000.

CATCA's goals are a mix of traditional bread-and-butter issues, as well as some broader concerns. The current president, Bill Robertson, has put forward the objective of making the total compensation package of controllers equal to that of airline pilots.[8] Since controllers' compensation, according to CATCA, is equal to only 50 percent of pilots', it will be quite some time, if ever, before this objective is achieved. CATCA's broader concerns involve such matters as improving MOT's handling of occupational health problems, improving controllers' retirement package, and providing better career development opportunities for controllers who leave operational controlling at an age early enough to begin another career.

In interviews with controllers, there was very little dissatisfaction expressed, even among francophones, with CATCA's performance in delivering economic benefits to its members. This perception that CATCA has bargained well is at least partially reflected in the fact that only twenty-nine controllers are not members of the union. Furthermore, public servants in MOT and the Treasury Board Secretariat express a grudging respect for CATCA's professionalism and success as a union.

CATCA's organizational structure is quite simple. Each control unit has an executive, elected by its members. In addition, CATCA has a national structure which mirrors MOT's flight information regions: there is one regional director, elected by the regional membership, for each of the regions.

CATCA has a national executive, consisting of a president, two vice-presidents, and a secretary-treasurer. The national executive is elected at a biennial convention, by about 100 delegates from the units. CATCA's major policy-making body is the national council, which includes the executive and the regional directors, and which meets regularly every few months, and on other occasions by conference call. Except for the president, who works full-time for the union, all CATCA executives and regional directors are active controllers, with CATCA paying their salaries for the periods when they are on leave for union business. CATCA has a small office in Ottawa. In addition to the elected executives, there is a managing director, who is an employee of the union and chosen by the executive, and two or three secretaries.

Since its establishment as a union, CATCA has had four presidents: J. D. Lyon from 1967–71, J. R. Campbell from 1971–73, Jim Livingston from 1973–79, and Bill Robertson, who took office in 1979. All three past presidents have remained in air traffic control, Lyon and Campbell at MOT headquarters and Livingston as an operational controller in the Halifax terminal control unit.

THE AIRLINE PILOT'S WORK

Most airline pilots in Canada start flying either privately or in the military, and thus their initial training costs are not borne by the airlines, which simply recruit the best. Airlines do not impose formal educational requirements but look for people with flying experience and skill, intelligence, mechanical aptitude, good eye-hand coordination, good health, and emotional stability.

There is a very rigid seniority system for pilots, with priority for promotion determined by when a pilot joined the airline, and priority for those who joined at the same time determined by age. Pilots are ranked as captains, first officers, or second officers.

The airlines, together with the government, maintain rigid testing and retraining requirements. Pilots' flight skills are tested, both on simulators and on real aircraft, every six months. Pilots must also pass physical examinations twice a year. Failure of the physical or the flying tests results in loss of licence.

Certainly, the pilot's work has been romanticized: there is, of course, the exhilaration of flying, the excitement of travel, and a substantial salary to account for the image. On the other hand, continual changing of time zones and climate is physically disorienting. As well, the "exhilaration of flight" has become ever more constrained. As discussed previously, less and less of a flight is now under the pilot's control. Also, pilots often feel that they are under pressure from the airlines, which are willing to compromise a little on safety in order to make money. Pilots are partially protected from unreasonable demands by the seniority system, as well as by their right (under the Aeronautics Act) to refuse to fly under unsafe conditions. On the other hand, they know that the airlines can make life difficult if they exercise this right too often.

The nature of a pilot's work is quite different from the controller's. The controls of modern aircraft are becoming more and more automated. In this situation, pilots' work has become similar to that of engineers responsible for operations at highly automated factories. Like the engineers, the pilot provides a final backup system. He must have an intimate knowledge of the aircraft so that, if all else goes wrong, he can make a last attempt to bring it down safely. Much of a pilot's training is designed for the relatively few times in his career when he is called upon to play this role. Unlike the engineer, the pilot's own life is at stake. The stress involved in providing this last backup system is undoubtedly increased by the pilot's knowledge that, if he should fail his semi-annual flight tests, he will not be prepared for any other career.

The relationship between pilots and controllers is a subtle one. They need each other to exist, but there are numerous causes of tension. Pilots are a higher income and status group than controllers. Given the status difference, and given that the work rarely brings the two groups into physical contact, there is almost no social contact between pilots and controllers. Despite this, it is necessary for them to work together closely. On any flight, a pilot deals with a dozen or more controllers, none of whom he knows personally. At any time, a controller deals with up to a dozen pilots, none of whom he knows personally. In order for the system to work, all interchanges between the two groups must be calm and professional. Aviation terminology has been developed to be economical, clear, and unambiguous, in order to further this end. The complicating factor is that the workload for both groups is sometimes too heavy for complete information to be passed along. In this situation, pilots, especially if they are flying IFR in bad weather, must trust the controllers' commands. Controllers, if asked questions by pilots, must feel that these are genuine requests for information, not challenges or obstructions. In a world where information is less than complete, situations can be ambiguous and either party can see what he thinks are mistakes by the other. Both controllers and pilots make disparaging comments about the other group, and each will find instances where they are sure that the other made a mistake or did his job less than adequately.

THE ROLE OF CALPA

CALPA, the Canadian Air Line Pilots Association, is the union to which airline pilots in Canada belong. CALPA was first organized as a voluntary association in 1937, and it was certified as as a collective bargaining agent in 1944. In 1981, CALPA had about 2,800 members. CALPA's annual dues are 1½ percent of salary. Given an average income of $45,000, CALPA dues bring in an annual revenue of about $1,900,000, which is over twice as much as CATCA receives.

The basic unit in CALPA is the local council. For small airlines, all pilots belong to the same local council, while the membership of the larger airlines is organized into several councils, with one for each major pilot base. CALPA holds a biennial convention at which delegates of the local council choose the Board of Directors, which consists of a president, first vice-president, treasurer, and four regional vice-presidents.[9]

The responsibility for day-to-day administration of the organization rests with the Board of Directors, which meets in person four times a year and more frequently if necessary, by means of conference calls. CALPA executives have their salaries paid by the union for the time they are on association business. The president is at CALPA almost all the time, and does only enough flying to maintain his licence. CALPA is a fairly wealthy organization, and can afford a high level of office and executive support. The national headquarters in Brampton, near Toronto International Airport, has an executive director, a public relations director, an industrial relations director, an accountant, secretarial staff, and even summer students.

It is clear from CALPA's literature that the pilots' professional ethic emphasizes safety. For example, CALPA's code of ethics begins with the assertion "An airline pilot will keep uppermost in his mind that the safety, comfort and well being of the passengers who entrust their lives to him are his first and greatest responsibility." Safety is the first goal, comfort the second, and arrival on schedule the third, to be met only if the two previous goals have been satisfied.[10]

Chapter Two

French in the Air:
The First Steps

Men make their own history, but they do not do it just as they please; they do not make it under circumstances chosen by themselves, but under circumstances directly encountered, given and transmitted from the past. The tradition of all the dead generations weighs like a nightmare on the brain of the living.

Karl Marx, *The Eighteenth Brumaire of Louis Bonaparte*

This chapter deals with the initial events which led to the use of French by some controllers and pilots in Quebec, tracing the story into 1973. In this period the basis for the more dramatic events of 1975 and 1976 was laid: in the behaviour of the various actors, and in the issues raised, we can see a very clear foreshadowing of the themes of the following years.

THE ENGLISH TRADITION

In the post-World War II period the aviation world was dominated by English-speaking nations and individuals. Allied leaders organized a conference in Chicago in 1944 to lay the groundwork for the post-war global civil aviation system. Twenty-six nations, including Canada, signed the Chicago Convention, which led to the creation of the International Civil Aviation Organization (ICAO).

The founders of international civil aviation saw that success depended on the standardization of aviation procedures throughout the world. One area to be standardized was communications. Since the leaders of the allies were English-speaking, the major aircraft manufacturers were English-speaking, and the overwhelming majority of the western world's military pilots (who, after the war, would become its civilian pilots) were

English-speaking, the logical choice of a *lingua franca* for international aviation was English.

However, in formulating its policy for air traffic control language, ICAO recognized that many countries would wish to use their own languages in addition to English. ICAO first recommended that air traffic control be conducted in the national language of the state responsible for providing it. However, English was to be available at all control facilities serving international flights. ICAO envisioned this use of everyday English as a provisional measure until a more universal aviation language had been developed. The latter, ICAO suggested, would be a simplified form of English, which would be easy for non-anglophones to master.[1]

In the years after World War II, aviation in Canada was clearly a field dominated by the English. This domination was hardly atypical, and indeed it was the result of the same factors which, before the Quiet Revolution, led to English over-representation and French under-representation in business and technology. This pattern was intensified by the military origins of civil aviation, in a period when the military was primarily an anglophone institution. The use of English was so taken for granted that MOT never made any regulations requiring it. This is not to say that French Canadians were entirely absent from Canadian aviation industry at that time. They were present, though grossly under-represented. Furthermore, they had to be completely fluent in English. For them, French could only be the language of home and family.[2]

THE GROWTH OF THE FRENCH FACT IN QUEBEC AVIATION

VFR OPERATIONS AND THE GOODWIN MEMO

The use of French had to start somewhere. The logical place was not Montreal but some more distant part of the province where English was rarely heard and francophone pilots rarely came into contact with anglophones.

In 1962, one Georges Hamel opened a flying school in Baie Comeau (on the north coast of the St. Lawrence, east of Quebec City) and for that purpose bought a plane equipped with a radio. His students, mainly unilingual francophones, would be studying for private licences and flying only in the Baie Comeau region. Therefore, Hamel felt no need to teach aviation English. Louis Doucet, the chief controller at Baie Comeau and a person who later would be greatly involved in the bilingual air traffic control controversy, felt that it would be safer if Baie Comeau controllers could speak French with these pilots, rather than control only by means of signal lights. On April 10, he wrote a memo to the director of air traffic services for the Quebec region asking for permission to control in French. On April 17 the director responded, giving Doucet temporary authorization to control in French, but referring his request to the director of civil aviation in Ottawa for final approval.

The matter was settled on October 2, 1962, by a memo from R. W. Goodwin, the director of civil aviation. Goodwin based his answer on the ICAO recommendation that English be provided throughout the world to control international flights. He felt that Canada should not draw a distinction between international and domestic traffic (whereby the latter might be controlled in French) because of its geographical location on international air routes. He concluded that the use of two languages in Canada "would lead only to misunderstanding, confusion and a consequent lowering of the safety factor."[3]

On the other hand, Goodwin did not close the door to French entirely. He recognized that it would be impossible to prevent unilingual francophones in Baie Comeau, or presumably in equally far-flung parts of the province, from flying, and that safety would be enhanced if they were allowed to use the radio. Thus, he wrote: "It is recognized that in certain unusual conditions, such as those of emergency or stress, the French language may be used between controllers and pilots. However, whenever the French language is used, sufficient pertinent information shall also be broadcast in the English language to safeguard other pilots flying in the vicinity."[4] This decision was then communicated back down to the tower at Baie Comeau in a memo classified as "confidential." The rationale for keeping the memo confidential was the feeling that pilots did not "need to know" about it, and that, if they knew, there might be what Goodwin and his associates at MOT would have considered an undesirable increase in the use of French in air traffic control. They were willing to permit French under extreme circumstances, but did not wish to encourage its use.

This decision was not a particularly contentious one. Goodwin thought the matter sufficiently within his range of discretion that he did not discuss it with John Baldwin, the deputy minister of transport at that time.

In the years following the Goodwin memo, the use of French in air traffic control for private pilots flying VFR in more distant parts of the province continued. Since there were few anglophone pilots present to overhear these conversations, often the francophone controllers ignored the provision of the memo requiring them to inform other pilots of what they said in French. This use of French was not challenged by anglophone pilots, by CATCA, or the MOT bureaucracy: they all simply turned a blind eye to it.

Public policies often have unintended consequences. An example of this was MOT's Air Navigation Order Series V, Number 21, issued on May 20, 1969. This order, intended to improve aviation safety in the face of increased air traffic, instituted positive control zones (PCZ) around many Canadian airports. The order required VFR pilots operating in a

PCZ to accept instructions from air traffic control using two-way radio. In Quebec, PCZs were established at Dorval, St. Hubert, St. Jean, Sept-Iles, Quebec City, and Baie Comeau.

As a result of this order, unilingual francophone pilots began to acquire radios: the question that arose was which language they would use for air traffic control. Clearly, they preferred French. The controllers' response was somewhat hesitant, given the Goodwin memo which restricted the use of French to conditions of emergency or stress. Some francophone pilots tried to communicate in English, but with great difficulty. Controllers often felt that the only word of English these pilots knew was "Roger." After hearing pilots say "Roger" but ignore instructions in English, the controllers began to switch to French. However, some francophone pilots simply ignored the radio, and assumed that visual separation would be sufficient. Finally, some francophone flying clubs established small, uncontrolled landing strips in the vicinity of MOT-controlled airports.

RECRUITMENT OF FRANCOPHONE CONTROLLERS AND RADIO OPERATORS
In 1963, francophones were very poorly represented in technical aviation sector jobs in Quebec. Only nine of 110 air traffic controllers, fifteen of 135 radio operators, and twelve of 150 aviation electronics technicians were bilingual francophones.[5] All the rest were anglophones. This was because English was a requirement for the job, and because recruiting and job assignments had been conducted on a national rather than a regional basis.

In 1964, Maurice Baribeau took over the job of Quebec regional administrator. Baribeau was a pilot with the air force during World War II who joined Transport in 1948 and worked in Ottawa before his promotion to Quebec regional administrator. He was determined that francophones should play a greater role in the aviation sector in Quebec.

In 1962, MOT had changed its recruiting pattern for air traffic controllers. Thereafter, controllers were recruited by the regions, trained at the national school, and, if successful, returned to the region where they were recruited. This gave Baribeau the opportunity he needed. In 1965, he issued guidelines that all new controllers and aeradio operations in Quebec should be bilingual. Baribeau's francophone staff in Montreal took every opportunity to encourage francophones to compete for air traffic control positions. In addition, francophone examiners of air traffic controller candidates helped good francophone candidates by giving them questions in French if they had trouble answering in English. Baribeau's practice was really no more than an attempt to help francophones get a foot in the door: the francophone candidate who succeeded in the competition at the regional level still had to complete the air traffic control course at the national school, which was given in English. To succeed there, his English skills had to be high. Judging by the fact that a higher percentage of francophones than anglophones failed the course at the air traffic control school, many francophone candidates were not able to acquire sufficient skill in English.

By 1971, the Ministry of Transport legitimized the practice of the Quebec region in recruiting controllers. The most critical technical portion of the test, the set of true-false questions that tested a candidate's ability to think three-dimensionally, was given in French as well as English. Candidates who passed that section of the exam, but who failed other sections, were provisionally accepted into air traffic control school. However, they were required to take and pass English-language training before beginning practical training.

By the mid-1970s, the new policies and practices had proven successful. Of the 200 aeradio operators and 275 air traffic controllers in Quebec, only a handful of the former and about sixty of the latter were unilingual anglophones. Baribeau's policy was aided by the rapid growth of commercial aviation so that francophones could fill newly created positions, rather than having to wait for anglophones to retire or quit.

THE USE OF FRENCH AMONG CONTROLLERS

As the number of francophone controllers grew, a question that was being raised throughout Quebec also was posed in the control towers and centres—would the language of the workplace be English or French? Even though they were speaking to pilots in English, the bilingual francophone controllers felt more comfortable speaking French to one another. However, unilingual anglophones claimed that air traffic control involved such a high degree of teamwork that it was necessary for every controller to understand colleagues at all times: therefore, English should be used. This, of course, would perpetuate an old fact of life in Quebec: in any situation involving both linguistic groups, the *lingua franca* would be English, even if all but one of the people there were francophone.

The language issue was resolved differently in Montreal than in the towers of small airports. At the latter, the controller positions were relatively junior and the majority were held by francophones by the late 1960s. Furthermore, many supervisors were also francophone. As a result, the increasing use of French among controllers was quietly accepted. On the other hand, the Montreal area control centre had the greatest concentration of senior controllers' jobs: a large number of these jobs, as well as the supervisory positions, were held by unilingual anglophones. They strenuously resisted any attempt by the more junior francophones to use French on the job and threatened them with disciplinary action. They also informed CATCA, which raised the issue in consultations with the Ministry of Transport in April 1969. The situation was growing tense, and controllers were exchanging harsh words.

After a few months of uncertainty, the problem was resolved in a number of ways. Some members of both language groups left the centre, the anglophones transferring to English Canada and the francophones to other Quebec airports. On July 28, 1969, G. A. Scott, the assistant deputy minister of transport in charge of air operations, decided that English alone would be used at the Montreal centre for discussions dealing with operational matters.[6] Since the unilingual anglophones could not distinguish operational from non-operational matters when discussed in French, the actual result of Scott's memo was that English was used exclusively at the Montreal centre. Finally, an occupational study of air traffic control, headed by R. R. Lisson of the Department of Supply and Services' Bureau of Management Consulting, had just been commissioned, and it would also deal with the question of bilingualism.

THE LISSON REPORT AND THE LOGIC OF THE OFFICIAL LANGUAGES ACT

Lisson quickly began to realize that the issue of bilingual air traffic control was thorny indeed. To begin with, the anglophone controllers, CATCA, and MOT officials all were opposed to it. Their position was based on the argument that it is safer if all pilots understand all conversations with air traffic control and on ICAO's recommendation that English be the *lingua franca* of international aviation. In addition, unilingual anglophone controllers who wished to retain their jobs clearly had an interest in preventing the acceptance of French in air traffic control. The anglophones argued that they had agreed to work in Quebec after receiving assurances that they would not need to speak French. Francophone controllers and the Quebec regional administration argued that the use of French would enhance safety for the unilingual francophone pilot flying VFR, an ever more frequent concern. Finally, the Official Languages Act, which was enacted in July 1969, committed the government and its agencies and Crown corporations to provide services to the public in both official languages at its principal offices in bilingual districts, elsewhere where warranted by demand, and to the travelling public where warranted by demand.[7]

To sort out this conflict, Lisson visited European air traffic control centres, where he saw bilingualism in action. He felt that the Official Languages Act, with its emphasis on the availability of both languages to the travelling public, provided a clear mandate to MOT to go beyond the Goodwin memo, which he judged as "contrary to the spirit and the intent of the Official Languages Act [which] begs a broader interpretation."[8] On the other hand, he was unclear as to what the ultimate implications of this newly enacted legislation would be for the geographical extent of French service or the speed with which it would be implemented. Like many Canadians at that time, he was optimistic that the Official Languages Act would be the core of a policy which would hold the country together. His optimism was reinforced by assurances from the civil servants in charge of implementing the act that anglophone controllers would need only a limited amount of very technical French which they could easily learn.

Lisson attempted to come down with a balanced report. The Official Languages Act convinced him that francophone pilots had a legitimate claim, and his experience in other countries demonstrated that air traffic control could be provided safely in two languages. As he put it, "the argument about safety is relative rather than absolute and does not work only in one direction."[9] Based on what he saw in Europe, he felt that the translation of messages for the benefit of unilingual pilots would be made "at the discretion of the controller when they feel it is safe to do so." Lisson made no distinction between the use of French for VFR and IFR operations. However, he recommended the use of French only in bilingual districts, rather than throughout the entire country. He doubted that there would be substantial demand for French outside bilingual districts and he felt that it would be very difficult to implement bilingual air traffic control in the entire country.

Lisson realized that the opposition of anglophone controllers and pilots would complicate implementation. Therefore, he proposed gradual implementation in order to avoid disrupting the careers or limiting the opportunities of unilingual anglophones.[10] He recommended that MOT be given five years, until 1975, to provide bilingual supervisors in bilingual districts and until 1980 to ensure that all controllers in bilingual districts were bilingual. He proposed that French-language training be made available to unilingual anglophone controllers who wished to remain in bilingual districts. However, he recommended that MOT transfer unilingual anglophone controllers who could not or would not become bilingual to English-only regions and, in response to the problems of the unilingual anglophones at the Montreal area control centre, urged that they be given priority in filling IFR controller positions elsewhere.

Lisson's report was made public in July 1970. It drew particularly angry opposition from pilots, because it took the position that controllers, rather than pilots, should have the discretion in determining when translations should be provided. In addition, Lisson had laid out very clearly the personnel implications of bilingual air traffic control: the question controllers asked was whether MOT would actually implement the report.

MOT's response to the Lisson report was cautious: the department "tended to favour" some of his recommendations, but would not implement anything without further study. An air traffic control implementation team was established to undertake further study of the Lisson report.

THE FIRST SKIRMISHES

At the same time the implementation team was studying the Lisson report, other parts of the government were moving to implement bilingualism. In September 1970, the Treasury Board issued a circular to all federal government departments calling for the establishment of French-language units within the public service. The objective of the circular was to ensure that French would be the language of work in many parts of the civil service, thereby expanding opportunities for francophones. Departments were to respond to the circular by proposing French-language units. The MOT Personnel Branch, which is not part of, or controlled by, the air administration, proposed sixty-two French-language units, with a total of 1,742 employees. Included among these were the control towers in Quebec City, Baie Comeau, and Sept-Iles. Treasury Board accepted the MOT proposals and on August 11, 1971, designated all the groups as French-language units.

At this point, CATCA responded. On August 24, its president, J. R. Campbell, sent a memo to CATCA branch chairmen, discussing the implications of bilingualism for controllers' career development. He argued that the Official Languages Act should not create hardship for individuals, limit their promotions, or interfere with the merit principle. He claimed that the unilingual anglophone controllers in Quebec, despite the assurances that they would have no need for French, received when they took jobs in Quebec, were now being told candidly by the Quebec regional administration that they had no prospects for promotion within that region. Finally, Campbell cited with alarm the increased use of French in controlling VFR aircraft.[11]

CATCA's collective agreement was to expire at the end of 1971, so it was logical to raise the bilingualism issue in the context of collective bargaining. President Campbell placed on the agenda of a CATCA national council meeting in November a proposal to add to CATCA's bargaining position a clause calling for the provision of air traffic services in English only. The francophones in the Quebec City branch sent Campbell an angry telegram which insisted that CATCA drop its opposition to the recommendations of the Lisson report and threatened to raise the issue directly with federal Cabinet ministers.[12] However, the CATCA national council sided with the anglophones in Montreal, passing a resolution urging MOT to adopt an English-only policy for air traffic control and urging the government to amend the Official Languages Act.[13] The Quebec City controllers made good on their threat, and wrote to Gérard Pelletier, the minister responsible for the Official Languages Act (and a close friend of the prime minister), urging his intervention.

On November 26, the CATCA negotiating team met with Don Jamieson, the minister of transport, O. G. Stoner, the deputy minister, and Walter McLeish, the director-general of civil aeronautics, in an attempt to resolve the issue outside the collective bargaining procedure. Jamieson, Stoner, and McLeish were successful in mollifying CATCA. The astute Jamieson immediately began the meeting by assuring CATCA that safety was his prime objective and stating that the Ministry's policy on the use of English was the same as CATCA's. On the other hand, he justified the designation of air traffic control positions in Quebec as bilingual in order to ensure the complete availability of emergency bilingual services in accordance with the Goodwin memo. Jamieson indicated a willingness to investigate any evidence CATCA could gather of clear breaches of aviation regulations through the unwarranted use of French. Stoner and McLeish confirmed that a growing number of Quebec control positions would be designated bilingual, but were vague about the details or about what would be done to assist unilingual anglophones who wished to transfer. The meeting ended with an agreement to establish regular meetings between McLeish and CATCA to deal with continuing problems relating to bilingualism.[14]

In the weeks following this meeting, collective bargaining over monetary issues was completely deadlocked. Campbell and the negotiating team came to feel that the important issue was money, that a strike was likely, and that full union support was essential. On new year's eve, Campbell had a long meeting in Montreal with francophone controllers. He promised to drop bilingualism from CATCA's set of bargaining proposals, and was now sympathetic to the francophones' desire to use French in controlling VFR aircraft. The francophones thus agreed to support a strike, and in January, CATCA went on strike. At first it had good public support, but that waned as the strike went into a second week. The strike ended with the appointment of an arbitrator, who ultimately recommended a two-year contract, and substantial pay increases.

In July 1972 the air traffic control implementation team finally reported. The members of the team, mainly air traffic controllers, approached the problem with their expected professional concern about the feasibility of developing procedures to control traffic in two languages. The team concluded that Lisson had not proven the feasibility of bilingual control and that a detailed study should therefore be commissioned. Until the study was completed, existing language policies should not be changed. One of the members of the team was Pierre Proulx, a francophone who began his career as a controller in Quebec City in 1957 and moved to Montreal in

1966, and whom we will meet again later in the story. Proulx argued long and hard with a number of anglophone members of the team who wished to dismiss bilingual air traffic control as simply unfeasible: he felt that the commitment to further study was an important victory for francophone controllers.

The study also dealt with the question of staffing air traffic control positions with bilingual people. It accepted as a long-run goal that all supervisors and controllers in Quebec should be bilingual, but questioned how rapidly this could be done. The team felt it was important to determine soon which air traffic control units outside of Quebec would be designated bilingual, so as to relieve uncertainty for unilingual anglophone controllers throughout Canada. The team doubted that bilingualism could be implemented outside of Quebec on the basis of Lisson's schedule.[15]

This report did not disturb the status quo in air traffic control language. Walter McLeish, the director general of civil aeronautics, moved slowly on the formation of a team to study the safety and operational implications of bilingual air traffic control. He himself had strong doubts about its desirability and was unenthusiastic about raising this most divisive issue.

Meanwhile, the factors providing the basis for change continued to evolve: more Quebec controllers were francophone, more VFR pilots in Quebec were francophone, and more French was being used. In June 1973, Parliament adopted a resolution which outlined a process by which the Treasury Board would identify bilingual civil service positions and then take steps to ensure that they would be appropriately filled by the end of 1978. However, unilingual civil servants holding positions designated bilingual and who could or would not take language training were given the "incumbent's right" of remaining in their jobs.

During this period, another of the major actors in this story entered the scene. On June 1, 1973, Jim Livingston became president of CATCA. Livingston had first become interested in air traffic control as a boy operating a wireless set in Halifax. After a number of unsatisfying jobs, he trained as an air traffic controller and started at the Halifax tower in 1959. Livingston had the reputation of being a hard-nosed union man: he was elected vice-president of CATCA in 1969. In 1971, he ran against the incumbent president, J. R. Campbell, and lost: some of the delegates to the convention felt that Livingston was too militant. In 1973, Campbell decided not to run again because of poor health, and Livingston was elected.

One difference between the two men concerned the question of signing CATCA's contracts with the government in both languages. During his term as vice-president, Livingston had been asked to sign both English and French versions of the collective agreement negotiated with the Treasury Board. He had initially refused, arguing to his rather astonished fellow executives that, even though the negotiations had been conducted in English, the government might use discrepancies between the two versions of the contract to its advantage in dealing with CATCA. Furthermore, he did not want to sign anything he himself did not understand. Ultimately, the other executives pressured Livingston into signing the contract: however, he vowed to himself that he would never again sign the French version of collective agreement. Campbell headed the negotiating team in 1972 and the agreement was signed in both English and French, after MOT acceded to CATCA's demand that the official French version be produced by a translator chosen by CATCA, but paid for by MOT.

Very shortly after taking over as president of CATCA, Livingston began to challenge the government on the bilingualism issue. On November 19, 1973, he sent out an information bulletin to his members in which he urged them to report to his office deviations from the existing language rules (i.e., the Goodwin memo) by obtaining the names and licence numbers of pilots whose English appeared to be inadequate. In that same bulletin, Livingston noted that Treasury Board was beginning to identify bilingual air traffic control positions. Members of CATCA were "urged to initiate grievances against identifications inconsistent with safe and efficient air traffic control."[16] Livingston was quickly beginning to express the fears of the anglophone majority of his union. The controllers were concerned that, despite the absence of any formal policy change by MOT and despite the bland assurances of Walter McLeish and other civil servants, French in air traffic control was becoming a fact in Quebec and possibly elsewhere in Canada, with serious consequences for safety and employment prospects of CATCA's predominantly unilingual anglophone membership.

Chapter Three

Bilingual Air Traffic Control: Pro and Con

I grow daily to honour facts more and more and theory less and less.

Thomas Carlyle, letter to Ralph Waldo Emerson, April 29, 1836

The previous chapter has shown how the application of the Official Languages Act to communications between pilots and controllers would require controllers to be bilingual. This drew the opposition of unilingual anglophone controllers who wanted to retain their jobs. However, the issue of bilingual air traffic control was more than a question of jobs. Members of the entire Canadian aviation community argued heatedly over whether bilingual control was safer and / or more efficient than unilingual control. Therefore, this chapter presents both sides of each argument. In the following chapters, we will refer to the various arguments by name, without repeating them in detail.

THE LISTENING WATCH

Pilots who have two-way radio are required to keep a listening watch at all times on the appropriate frequency. They are to listen not only for messages addressed to themselves, but for messages to and from other pilots so as to gather information on the precise locations of other aircraft in their vicinity or to catch errors made by other pilots or controllers. The indirect use of radio is referred to by pilots as the party line aspect of the listening watch, or "redundancy." Redundancy is a basic principle of aviation. In order to prevent disaster, the aviation system is built with many backup systems or redundant pieces of equipment. Only when all systems fail simultaneously will disaster occur. Thus, the listening watch can be thought of as the backup system for the controllers.

The listening watch argument against bilingual air traffic control is quite simple. When pilots use two languages to communicate with controllers, unilingual pilots will not understand messages in the other language, and the value of the listening watch will be decreased.

The opponents of bilingual air traffic control claimed that the loss of the listening watch would decrease not only safety but also efficiency. For example, a pilot flying en route may monitor messages on the frequency in the area into which he is flying, thereby learning of weather and traffic conditions without having to request the information from the controller.

Because the listening watch enables pilots to catch the errors made by controllers, its most enthusiastic exponents are pilots. The listening watch, in a sense, justifies the pilot's position of superiority vis-à-vis the controller. In an interview in the Canadian edition of *Time*, CALPA President Ken Maley expressed this perspective clearly: "The only way to know what's going on around you is to listen to all communications on the frequency. If you start feeding in another language, you lose comprehension. It puts safety in the hands of the controllers in the tower, not the pilot, which is very wrong."[1]

The proponents of bilingual air traffic control conceded that the listening watch can help to avert collisions. However, they claimed that it is a very ineffective backup system for air traffic control. To begin with, the listening watch plays a different role under IFR and VFR. When weather conditions are clear enough for VFR flight, then pilots, whether they are flying VFR or IFR, have another backup system—their own eyes. Advocates of bilingualism claimed that the value of the listening watch to aircraft flying IFR had been greatly reduced in recent years and would be further reduced in the future. Because pilots change frequencies often, especially in the vicinity of airports, they do not overhear all communications with aircraft near them. The increased volume of traffic has meant that controllers often tell pilots to "omit position report," with the result that pilots do not overhear the location of other aircraft. With JETS radar displays, installed in 1981, controllers read pilots' speed and altitude on the radar, and do not need to ask for that information, which also reduces the amount any pilot can overhear. Finally, there is the possibility that the listening watch itself might lead to disaster if a pilot, on the basis of an overheard conversation, independently takes inappropriate action. The attitude of the proponents of bilingual air traffic control is that, in the present and future aviation environment, the responsibility for maintaining separation must rest with the controller, and that as much as possible should be done to permit the controller to discharge that responsibility effectively.

MINORITY RIGHTS OR MINORITY ASSIMILATION?

Even the most ardent proponents of bilingual air traffic control accepted the claim that the best system would be one in which all pilots were fluent in and used the same language. However, in the next breath, they said this ideal is hopelessly utopian. In the Canadian context, there are francophone pilots with VFR licences whose command of English is very limited. If one accepts that these individuals have a right to fly in Canada, or simply that it is politically impossible to prevent them from flying, then the safest way for them to fly is to provide air traffic control services for them in French. Generally, the opponents of bilingualism, especially airline pilots, were willing to accept the minority rights argument as it pertained to VFR traffic speaking French and using small airports.

Where the minority rights argument became controversial was in its application to IFR flying. At the time, all francophones with IFR licences were sufficiently fluent in English to fly in English: nevertheless, some would probably have preferred to use French if it were available. Furthermore, if French were available, unilingual francophones would also have been able to get IFR licences.

On the other hand, the opponents of bilingual air traffic control claimed that it would be less expensive (and safer, because of the listening watch argument) to train the small minority of IFR pilots who were francophones to use English than to institute a system of complete bilingual air traffic control. This is an example of the standard economic argument against bilingualism: costs are minimized if the minority goes along with the majority, rather than if a double linguistic infrastructure is established.

INTERNATIONAL STANDARDS

Opponents of bilingualism, particularly pilots, cited ICAO's overall objective of standardizing aviation practices, including the introduction of a universal lexicon. They resisted the introduction of bilingual air traffic control because they saw this as the first instance when a major western country moved away from the objective of standardization. They felt that the western countries should be at the forefront of an international movement to improve standards, and bring the rest of the world along. They pointed to countries such as Germany and the Netherlands, which have adopted English as their exclusive language for IFR air traffic control.

The international standards argument did not cut much ice with the proponents of bilingualism. They cited ICAO's acceptance of two languages in air traffic control, and pointed out that there were western countries in the forefront of the aviation world (France, Switzerland) which use two languages in air traffic control. In response to this argument, opponents claimed that it was not as safe to fly in Switzerland and France as in Germany or the Netherlands. Proponents responded that such statements were unproven. However, neither side provided accurate information to compare the safety records of unilingual and bilingual countries, or even an enumeration of which countries are bilingual and which are unilingual.

CONTROLLER WORKLOAD

Opponents of bilingualism claimed that the use of two languages would complicate the controllers' work because they would have one more fact to remember about each aircraft, they might address pilots in the wrong language, and they would have to translate messages for the benefit of unilingual pilots. They also argued that the increase in controllers' workload would result in more controller errors and therefore a decrease in safety if the same volume of traffic were handled as in a unilingual system, or a decrease in the efficiency of a bilingual system if the same standards of safety as in a unilingual system were maintained. Given the pressure by the airlines and the travelling public to keep up the volume of traffic and to minimize delays, they claimed that one could more realistically expect lower safety standards than reduced traffic volume.

Those favouring bilingualism claimed that this argument was erroneous, in that it stemmed from a unilingual person's inability to conceive that it was possible to switch languages fluently. They cited examples of bilingual people in other jobs who could alternate languages with ease and bilingual controllers claimed that they could do likewise.

Very quickly, this argument descended to the level of "No, you can't" and "Yes, we can." It could not be resolved without some empirical testing, and for most of the debate over bilingualism no such tests were performed.

HEAVY TRAFFIC

Closely related to the controller workload is the heavy traffic argument. Opponents of bilingualism claimed that a bilingual air traffic control system would be most likely to break down when there was a high volume and complicated mix of traffic. As support for this statement, they were fond of citing statistics which showed that the traffic volume at certain high density North American airports is much greater than that experienced in bilingual European airports. They also quoted statistics showing that the number of aircraft, both total and per capita, is much greater in Canada than in any of the countries that have bilingual air traffic control.

Proponents of bilingualism responded to this argument in the same way they had responded to the previous argument: they had no doubt that they could handle heavy traffic in a bilingual system, with little loss in efficiency, relative to a unilingual system. They did not quote statistics of their own, but they felt that the statistics quoted by the other side were misleading. For instance, the fact that Chicago's O'Hare Airport is unilingual and the busiest in the world is irrelevant, since no one had proposed making it bilingual. The relevant question was whether there were bilingual airports with approximately the same traffic flow as Montreal's Dorval and Mirabel. If there were, and if they could handle that traffic volume safely and efficiently, then one would think that Dorval and Mirabel could do likewise. The statistics about aircraft registrations were claimed to be misleading because they did not translate directly into controller workload. Once again, the question was an empirical one, and the debaters did not have the data to come to a convincing conclusion.

THE STRAY UNILINGUAL FRANCOPHONE PILOT

The opponents of bilingual air traffic control were worried that once bilingual air traffic control was provided in part of Canada, unilingual francophone pilots might stray into other parts of Canada and the United States where air traffic control was in English only. This might happen if a pilot was forced by sudden bad weather to leave the area where French was provided, or if he overestimated his knowledge of English.

The proponents of bilingual air traffic control responded with a number of arguments: first, that the hypothetical situations offered were, in practice, very rare, and second, there are landing procedures for pilots flying either IFR or VFR in the event of a total communications failure. These procedures could be applied in such cases, or, better still, less drastic procedures could be devised to deal with such situations. These procedures might involve special clearances issued by air traffic control in the bilingual area as the pilot was leaving. Also, some bilingual capability, such as one controller on every shift, could be provided along the borders of Quebec. Proponents claimed that in the United States, air traffic control units in places like Texas and California had some Spanish-speaking personnel to handle Mexican pilots who were insufficiently fluent in English. In this instance again, the empirical question of how often this problem occurs was of some importance; however, the debate went on without any convincing answer to the question.

This, then, is a short summary of the arguments on both sides of the issue. Both sets of arguments are theoretically plausible. Therefore, the problem could only be resolved empirically, with data on the effectiveness of the listening watch as a backup system, data comparing traffic volumes,

Chapter Four

The Battle for Bilingualism: The Early Victories

It doesn't take a majority to make a rebellion; it takes only a few determined leaders and a sound cause.

H. L. Mencken, *Prejudices*

BIRTH OF AN ORGANIZATION

During the early 1970s, the question of the language of air traffic control was often discussed by the francophone controllers in Quebec City. Because the unit was small and the pace of work rather unhurried, the men knew each other quite well and expressed their feelings openly. A number of them had spent some time at the Montreal centre, and spoke bitterly of their experience with anglophone domination. Jean-Luc Patenaude, who was the head of the CATCA local, went from high school into the air force, and had spent his whole career working in English. When he thought about the language question, he began to feel ashamed that he could not perform his trade in his mother tongue, simply because he had not been trained to do so. Finally, Patenaude and the others came to believe that the use of French would increase safety for unilingual francophone pilots. As he put it in an interview some years later: "No one would have used French had they not believed it was safe. You can't live with this type of thing, working day in and day out, if you're not sure what you're doing is correct. You would be jeopardizing your whole career, your family, everything you live for."[1]

These sentiments formed the basis for a challenge to the anglophone domination of air traffic control. However, to do this, the francophone controllers had to create an organization able to apply pressure for change. For a number of reasons, Quebec City was the most fertile ground for forming such an organization.[2]

By 1973, the francophone controllers in Quebec City had developed a great deal of internal cohesion and self-confidence. All but a handful of the forty controllers there were francophone. All the supervisors were francophone: one of these was Louis Doucet, the former Baie Comeau tower chief who first requested that the use of French be allowed. These supervisors supported the increased use of French in communications with francophone VFR pilots and ignored the complaints of anglophone pilots. The controllers also got support from francophone VFR pilots, as well as from IFR-licensed pilots of the Quebec Government Air Service, which was based in Quebec City. In short, for the Quebec City controllers there was a growing disparity between the French surroundings and pilot clientele, on the one hand, and the formal English-only nature of their job, on the other.

The situation in Quebec City also had aspects of a revolution of rising expectations. At the same time that the controllers' self-confidence was growing, CATCA and MOT were treating them with hostility. For its part, CATCA was unwilling to use French for union business: the Quebec controllers were offended by the absurdity of the CATCA Quebec region newsletter which came out of Montreal, written entirely in English, even though many of the contributors were French. The controllers were angered by Jim Livingston's urging of the membership to oppose the designation of Quebec air traffic control positions as bilingual and by his request that pilots using French be reported to MOT for disciplinary action. As for MOT, the controllers saw a mixture of blatant racism at the lower levels and temporizing at the upper levels. An example of the former, recounted by a Quebec City controller, concerns two MOT inspectors visiting the Quebec centre, who were upset to hear the controllers talking among themselves in French; their muttered comments about "goddamned long-haired Frenchmen" were easily overheard.

MOT's management had begun two studies of the bilingualism problem. Maurice Baribeau, Quebec regional air administrator had received Ottawa's authorization to learn precisely how much French was being used in Quebec air traffic control. In late 1973, as a result of the air traffic control implementation team study completed in 1972, Walter McLeish, director-general of civil aeronautics, chose a seven-member task force, called the Bilingual Communications (BILCOM) Project, to study the problem. Four of the members of the BILCOM team were francophone, one being Louis Doucet. Despite this undertaking, the Quebec City controllers were impatient: why were studies necessary to prove what by then was self-evident to them?

In early 1974 a group of about thirty controllers met one night at the Aero Club—an old hangar—and formed the Association Québécoise des Contrôleurs de la Navigation Aérienne (AQCNA). Their fundamental objective was to have French as well as English used in air traffic control. They set a low membership fee of three dollars in order to build up a large membership as quickly as possible. The president of AQCNA was Guy Charette, a veteran controller with experience at various airports in Quebec since 1957. Charette had long been active in CATCA, and therefore had legitimacy in the eyes of his anglophone colleagues. The vice-president was Pierre Beaudry, and the treasurer, Roger Buisson. Both were energetic young men, who had begun controlling in the early 1970s. Another moving spirit in AQCNA was Louis Doucet, although, since he was a member of the BILCOM Task Force, he could not serve as an executive of AQCNA. However, he was sufficiently skeptical that change could be achieved by yet another task force that he urged the controllers to organize.

The members of AQCNA decided to advance the cause by attacking on a number of fronts. They would put pressure both on politicians and on CATCA. They would seek publicity. Finally, they would take direct action by using French as much as possible in their work. They did not feel that in this they were doing anything illegal: there were no acts of Parliament or Cabinet orders prohibiting the use of French—there was only custom. The one administrative directive on the subject—the Goodwin memorandum—they interpreted broadly.

Jean-Luc Patenaude, the chairman of the CATCA local, was successful in bringing CATCA's spring national council meeting, scheduled for the weekend of April 29–May 1, to Quebec City. Throughout the spring, CATCA had been in the midst of collective bargaining, and would be in a strike position by late April. Guy Charette informed Livingston that the controllers in AQCNA would not support a strike unless CATCA was willing to support their desire to use French. Like his predecessor, Livingston was anxious to maintain solidarity and he agreed that the upcoming council meeting would hear a presentation by AQCNA on the language question.

AQCNA's approaches to the politicians were more disappointing. Whenever Jean Marchand, the minister of transport, who was the MP for the Quebec City riding of Langelier, flew home, controllers met him at the airport to urge that he authorize the expanded use of French. Marchand assured them he was on their side and had spoken to his civil servants about bilingual air traffic control. He urged them to be patient while the problem was being studied. Meetings with Quebec Cabinet ministers were equally inconclusive. Disappointed, the controllers decided to go public.

Charette held a press conference in Quebec City on March 13, 1974, at which he announced the formation of AQCNA, stated its objectives, and claimed that it represented 250 Quebec controllers. In response to this press conference, an MOT spokesman said that he had never heard of AQCNA. Ed Lesage, Quebec regional director of CATCA and—despite the name—an anglophone controller from Montreal, had heard of the association, but claimed that Charette represented only thirty or forty controllers, mainly in Quebec and Sept-Iles.[3] Roch Desgagne of *Le Soleil*, manifesting the advocacy journalism common in Quebec, followed his first article about AQCNA with one five days later with the headline: "What is Marchand waiting for before coming out in favour of the use of French in air traffic services?"[4]

The controllers began to step up the use of French at work, partly because at the same time that MOT's Civil Aeronautics Branch was studying the bilingualism problem, its Personnel Branch was taking action by carrying out, step by step, the bilingualization of air traffic control positions in Quebec. On March 24, just days after AQCNA made its first public statement, P. A. Cordeau, director of the Personnel Branch, wrote all unilingual Quebec controllers informing them that, even if they were unwilling to become sufficiently bilingual to satisfy the job requirements, or to transfer out of Quebec, MOT would nonetheless take measures necessary to provide the bilingual services required by the job. The francophone controllers chose to interpret the Personnel Branch's action as encouragement to use more French and chose to ignore the Civil Aeronautics Branch. This episode is an instance of the tendency of large organizations to function with less than perfect coordination, so that contradictory policies are followed.

On April 10, Charette announced that his members had begun to call pilots for Air France, Swissair, Sabena, the Quebec Government Air Service, and even Air Canada in French, and that many of the pilots were responding en français.[5] Thus, AQCNA was extending the use of French to pilots who were perfectly fluent in aviation English, which went far beyond communications with francophone VFR pilots who were marginally fluent in English. In order to give some credence to the use of French, AQCNA members contacted Air France pilots and ICAO for French lexicons, modified them to be consistent with Canadian usage, and distributed an unofficial lexicon of their own to francophone controllers and pilots.

Finally, AQCNA had not given up on Jean Marchard. On April 14, they presented him with a brief, which stated that AQCNA did not wish to break away from CATCA, but that its members simply wanted the Official Languages Act applied to their work. They also asked that MOT produce an official French air traffic control lexicon and other technical materials as soon as possible.[6]

THE RESPONSE TO AQCNA

The response of airline pilots to the controllers' initiative was complete opposition. They were particularly upset at the prospect of hearing French on IFR frequencies. On April 4, CALPA President J. B. Wright sent a telegram to Jean Marchand stating that "CALPA is unalterably opposed to any departure from the exclusive use of English in air traffic control."[7] A more informal expression of pilot opinion came from Guy Charbonneau, a francophone Air Canada pilot who wrote the *Montreal Star* on March 27 supporting unilingual English air traffic control. He claimed that "the English language is simple and to the point [while] French is a very flowery, beautiful language [which] is not, however, suited to conducting fast, explicit and efficient cockpit commands. I would not dream of using French in my cockpit any more than I would contemplate using English to make love."[8]

CATCA responded to AQCNA at the national council meeting on April 29 in Quebec City. MOT representatives and federal government mediator Stanley Hartt had also come to Quebec City for last-ditch negotiations. The council decided to hear a presentation of AQCNA's case by Guy Charette and Louis Doucet before bargaining with the government. Doucet and Charette emphasized the problem of unilingual francophone pilots, the growing use of French, and the ability of Quebec controllers to work in both languages. In answering questions, they were conciliatory in expressing their willingness to work within CATCA and their support for possible CATCA proposals to MOT for special licences restricting unilingual francophone pilots to flying only within Quebec. On the other hand, they were quite explicit about their desire to provide service in French for both VFR and IFR traffic.

After the presentation, the national council passed a resolution stating: "provided that MOT will limit unilingual French pilots to operation within the geographical confines of Quebec, exclusive of the Montreal International Airport and the Mirabel control zones and TRSA's, by means of specially endorsed licences, CATCA will not oppose the use of the French language in the provision of VFR services at airports within the Province of Quebec." The resolution attempted to strike a balance between the positions of AQCNA, on the one hand, and the unilingual anglophone controllers, especially in Montreal, on the other. The council, sympathizing with the francophone controllers who were being harassed by anglophone pilots, felt that accepting the reality of air traffic control in French at the smaller Quebec airports would end the harassment. On the other hand, by restricting unilingual francophone pilots to certain parts of Quebec, it was hoped that the jobs of unilingual anglophone controllers in

Montreal and elsewhere would be protected from a bilingual requirement. In addition, the council passed a resolution urging MOT to clarify its position on bilingualism.[9]

The council then heard a presentation by Jean-Luc Patenaude, urging greater use of French within CATCA. The council passed a resolution that CATCA would accept correspondence and grievances in either language, publish articles in CATCA publications in the language in which they were submitted, provide contract proposals to the branches in both languages, and publish the CATCA policy manual in both languages. This satisfied most of Patenaude's requests. However, concern was expressed over the cost of creating a second linguistic infrastructure for CATCA, especially because it would benefit only a few members. Therefore, the council went on record as urging bilingual members to use English in the interest of economy.[10]

In response to these decisions Charette declared himself satisfied, "for the moment," and promised that AQCNA members would join their CATCA colleagues in the event of a strike. However, he said that the resolution had not satisfied AQCNA totally and that its members might still take action to advance their cause.[11] The CATCA council's next order of business was collective bargaining. An agreement was reached on May 1, and ratified by the membership on May 6.

The next focus of AQCNA's pressure campaign was MOT. The person at whom the pressure was ultimately directed was Walter McLeish, director-general of civil aeronautics. The problem came to rest with McLeish because his superior, William Huck, the head of the air administration, did not have the aviation expertise to handle it. Huck had been trained as an accountant and entered the government as one of "C. D. Howe's boys" in the Department of Munitions and Supply. He rose to the position of assistant deputy minister in the Department of Supply and Services. In 1970, Deputy Transport Minister Stoner brought Huck to MOT to reorganize the air administration and implement a new financial control system.

Bilingual air traffic control thus was delegated to Walter McLeish. McLeish, who had served in the Royal Canadian Air Force as a flying instructor in World War II and later as an engineer, joined MOT in 1964 as chief aeronautical engineer and in 1970 was appointed director-general of civil aeronautics. McLeish is a most imposing fellow: tall and athletic (an expert skier and tennis player), with steel-grey hair and a craggy but youthful face and an air of authority. One journalist described him as "the sort of man you could see inspiring young pilots to screw up their courage, go into battle, and not crap out." One of my former students who joined MOT as a junior staffer recounts that he first saw McLeish at a meeting: "No one told me who he was, and he didn't say very much, but it was very clear to me who was in charge."

McLeish recognized how difficult an issue air traffic control would be. He knew how thoroughly opposed his anglophone staff were to the use of French and had spoken with Jean Marchand about the matter several times. Marchand's style was not to give his officials detailed orders, but rather to indicate the direction in which he wanted them to move. He told McLeish that he wanted something done to enable francophone pilots and controllers, like francophones in all walks of life, to address each other in French within Quebec.

In organizing the BILCOM study, McLeish had devoted a lot of effort to assembling a team of people who could take a dispassionate and unbiased look at the problem. For example, the leader of the team, Ross Wickware, was a bilingual anglophone, a former pilot, with a background in personnel management. Louis Doucet was chosen to express the Quebec controllers' viewpoint. The team was balanced between anglophone and francophone, and MOT headquarters staff and the Quebec region. Its mandate was to determine the demand for bilingual air traffic services and to make recommendations on how to meet that demand, taking into consideration the implications for aviation safety and human and financial resources. The study was to be completed by December 31, 1974.

On January 22, 1974, shortly after the BILCOM study got underway, Maurice Baribeau reported on the use of French in Quebec air traffic control.[12] His survey showed that 10 to 15 percent of the control transmissions in Quebec control towers other than Montreal were in French. While he listed Montreal as 100 percent English, he added the caveat that "there is no assurance that French is never used at the Montreal tower." Baribeau's memo continued: "There is no one in this Region who believes that safety is in jeopardy" because radio operators and controllers respond to pilots in French. McLeish passed Baribeau's memo on to the BILCOM team to use in their deliberations. His hopes that the problem would not get worse before the team's report might resolve it, were dashed by the Quebec City controllers' insistence on using French, which two MOT pilots forcefully brought to his attention.

On April 3, pilots Desmond Peters and Paul Saunders were sitting on the taxi-way in Quebec City, waiting to take off for Ottawa. A small plane was on the runway cleared for takeoff, but for some reason was unable to take off and turned back. This forced a small jet aircraft which had been cleared to land to overshoot the runway and circle back. Peters was then cleared for takeoff and began to taxi onto the runway. By this time the jet was again on its final approach; all Peters could do was to take off hurriedly before the other plane landed. Peters and Saunders were very upset because the transmissions to the small plane which had been unable to take off were given in French, and they therefore did not know what was happening. In addition, the controller had cleared them to take off at the same time that the small jet (albeit, with a pilot who used English) was on final approach. Peters blamed the entire incident on the use of French and on April 5 wrote a memo, which concluded: "This was an example of utter confusion in that pilots airborne and on the ground were unaware of what was going on due to the extensive use of French... unless something concrete is done in this regard it is only a matter of time before an accident will occur."[13]

When McLeish read Peters' memo, he concluded that the situation at Quebec City was becoming too serious to await the report of the BILCOM Task Force: he decided to set up a special study. Within days, Jean Marchand, who had just received the AQCNA brief, called McLeish to ask what he was doing to recognize the fact that French was now being used frequently at Quebec City.[14] McLeish informed him that he was setting up a safety investigation: Marchand asked to hear the results as soon as possible.

Walter McLeish is an unusual manager in that he is inclined to take risks and prefers to confront rather than avoid controversy. When organizing a study, he often brings in a subordinate who is knowledgeable of the problem, regardless of his biases. Thus, he appointed Desmond Peters to head the safety investigation. To balance the team, he appointed as members Gilles Foy, a francophone member of the BILCOM study, and J. M. R. Langlois, a francophone from the Quebec region. The team visited Quebec City airport from April 24 to 26, and completed its report by May 2.

The visit to Quebec City was very tense. Peters, who saw himself as an apolitical pilot and technician, was distinctly uncomfortable. When the team presented itself at the tower, the tower chief spoke to AQCNA President Guy Charette, who then called McLeish in Ottawa. Charette requested that two AQCNA members be present as observers at the interviews with air traffic controllers, and McLeish agreed. Peters felt their presence decreased the candour of the interview.[15] In the initial discussions, Charette referred to a tape he had made of a telephone conversation between Jean Marchand and himself: Peters felt it was entirely inappropriate for a civil servant to go over his superior's head to contact his minister and then use a record of such contact as a pressure tactic. However, the visit made Peters more sensitive to the problem of unilingual francophone pilots, and to the ability of controllers to handle both languages.[16] Reflecting on the incident of a few weeks earlier, Peters decided that the real problem had been in the controller's clearing him to take off when another plane was approaching, an error not related to language, since both pilots involved had been using English.

Peters reluctantly agreed with Foy and Langlois that, as an interim measure, pending the results of the BILCOM study, French could be used safely for VFR operations at Quebec City if a number of conditions were met. A proper lexicon would have to be provided for all controllers and pilots, the language used would be at the discretion of the pilot, not the controller, and controllers would pass along traffic information requested by unilingual pilots.

The rest of the report consisted of thinly veiled criticism of the Quebec controllers. Peters was particularly disturbed by the controllers' practice of initiating communications in French, especially with international flights. The recommendations included one that English alone be used to communicate with IFR traffic and another that "MOT Headquarters closely monitor the operational services provided by Quebec Tower / TCU in the French and English languages."[17] The AQCNA leaders recall that, before leaving, Peters summed up his position by saying that French was fine for VFR operations, but warning them not to "spoil the upper air space."[18] The two AQCNA representatives who sat as observers refused to sign Peters' report, issuing instead a minority report which recommended that bilingual air traffic services be provided at all airports in the province, for both VFR and IFR operations, immediately.[19]

After receiving Peters' report, McLeish was inclined to support its recommendations. On May 15, while still deliberating, McLeish wrote to Captain Wright, the president of CALPA, in response to Wright's telegram of April 4 to Jean Marchand. In his letter, he defended the francophone pilots' use of French for VFR operations, since restricting them or forcing them to learn English would be treating them as second-class citizens. On the other hand, he said that MOT's "preliminary thoughts suggest that IFR operations must remain English only" and assured Wright that "the use of French will not interfere with air transport operations."[20] Later in the struggle, the pilots would make this letter public in order to show McLeish's inconsistency, which they would claim was politically motivated.

After consulting Jean Marchand, McLeish proposed that VFR air traffic control at Quebec City and four smaller Quebec airports (St. Jean, Sept-Iles, Baie Comeau, and St. Honoré) be provided in both English and French, but that IFR operations remain in English. Marchand felt this was a reasonable solution.

On June 19, 1974, McLeish issued a notice to airmen (NOTAM), a temporary order authorizing the use of French for VFR operations at the five Quebec airports, pending the results of the BILCOM study, and subject to the conditions recommended in Peters' report.[21] Appended to the notice was a French lexicon.

After barely three months of organizational existence, the members of AQCNA had won some real victories. Five Quebec airports now permitted the use of French for VFR flights and all air traffic control positions in Quebec were in the process of being classified as bilingual. However, their ultimate objective—totally bilingual air traffic control throughout Quebec—had not been achieved, and CATCA, CALPA, and MOT appeared to be digging in to resist it.

<h2 style="text-align:center">MID-1974 TO MID-1975: A YEAR OF GROWING TENSIONS</h2>

On August 22, CATCA signed its collective agreement with the Treasury Board. Livingston told the Treasury Board he would not sign the French version of the contract unless it contained a clause stating that, because the contract had been negotiated in English, the English version would prevail in the event of any discrepancies between the two versions. When Treasury Board refused to add such a clause, Livingston refused to sign the French version. This refusal made the Quebec controllers doubt the sincerity of CATCA's commitment to expand the use of French internally. Their doubts were not assuaged by Livingston's explanation at a meeting with the Quebec local in February 1975 that the bargaining team had to devote a good deal of time to studying the English version of the contract prepared by MOT, did not have time to study the French version, and therefore had no intention of signing it then or in the future. The Quebec controllers took this to mean that Livingston was laying down a policy that CATCA would never sign the French version of any future collective agreement.[22]

CATCA decided to contest the designation of the 184 operating-level IFR controllers at the Montreal area control centre as bilingual, arguing that the only public the IFR controllers serve are pilots who are authorized to speak only English. However, because the power of designating positions is in the hands of the Treasury Board alone, CATCA could do little. By April 1975, CATCA had appealed the designation up to Gordon Osbaldeston, the highest-ranking civil servant in the Treasury Board's Secretariat, and had been rebuffed. The next appeal would have to be to the political level.

At the same time CATCA was fighting a losing battle with the Treasury Board, CALPA pilots were venting their feelings to the BILCOM Task Force. The task force held a public meeting in Dorval on December 4, 1974, at which CALPA organized a contingent of fifty pilots who vociferously opposed the use of French at any airport which served commercial traffic. At one point a pilot stood up, and angrily shook his fist at Louis Doucet, shouting: "You are the guy who started all this, aren't you!" Doucet wisely said that his role was to listen to the pilots and not present his own views.

On the other hand, the Quebec City controllers were not silent during this period. In March, Jean-Luc Patenaude, the chairman of the CATCA local, filed a complaint with the Public Service Staff Relations Board against his own union alleging that it was discriminating against its French-speaking members by failing to sign its collective agreement in French. The AQCNA members also began to proselytize among the francophone controllers in Montreal, using the direct phone lines between the two units to make their case. In November 1974, Roger Buisson, the treasurer of AQCNA, was transferred from Quebec to the Montreal centre, and he started to look for new recruits.

BILCOM: THE RESEARCH, THE REPORT, THE REACTION

Ross Wickware and the BILCOM team conducted fairly extensive research activities, including consultation with aviation organizations, a pilots' questionnaire, public meetings in Quebec, Ontario, and western Canada, visits to airports and the aviation industry in Quebec, and visits to air traffic control facilities in Europe. Despite the research, the BILCOM report itself was a rather cursory document, consisting of a survey of European practice, the results of the pilots' questionnaire, and a set of recommendations supported by rather brief justifications.[23]

The European survey mentioned the use of two languages for air traffic control in France, Belgium, Italy, Spain, and eastern Europe. Germany and the Scandinavian countries normally use English, but provide their own language on discrete frequencies for VFR pilots not using English.

The BILCOM questionnaire was sent to 7,500 pilots in Quebec, of whom 2,700 replied, a relatively high response rate of 36 percent.[24] The two major questions posed were whether pilots considered both English and French necessary for domestic air / ground communication, and which language pilots would use, if given the choice. The last question was designed to measure the latent demand for French on the part of francophone pilots.

These two questions present a good picture of the preferences of the pilots active at that time. The anglophones were almost unanimous (98 percent) in preferring English. On the other hand, a noticeable minority (13.3 percent) of the anglophone commercial and private pilots thought it necessary to have service provided in both languages. Among francophones, a clear majority of 68.5 percent preferred to have service available in both languages. A slight majority of the francophones (52.3 percent) preferred to use English themselves. As might be expected, the preference for the use of English was stronger among francophone commercial pilots than private pilots.

In their analysis, the BILCOM team accepted francophone arguments against the effectiveness of the listening watch and about the need to accommodate unilingual francophone pilots. As a result, they recommended a significant expansion of bilingual VFR air traffic services to include the other small airports in the province, either existing (St. Hubert, Val D'Or, Bagotville) or planned (Drummondville, Mont Joli, Sherbrooke, Trois-Rivières). They also recommended that the Montreal TRSA, national capital region, and all aeradio stations in northern Quebec provide VFR service in both languages. Because St. Hubert, located near Montreal, is a very busy VFR airport, they recommended reviewing the performance of bilingual operations there after a year.

They reached a different conclusion about bilingual IFR operations. Interpreting the survey, as well as the expressed willingness of francophone VFR pilots to learn aeronautical English in order to attain higher qualifications, as evidence of insufficient pilot demand for French, they recommended that IFR communications remain in English. Finally, they recommended that VFR operations into Dorval and Mirabel (which were heavily used by IFR traffic) also remain in English.

Despite the urgings of McLeish and Wickware, Louis Doucet wrote a minority report of his own. He argued that francophones should have a right to make a career of IFR flying within Quebec even if they are unable or unwilling to learn English. To fail to allow this would perpetuate the distinction between French as a language of culture and leisure and English as the language of work.

Doucet took issue with the very notion of surveying active pilots to determine the demand for French, because it ignored the latent demand on the part of the 4,000,000 unilingual francophone Québécois, some of whom might wish to fly if greater service were provided in French. He felt that the failure to provide service really put francophones in a vicious circle, whereby their demand could never justify an extension of service. As he put it: "pas de demande, pas de service, pas de demande." Doucet therefore recommended that all air traffic control service, both IFR and VFR, in Quebec be bilingual.

By April 1975, the BILCOM report had been completed and was awaiting release. On Sunday April 13, Louis Doucet met with Transport Minister Marchand for an hour, urging upon him the minority position of the task force. As Marchand's response was non-committal, AQCNA, which had received a copy of the report from Doucet, made it available to the separatist newspaper *Le Jour*. On Wednesday, April 16, *Le Jour* began publishing excerpts. That weekend, pilots for Quebecair and the Quebec Government Air Service and Quebec City controllers all sent telegrams to Jean Marchand demanding the right to use French for IFR operations. Quebec Premier Bourassa and Fernand Lalonde, the minister responsible for L'Office de la Langue Française, when asked for their reactions, tried to support the controllers and pilots without being overly critical of their federal colleagues.[25] Bourassa approved of the use of French "to the extent there are no technical objections," and Lalonde approved "to the extent that international rules permit."[26]

Keith Spicer, the commissioner of official languages, had been watching this issue for quite some time. In his 1974 annual report, he identified MOT as one of the government departments that was most sluggish in implementing any aspect of bilingualism.[27] In response to the controversy over the BILCOM report, he made an information-gathering visit to the Quebec City control facilities.[28] The next day, he called McLeish, Wickware, and the leaders of AQCNA together in Ottawa. The meeting was not very successful. The Quebec controllers were angry because the BILCOM report did not go far enough: Pierre Beaudry told McLeish that they were using French for IFR operations and would continue to do so, whereupon McLeish angrily threatened disciplinary action. However, he promised that the BILCOM report would not be the end of the matter and there would be additional studies of the use of French for IFR operations. AQCNA told McLeish that they were fed up with studies. In his announcement after the meeting, Spicer tried to put matters in the best possible light, saying that the meeting had led to an agreement that MOT would "work with a sense of urgency" on further studies with the Quebec controllers.[29]

CALPA responded to the activities of the Quebec aviation community with a statement that "the introduction of a second language in air traffic control can only be regarded as a step backward" and that "to deliberately downgrade an existing system for political expediency is to take an active part in the shaping of a potential disaster."[30] Copies were sent to all members of Parliament, and meetings were arranged with McLeish, Spicer, and interested MP's.

CALPA's spokesman who issued these strong words was Kenneth Maley, who had been elected president in November 1974. Maley is a unilingual anglophone who went from high school to the air force in 1952 and then to CP Air in 1966. In his late thirties, Maley was the youngest person ever elected president of CALPA and, as a first officer, was the only president who was not a captain. His unassuming and open manner, accompanied by a sincere demeanor and friendly smile, quickly won him support and he rose to president by 1974.

All the time that this debate was going on, the BILCOM report had still not been released. McLeish, still of the opinion that IFR air traffic control should remain unilingual, in April commissioned his staff to "present logical and conclusive arguments against the recommendation of the BILCOM minority report to provide bilingual communications in IFR operations." This report, completed on May 23, opposed bilingual IFR communications on the basis of the listening watch argument and the possibility of stray unilingual francophone pilots and also argued that IFR bilingualism would increase costs to the public, slow the flow of traffic, and limit the career aspirations of unilingual francophone pilots.[31] On May 25, Transport Minister Marchand tabled the BILCOM majority and minority reports, but not the report of McLeish's staff, in the House of Commons. Marchand announced that no action would be taken until this contentious question received further study and the aviation organizations had been consulted.

Though CALPA and CATCA both opposed the extension of French VFR services recommended in the BILCOM report, the report did contain some good news for CATCA in recommending that IFR operations use English alone. Livingston made a last effort to fight the bilingual designation of all Quebec controller positions, citing this recommendation as support for CATCA's position. On June 5, he wrote Jean Chrétien, president of the Treasury Board, asking for a final review. On July 17, Chrétien replied, informing CATCA that he upheld the bilingual designation.

At the time the BILCOM report was being released, a new deputy minister of transport was becoming acquainted with his job. On May 1, Sylvain Cloutier, former deputy minister of national defence, became deputy minister of transport. Regarded as a "rising francophone superstar" in the bureaucracy, Cloutier was respected by many for his intelligence and decisive administrative style. However, many of the anglophones in MOT feared that his objective was to shatter their grip on Transport, just as they felt he had attempted to do in National Defence. However, Cloutier's main priority at the outset was to implement the recommendations of the Davey Task Force on Transportation Policy.[32]

In learning about the bilingual air traffic control problem, it very quickly became apparent to Cloutier that William Huck was not interested in it, and thus he began to deal directly with Walter McLeish. Cloutier made it clear to McLeish that he had a strong sympathy for the francophone pilots and controllers and wanted to do everything possible to allow them to use French in all phases of air traffic control. McLeish with equal firmness responded that he did not believe that bilingual air traffic control was as safe as unilingual control. The forthright nature of this disagreement led the two men to respect each other's character and professionalism. McLeish came to understand Cloutier's objective, and Cloutier agreed that McLeish would be responsible for determining what was technically possible.

Otto Lang

Sylvain Cloutier

Walter McLeish

Jim Livingston

Ken Maley

Pierre Beaudry

Roger Demers

Jean-Luc Patenaude

Someone could see some humour in the situation. Cartoon by Aislin, *The Gazette*, December 16, 1975

Chapter Five

From Angry Words to Clenched Fists

The Canadian community must invest for the defence and better apprecia-
tion of the French language as much time and energy and money as are
required to prevent the country from breaking up.

Pierre Trudeau, *Federalism and the French Canadians*

This chapter discusses the growth of the bilingual air traffic control controversy between June and December 1975. At the outset of this period,
MOT tried to play the role of mediator, initiating studies and setting up
forums in which the opposing sides could iron out their differences. However, the francophone and anglophone controllers had no such desire:
rather, they took unilateral action, and began to mobilize both pilots and
public opinion to support them. By the end of the period MOT's role had
changed, and it too became a partisan, shifting towards the francophone
side in the dispute.

CONSULTATION ABOUT THE BILCOM REPORT

As director-general of civil aeronautics, Walter McLeish had the authority
to implement the BILCOM recommendations. However, because of the
disagreement between the two aviation communities, he decided to act
cautiously. In order to calm the situation, he called a meeting with representatives of all interested aviation organizations to discuss the BILCOM
report on June 26, 1975, at MOT Headquarters in Ottawa.

Transport Minister Jean Marchand began the meeting with a short
speech in which he affirmed the importance of safety, urged goodwill and
compromise, but made no specific suggestions. He then left, turning the
meeting over to McLeish, who acknowledged both positions, initially stat-

ing that "the use of one language is the safest approach" but then asking the anglophones, "can you deny a unilingual francophone the right to exercise a career in aviation in Quebec?" Finally, he urged the organizations to "look at the other side of things, the social justice side. Look for a solution between the extremes."[1]

The anglophone-dominated organizations had worked out a common approach in advance of the meeting. They would resist being drawn into any discussion about specific recommendations because they feared such discussion would be taken by McLeish to imply acceptance of them.[2] Their spokesman at the meeting, CALPA Vice-President D. Bruce Yake, rejected the entire BILCOM report, arguing that it had completely failed to conduct an objective analysis of the safety question. Benoit Ste.-Marie, of the Quebec Government Aviation Service, the unofficial spokesman for the francophones, recommended that all Quebec airports as well as the Ottawa airport provide air traffic control in both languages for both VFR and IFR pilots.[3]

Given this impasse, an embarrassed Walter McLeish brought the meeting to a quick conclusion. He announced that MOT would continue to study the most controversial BILCOM recommendations, would formulate plans for implementing the less controversial recommendations which he himself had approved, but would not implement anything until there had been another round of consultation with the organizations.

The francophones left the meeting very upset, having seen an opposition that was both united and vociferous. Ste. Marie was furious; Gilles Simard, the chief instructor for the Quebec Government Aviation Service, said it was the first time he was ashamed of being a Canadian.

The anglophone aviation leaders adjourned to a nearby hotel to analyse the meeting and discuss future strategy to block bilingual air traffic control. One of the people present at the meeting was John Keenan, CALPA's lawyer. Keenan, a fluently bilingual Montreal lawyer specializing in aviation law, prepared notes for CALPA on both the meeting at MOT and the post-mortem that followed.

The anglophones perceived that the MOT bureaucrats were sympathetic to their cause. Keenan wrote: "One could read between the lines that Mr. McLeish was under considerable political pressure on this issue. Indeed, the privately expressed views of MOT bureaucrats there were that BILCOM was an absolute waste of time, that MOT was backed into it and that they hoped we would serve as their scapegoats and 'scream like hell.'"[4] Conversation then shifted to strategies to fight its implementation. Keenan summarized a number of suggestions for normal lobbying activities. Two particular suggestions, however, stand out. One was to draw up a "special, simple incident form for all pilots flying into Quebec so that they may report any incidents of confusion, bilingualism, etc. for use by CALPA in supporting its position." This would go beyond standard practice whereby individual pilots would report such situations to MOT. The second was made by Russell Beach, president of the Canadian Owners and Pilots Association (COPA), which represents private pilots. Beach, a vehement opponent of bilingual air traffic control, suggested pilots who fly to Quebec and find the situation unacceptable could abort their flights. Keenan transcribed this suggestion as, "If necessary, a flight to Quebec, faced with a 'chaotic situation' could be aborted for safety's sake." It is not clear from the context whether this meant that pilots should abort flights to Quebec only if they felt the situation truly was unsafe, or whether they might abort flights on the pretext that it was unsafe, in order to gain publicity. The latter would of course be dishonest and irresponsible. Aware of this ambiguity, Keenan added the caveat "one must be careful here."

Keenan's notes on the meeting were presented to the CALPA Board of Directors a few days later. They endorsed the lobbying tactics and the creation of their anonymous incident report form, but were naturally hesitant about aborting flights to Quebec. They decided that pilots should only do this if they felt a flight truly was unsafe, and not as a pretext to draw publicity.

A Summer of Discontent

A few days after the BILCOM meeting, Walter McLeish left for Quebec City to take a French immersion summer course at Laval University so that he could meet the language requirement for his job. McLeish had grown up in Montreal, and had spoken some French as a child, but this knowledge had long since been lost. He left R. W. Dodd, the assistant director-general of civil aeronautics to act in his absence, warning him to be careful about the bilingualism problem. Dodd preferred to steer clear of it, since he opposed the limited steps to implement bilingual air traffic control which McLeish was taking and did not want to be in a position of conflict with his superior.

On July 14, Dodd sent out a letter to all the organizations which had been represented at the BILCOM meeting, reiterating what he understood to be the conclusion of that meeting, namely, that MOT would study some of the BILCOM recommendations, but that it would implement others without delay! Upon receiving this letter, CALPA, CATCA, and COPA felt that MOT had betrayed them by going beyond the sense of the meeting and angrily called Dodd. After consulting with McLeish, Dodd admitted his mistake. While this resolved the matter, it left Jim Livingston of CATCA, Ken Maley of CALPA, and Russell Beach of COPA somewhat suspicious of MOT's true intentions.

Their apprehensions grew as a result of a question in the House of Commons two weeks later. On July 29, Gordon Towers (PC, Red Deer) aggressively asked Jean Marchand: "in view of a statement made by CALPA.... that the very concept of bilingual air traffic services should be rejected..., will the Minister assure the House that the government will not take any unilateral action which would jeopardize complete and rapid comprehension of all communications by all pilots?"[5] The burdens of office (as well as a conviction for impaired driving) were resting heavily on Jean Marchand that summer, so much so that he was hospitalized a month later for exhaustion. Out of fatigue or possibly anger, he refused to take Towers' question seriously and simply replied "No, Mr. Speaker." Livingston, Maley, and Beach read this interchange and felt that they had again been told that unilateral action by MOT to implement bilingual air traffic control was a definite possibility.

Ken Maley's membership was troubled less by the statements of politicians and bureaucrats than by a very visible change in the work environment. Some of the francophone controllers at the Montreal area control centre had begun to use French in their conversations with one another and in their transmissions to francophone pilots. While this was not causing losses of separation, it was making the anglophone pilots insecure, confused, and angry. They retaliated by asking for translations. The controllers of course felt that these requests were a form of harassment and responded by telling the pilots that the conversations were of no concern to them. This reply, coming from "upstart" francophone controllers, greatly angered the anglophone pilots. Some were so incensed that, when they overheard transmissions in French, they pressed down the call button on their two-way radios which jammed the frequency, making all communications impossible. In short, there was a vicious circle of escalating misunderstanding, mistrust, and hostility.

In early August, the Canadian aviation community always gathers for the air show in Abbotsford, British Columbia. The CALPA Board of Directors met on August 7. They felt their membership was so incensed that, if they failed to act, the membership would "crucify" them. Some of Maley's predecessors had been criticized as being "too soft" vis-à-vis the government on a number of issues, and there was even talk among some Air Canada pilots of setting up a new association to replace CALPA. Its directors decided to take a hard line, and voted to order a twenty-four hour cessation of operations by all members unless the government withdrew the NOTAM authorizing the use of French at the five small Quebec airports and insisted on the use of English only for IFR operations. Furthermore, they threatened additional work stoppages if any of the BILCOM recommendations were implemented.

This decision was supported unanimously by the directors, but was questioned by two of CALPA's "civil servants," lawyer John Keenan and Director of Industrial Relations Ron Young. The two men, both experienced negotiators, were concerned that the resolution, which demanded that MOT completely reverse its policies left MOT with no bargaining room and put it on a collision course with CALPA. The directors responded by criticizing Keenan and Young, neither of whom were pilots, for their political approach to a question of professional ethics. However, the board did recognize the tactical validity of Keenan and Young's argument, and set the work stoppage for October 17, which would at least give the government some time to respond.

Ken Maley announced the decision to a crowded press conference after the day-long directors' meeting. A tired Maley, answering a question about support for the work stoppage, claimed that his membership, just like his Board of Directors, was unanimous in its support for English-only air traffic control. Upon hearing this, Jack Desmarais, a francophone Air Canada pilot who supported English-only air traffic control, slapped his forehead in dismay. He knew that there was substantial opposition to this position among francophone airline pilots based in Montreal, and he was certain that Maley's statement had just challenged the opposition to come forward.

Hart Finley, a former air force pilot (who looked every inch the part) and the director of MOT's Aviation Safety Bureau, was also present at Maley's press conference. Finley had long been interested in aviation safety and was instrumental in the establishment of the bureau in the late 1960s. After the press conference, he emphatically told the CALPA directors that he completely supported their view, and would do what he could to help.

Walter McLeish's reaction to the CALPA decision to hold a work stoppage was very different. The discussions with Sylvain Cloutier contributed to his rethinking of the bilingual air traffic control problem. In June, he had been dismayed at the way the anglophones had "ganged up" to prevent any serious consideration of any part of the BILCOM report. While studying French, he was still mulling over the question of bilingual air traffic control. The day after the pilots' announcement, the Quebec newspaper *Le Soleil* carried a story with the headline "Francophone air traffic controllers say we will not give in to pilots' blackmail."[6] His French teacher started class by asking McLeish, as the man in charge of the problem, to explain, en français, what the story was about and why francophone pilots should not be allowed to speak French with francophone controllers. McLeish had great difficulty justifying restrictions on the use of French because he was beginning to change his mind. As he said in an interview some years later:

As someone who has spent his whole life flying or working in aviation research and development I really had to search my soul. I was used to doing research and development [but on] the question of bilingualism, which remember is new to most of us, I was not using the same objective method of assessing the problem as I had for all the others. I was reacting instinctively, I realized, to my own background. I decided that the very least I could do was apply all my professionalism, divest myself of all other baggage. Once I did that, I began to define the problem differently. I began to realize that we could solve it.[7]

McLeish realized that the government would have to move to an air traffic control system in Quebec which would be increasingly bilingual. However, he still doubted whether bilingual IFR operations were either necessary or desirable. He asked himself whether he could support the introduction of more French into the system, and realized that if he could not, he should resign. On the other hand, he could not have been unaware that, given Cloutier's position, if he took the responsibility, he might well advance his career. He concluded that he was the man to do the job, and resolved that he would handle the problem, wherever it led him.

The battle between francophone and anglophone aviators continued. In mid-August, a French-speaking pilot flew a small aircraft to Toronto International Airport, landed on a runway being used for takeoffs, passed two jets waiting to take off, and then took off again without permission. Ken Maley drew this to the attention of the press.[8] A few days later, he gave a wide-ranging interview to the Canadian edition of *Time* magazine. Maley's unassuming and open manner, which appealed to his fellow pilots, made him an easy mark for a journalist's questions. After dealing with the aviation issue, he was asked by the interviewer to speculate on the broader implications of CALPA's action. An experienced politician would have dodged the question, but Maley was forthright, replying: "If we're successful and the Government withdraws this French program at the airport, it's going to be felt in other areas, particularly the civil service where this bilingualism and biculturalism thing has gone too far."[9]

The American aviation community also began to get involved, with Captain John O'Donnell of the United States Airline Pilots Association informing CALPA of their complete support[10] and Frank McDermott, an aviation consultant, telling an aviation workshop at the Canadian Bar Association meetings in Quebec City that all air traffic communications throughout the world should be in English.[11] Finally, John Keenan, CALPA's counsel, joined in, when he said in an interview at the aviation workshop, "there are Canadian pilots who won't fly to Paris" and that bilingual communications in Canada "are actively changing a good situation for the worse."[12]

The English press, for the first time, expressed itself editorially on this issue. There was near-unanimity in support of the pilots.[13] In sharp contrast to the editorial support the pilots and controllers received over the bilingualism issue was the editorial response a few weeks later to a threatened air traffic controllers' strike the day before Labour Day, to protest MOT's plan to give more responsibility to air traffic control assistants (who are not members of CATCA). Despite Jim Livingston's claim that the assistants were insufficiently trained and would therefore jeopardize safety, the English press was not impressed, and roundly denounced the controllers.[14] The *Globe and Mail*'s editorials present clearly contrasting responses to the two threatened strikes. The *Globe* looked at both threats, not on their own merits, but through the prism of its views on larger issues. The editorial on the pilots' threat was really an attack on what was felt to be the over-zealous interpretation of the Official Languages Act.[15] The editorial about the air traffic controllers' strike threat interpreted the issue as one of excessive power in the hands of the public service unions. The controllers' strike was ultimately averted in a last-minute compromise negotiated by Transport Minister Marchand. The *Globe and Mail* was distressed by this outcome, editorializing that "the federal government has once again yielded to a union which was using the people of Canada as hostages to gain its own ends."[16]

The dissatisfaction among Air Canada pilots in Montreal which Jack Desmarais foresaw after Maley's August 7 press conference, indeed occurred. On August 22, sixty-two pilots signed a letter to the chairman of their local which said that they believed that bilingual air traffic control would not impair safety and that they therefore opposed CALPA's one-day strike.

It was at this point that the francophone pilots and controllers began to recognize the extent of their common interests, and thought about forming a common organization to fight for the use of French in air traffic control and, more generally, for the expansion of opportunities in aviation for francophones.

The new organization chose the name l'Association des Gens de l'Air du Québec (AGAQ), and elected as its president Roger Demers, a pilot for the Quebec Government Air Service, as its vice-president Pierre Beaudry, the former vice-president of AQCNA, and as its publicity director Jean-Luc Patenaude, the chairman of the CATCA local in Quebec City. The founders envisioned that AGAQ would encompass francophones in all sectors of aviation in Quebec, but that its members would continue to belong to CALPA, CATCA, or any of the other national aviation organizations. AQCNA was subsumed in AGAQ, becoming the

Air Traffic Control Section. A recruiting drive among pilots, controllers, clerks, cabin attendants, and mechanics was launched immediately.

The original executive group of AGAQ present some interesting contrasts. Demers was by far the eldest, a rather phlegmatic person, termed by one interviewee as a "bon père de famille," a mediator, and a spokesman. Beaudry and Patenaude were much younger, Beaudry in his late twenties, Patenaude in his early thirties. Beaudry was thin, long-haired, ascetic-looking, articulate, intense, and occasionally excitable: many of the anglophone interviewees considered him a radical with whom it was difficult to deal. Beaudry's ambitions went beyond operational air traffic control, as he was taking part-time courses in law and management at Laval University. Patenaude was also a political activist, given to embarking on solitary crusades, such as his complaint to the Public Service Staff Relations Board about CATCA's refusal to sign its contract in French. Like Beaudry, Patenaude wore long hair (which in itself aroused suspicion among some anglophones), but was more even-tempered and pragmatic.

The origins of the name "Gens de l'Air" are rather unusual. On August 21, Patenaude and Beaudry were flying to Ottawa to attend the hearing of the Public Service Staff Relations Board dealing with Patenaude's complaint about CATCA's refusal to sign its contract in French. They were joking about the name for a fictional airline and came up with the pun "Légendaire." After the hearing, Patenaude was asked by CBC reporter Frank Hilliard whom he represented, and the first name he thought of was "Les Gens de l'Air." The name is also similar to "l'Association des Gens de la Mer," or the seafarers' union. The name stuck.

KEITH SPICER'S INITIATIVE

With the dispute mushrooming, and with an apparent vacuum at MOT, due to McLeish's temporary absence, Huck's reluctance, and Marchand's discomfiture, Commissioner of Official Languages Keith Spicer attempted to step into the breach and bring about a compromise.

Keith Spicer, who had been a professor of political science at the University of Toronto, University of Ottawa, and York University, was named the first commissioner of official languages when the position was created in 1970. Along with a staff of approximately eighty, Spicer's mandate was to advise the government on the implementation of bilingualism within the public sector, to respond to linguistic complaints by civil servants and the public, and, in general, to serve as an advocate for bilingualism. According to government thinking, the crux of the bilingualism problem was English Canadians' unwillingness to learn French and their resistance to French Canadians' aspirations. It was felt that Spicer, a man whose mother tongue was English but who had become perfectly bilingual, could exemplify tolerance and linguistic competence for English Canadians. Furthermore, he was witty and articulate in both languages, and could use his persuasive abilities to further the cause of bilingualism. Spicer used humour to advantage. As a professor, he once advised unilingual anglophones to learn French by finding francophone lovers: his annual reports were full of jokes, catchy titles, and cartoons, in order to attract public attention. Spicer felt it was crucial to increase the acceptability of his young institution: to do this he had to establish his *bona fides* as a linguistic ombudsman, rather than as a mouthpiece for government policy. This meant that he had to consider carefully when to work behind the scenes to influence government policy and when to make public statements.

Spicer spent part of August in Europe, visiting control towers and centres in countries which had bilingual air traffic control. Upon his return, he approached the various parties to the dispute to persuade them to meet and reconcile their differences. Ken Maley was receptive: the article in *Time* magazine had portrayed him as a bigot and had stirred up opposition within CALPA. He therefore wished to make a conciliatory gesture. Jim Livingston vigorously argued to Spicer that the controllers were not resisting bilingual air traffic control out of bigotry or self-interest but because of serious technical objections. Ultimately, Livingston, Beaudry and Patenaude of the Quebec controllers, and Russell Beach of COPA, agreed to carry discussions further.

Spicer convened a tense, day-long organizing meeting in Ottawa on September 5, attended by representatives of CALPA, CATCA, COPA, the Quebec pilots and controllers, and William Huck and Walter McLeish. Huck's major concern was territorial: bilingual air traffic control was MOT's jurisdiction, not Spicer's. Livingston was not willing to negotiate face-to-face with the Quebec controllers because as president of CATCA, he claimed to represent all members of the association. These concerns were ultimately incorporated in the terms of reference they hammered out for a special committee on bilingual air traffic control. The terms were:

1. Each interested organization (CATCA, CALPA, COPA, Quebec Government Aviation Service) should, if possible, be represented by one anglophone and one francophone. The Quebec controllers therefore were not represented in their own right, but as members of CATCA, which satisfied Livingston's concern.
2. The committee would deal with technical aspects of the bilingual air traffic control problem, with the sole objective of maximizing aviation safety, and attempt to reach agreement as soon as possible.
3. The committee would be chaired, not by Keith Spicer, but by a representative of MOT, who, it was hoped, would be perceived by all the participants as neutral.

4. The committee would issue a unanimous report and no minority reports.
5. All parties to the committee would refrain from public statements until after the report was complete.[17]

McLeish named as chairman Hart Finley, the director of the Aviation Safety Bureau, who in August had been in such vigorous agreement with CALPA at the Abbotsford meeting. McLeish followed the same strategy he employed in appointing Peters to head the aviation safety study in Quebec in 1974: he hoped that Finley would confront his prejudices and deal with the issue technically and professionally.

The committee held two key all-day meetings on September 23 and 24. The only results by the end of the second day were an agreement that aeradio stations in Quebec could use French for communications with aircraft flying VFR, and a decision to invite Keith Spicer to their next meeting for a pep-talk. The transcript of these meetings indicates why so little progress had been made that it was felt necessary to recall Spicer.

COPA's anglophone executive director, William Peppler, displayed a total incomprehension of the francophone position. At the outset of the meetings, he said, "I feel the injustice is our failure to help francophones to learn sufficient phraseology to communicate in the most normal manner."[18] The francophones responded to this with some exasperation. Jean Guertin, a pilot for Quebecair replied: "We are not happy to be compared to Canadian minorities. We speak one of the official languages."[19]

Given the dissension within his ranks, Jim Livingston instructed CATCA's anglophone representative, Vice-President Mike Tonner, to say little, except about matters directly pertaining to controllers' operational responsibilities.

With CATCA taking a back seat, CALPA tried to play a major role in the committee. Its two representatives were President Ken Maley and Robert MacWilliam, an Air Canada pilot and CALPA director of the central region (Ontario and Quebec).

CALPA presented several proposals. Their main thrust was that unilingual francophone pilots should be restricted to certain Quebec airports as part of the licensing process. CALPA did not indicate which airports, but said that they ought to be designated on the basis of traffic mix, presumably those airports with substantial commercial traffic not being open to the unilingual francophone pilot. Maley suggested providing materials for student pilots so as to encourage them to learn standard English terminology. Finally, he suggested that bilingual air traffic control units be established throughout Quebec and on its periphery.[20] CALPA felt that this approach would contain the unilingual francophone problem, while the bilingual controllers could handle any emergencies. CALPA's differences with controllers were made clear by its advocating that all Quebec controllers be bilingual. Its attitude towards the accommodation of unilingual francophone pilots was very unsympathetic; as Maley told Jean Guértin: "You are saying if we have cowboys breaking rules then we should accommodate them by changing the rules."[21]

Maley and MacWilliam were so belligerent because they had backed themselves into the corner of which Keenan and Young had warned them in Abbotsford. To be consistent with their call for the revocation of the NOTAM designating five Quebec airports as bilingual for VFR services, they had to object to the use of French at least at one of the five airports, of which Quebec City was the logical one, since it was served by commercial airlines. Privately, Maley had told Keith Spicer, McLeish, and some of the francophones that he could live with bilingualism for VFR operations at the five Quebec airports, but that he could not say that openly until after the October 17 work stoppage. However, Jean Guertin was unwilling to accept this promise, given the combative tone of the two meetings. Towards the end of the second meeting, he told Maley, "We should clarify the issue of the five airports. We are not ready to give up bilingualism.... If you want them unilingual, we will pack up our bags and go home."[22]

The crucial role of trying to keep the meetings together fell to Hart Finley, who tried to take a neutral position, one in which safety was his prime concern and in which he was skeptical of all undocumented claims. He did not accept the francophones' claim that experience in Quebec had proven that the use of French for VFR operations increased safety, saying, "we have had 16 months of [French in VFR operations]. This may or may not be representative. There could be a hazard we have not come across."[23] Very quickly, the francophones became frustrated with this approach. Roger Demers, representing the Quebec Government Air Service, asked: "Would anyone have an objection to using French in VFR?", and Finley responded: "On the view expressed here we are not in a position to comment."[24] Guertin followed by sarcastically asking Finley why MOT allowed high performance military aircraft using UHF frequencies to share airports with civilian aircraft on VHF. "Why do you tolerate this?... What is happening? Is this not dangerous?" Finley lamely backed off, saying, "I cannot comment on this, I do not have sufficient knowledge."[25] Finley tried to keep the meetings moving constructively, by shifting the conversation to technical aviation concerns as opposed to broad discussions of linguistic rights. He was willing to volunteer any data MOT had available. However, the francophones, with considerable justification, saw him as an anglophone who was taking an unduly skeptical position, and who could never be convinced that bilingual air traffic control could be safe.

The francophones grew more and more exasperated with what they perceived to be the mixture of intolerance and delaying tactics displayed by the anglophones. At the meeting on September 30, Roger Demers announced that all the francophones on the committee henceforth would be representatives of AGAQ. He then put forward a proposal that "the special committee discuss implementation and enforcement dates for the introduction of bilingual air traffic control at all airports in the Province of Quebec where it is not already in progress."[26] The proposal was strongly opposed by the anglophones, and the meeting broke up, with only an agreement to meet one last time on October 9.

At that meeting, Roger Demers presented a memorandum written by AGAQ, which ended with this impassioned plea.

But who is opposed to bilingualism? Many people outside the Province of Quebec are opposed. Certain of them are simply psychologically blocked. Others who are more experienced have been trying objectively to understand. But what is their problem? Perhaps, as privileged unilingual anglophones, they cannot perceive the problem of comprehension, because they have always understood everything.... Rather than reflect and discuss the problem, CATCA and CALPA prefer to instigate incidents and sow panic among the Canadian public. Does the psychological discomfort that they feel due to the use of a second language outweigh the injustice imposed on francophones who are eliminated completely from flying or often restricted to careers as bush pilots? Let's get to the point...IFR flights in Quebec: bilingual or not. Does the pilot, where it is possible, choose his language of work or does MOT choose it for him?[27]

In response, Finley proposed looking at MOT's technical studies. The anglophones supported him, the francophones would have none of it, and the committee disbanded.

Spicer's initiative in forming this committee was a noble one, but the structure made it unworkable. The representatives of a number of the organizations were constrained in various ways. Any agreement the COPA and CATCA representatives made would have to be ratified by their executive and membership, so they therefore had no real authority. Ken Maley's authority as president of CALPA was restricted by his Board of Directors' commitment to stage a work stoppage. The francophone individuals found their role as representatives of unsympathetic organizations most unnatural, and they responded by regrouping under the banner of AGAQ. What the committee could do was itself unclear. Its aim was to reach agreement within the shortest possible time. Given the divergence in views, no agreement could occur except after prolonged study. There were no resources or mandate to undertake such a study and the representatives had other organizational commitments which precluded their involvement for any prolonged period. Given this situation, it was not surprising that the individuals chose to ignore the possibility of acting in unison as a study group, and simply restated their original opinions. Thus, there was no movement to a consensus, only an exacerbation of the feelings of distrust and bad faith with which the process had begun.

LANG, CLOUTIER, AND McLEISH:
BETWEEN AN IRRESISTIBLE FORCE AND AN IMMOVABLE OBJECT

On September 25, as part of a major Cabinet shuffle brought about by the resignation of Finance Minister Turner, Prime Minister Trudeau made his close friend, the ailing Jean Marchand, minister-without-portfolio and appointed Otto Lang minister of transport. Trudeau felt that the Transport portfolio needed someone with the analytical ability to master its complexities and the administrative ability to manage its day-to-day problems at the same time that he would be implementing the recommendations of the Davey Task Force. Finally, given the importance of transportation issues in western Canada, a westerner would be preferable. Otto Lang was precisely the person needed. Like Trudeau, Lang had been a law school professor (and dean of Law at the University of Saskatchewan) before entering politics. In previous portfolios, such as Justice, Lang had impressed Trudeau and the rest of the Cabinet with his analytical grasp of the most complicated policy problems, his decisiveness in choosing solutions, and his tenacity in implementing them. However, the decisiveness and tenacity which Trudeau admired in Lang were perceived by his detractors as stubbornness and inflexibility. Some of Lang's actions while minister of justice—such as his steadfast opposition to abortion and his repeated prosecution of Dr. Henry Morgentaler—were seen by his critics as examples of dogmatic rigidity, and an attempt to impose his Catholic beliefs on the nation.

Bilingual air traffic control was one of the initial problems facing Lang in his new portfolio. After being briefed by McLeish, one of Lang's first visitors was Ken Maley, who expressed dismay over the Finley committee, which was then on its last legs, and reiterated his strike threat. As Lang told broadcaster Patrick Watson some months later: "I remember going home and saying that I had just observed the immovable object and the irresistible force, and was squarely in between the two of them."[28]

The first priority for Lang, Cloutier, and McLeish was averting a pilots' strike. They tried to convince the pilots that MOT had no imminent plans to make IFR air traffic control bilingual, and that any extensions of bilingual control would be done only after having been proven completely safe. On October 3, after it had become clear that the Finley committee would fall apart, McLeish and Finley appointed a three-person team to study facilities and operational procedures at Quebec City airport, which had been the subject of most pilot complaints. The report was due October 10. The study found that there were a number of problems at Quebec City, but that they were not language-related.[29]

On October 15, just two days before the threatened work stoppage, McLeish and Finley met the board of CALPA at the Montreal Airport Hilton to convince them to stay on the job. The CALPA board stated that the Quebec City airport study was irrelevant to their concern, which was the accelerating use of French at Quebec airports, which they felt McLeish and his staff were unable to control. They were not persuaded to change their plans. However, at the same time McLeish was attempting to persuade the pilots not to walk out, the airlines were enlisting the force of the law. Air Canada obtained an injunction in Quebec which ordered CALPA to ensure that pilots reported to work. CALPA's problems of internal cohesion once again became apparent. John Keenan's memo summarizing the BILCOM meeting the previous June had found its way to the Montreal CALPA local, and from there into the hands of the Quebec press. On October 16, both Le Devoir and La Presse published articles quoting from the document. Le Devoir's article, entitled, "Disguised protest against the use of French: CALPA tells pilots to increase the number of incidents," drew the most unfavourable interpretation possible of the memorandum.[30] Otto Lang was asked about the Keenan memorandum and he replied, "Obviously it isn't a fact that [the Quebec aviation environment] is unsafe and therefore [the recommendations] seem to be an unnecessary and provocative move. But I have only seen reports of this."[31] Thus Lang was aware, if only for a fleeting moment, of the Keenan memorandum, a piece of paper which would turn out to be extremely significant a few months later.

Faced with the court action and the possibility that francophone pilots would not support the work stoppage, the CALPA directors decided to cancel it. Furthermore, the pilots' threatened work stoppage did not seize the nation's attention. On October 15, Prime Minister Trudeau announced the imposition of wage and price controls, a controversial policy which would be the focus of political attention during the fall and winter.[32]

Throughout the fall, Lang, Cloutier, and McLeish were struggling to keep the issue under control. On the one hand, the pilots and controllers in Quebec were attempting to make bilingual air traffic control a de facto reality, simply by speaking French. On the other hand, the anglophone pilots and controllers watched MOT very suspiciously for any sign that it was giving in to the francophones. In this delicate situation, they attempted to enunciate a policy of proceeding with caution. McLeish would initiate additional studies of various aspects of the language problem to satisfy the francophones. However, no changes in existing policies would be made until the studies were complete, the aviation community had been consulted, and McLeish was satisfied that new procedures had been worked out so as to ensure the same level of safety in a bilingual air traffic control system as in a unilingual one: it was hoped that this would satisfy the anglophones. In discussions with Maley and Livingston during the fall, McLeish did not mention the change of heart he had had over the summer: rather, he emphasized that he did not think MOT would want to implement bilingual IFR air traffic control. Publicly, MOT took a similar line. In response to a speech by Jack Murta (PC, Lisgar) criticizing bilingual air traffic control, the government's policy was expressed in the House of Commons by Ralph Goodale (Liberal, Assiniboia), Lang's parliamentary assistant, on October 27: "The decision to introduce further changes to the existing situation will not be made before the most exhaustive examination clearly indicates that such changes will appear to be safe and will in fact be safe."[33]

At that time, McLeish asked Archie Novakowski of the Air Traffic Services Branch to prepare a report on how some of the BILCOM recommendations might be implemented. In dealing with bilingual IFR operations, Novakowski suggested that MOT set up a thorough study of the effects of two languages, using MOT's newly opened air traffic control simulation centre.[34] McLeish agreed that the logical next step would be the simulation studies, and began to plan them.

The Treasury Board's upholding of the designation of all Quebec control positions as bilingual meant that it was inevitable that Quebec controllers would be permitted to speak French among themselves, even if they only spoke English to pilots. Therefore, on November 6, McLeish asked the Quebec region to formulate recommendations concerning the use of French in communications among controllers: the region established a committee on "Inter- and Intra- Air Traffic Control Unit Communications" which had a mandate to report by early January.[35] At the same time that McLeish was attempting to start planning for future changes, he felt it was necessary to assert control over the existing situation. He was particularly concerned about the unauthorized and irregular use of French for IFR communications by Montreal controllers and some pilots. He convinced Cloutier that MOT's existing policy had to be restated as emphatically as possible. McLeish and Cloutier drafted a NOTAM which was then issued by Otto Lang on November 12. It "[prohibited] IFR flights except where a continuous listening watch is maintained on the appropriate air traffic control frequency, and two-way communication in the English language only is established and maintained with the air traffic control unit concerned."[36]

In justifying the issuance of the NOTAM, McLeish drafted a memorandum signed by Huck and sent to Cloutier. The memorandum advocated, without qualification, a restriction on bilingual air traffic control: "A mix of two languages introduces factors of misunderstanding, communications delays and retarded compliance in flight control procedures, and consequent deterioration of safety."[37]

This NOTAM was received very angrily in Quebec. On November 16, Roger Demers sent an outraged telegram to Prime Minister Trudeau calling it "the summit of the racism of the senior civil servants of MOT." He asked Trudeau to intervene personally in the matter, and expressed the fear that "the air traffic control system in Quebec would be gravely disrupted if MOT becomes embroiled in so shameful a display of anglophone hegemony."[38] Trudeau's initial response, conveyed through his office, was to tell AGAQ that he supported them, but to urge them to show patience and serenity. Demers gave copies of the telegram to the press, along with copies of the memos that had been sent to controllers in Quebec demanding that they use English. A spate of headlines and front page stories followed.[39]

Pressure mounted within the House of Commons as well. Pierre De Bané, (Liberal, Matane), on November 18 asked Otto Lang what his policy was in the light of the recent NOTAM. Lang simply reiterated that the use of French for IFR services was still under study.[40] De Bané's question in the House was just the tip of an iceberg. The Quebec caucus was putting great pressure on Otto Lang to reverse his policy, so much so that Liberal MP Bryce Mackasey mused to the press that "the caucus was guilty of unfairly attacking newly-appointed Transport Minister Otto Lang for the government backtrack on the use of French in air-ground communications at Quebec airports."[41] Resolutely, Lang, Cloutier, and McLeish resisted the pressure to extend bilingual air traffic control before they thought it had been studied thoroughly. Patrick Watson, himself the holder of an IFR instructor's licence, was well aware of the turmoil within the aviation community. On December 4, he interviewed Walter McLeish on the CBC television program "The Watson Report": the interview clearly presented McLeish's ambivalent thinking at the time. Watson asked him about whether French would be used for IFR traffic, and he replied: "We have not found an urgent need to introduce the second language, for example, under instrument flight rules...we find that all instrument-rated pilots who are French speaking have a good command of English because they had to be able to pass their instrument test in English."[42] McLeish's answer to Watson's question about the effect of bilingualism on operational efficiency shows the extent of his uncertainty:

If we were to introduce the second language into IFR operations in Montreal, we would have to curtail the present number of operations, which I would say with parallel runway systems, can be as high as 60 an hour. We'd probably have to pare it back to something,... it would probably drop back to 40 an hour, so there's an economic penalty, for using two languages.... Well I can't give you that figure, because we're still studying the problem, but we know we're going to have to cut it back. I'm just guessing. It might have to be cut back by about one-third, and it may even be as much as half initially, then we'd work it up to some higher figure.[43]

These statements gave CATCA and CALPA some confidence that the status quo would be preserved. Ken Maley, in his newsletter to CALPA members dated December 12 (but which was written several days earlier) observed that

Public pressure and political uneasiness created by CALPA's protests would appear to have brought about a much more conservative approach [to bilingual air traffic control].... Otto Lang has, to date, at least, given CALPA assurance of a truly objective re-evaluation of the entire program, while Walter McLeish continues to state that no further moves will be made without full consultation with the industry and affected parties.[44]

As we shall see, the status quo which Maley thought was being preserved had, by the very date of his newsletter, completely been transformed.

CONFRONTATION AT THE MONTREAL CENTRE

The unauthorized use of French by some Montreal controllers had opened a rift between those who favoured bilingual control and those who opposed it. With the issuance of the NOTAM on November 12, the rift became a chasm. The core of the former group were the Gens de l'Air activists and the core of the latter the unilingual anglophones. However, there were a large number of partially bilingual anglophones and bilingual francophones who were now being forced to take sides. This group split primarily on linguistic lines, with the francophones supporting bilingual air traffic control and the anglophones unilingual control. However, a few francophones split with their linguistic confrères and sided with the unilingual proponents.

The group that favoured the use of French realized that, because of the teamwork necessary for air traffic control operations, as long as there were unilingual anglophones at the Montreal centre, the language of operations would be English. Thus, they began to use French, in order to provoke a situation in which the anglophones would either have to conform to the practice of the francophone majority in the centre, or leave. As a consequence, tension between the groups grew. Members of each group grew sloppy in making "handoffs" of aircraft to members of the other group. Both groups were looking, almost with anticipation, to the one small insult that would justify fisticuffs. It almost happened when a francophone called an anglophone a "maudit juif," and another anglophone pulled the francophone from his chair. In addition, there were threats of violence against Ed Lesage, the anglophone Quebec regional CATCA director: police were posted at his house for protection.

The air traffic control supervisors were in a terribly difficult position. As early as August, William Huck had requested that they take disciplinary action, if necessary, to ensure that English only was used.[45] While the supervisors had relayed Huck's threat to the controllers, they were unwilling to act. To begin with, both the tower and the centre were seriously under-staffed. Francophone managers like Maurice Pitre, director of air traffic control for the Quebec region and Louis Desmarais, the chief of the control centre, had some sympathy with the desire of the francophone controllers to speak French and some resentment towards the anglophone administration in Ottawa which was ordering them to put themselves on the line by disciplining individuals. Their reluctance grew after they received phone calls threatening violence if controllers were disciplined. Pitre and Desmarais, along with their families, moved to hotels, with RCMP protection.[46]

For several weeks, Jim Livingston warned Walter McLeish that violence could erupt in the Montreal centre at any moment. However, the Quebec regional administration, fearing Ottawa's intervention, reported that discipline was being maintained.

In the absence of any action by the Quebec regional administration or MOT headquarters, both sides felt that something had to be done to signal to the outside world how serious matters had become, and to resolve the dispute. On Friday, December 5, an anglophone controller on the James Bay sector heard a francophone radio operator speaking in French to a pilot. The controller was so upset that he stopped work and asked unit chief Louis Desmarais to relieve him of his duties. Desmarais did so, without suspending his pay. On Saturday, a francophone and an anglophone got into a heated argument over the use of French. A few hours later, another argument arose among another anglophone controller, a francophone trainee who was using French and the trainee's francophone monitor. The anglophone was sent home, also with pay, by the supervisor. Later that day, another anglophone, who had been threatening not to work, upon hearing a francophone using French, got up from the radar and carried out his threat. He was sent home on leave without pay. On Monday, December 8, two francophone controllers, Serge Cormier and Roger Buisson, were suspended without pay for one day for speaking French, after having been warned not to do so.[47]

After weeks of inaction, Louis Desmarais and his supervisory staff had finally been forced to act. There were immediately reverberations throughout the province. Serge Cormier contacted MP Serge Joyal (Liberal, Maisonneuve-Rosemont) who happened to be a friend of his brother. The Gens de l'Air issued a statement denouncing the suspensions and demanding that the civil servants in Ottawa cease bowing to anglophone lobbying, that the members of Parliament rise up against this aberration, and that Otto Lang enforce the Official Languages Act. Pierre Beaudry told the press that AGAQ would not suggest timid measures, such as work stoppages, but that the controllers would keep speaking French, and would dare MOT to suspend them all.[48]

The issue was picked up by the Quebec government, the journalists, and Quebec MPs. On Tuesday, Premier Bourassa, who until then had said nothing about this issue that might antagonize his federal colleagues, told the National Assembly that it was unacceptable that controllers could not use French and that he would make representations to Ottawa concerning Buisson and Cormier. That same day, Quebec MPs of all parties posed questions to Lang about the suspensions, with the questioning led by Serge Joyal and Pierre De Bané. Lang continued to hold his ground, stating that "in each case it is necessary for us to enforce the regulations as they stand," but indicating that the government was studying the bilingualism problem and hoped to make progress "to allow for the use of French where reasonably possible, but we have to do so with serious consideration of safety."[49] On Wednesday night, Keith Spicer decided to call public attention to the situation by visiting the Montreal centre. He then wrote a public letter to Sylvain Cloutier, discussing the factors which had led to the suspensions and recommending that French be used for communications among controllers in Montreal and that financial penalties against individuals be waived.[50] He visited Otto Lang the following evening to warn him of the seriousness of the situation at the Montreal centre. On Friday, *Le Devoir*'s associate editor Michel Roy justified Cormier and Buisson's action by saying: "When a francophone civil servant sees himself forbidden to use the language of Quebec because of a federal regulation invoked five years after the adoption of a law [i.e., the Official Languages Act] which the authorities have forgotten to apply to his work, he has no recourse other than to disobey the regulation in order to denounce this absurdity. Mr. Trudeau himself would have done that."[51]

This new situation brought about changes in opinion within the Liberal's Quebec caucus. Moderates like caucus leader and Health and Welfare Minister Marc Lalonde were now in agreement with linguistic nationalists like Joyal and De Bané that MOT had to hasten the implementation of bilingual air traffic control. Lang could no longer resist the pressure of the entire Quebec caucus. On Thursday, December 11, he agreed to change the thrust of his policy, in that he would set forth publicly the goal of total bilingual air traffic control in Quebec, including IFR operations, and would enunciate a timetable for achieving it.[52] Speaking in the House of Commons on Friday, December 12, Lang announced that "[the government] fully appreciated the aspirations of French-speaking members of the aviation community to use their own language and that with the co-operation of all concerned, we believe that we could make rapid progress in meeting these aspirations."[53]

In order to announce the shift in his policy to the aviation community and to see first-hand the extent of the discipline problem at the Montreal centre, Lang, Cloutier, and McLeish decided to visit the centre on Saturday, December 13. Lang would give a formal speech announcing the change in direction. McLeish and Cloutier drafted the text Thursday night, over a bottle of Scotch. McLeish provided the most rapid implementation timetable he could live with. It was very optimistic, in that, contrary to Murphy's Law, it assumed that whenever something could go wrong, it would not.

On Friday, Marc Lalonde checked over the draft prepared by Lang and McLeish. He was pleased with the strong tone and the rapid timetable: the speech embodied the position taken by the caucus. Word of Lang's impending visit spread rapidly, and a number of MPs (Marc Lalonde, Serge Joyal, and Rod Blaker, the member for Lachine-Lakeshore, in whose riding the airport was located) decided to accompany Lang. Provincial Liberals, the leaders of the Gens de l'Air, anglophone controllers, and the press were also informed of the event.

On Friday afternoon, Otto Lang went to a Christmas cocktail party given by CATCA. He exchanged pleasantries with Jim Livingston, whom he had met once before, but said nothing about what was to happen on Saturday.

On Saturday morning, in a crowded air traffic control centre, Lang announced the progressive implementation of a number of measures that would bring about full bilingual air traffic control service in Quebec.[54] They included an eight-week simulator study of bilingual IFR control, and then the development of procedures for bilingual IFR and VFR operations at Dorval and Mirabel. The speech set a strong tone, indicating that the government would be moving rapidly ahead. While it mentioned many opportunities for consultation with the aviation community, its tone indicated that MOT would be making the ultimate decisions and that the aviation industry would not be able to veto implementation. Finally, Lang reiterated "the need for good will, co-operation, and active participation for all interested parties in the program of consultations in the months ahead,"[55] and, in order to show his own spirit of good will, announced that he would reduce the financial penalties for the controllers who had been suspended or given leave without pay. Lang's speech squarely moved the government's role from that of neutral arbiter to committed participant.

The francophone controllers responded to the speech joyously: they had won a victory. Ed Lesage, the anglophone Quebec regional director of CATCA, while walking out of the meeting, turned to Jean-Luc Patenaude, told him he was exhausted, and offered Patenaude his CATCA position. The anglophones at the centre were crushed and some were in tears: it was now clear to many of them that, with a government commitment to increasing the use of French, there was no place for them in Quebec. They demanded a meeting with Lang and McLeish, to explain their version of the events of the previous few weeks. Lang and Cloutier listened sympathetically for a while, and then returned to Ottawa to pursue other commitments. McLeish remained behind to continue the discussion. For the first time he saw the anglophones' despair and heard the stories of threats and near-fights, which shocked him deeply. McLeish gave the men a commitment that he would become personally involved in resolving their problems. He promised that there would be meetings the following week, that he would set up direct lines of communications with them, and that he would monitor the control centre on a day-to-day basis until the situation stabilized. McLeish let it be known that if stability could not be restored at the Montreal centre, he would order it closed, and traffic handled by the other centres. Late Saturday evening, McLeish, shaken, returned to Ottawa.

In contrast, upon returning to Quebec City after the meeting, Demers and Patenaude toasted their victory with champagne. Louis Doucet partook, but voiced the premonition that they might be acting prematurely.

The reaction in the anglophone aviation community was that they had been betrayed. Ken Maley telephoned Walter McLeish on Sunday and asked him to explain why MOT had changed its position overnight. McLeish replied that the initiative for the rapid implementation timetable had come from Lang for political reasons, but that he himself felt the timetable was reasonable. However, he assured Maley that bilingual IFR operations would not be implemented until they were certified as safe. Maley no longer felt he could believe McLeish: he was sure that if the Montreal control centre was to be taken over by bilingual francophones, the pressure to use French in IFR operations in the very near future, whether or not it was safe, would be overwhelming.

Maley and Livingston, after conferring, requested a meeting with Otto Lang on Monday, where they pressed him to make a public statement that MOT was not irrevocably committed to the expansion of bilingual air traffic control into IFR and VFR operations in the Montreal area unless studies proved they were safe. Not only did Lang refuse to make such a statement, but Sylvain Cloutier, who was also present, said that there was a possibility bilingual air traffic control could be expanded to Ottawa and Moncton.[56] Livingston and Maley told Lang that they were completely unsatisfied with his position, and that they would take all possible steps to resist MOT's new policy.

At this point, CATCA did not feel bilingual air traffic control had been rammed down their throats, but rather that it had been implemented by stealth behind their backs. CATCA had appealed the bilingual designation of all Quebec air traffic controllers right up to Treasury Board President Jean Chrétien, and lost. Because the supervisors in the Montreal control centre had not been willing to enforce the language rules, CATCA felt it was inevitable that the anglophone controllers would have to leave Montreal and be replaced by bilingual francophones. Vice-President Bill Robertson, who had been assigned the task of monitoring the situation at the Montreal centre, reported to the national council on December 18, that CATCA "should make every effort to expedite the transfers of those persons wishing to leave Quebec not only for the sake of their peace of mind and health but also for the safety of the flying public."[57] Lang and McLeish were now moving ahead on their bilingualization policy step by step, and consultation would not stop them. One CATCA executive described CATCA's position then as one of "playing catch-up ball." Then he thought of the contract negotiations with MOT. CATCA's contract expired on December 31, 1975. Negotiations had begun in November, and in mid-December recessed until the new year. On December 23, the CATCA negotiating committee met and decided that in January they would introduce the question of bilingualism into the negotiations. They knew that MOT would not accept this, because the Public Service Staff Relations Act does not permit collective bargaining about matters of government policy, such as bilingualism. However, it was the best card in their hand, and they were determined to play it.

Maley, Livingston, and Beach began calling each other more frequently. The response to their public statements in English Canada in the previous months convinced them that there was widespread opposition to the government's bilingualism policy, which could express itself as public support for their position. They began to discuss organizing a publicity campaign to build public support for their position: perhaps that support could force the government to back down.

A number of Conservative backbenchers, who were identifying ever more closely with the positions of CALPA and CATCA responded to the events with questions in the House. Jack Murta (PC, Lisgar) who had spoken with disaffected MOT bureaucrats, asked Lang to "table the reports from the department which led him to the conclusion that air communications would gradually become bilingual."[58] Lang offered only a copy of his statement at Dorval.

Lang's statement at the Montreal control centre drew a good deal of editorial reaction throughout the country. The French press gave its full approval. The English press was split, with the *Montreal Gazette* in full support of Lang, the *Montreal Star* and the *Ottawa Citizen* taking a moderate position, and the *Winnipeg Free Press* and the Toronto *Globe and Mail* in total opposition.[59]

At the same time that so many public reactions to Lang's new policy were being voiced, the Montreal controllers, behind closed doors, were attempting to deal with their problem. On Monday, Walter McLeish returned to the Montreal control centre to meet with the managers and supervisors. He found a group that was both demoralized at the breakdown of discipline and resentful of the intervention by headquarters, which they considered to be "overkill." McLeish repeated his threat of closing down the centre if discipline was not restored and suggested that the situation had deteriorated sufficiently that some "overkill" would not be a bad thing. On Tuesday, there was a general meeting of seventy-seven controllers favouring unilingual air traffic control. This group began to consider its alternatives and identified three major options: taking early retirement, seeking French language training, so that they could remain in Quebec, or requesting transfers to other parts of the country. Upon discussing the options, it was clear that there was great uncertainty about some highly important issues. For instance, staffing of air traffic control positions was usually handled regionally, rather than nationally: how would a large number of transfers be handled within such a system? The controllers decided to set up an executive committee of eight members who would be in charge of negotiations.

The Committee of Eight met for the first time the following day, Wednesday, December 17, and began to formulate tactics.[60] Insofar as possible, it would bypass the regional administration, which it no longer trusted, and deal directly with MOT Headquarters. The chairmanship of the committee would rotate among its members, for fear of reprisals against any individual who developed too high a profile. Finally, the eight decided to keep their discussions out of the public arena for the moment, in order to preserve the threat of going public at some later date if their negotiations bogged down.

The Committee of Eight spent the entire day Thursday meeting with McLeish and his staff. Much of the day's discussion dealt with the three options. Early retirement did not appear to be feasible since most of the controllers, while veterans by air traffic control standards, were far from normal public service retirement age. It would be very problematic for unilingual controllers to remain in Quebec, even though under the 1973 House of Commons resolution on civil service bilingualism they had the "incumbents' rights" to do so. The usual method of handling unilingual individuals who wish to remain in bilingual jobs and who are unwilling or unable to become bilingual is to "double staff" their positions and reassign them to similar positions where they can work in one language. Neither alternative would work for the Montreal controllers: operational air traffic control positions could not be double-staffed, and the working language of the non-operational positions in the Quebec regional office was French. Linguistic training for unilingual and partially bilingual anglophones was discussed, and it was agreed that existing language standards and training programs were not adequate to meet the special requirements of controllers, and that something new would have to be developed. The underlying reason why it would be difficult for the controllers represented by the Committee of Eight to stay in Montreal – the antipathy towards them of the francophones who favoured bilingual air traffic control—was discussed in a different context. McLeish agreed that MOT would provide counselling for those controllers who had found the events of the previous weeks disturbing and traumatic. (For example, one of the anglophones had developed asthma.)

The alternative to which attention gravitated was transfer. The committee was concerned about such matters as how the transferring controllers could find comparable jobs elsewhere, given regional control over staffing, how priorities for transfers would be determined, and what financial compensation would be provided. The committee made it clear that if they were to renounce their incumbents' rights to remain in their present jobs, they would want to receive adequate compensation. The financial problems were complicated by the realization that housing costs were much lower in Montreal than in cities such as Toronto and Vancouver, where comparable positions would be found.

McLeish responded by assuring the controllers that headquarters would find ways to cross regional boundaries to expedite transfers, and would set up priorities for transfer on the basis of psychiatric assessments. He also suggested that MOT would be willing to enter into negotiations on financial questions. McLeish agreed to provide office space and cover costs for the committee and give its members time off with pay, when they were involved in committee activities. The meeting ended with an agreement to reconvene early in January.[61]

At the December meeting, McLeish had made it clear that he personally would be concerned with resolving their problems, regardless of what position he would hold in the new year. The last proviso was necessary because word had spread to the controllers that he had been promoted to the position of deputy air administrator, beginning January 1, to succeed the retiring deputy administrator. Air Administrator William Huck, who himself would be retiring on January 1, 1977, made sure that a new deputy administrator was chosen during the fall, so that he could groom that person to be the next administrator. The selection committee which chose McLeish felt that it was important that the next administrator have an aviation background, in contrast to Huck's financial background. They also felt that McLeish had both the necessary managerial skills and the respect of the aviation industry.

This opened up the position of director-general of civil aeronautics, for which Pierre Arpin, the Quebec regional administrator, was chosen. Some anglophones who were passed over were bitterly disappointed, and expressed their resentment to Tory backbencher Jack Murta. On December 9, in the House of Commons, Murta asked Otto Lang whether it was true that Arpin would be succeeding McLeish: Lang simply denied any awareness of the appointment.[62]

By late December, the holiday season was upon the embattled bureaucrats, the contrary controllers, and the argumentative association leaders: as if by common consent, all rested for a few days, putting out of mind the dispute which would so occupy their time, energy, and attention in the new year.

On the evening of December 28, Prime Minister Trudeau held his annual year-end television interview with Bruce Phillips and Carole Taylor of CTV. In it, recognizing his intellectual debt to John Kenneth Galbraith, he mused about the failings of the free market and the need for permanent government intervention. These "new society" musings touched off a storm of protest in the business community and contributed to a sharp decline in the Trudeau government's popularity. During the last half of 1975, the Liberals had led the Conservatives in the Gallup polls by 40 percent to 35 percent. But the March 1976 poll, the first to reflect this protest, showed the Liberals were down to 34 percent and the Conservatives up to 43 percent.[63]

Chapter Six

A Conflict on Many Fronts: January to June 1976

Turning and turning in the widening gyre
The falcon cannot hear the falconer;
Things fall apart; the centre cannot hold;
Mere anarchy is loosed upon the world,
The blood-dimmed tide is loosed, and everywhere
The ceremony of innocence is drowned;
The best lack all conviction, while the worst
Are full of passionate intensity.

W. B. Yeats, "The Second Coming"

INTRODUCTION

In previous chapters, our story focused on activity at specific points in time. However, by January 1976, many events were occurring simultaneously. For the next six months, the story can be likened to a tangled braid, with a number of distinct strands which sometimes ran independently of one another and sometimes intersected. This chapter identifies three major strands of the story: the implementation process, the collective bargaining process, and the publicity battle.

The implementation process involved the effort to develop procedures to permit controllers in the Quebec region to speak French with one another, the negotiations with the Committee of Eight to resolve the Montreal control centre crisis, consultation between MOT and the industry on the use of French for VFR operations at St. Hubert and the design of simulation studies of bilingual IFR control. The implementation battles were played by MOT's rules, since MOT had the legal authority to make the decisions, and the other parties had no veto or right of appeal.

The second strand to the story is the collective bargaining process, within which CATCA raised the issue of bilingualism. Here the ground was more favourable to CATCA, since the rules of this process allowed it to enter as an equal and possibly emerge as a winner. The third strand is the publicity campaign waged by CALPA and CATCA, and, to a lesser extent, by MOT and AGAQ, to convince the English and French publics of the rightness of their causes. For CATCA, the publicity campaign was a key tactic in the strategy of raising the bilingualism issue in the collective bargaining process. Since the ultimate weapon in that process, a strike, would greatly inconvenience the public, the controllers had to win public support, so that the strike threat would be credible.

This chapter, then, traces these three strands of the story up to early June, ending with the *casus belli*, the event which precipitated the pilots' strike against bilingualism.

IMPLEMENTATION: JANUARY TO MARCH 1976

Following the visits to the Montreal centre by Otto Lang and Walter McLeish, the atmosphere began to improve, instances of the unauthorized use of French decreased, and provocations between anglophones and francophones lessened. The francophones could afford to be magnanimous, since it now appeared that they had won their battle. The anglophones were reaching a consensus that relocation was the best option, and it appeared that McLeish was doing all he could to make the terms as favourable as possible.

On January 7, the study of language usage for coordination among controllers (referred to as the Inter and Intra Unit Air Traffic Service Co-ordination Report, or the "I and I Report," for short), which had begun in December, was presented.[1] The study recommended that all controllers who remained in Quebec be certified as bilingual. For the francophones, this meant merely a one-week course in the new French lexicon. Because of the large number of anglophone controllers who would require extensive training or who would probably leave Quebec, thus requiring the recruiting and training of bilingual replacements, it was estimated that the certification process would not be completed until December 31, 1978.

McLeish established an implementation team to maintain discipline at the Montreal centre, to implement the I and I Report, and to work with the Committee of Eight to handle the anglophone's problems. The leader of the team was John David (J. D.) Lyon, who was one of the founders of CATCA, and had been a very popular president from 1965 until retiring from the position in 1971. He then joined the managerial ranks in the air administration. Lyon's philosophy in serving on the team was to reconcile duty and conscience. One the one hand, he believed that air traffic control is intrinsically safer in one language than two: on the other hand, he accepted as immutable the political decision to implement bilingual air traffic control. He saw his job, therefore, as ensuring that the implementation was done as safely as possible. He served notice that he would neither tolerate its being rushed ahead so rapidly that it would compromise safety, nor countenance behaviour that would undermine the implementation effort. Lyon's deputy was Gilles Foy, a francophone staff officer who had been involved in the BILCOM study, the Peters study of bilingual operations at Quebec City airport, and the I and I Report. Together they set up an office at the Montreal Airport Hilton. Along with two psychiatrists, they immediately began to interview individual controllers and their families in order to establish priorities for relocation. On January 23, Air Administrator Huck informed the other MOT regions that English-speaking Quebec controllers were to be given priority in filling any appropriate vacancies, provided they could successfully "check out." As a result, by mid-March, the first transfers were accomplished.

Lyon and Foy chose a certification committee of francophone controllers (including Serge Cormier, who had been suspended in December) to develop a French lexicon and language courses for controllers. By March, the committee had completed these tasks.

At the same time that the Lyon project team was at work at Dorval, McLeish was initiating a joint government-industry study of the use of French at St. Hubert. The objective of the study, which would be chaired by David Cunningham of the Air Traffic Services Branch of MOT, was to determine how to implement safe bilingual VFR service at St. Hubert.[2]

A third activity also getting underway was the simulator study of bilingual IFR communications. McLeish and Pierre Arpin, the director-general of civil aeronautics, chose Ron Bell, the chief of radar and automation in the Air Traffic Services Branch and George Skinner, the acting chief of aeronautical planning and development to conduct this study. Bell had become an air traffic controller in 1960, after having served in the air force for six years as a navigator, flying mainly in Europe. Though he is a unilingual anglophone, Bell's European experience left him reasonably accustomed to a multilingual aviation environment; hence, he looked forward to his new assignment, as he was quite certain he could devise a bilingual system which was just as safe as the existing unilingual one. However, George Skinner, whose background was also air force, was not only skeptical about the viability of bilingual air traffic control, but was also very hesitant about becoming involved in a project having such obvious political overtones. As a result, Bell became the *de facto* team manager.

Bell spent February on the initial planning of the simulation study. MOT's recently opened air traffic control simulation centre was built around two large adjacent rooms. In one sat a number of controllers at radar positions. In the other, a number of clerks, trained to simulate pilots, sat at computer consoles, conversed over the radio with controllers, and entered data at the consoles which activated the fictional aircraft showing up on the controller's radar screens. Bell's task was to design exercises that would develop procedures for safe bilingual IFR operations. This entailed seconding people from many areas at MOT to work with the fledgling staff of the simulation centre. One difficulty he soon encountered was the shortage of Montreal controllers to participate in the exercises. The Montreal centre was already short-staffed, a problem which would be increasingly exacerbated by the departure of the anglophones and the heavy air traffic the Montreal Olympics were expected to generate later in the year. As he began to lay out the tasks before him, Bell realized that this project would take far longer than the eight weeks McLeish had anticipated, and he so informed McLeish.

THE PUBLICITY CAMPAIGN: THE SAFETY SYMPOSIUM

Having decided to fight bilingual air traffic control, the leaders of CATCA and CALPA embarked on publicity campaigns to build support among their own members and among the public at large. CATCA allocated $20,000 for newspaper ads opposing bilingual air traffic control, ads which appeared throughout the English press in late January. The advertising campaign was discussed in the privacy of the CATCA national council on February 5, and the minutes record the observation that "apart from the effectiveness [of the advertising campaign] in enlisting public support, it was the kind of thing expected by the majority of the membership and was fully supported."[3] Something of a vicious circle was created between CATCA's leadership and its membership: the members expected the leadership to be radical in its opposition to bilingualism; the leadership responded as hoped, which simply encouraged the membership to become more radical. Another CATCA tactic was to enlist the support of air traffic controllers throughout the world. For example, its national council decided to prepare a paper opposing bilingual air traffic control for presentation at the meeting of the International Federation of Air Traffic Controllers Associations (IFATCA), scheduled for April 1976.

On January 6, three CALPA directors sent a letter to all members, asking them to submit information in support of their opposition to bilingual air traffic control. The letter's assertion that "We cannot continue to state that we are opposed to bilingual ATC simply because it is unsafe without providing reasoned arguments supported by facts..."[4] was an admission that the pilots' opposition to that point had been based on their "gut feelings." Judging by the many pilots' responses to the letter, as well as the anonymous incident reports, CALPA acquired a fair bit of ammunition for its cause. Sometimes pilots wrote articles for newspapers, and sometimes they talked with their local MPs. The alliance between CALPA and the Progressive Conservative caucus strengthened. CALPA made its incident reports available to the Conservative Research Office, which packaged them for use in House of Commons questions and speeches.

On occasion, the MPs made use of the materials in ways which did not display a reasonable interpretation of the information. For example, Erik Nielsen (PC, Yukon), himself a pilot, quoted at length from an incident report in a speech on February 16.[5] The report described a situation in which an Air Canada aircraft in an undisclosed location was on its final approach while a United Airlines jet had been cleared to take off from the same runway. Because the Air Canada pilot had overheard the transmission to the United jet and saw it on the runway, he decided to execute a missed approach. From this, the pilot drew the following conclusion: "All ended happily. But now, and here is my point, just change the above into a bilingual situation. Now perhaps nobody is prepared... Disaster!" The report was signed, though flight numbers and the location were not indicated, and the pilot wrote "You may show this to anyone you wish—it's all true!" The CALPA office noted on the report's upper right-hand corner that it had been received January 25, 1976. However, Nielsen stated, "I am telling you something that actually happened in the air over Quebec air space on January 25 last." Furthermore, it should be noted that United Airlines has never had regularly scheduled flights into any Quebec airports. Nielsen's speech was nevertheless picked up on the CBC radio news the next day, and stories based on it appeared in the *Vancouver Province*, *Ottawa Citizen*, and *Ottawa Journal*.[6]

One speech that contained a prototypical non sequitur was made by Benno Friesen (PC, Surrey-White Rock). In the midst of a disquisition about the dangers of bilingual air traffic control, Friesen recounted a personal experience aimed at showing its perils, but which fell well short of the mark.

On my return [from Mexico City] I was privileged to sit in the cockpit of the plane while awaiting clearance from the tower for take-off. I was wearing a headset and listening to the instructions coming from the tower. Most of them were in Spanish but in the jumble of words coming from the headset there was one instruction in English. I did not catch it, but the pilot, with his more acute perception, had no difficulty in doing so.[7]

The leaders of CALPA and CATCA began to have more contact with the English media, and Jim Livingston was becoming well aware of the growing public support. In February, he had dinner with J. D. Lyon, at Lyon's request. Lyon was attempting to determine how serious CATCA was in its opposition to bilingual air traffic control. Livingston assured Lyon that CATCA was entirely serious, and claimed that public opinion in English Canada was so strongly opposed to the government's bilingualism policy that, if English Canadians were given a specific issue they could sink their teeth into, their opposition could bring down the government.

In addition to their independent pressure campaigns, CATCA, CALPA, and COPA decided to hold a media event, namely, a "Special International Air Safety Symposium." At the CATCA executive meeting on January 19, the minutes note that "the aim [of the symposium] was to achieve wide press coverage for a concerted view that the use of more than one language in air traffic control was a degradation of safety."[8] Over the following weeks, the concept evolved somewhat, and it was felt that the objective would be best achieved if the symposium were conducted as a serious inquiry to determine whether a bilingual air traffic control system in Quebec would have a beneficial or detrimental impact on aviation safety. It was decided that a panel of three experts would hear opinions on both sides of the issue and then pronounce their judgement. The symposium was organized under the auspices of IFALPA, the International Federation of Air Line Pilots Associations, and scheduled for March 2 and 3 in Ottawa. CALPA invited presentations from Transport Minister Lang, Keith Spicer, Jim Livingston, the Gens de l'Air (AGAQ), and representatives of the American aviation community. All members of CATCA, the press and many VIPs were invited to attend. The invitation to Transport Minister Lang also requested that as many as possible of MOT's officials in the civil aeronautics area attend as well.

Lang, Cloutier, and McLeish pondered how to respond to the invitation. They were well aware that the preponderance of the arguments at the symposium would oppose the government's position and that the panel would probably decide that unilingual air traffic control was safer. If the government tried seriously to convince the panel and failed, it would be much more difficult to convince the public. Furthermore, many of the staff in civil aeronautics were opposed to bilingual air traffic control, and the symposium would increase their discontent with the policy and give them opportunities to undermine it, certainly privately, and possibly even publicly. On the other hand, Lang knew that to ignore the symposium altogether would appear arrogant and unresponsive, especially in light of his commitment to industry consultation, no matter how perfunctory. Lang and McLeish settled on a compromise tactic. McLeish would attempt to pre-empt the symposium by holding a press conference the day before, Lang alone would appear at the symposium, make the introductory speech which would include a statement of the government's intentions, refuse to answer questions, and then leave.

On March 1, Walter McLeish held his press conference.[9] He announced that, based on Bell's planning, it would take a full eight to twelve months, not eight weeks, to develop a methodology to simulate bilingual air traffic control, and another six months or more to complete actual simulations. He expected that bilingual IFR service would be available in two to three years. He admitted that he had no idea of the cost of bilingualism, but did allow that the program would have to be halted if costs were unreasonable. He noted that the traffic volume at Quebec City had increased by 30 to 40 percent. Thus the vicious circle of "pas de service, pas de demande, pas de service" had been broken in that instance. When pressed as to whether this meant that increases in demand would lead to bilingual service throughout the country, he said that MOT had no plans to extend bilingual service beyond Quebec, either in the national capital region or northern New Brunswick. By that time, the Quebec press was claiming that MOT was discriminating against Quebec because so much of its airspace was controlled by the Moncton flight information region; in response, McLeish affirmed that there were no plans to shift this airspace from Moncton to Quebec jurisdiction.

McLeish faced some very tough questioning at the press conference, particularly from Hugh Whittington, the editor of *Canadian Aviation* and an opponent of bilingual air traffic control. He responded with a blustery performance, in effect, shouting down the opposition. To suggestions that francophones were making the air traffic control system unsafe, he stormed "there is no bloody way these guys are going to jeopardize this system." The press there, including Whittington himself, felt that McLeish was impressive. McLeish himself was troubled by his performance. He had had to resort to bluster because he did not have all the facts, figures, and background data he would have liked at his fingertips. He felt naked.

The symposium itself was a stormy affair. Anglophones were angry at the government, francophones at the anglophones, and neither group spoke much with the other. Otto Lang's keynote address was simply a recapitulation of present and planned measures, basically the same as his speech at Dorval in December. It was not well received. Keith Spicer's speech was a plea that the parties establish "a climate of serenity," and "replace confrontation with consensus." He admitted that he did not know whether one, two, or five languages is best, but felt that in this exceptional instance, bilingualism should be argued from a premise of safety only.[10]

After completing his speech, Spicer stayed at the symposium to make another attempt to settle the controversy.[11] He buttonholed Jim Livingston and asked him, in confidence, what it would take to settle the matter then and there. Livingston suggested a commission of inquiry on bilingual air traffic control. Spicer immediately called Otto Lang for his reaction. Not only did Spicer propose a commission, but he even had the name of a possible commissioner, Alberta Supreme Court Justice W. R. Sinclair. Sinclair, an anglophone, so enjoyed studying French that he wrote Spicer an enthusiastic letter in near-perfect French, proclaiming, "I now have before me, to be enjoyed for the rest of my life, the whole of French literature from the *Chanson de Roland* to the new novels of Butor and Robbe-Grillet."[12]

Lang was never enthusiastic about commissions, believing that the government itself should solve problems. In this instance, he saw no reason to yield to pressure and accept a commission of inquiry which would only delay implementation. From Lang's point of view, Spicer's interventions were more of a hindrance than a help. Spicer's motherhood statements about the need to argue the issue from a standpoint of safety and his confessed confusion as to what was the safest air traffic control system simply cast public doubt on MOT's capability. Lang and McLeish had convinced themselves that they could implement a bilingual air traffic control system that was just as safe as any unilingual system. Why did Spicer doubt them, especially after having studied the problem and after having visited bilingual air traffic control centres in Europe? Lang was in no mood to accept the proposal of this doubting Thomas and relinquish the issue to a commission of inquiry. Regretfully, Spicer conveyed this message to Livingston.

The most intense opposition to bilingualism was expressed by the American speakers.[13] Captain J. J. O'Donnell, president of the Air Line Pilots Association flatly stated that a two-language system is simply not as safe as a one-language system and that anyone who would not admit that was a coward. When asked if he had any figures on near-misses in Europe due to language, he admitted that he did not, but went on to say that figures were not necessary: it was self-evident that one language is safer! Max Karant, vice-president of the American Owners and Pilots Association, could not believe that Canadians, "otherwise reasonable men," would take so retrograde a step as using two languages.

Jim Livingston had no desire to compete with the Americans in histrionics. He simply repeated the standard arguments. To end his speech, he chose an approach that was just the opposite of Ken Maley's August

1975 declaration that bilingualism and biculturalism had gone too far. He said: "It is seemingly impossible to protest on grounds of safety without being branded as bigots. We only hope that Canada will not act like some municipalities do...wait until several people are killed at one intersection and then put up a traffic light."[14]

AGAQ was represented by Roger Demers and Pierre Beaudry. Receiving invitations only two weeks before the event, and anticipating the nature of the discussion, they were initially hesitant about attending. Keith Spicer urged them to attend, saying, "Those who are absent are always wrong." They ultimately decided it was important that their position be represented, and drafted speeches in French, which were translated by MPs Pierre De Bané and Serge Joyal and some of Spicer's staff. Joyal and De Bané had become de facto advisers to AGAQ at this point: they suggested that AGAQ hire a lawyer, and recommended Clément Richard of Quebec City, a Parti Québécois activist.

Demers gave a low-key speech, emphasizing the arguments for the development of bilingual air traffic control in the context of Quebec. Pierre Beaudry had also prepared a speech. Knowing Beaudry, Livingston had suggested that he either not speak or tone down his remarks, in order not to exacerbate tensions at the Montreal centre. Beaudry took the suggestion as a threat of disciplinary action, and defiantly delivered his prepared text. He accused CATCA and CALPA of expounding "all kinds of unfounded opinions, theories, and assumptions in order to spread panic among the Canadian public." He described their attitude towards francophones as "obsolete paternalism." His parting shot was reserved for the pilots: "IFR is the most interesting, lucrative and important part of modern aviation. Is safety the real reason for this meeting? Something is at stake that not many laymen know about, namely the responsibility of each occupation, the pilot's and the controller's...The responsibility [for maintaining separation between aircraft] is now in the hands of the controllers and it is high time that everyone acknowledged it."[15] Beaudry's speech left the pilots—especially the Americans—seething, and "young punk" was one of the kinder epithets they had for him.

Finally, the three panel members summed up. Henk Vermeulen, a Dutch pilot and IFALPA vice-president, gave a rambling, emotional speech in favour of language standardization. The flavour of his remarks is best shown in a comment such as

A task force [BILCOM] was sent out to other countries. That is good and wise. But what is that we learn from other people? Are you doing away with central heating because you have found a state where it is not a common good as yet—or are you going to stimulate living in open huts because somewhere else they do this?

Then came the peroration.

> I will end with a strong plea to those who can see...towards the shiny
> future which we all have to work for...to those men who are attri-
> buted with power to lead this fascinating country towards that goal.
> Help us, who have become world citizens, who, suspended above the
> earth, need each other when the going gets rough; help us under-
> stand each other; help us to make communication easier, not for the
> individual, but for all of us from the North to the South Pole.[16]

This evocation of the spirit of St-Exupéry drew the greatest applause
of the symposium. On the other hand, J. D. Monin, the Swiss president of
IFATCA, condemned the emotionalism, and even passion "which is
incompatible with the objective approach required to the subject under
discussion." He did not hear proof that the use of more than one language
contributed to any aircraft incidents, and he said he could not accept the
unproven claims that air traffic control in France was less safe than in the
United States. Captain O'Grady, the Irish president of IFALPA, concluded that the Canadian government had made an error, but the error
was not likely to be reversed, and that therefore the responsibility for a
language-related accident would rest with the government.[17]

The symposium got good press coverage. The French press emphasized
Otto Lang's and J. D. Monin's contributions and what they felt was the
emotional fanaticism of the anglophone aviation community. The English
press continued to split the regional lines that were developing previously.
Western and Ontario papers supported the pilots, while the two English-
language Montreal papers were more inclined to take the government
view. Probably the affair was summed up best by the headline in *Montreal-
Matin*: "Dialogue of the Deaf."[18]

In the midst of their day-to-day tactical considerations of how to
respond to the symposium and the questions in the House, Lang, Cloutier, and McLeish (as well as Lang's wife, and unpaid press secretary,
Adrian) were forced to deal with the strategic question of whether to
respond to the publicity campaign with one of their own, but ultimately
rejected the idea. Instead, they chose not to dignify the CATCA-CALPA
campaign with a response, and simply worked on the implementation.
There are a number of reasons for this. First, Lang and Cloutier were
supremely self-confident. Though they did not have empirical data comparing bilingual and unilingual air traffic control systems, they were
convinced by the theoretical logic of their position. Also, they underestimated the extent to which the pilots' publicity campaign was winning over
public opinion in English Canada, and failed to recognize the urgent need
to respond. Second, a proper publicity campaign would have required staff

work to gather information on language use, traffic levels, and accidents at airports in countries having either bilingual or unilingual air traffic control systems. McLeish's staff in civil aeronautics was not very loyal to his position: they did not on their own initiative do anything to help McLeish, they were slow in responding to his requests, and they leaked embarrassing information to CATCA, CALPA, and the press. In this difficult situation, McLeish feared that any publicity campaign would be undermined from within: therefore, he put the loyal staff members he did have onto the implementation problem. Thirdly, the trio still thought of themselves, at least partially, as mediators, and considered that adopting a publicity campaign would be inconsistent with this role. Fourthly, Otto Lang was aware that the government had made the anti-inflation program its major political priority at that time, devoting substantial amounts of ministers' time and advertising expenditures to gaining public support for its position. There is a limit to how many government publicity campaigns the public will tolerate, and Lang felt that the anti-inflation program then occupied centre stage.

COLLECTIVE BARGAINING: TOWARD CONCILIATION

Very shortly after he arrived at his office on Monday morning, January 5, Peter Dawson, director of employee relations at MOT and the man in charge of bargaining with CATCA, received a telephone call from Jim Livingston, asking him to await a hand-delivered letter. In the letter, CATCA presented two additional demands in the area of bilingual air traffic control. The first was that bilingual service would be limited to the provision of VFR services in Quebec, but excluding Dorval, Mirabel, or St. Hubert airports. The second was that MOT would issue regulations limiting unilingual francophone pilots to airspace where bilingual service was provided. Dawson, a bilingual anglophone with years of experience representing management in tough negotiations with Quebec forestry workers and miners, was not at all surprised. He had expected that Otto Lang's Montreal speech in December would arouse CATCA.

Government negotiators like Dawson have fairly limited autonomy, since their bargaining positions are worked out carefully with the Treasury Board Secretariat. Dawson called Tim McShane, the Treasury Board Secretariat official who was in charge of negotiations with CATCA. McShane and his superiors quickly worked out their response to CATCA's new demands. Their position was based on the Public Service Staff Relations Act, which permits collective bargaining about wages and working conditions, but not about questions of public policy.[19] They felt that air traffic control bilingualism was a policy area which MOT had the power to regulate under both the Aeronautics Act and the Official Languages Act.

At their next negotiating session, Dawson informed the CATCA negotiating team that he would not discuss bilingualism. Jim Livingston, head of CATCA's team, replied that he was going to talk about bilingualism, regardless of Dawson's position, and that without negotiations on this issue, there could be no settlement. Though Livingston and Dawson had good personal rapport, the negotiations went downhill from that point, and on February 5, both sides agreed that they were at an impasse. Twenty-five issues had not be resolved, including the bilingualism question. Indicative of the relative importance of the unresolved issues was a comment Livingston made to CATCA's national council meeting, on February 29, "Without the language issue, the agreement would by now have been signed."[20]

When negotiations reach an impasse, the Public Service Staff Relations Act provides two mechanisms for resolution—binding arbitration or conciliation. Binding arbitration is conducted by an arbitrator appointed by the Public Service Staff Relations Board (PSSRB) and precludes a strike. In conciliation, a board of three conciliators is established. One is nominated by the government, the other by the union, and the third by the first two conciliators. The board hears the arguments on each side, and attempts to persuade them to reach an agreement. If the two sides remain too far apart, the conciliators conclude their work by publicly releasing a report containing their recommendations on how each issue should be settled. The report is not binding on either side, and seven days after it has been issued, if no agreement is reached, the union can go on strike. CATCA, sensing that it was in a strong bargaining position, chose conciliation.

Before conciliators can be chosen, two matters must be settled. The issues the conciliators may deal with must be decided, and a list must be made of designated employees who will stay at work to provide, in the words of the Public Service Staff Relations Act, section 79 (1), "duties the performance of which at any particular time or after any specified period of time is or will be necessary in the interest of the safety or security of the public." If the government and the union cannot agree among themselves on these matters, then the Public Service Staff Relations Board must determine them.[21]

The MOT and CATCA negotiators agreed without too much difficulty on a group of 230 controllers throughout the country who would provide essential service for emergency flights, search and rescue missions, and northern supply flights.

After this issue was resolved, on February 12, Pierre Arpin, the new director general of civil aeronautics invited Jim Livingston and Bill Robertson to his office to propose that the controllers at the Gander centre, most of whom had not been designated, in the event of a strike should continue to provide normal service to aircraft flying over the North Atlantic.[22] Since most aircraft flying between the United States and Europe use airspace controlled by Gander, the American Federal Aviation Administration had made it very clear to MOT that it expected normal service to be maintained. The implicit threat was that if Canada could not provide uninterrupted North Atlantic service, then perhaps ICAO would have to assign it to another country that could, thus leading to the loss of perhaps seventy-five air traffic control positions in Gander. Jim Livingston wanted to discuss this with his membership before making any commitments, and suggested another meeting on the subject in late February with Walter McLeish.

The next day, Jacob Finkelman, Chairman of the PSSRB, held a hearing in which MOT and CATCA argued about the terms of reference for the conciliation board. CATCA was willing to drop the clause restricting unilingual francophone pilots, but would not drop its demand that the application of bilingual air traffic control be limited to VFR operations in the smaller airports. Finkelman listened to the arguments and announced that he would hand down his ruling in several weeks.

While awaiting Finkelman's decision and the meeting to resolve the Gander problem, the two sides chose their conciliators. MOT chose Edward Stringer, a labour lawyer from Toronto with a reputation for being tough and management-oriented. CATCA chose Peter Sadlier-Brown. Sadlier-Brown, who was then working for the NDP caucus as a policy coordinator, in the past had worked for the International Association of Machinists and had thrice been a member of conciliation boards involving dockyard workers. Sadlier-Brown and Stringer then chose Thomas O'Connor, a labour negotiator, as the third member of the board.

As CATCA's policy of using both a publicity campaign and the collective bargaining process to oppose bilingualism was evolving ever more clearly, the Gens de l'Air attempted a counter-attack. On February 25, the controllers' section of AGAQ wrote Treasury Board President Jean Chrétien, informing him that they would not participate in any strike, whether legal or illegal, against air traffic control and urging the government to use an injunction to prevent such a strike. They also asked Chrétien to establish an inquiry to investigate their charges and decide whether a new union to represent Quebec controllers should be formed. Vice-president Pierre Beaudry held a press conference to publicize their quarrel with CATCA.[23]

The CATCA national council gathered in Ottawa in late February to plan its strategy, to meet with Walter McLeish, and to listen to the symposium.[24] McLeish met the council on February 29 to discuss both the implementation of bilingualism and the question of providing service for the North Atlantic at the Gander centre. McLeish began by reviewing the activities of Lyon's implementation team and made it clear that the team's work would not be delayed by any objections from CATCA. Soon McLeish was tripped up on a small factual error, which began to undermine his credibility. Shortly thereafter, he asserted that the rights of the anglophone controllers in Quebec were being protected adequately. Livingston interrupted, accusing McLeish of ignoring their incumbents' rights and of ignoring aviation safety. McLeish responded with a long oration on the technical and sociological background to the decision to implement bilingual air traffic control. In a fit of high dudgeon, he heatedly reminded CATCA that the people at MOT were professionals and would not yield to political pressure.

McLeish, however, continued to exemplify the ambivalence of the government and of his own feelings on the question. At times he became more conciliatory, conceding that bilingual IFR air traffic control would create delays for aircraft, and that this might have an impact on government policy. In response to questions, he stated that bilingual IFR air traffic control was an objective for some time in the future, and that all steps would be slow and deliberate. The members of the council interpreted McLeish's ambivalence by concluding that his true loyalties were with them, but he was being forced to support bilingual air traffic control by his political masters. This heightened their concern that bilingualism would be implemented even if it were not proven safe.

Finally, the discussion turned to the question of keeping Gander open during a possible strike. The CATCA council members wondered whether this was the thin edge of the wedge and whether McLeish would next ask CATCA to provide service to all international flights travelling over domestic Canadian airspace: McLeish said that was not under consideration but did not exclude the possibility. At that point McLeish left and the council began to discuss the issue, examining it on purely political terms. Refusing to provide service could jeopardize the air traffic control jobs in Gander and thereby reduce CATCA's support for a strike vote from the Gander members. On the other hand, maintaining service would undermine morale throughout the entire union during a strike. They decided to propose an agreement that would keep Gander open and, at the same time, get as much as possible from MOT. They would keep Gander open under the following four conditions: first, the justification for such service would not be based on a need for "safety and security" of the public; second, the employees providing this service would not be designated, but (third) would be provided on the basis of consultation between CATCA and the local management; and fourth, MOT would suspend all other VFR and IFR control service in Canadian airspace.

The first term was designed to ensure that only CATCA could use safety as a rationalization for its actions, the second and third, to avoid the precedent of designating CATCA members in Gander, and the last—and most important—to make it impossible for Quebec members to provide service if the rest of CATCA went out on strike. The national council also discussed the implementation of bilingual communications among Quebec controllers, realizing that there was little they could do to stop the government on this issue: furthermore, support for bilingual communication among Quebec controllers might possibly quiet their internal opposition. After much debate, and a vote of six to five, they adopted a resolution indicating that CATCA was not opposed to bilingual communication among Quebec controllers, provided that MOT demonstrated that safety would not be diminished. This resolution effectively ended CATCA's opposition to making all air traffic control positions in Quebec bilingual.

On March 3, Arpin replied to CATCA's four conditions for continuing service at Gander. He was willing to accept the first three, but not the fourth. Arpin and McLeish wanted to preserve the option of having controllers who disagreed with a strike still able to work, which could be a useful tactic in fighting a strike. Livingston responded that Arpin's offer was unacceptable, and told him CATCA would simply wait until MOT accepted its conditions.[25]

The following day, March 4, PSSRB Chairman Finkelman handed down his ruling about the terms of reference. His attitude towards the bilingualism problem was pragmatic. He felt it was unrealistic to think that the problem could be avoided in the negotiations and, because the controllers and the government had to live with one another, some accommodation would have to be reached. Finkelman recommended that the controllers rephrase their bilingualism clause to deal with the impact of bilingualism on labour conditions, which would be a legitimate subject for negotiation under the act. Finally, he advised the board to "devote some, but not an undue amount of time, to seeking a formula . . . that would allay the fears of the employees."[26]

A week later, the Public Service Staff Relations Board had more good news for CATCA. On March 12, it handed down its ruling on Jean-Luc Patenaude's petition that CATCA be forced to sign its previous collective agreement in both English and French. The board dismissed the petition because the Official Languages Act makes no specific requirement that public service unions sign collective agreements in both languages. Nevertheless, they roundly condemned CATCA's behaviour as being contrary to the spirit of the law: "This is the only instance in the period of almost nine years since the Public Service Staff Relations Act came into force that we have ever heard of a bargaining agent refusing to sign a collective agreement in both official languages. The course adopted by [CATCA] flies directly in the face of the spirit of the declared policy of Parliament regarding the two official languages of Canada and is deplorable."[27]

On March 20, the CATCA executive met to consider a response to Finkelman's ruling on the terms of reference. They agreed that they could bring the bilingualism clause to refer to conditions of employment by rewriting it in terms of potential lawsuits against controllers resulting from the increase in accidents in a bilingual environment. However, they decided not to change it because they wished to fight the issue in terms of safety, narrowly defined, and because they felt the decision gave them enough latitude to talk about bilingualism, even without rephrasing the clause. Thus, the terms of reference for the conciliation board were complete.[28]

On March 26, Pierre Arpin finally agreed to CATCA's fourth condition for keeping the Gander control facility open, namely that all IFR and VFR services throughout the rest of Canada would be closed in the event of a strike.[29] Foreign pressure to keep Gander operating had forced MOT to give in.

The Gens de l'Air, who had not been winning many battles during the first stages of the conciliation process, received more bad news on April 1. Jean Chrétien replied to the letter of February 26, saying that the government could not intervene because CATCA was an accredited bargaining agent and it was up to the employees themselves to affect a change in representation. The government could not obtain an injunction to halt a strike because the conciliation process was underway and there were a substantial number of legitimate issues under discussion which, if unresolved, could lead to a legal strike.[30]

CATCA AND CALPA PREPARE FOR BATTLE

By March, the CATCA-CALPA publicity campaign was so successful that it took on a life of its own: Livingston and Maley were nationally-known figures, sought after by the media for interviews. They now turned their attention to increasing solidarity within and between their unions, and winning the support of pilots and controllers in other countries.

Maley and Livingston realized that there was a possibility that the government would attempt to use the courts or special legislation to keep the controllers from striking. In order to forestall these possibilities, they agreed that CALPA would support any strike by CATCA and would call upon international pilots to do likewise. Maley was also considering having his pilots refuse to fly if CATCA was legislated back to work.[31]

Throughout, the anglophone pilots were growing ever more incensed by the use of French between francophone pilots and air traffic controllers, and they began reporting incidents to their airlines. There were other manifestations of their anger: many pilots began wearing "English is the international language of the air" buttons, and on December 20 one pilot flying into Quebec City said to his copilot "it's a beautiful city— too bad there are so many fucking Frenchmen to ruin it." Unfortunately, his radio line was open, so the statement was heard by air traffic control, and passed on to the media.[32]

Late in March, the directors of CALPA sought their members' approval for possible strike action, sending out a ballot asking for a blank cheque, in these words: "I hereby authorize the President and Board of Directors of CALPA to take any action deemed necessary in support of CALPA's position in the matter of the bilingualization of Canada's air traffic control system."[33] Of CALPA's 2,644 members, 2,274, or 87 percent, voted. Of those voting, 2,083, or 92 percent, voted yes and 161, or 7 percent, voted no.[34]

On April 7, the CALPA executive also took their case to the annual conference of IFALPA, the International Federation of Air Line Pilots Associations. The conference passed by an overwhelming majority a resolution proposed by the Swiss Air Line Pilots Federation strongly condemning MOT.

The CATCA executive worked to increase solidarity among the anglophone controllers by informing the membership of CALPA's support, and by publishing in CATCA's Journal excerpts from the symposium, weighted heavily in favour of the anti-bilingualism position.[35]

The CATCA national council had agreed to say nothing, either publicly or within the union, about the negotiations of the Committee of Eight with MOT. However, rumours had been circulating within CATCA for months. Air traffic controllers have a network which provides for the rapid dispersion of rumours: each unit is linked to geographically contiguous units by telephone "hot lines." Controllers talk freely on these hot lines, and (as in the game of "broken telephone") by the time stories have been passed along several times, they may be quite inaccurate. By late March, negotiations between the Committee of Eight and Lyon and McLeish on the relocation package were going sufficiently well that the committee permitted Livingston to release some information. On March 30, Livingston sent a one-page memorandum to all units describing the tensions which had built up at the Montreal centre: the threats, religious slurs, near fist fights, police surveillance, and McLeish's near decision to close the centre.[36] The report also mentioned that many anglophone controllers would be transferring out of Quebec.

Livingston based this memo almost entirely on information from Ed Lesage, CATCA's former Quebec regional director, and one of the anglophones planning to leave Montreal. His relations with the leaders of AGAQ had deteriorated so badly that he did not trust them to tell him their version of the story. As a consequence, the memo is quite one-sided, leaving the clear impression that the francophones were completely at fault for the situation at the Montreal centre. This memo, which Livingston afterward regretted, contributed to the heated opposition to bilingual air traffic control and paranoia about MOT's intentions which were by then rampant within the air traffic control units in English Canada.

In April, Bill Robertson, a CATCA representative at the IFATCA Conference in Lyon, France, presented a paper on air traffic control language which urged IFATCA to accept English as the universal aviation language. The CATCA proposal met with strong opposition from controllers in countries using two or more languages, such as Switzerland and France. Ultimately, no resolution was adopted. Robertson felt that IFATCA President J. D. Monin (who had attended the symposium in Ottawa in March) and who sided with the delegation from his home country of Switzerland, had exercised undue influence to achieve the final outcome.[37]

Meanwhile, Lang, Cloutier, and McLeish continued refusing to conduct a publicity campaign of their own. However, MPs were receiving so many letters from constituents about bilingual air traffic control that on April 5, Lang issued a rather ineffectual three-paragraph memorandum to all MPs and senators for use in replying to constituent inquiries.[38]

Lang and Cloutier also tried to get their message across by holding private meetings with senior members of the English press and arranging meetings between English and French journalists. However, the meetings did not result in any positive publicity. For the media, the context of an issue, especially if it is complicated and technological, is often as important as its substance. With weak public support for the Liberal government and strong public opposition to bilingualism in English Canada, the English writers (or their publishers) did not find Lang very credible.

By the time the strike deadline approached, the pilots and controllers had successfully linked their cause to anglophone opposition to the government bilingualism policy and had English Canada solidly behind them. A Gallup poll, released on May 19, asked whether the government was putting too much or insufficient emphasis on bilingualism. In part as a result of the publicity campaign, 73 percent of the anglophones asked thought there was too much emphasis on bilingualism, while only 12 percent thought it was about right, and 10 percent thought there was too little. Among francophones, the results were just the opposite, with 16 percent saying there was too much emphasis, 26 percent saying it was about right, and 50 percent saying it was insufficient.[39]

THE CONCILIATION PROCESS

Conciliation began on April 1 with formal presentations in which each side laid out for the commissioners and for the other side its position on each issue. Peter Dawson once again argued that language should be excluded from the terms of reference. Jim Livingston responded that he did not care whether language was or was not excluded—it remained an issue, and the dispute would not be settled unless it was settled. O'Connor, the chairman of the conciliation board, pointed out Finkelman's terms of reference and told the parties that the board would be dealing with language.

After the formal meeting, the conciliators began to hold separate meetings with each side over the next two weeks. One objective of these meetings was for O'Connor to establish trust on both sides. O'Connor's strategy (especially with the union) was to present himself as a down-to-earth ordinary fellow, intent on listening to both sides of the story. It also gave him a chance to size up personalities and feelings on both sides as well. Later on, he would start to exert pressure to reach an agreement. Since he was trying to get the confidence of both sides, he avoided the language issue at first and concentrated on some of the other issues which could be resolved more easily.

Almost the entire Easter weekend (April 14–17) was spent in meetings. A number of minor issues were resolved, and the two sides moved closer, to within one percentage point, on the pay increase. MOT was ready to grant close to the maximum increase that the Anti-Inflation Board would allow.

O'Connor and Sadlier-Brown felt it would be impossible for them, as conciliators, to solve the immensely technical bilingualism problem. The best they could do would be to establish some ongoing mechanism, such as a commission of inquiry, to handle it. They approached Jim Livingston, and asked what terms of reference for such a commission would be acceptable. CATCA had not prepared a formal position for such a contingency, but Livingston's ad lib response was very thorough. The bilingualism issue would have to be turned over to one impartial commissioner acceptable to CATCA (Vice-President Mike Tonner suggested Ken Maley) who would have the power to launch a full inquiry into all aspects of the problem, including implementation costs and IFR bilingualism. Furthermore, the entire implementation process would have to be delayed until the commissioner had completed his report. It was obvious to Sadlier-Brown that the CATCA negotiators had lost all trust in MOT's handling of the issue. They did not want multiple commissioners, because they were certain that if they were not unanimous in their recommendations, MOT would simply act on the basis of that which was most favourable to its position, and ignore the others. The request for delaying implementation was also a reaction to the experience of the last few months, during which they saw McLeish moving forward step by step and interpreting consultation to mean only informing CATCA, asking for comments, and then ignoring them.

Sadlier-Brown and O'Connor then approached Stringer with CATCA's proposal. Stringer said that he was very reluctant to present it to the government side, but finally agreed to step outside what he considered to be his terms of reference and persuade MOT to accept some form of inquiry. However, in exchange, he asked the other conciliators to accept, then and there, whatever type of commission MOT recommended. He would not take CATCA's response to this proposal back to MOT for a second round, as that would be tantamount to bargaining over bilingualism.

Stringer and O'Connor thus approached Dawson with CATCA's proposal. It was outside his authority, so he suggested they see Sylvain Cloutier. On Easter Sunday afternoon, they met with Cloutier. Cloutier now realized that CATCA was determined and had strong public support: he said that a commission was a possibility, and suggested further consultations.

A few days later, Stringer and O'Connor met with a number of civil servants on the government side, including Cloutier and McLeish, Dawson, and representatives of the Treasury Board Secretariat. Stringer and O'Connor argued that no settlement would be reached without some resolution of the language problem and suggested setting up a commission. They also warned that CATCA was certainly ready to strike. To ensure that the strike would be legal, it was clear to them that CATCA would refuse to settle some of the other outstanding issues. McLeish expressed dismay at the possibility of *his* implementation program, to which he was so deeply committed, being delayed and possibly taken out of his hands and put into those of a commissioner.

A final decision would now be up to the politicians. Otto Lang pondered the alternatives. On the one hand, he was reluctant to face a controllers' strike, especially when the issue had been so skilfully exploited in English Canada, when support for the government's bilingualism policy in English Canada was very weak, and when the government's standing in the public opinion polls was very low. (The Liberals trailed the Conservatives in the April Gallup poll by 46 to 31 percent.)[40] On the other hand, by agreeing to a commission of inquiry, the government would be perceived in Quebec as going back on a promise to implement its bilingualism policies. This would be a dangerous precedent which could be exploited by the Parti Québécois. It would also lead to discontent on the part of the Quebec controllers, and possibly more situations like those encountered in the Montreal centre the previous December. Lang chose a middle road. The government would appoint one commissioner, but the terms of reference would be more circumscribed than CATCA desired. Furthermore, the commissioner would have a tight deadline for finishing his report, and implementation would not be postponed until he completed his work.

Stringer told O'Connor of the government's response, and O'Connor then told Sadlier-Brown. Both men knew that CATCA would not accept the government position: they did not even bother asking. Furthermore, they recognized that there was no reason to continue bargaining on the other issues, since CATCA would refuse to settle them without a settlement on bilingualism.

By late April, when it was becoming clear that the conciliation board was going to recommend a commission of inquiry, Lang, Cloutier, and McLeish decided that it was essential to announce the name of a commissioner and his terms of reference as soon as the board's report was made public. They hoped to resolve the problem expeditiously, so that the other issues could be dealt with in direct negotiations between Peter Dawson's team and the CATCA negotiators. By this point, Lang, Cloutier, and McLeish were quite anxious to "head the other side off at the pass," as one participant put it.

While this was happening, Walter McLeish went to Montreal one evening to give the after-dinner speech at an alumni dinner for the Institute of Air and Space Law at McGill University. The president of the institute was John Keenan, CALPA's lawyer. McLeish got an idea. He called John Keenan the next day, and mentioned to him that the conciliation board was going to suggest a commission of inquiry. Understanding McLeish to be asking him for the names of possible commissioners, Keenan agreed to think of some and call him back. McLeish replied, however, that Keenan had missed the point, that he was asking if he himself wished to be the commissioner. Keenan was doubtful, thinking he would not be acceptable to all the parties, and even suggested that the government should name three commissioners. McLeish wanted only one, and was quite certain that Keenan would be acceptable. Keenan then arranged to go to Ottawa the following day to speak with McLeish and Otto Lang.

McLeish's choice of Keenan emanated from the same philosophy that had led him to appoint Louis Doucet to BILCOM, Desmond Peters to investigate the use of French at Quebec City, and Hart Finley to chair the committee of aviation organizations, which met the previous September. Confident that bilingual air traffic control could be made as safe as unilingual control, he was sure that any unbiased professional would also come to that conclusion. McLeish had seen Keenan in action, knew that he was a most competent professional, and surmised that the fact that he had once represented CALPA was completely irrelevant. Finally Keenan's bilingual background equipped him to deal with both language groups.

Keenan met first with McLeish and Cloutier. They spent some time discussing his mandate, which was primarily to review MOT's simulation studies. Then it was Keenan's turn to raise a different matter. He reminded Cloutier and McLeish of his involvement with CALPA, and particularly of the memo he had prepared on the BILCOM consultation meeting, which could be very embarrassing, if made public. McLeish and Cloutier were not worried, and, to further reassure Keenan, they took him to meet Otto Lang. Keenan again mentioned the memo, telling Lang that there would be all hell to pay if he was appointed. Lang simply said "we'll handle that." Keenan stipulated that his association with CALPA be mentioned in the press release announcing his appointment. He also asked them to make sure he was acceptable to AGAQ and the Quebec government, and McLeish assured him that they would take care of that as well. With these assurances in hand, Keenan began to think about the positive side. He had a unique opportunity to handle a major judicial inquiry and to solve an important policy problem. He was also aware that, at this early stage in his career, it was sure to enhance his reputation. He decided to accept the appointment. In order to negate any charges of conflict of interest, he would sever his ties with CALPA and give up his partnership in a prestigious law firm.

During the previous few months, Fernand Lalonde, the Quebec solicitor general, had taken an interest in the bilingual air traffic control issue and had become an interlocutor between MOT and AGAQ. McLeish called Lalonde for his reaction to the suggestion of a commission. Lalonde replied that AGAQ was opposed; McLeish argued that there was no alternative and, besides, it would be a good opportunity to examine CATCA's arguments critically and demolish them. McLeish then told Lalonde about MOT's choice for a commissioner, emphasizing that Keenan was a bilingual Montreal lawyer, who would be acceptable to the anglophone aviation community, but who was sufficiently professionial and unbiased that he could be expected to hand down a report favourable to bilingualism. He did not, however, mention the potentially embarrassing memo. Lalonde sensed that McLeish was implicitly asking him not to oppose Keenan, and he replied non-committally, reminding McLeish that transport is ultimately an area under federal jurisdiction. Both men were somewhat reticent in this interchange. Lalonde did not probe too deeply, nor did McLeish offer too much information. If things worked out well with Keenan, there would be no need for it: if things did not work out well, McLeish would emphasize the fact that Lalonde had not disapproved of Keenan and Lalonde would emphasize the fact that he had not given his approval.

A few days later, Keenan called Ken Maley to inform him that he would no longer be representing CALPA because of his new assignment. Maley was incredulous, and started laughing loudly, saying that the francophones would never accept him as commissioner. Keenan said, au contraire, that McLeish had resolved that problem. Keenan asked Maley not to say anything until the appointment was made public. Maley thought about the appointment and concluded that the devil he knew was better than the devil he did not know.

The last step in making the Keenan appointment official was to clear it through Cabinet. MOT prepared a memorandum to Cabinet which contained both the limited terms of reference and Keenan's nomination. The commission would investigate the implications for aviation safety, implementation costs, and operational efficiency of the bilingual IFR simulation studies. The commission would not evaluate the need for bilingual IFR operations in Quebec, or discuss bilingual VFR operations, whether actually implemented (such as at Quebec City airport) or being planned (such as at St. Hubert). As for the conduct of the inquiry, Keenan would be allowed to ask the assistance of the civil servants of MOT, to have representatives of the organizations participate in his inquiry, and to engage consultants. He was to report no later than ninety days after MOT provided him with the final results of the simulation studies.[41]

There were some questions asked of Lang in Cabinet over his choice of Keenan. Some ministers were aware of Keenan's ties with CALPA, and pointed out that there was something of a "downside risk" involved. What would happen if Keenan came to the conclusion that the procedures MOT had developed were unsafe? Given his background, would he then be believed, especially by the francophones? Lang's response was that this was not a problem, because there was simply no way a reasonable man could draw such a conclusion. Lang emphasized Keenan's complete bilingualism, aviation background, and his acceptability to the anglophone aviation community, which was the real source of difficulty at that time. The Cabinet ultimately deferred to Lang, as it often defers to the judgment of a minister about a matter involving his own portfolio, especially if the minister, like Lang, is regarded as a heavyweight. Lang, while not universally liked, was certainly respected.

The conciliation board held a perfunctory final meeting with both negotiating teams on May 6. Since an agreement had not been reached, O'Connor, Stringer, and Sadlier-Brown sat down together to write the final report, which they would release publicly. The report itself was the product of a bargaining process among the three conciliators. A unanimous report would have had more persuasive force on both sides, but the differences among the three were deep enough that unanimity was not possible. The conciliators recommended a one-year contract. On a number of complex issues, they simply recommended continued consultation between the parties. Given the anti-inflation regulations, which involved limitations on employees' total compensation, the board did not support CATCA's requests for a cost of living allowance, a higher rate of overtime pay, and increased vacation entitlements (five rather than four weeks for employees with between twenty and twenty-five years' experience). On basic salary, the majority of the board was more generous to the union. O'Connor and Sadlier-Brown recommended a pay increase of 10.5 percent (subject to the Anti-Inflation Board's maximum of $2,400 for any individual). However, Stringer was less generous, recommending the government's final offer be 9.5 percent.

On the commission of inquiry, the recommendation was: "After much discussion the members of the Conciliation Board unanimously agree that the parties will only be able to solve the problem if they set up an independent public commission of inquiry into all aspects of the question of language use and safety in air traffic control."[42] Sadlier-Brown had to argue emphatically to have the words "independent" and "all aspects" included. He added an addendum of his own to the report in which he criticized the government for its inflexible position on the terms of reference for the commission.[43] This report was released on May 11.

Otto Lang announced the Commission of Inquiry and the appointment of John Keenan as commissioner on May 12. A few hours prior to the announcement, Keenan called Livingston to inform him. Livingston was skeptical, as Maley had been, but said nothing. Lang's announcement was accompanied by the first package of background material on bilingual air traffic control that MOT had ever prepared.[44] It included a history of the implementation of bilingualism to that point, a list of relevant laws and studies, information about the relocation of the Montreal controllers, some details of language usage in other countries, and a short discussion of the simulations. It was ignored by the English press.

The reaction to Keenan in Quebec was negative. The francophone pilots doubted his objectivity, and one called him "in the past one of the fiercest opponents of the use of French in air / ground communications." AGAQ said it had previously been willing to participate in the simulation exercises, but was now opposed to participation in Keenan's study. While AGAQ had a copy of the Keenan memorandum, it was decided not to release it to the press, in order to save it for the most opportune moment. However, there were already questions about the memorandum being asked in the House of Commons. On May 14, René Matte (Créditiste, Champlain) called the prime minister's attention to the newspaper reports in *Le Devoir* the previous October about it.[45] Trudeau simply denied that Keenan was the originator and promoter of a strategy to oppose bilingual air traffic control.

The CALPA Board of Directors was amazed and angered by the choice of Keenan. They felt that the only way the government could have agreed to choose him was if some deal had been made with him to come up with a report favourable to the government.[46] They were angrier still at Maley because he had not consulted them. Maley assured the board that no deal had been made, that Keenan would be impartial and, accepting their condemnation for his failure to consult them, promised that he would consult them more closely in the future.

Jim Livingston's initial reaction was cautious. He told the press that CATCA had rejected the 9.5 percent wage offer of the government, and said that its executive would have to know more about the terms of the commission before deciding whether it was acceptable.[47]

Negotiations were now back in the hands of CATCA and MOT. Before discussing the final negotiations, we return to the several aspects of the implementation problem: the anglophone controllers in Montreal, the study of bilingual IFR communications, the St. Hubert study, and the pilots' concern about the use of French on the flight deck.

IMPLEMENTATION: ONE STEP FORWARD, THREE STEPS BACK

The step forward was being taken by J. D. Lyon's implementation team at Dorval. The lexicon committee finished its work on schedule, and MOT issued a new NOTAM authorizing the use of French for VFR communications with the five original airports and with the aeradio stations in northern Quebec. The NOTAM superceded the provisional 1974 NOTAM, and contained an expanded French lexicon. In addition, the first group of thirty controllers completed the one-week course in the new lexicon, and on April 30 they received their bilingualism certificates.

During March, Lyon's team completed the interviews of the controllers who wished to leave Montreal: sixty-two had asked for transfers, and another thirty-eight had reserved the right to do so in the future. A relocation schedule stretching into July 1977 was formulated. MOT obtained the approval of the Treasury Board on April 8 to pay transferring controllers a special relocation allowance consisting of two amounts:

1. A lump sum payment equal to 1 percent of the controller's current salary for each year of service, with a minimum of $500.
2. A housing allowance equal to the interest, at current rates, for five years on the difference between the price of accommodations similar to his accommodation in Montreal in the city to which the controller would be moving, and the price of his accommodation in Montreal.

The second provision was designed to satisfy the controllers' demand of "a house for a house," given that housing is much more expensive in most of the destinations to which they were moving than in Montreal.[48]

The controllers were not satisfied with this offer, primarily because they wanted the housing allowance to be payable in a lump sum, rather than over five years, as offered, and because they wanted both allowances to be exempt from income tax. Late in April, word of the negotiations got out to the press. André Dumas, the new Quebec regional administrator, was interviewed on April 30, after announcing the completion of the lexicon course by the first group of thirty controllers. Asked by a reporter "What is the future for an English-speaking air traffic controller who refuses to learn French in Quebec?" he replied with unfortunate frankness: "Let's call a spade, a spade; none."[49] This greatly angered the Committee of Eight: the controllers felt that MOT had broken the gentlemen's agreement to keep the relocation negotiations out of the press. In consequence, Jim Livingston's dramatic March 30 memorandum to CATCA describing the tensions at the Montreal control centre appeared, almost in its entirety, in the *Montreal Star* on May 5.[50]

After this airing of dirty linen, the Committee of Eight was ready to negotiate seriously again with MOT. Sylvain Cloutier argued the controllers' case for income tax exemption before the Treasury Board on May 10, but lost: ministers were already concerned about the size of the payments (which, for an experienced controller, could exceed $25,000) and the precedent that could be set. However, Cloutier was able to convince the Treasury Board to agree to a lump sum payment of the housing allowance, and he promised the controllers that MOT would administer the entire relocation package in as favourable a manner as possible. Given that there was no more Cloutier could do for the relocating controllers, almost all of them accepted his offer. By the end of May, ten controllers had transferred. By the end of the relocation program in 1980, seventy-eight, representing 65 percent of the accumulated experience of the entire Montreal area control centre, left under its terms.

By accepting the relocation allowance the controllers were *ipso facto* waiving their incumbents' rights to their jobs at the Montreal centre. Only one anglophone controller, Don Kelso, attempted to assert his right to stay at the Montreal centre. Kelso did this for two reasons: first, he lived on a farm outside of Montreal, which he did not wish to sell and which was not covered under the special relocation allowance, and, second, he is by nature a person who takes stands on principle, regardless of the consequences. For a while, he was consigned to rather menial administrative work at the centre. His relations with the Quebec regional administration deteriorated, and he was threatened with dismissal unless he took a position at the air traffic control school in Cornwall. However, he accepted the Cornwall position only under protest, and began the lengthy process of fighting MOT's action in the courts.

The three steps backward in implementation came in the areas of the study of bilingual IFR operations, the use of French on the flight deck in Air Canada, and the study of bilingual VFR operations at St. Hubert.

During March and April, Ron Bell made substantial progress in designing the simulation study. He hired Paul Stager, an experimental psychologist at York University (and also a pilot) to help design exercises in which bilingual controllers and pilots using both English and French would simulate bilingual air traffic control in various traffic configurations. Arrangements had been made to link a number of aircraft simulators to the simulation centre. People had been seconded from a number of groups within the air administration: the only unit that was dragging its feet on co-operation was Hart Finley's Aviation Safety Bureau. Bell began consultations with CATCA, CALPA, AGAQ, COPA, and the airlines for participation in the exercises. He planned to conduct a preliminary simulation exercise for the aviation organizations on May 6 and repeat it the next day for the media. Bell briefed McLeish a number of times on the progress he was making, and frequently referred to the simulations as a marketing exercise, designed to convince the anglophones to accept bilingual air traffic control. The phrase "marketing exercise" stuck in McLeish's consciousness.

It was felt that there should be a number of impartial observers from other countries present at the simulations. One person who came to McLeish's mind was J. D. Monin, the president of IFATCA. J. D. Lyon had even gone to the air safety symposium for a few minutes to hear Monin speak, and concluded that his calm and rational call for empirical evidence showed the attitude MOT needed.

Before leaving for the IFATCA conference in Lyon, Jim Livingston heard a rumour from one of his MOT sources, that Monin would be invited to Canada as an observer to the simulation exercises. Livingston expected that Monin would approach him about this at the conference, since IFATCA policy was that its executives would not deal with the government of a member nation without the approval of the nation's association. However, Monin said nothing, even after Livingston broached the subject to him obliquely. On May 4, a few days after Livingston's return to Canada, Lyon called CATCA, asking for a reaction to having Monin as an international observer.[51] Lyon wanted an answer by May 6, the day the simulations were to be demonstrated to the organizations. Jim Livingston then attempted to contact Monin in Switzerland, learned that he was already in Canada, and found out he was at the Skyline Hotel in Ottawa! Livingston was coldly furious, feeling that he had been tricked by both Monin and MOT. He had no desire to speak with Monin; he simply wanted him out of the country immediately. However, Monin prevailed upon Livingston to meet him the next day, and said, in his own defence, that MOT had asked him not to inform CATCA, since they would "handle that." Livingston's anger remained unabated. Monin no longer had any legitimacy, and immediately returned to Switzerland. Despite the

Monin episode, Livingston sent Vice-President Tonner to the demonstration of the simulation exercises the next day; however, the Monin affair only served to heighten CATCA's opposition to bilingual IFR air traffic control and its suspicions about the way the simulation exercises would be conducted.

Bilingualism on the flight deck also became a greater problem at that time. In response to anglophone pilots' protests about francophone pilots using French, Captain Kent Davis, Air Canada's vice-president in charge of operations, on April 20 inserted a simple new rule in the airline's operating manual. Rule 14A read, "English only will be used on the flight deck, with the exception of passenger announcements." The francophone pilots found this rule totally unacceptable, since, interpreted literally, it could prohibit something so innocuous as flirting in French with a francophone stewardess. On May 10, the pilots' section of AGAQ denounced it as showing "scorn for the French language" and threatened to launch a campaign to boycott Air Canada.[52]

Air Canada management asked Captain Davis to remove or modify the rule. Davis refused and even threatened to resign in protest. CALPA pilots supported him and CALPA's Air Canada locals, on May 20, passed a resolution that they "cannot accept political interference" and threatened that if the rule were revised as a result of external pressure, Air Canada pilots would go on strike.

Francophone pressure on Air Canada increased. On May 26, MP Serge Joyal and Louis-Phillippe Ally, an Air Canada pilot, sought an order in the Quebec Superior Court, requiring Air Canada to permit francophone pilots to use French in the cockpit and in communication with aeradio operators and air traffic controllers and to require Air Canada to translate its complete flight operations manual into French within thirty days. On May 30, Pierre Nadeau, who had been the announcer for Air Canada's French commercials, announced that he would no longer appear in the commercials in protest against the restrictions on the use of French.[53] L'Office de la Langue Française also contacted Air Canada, with a view to taking action to modify its language policies.

Once again, MOT, this time accompanied by Air Canada management, was caught in the middle. On June 4, Pierre Arpin announced a new policy on language use by pilots, which gave entirely francophone crews the right to use French internally for operational matters, but required mixed crews to use English. This expansion of rights for francophones was somewhat hypothetical, because the paucity of francophone pilots and the airlines' practice of permitting pilots to change routes every month meant that there would be very few, if any, entirely francophone crews.[54]

The St. Hubert study, which was conducted by a task force with representatives from the aviation organizations, got underway in mid-March.

By the end of March, the CALPA, CATCA, and COPA representatives felt that MOT was pushing the task force to a predetermined answer. Rather than dissociate themselves from the study immediately, they decided to await the final recommendations.

The St. Hubert task force took a number of initiatives. It sampled tapes of 7,562 air traffic control transmissions on March 20 and 24 and found that, even without any formal authorization, 5.4 percent were in French. The French transmissions were almost always initiated by the pilots: controllers only used French to increase comprehension. A safety study was performed, which concluded that controllers at St. Hubert were providing excellent service. D. J. Douglas, the officer who did the study, felt that the existing limited level of French could be authorized formally. The task force then conducted a test of the impact of increased use of French. On April 28, a number of bilingual flying instructors based at St. Hubert joined the regular traffic in the circuit, but used French, so that about half of all traffic that day was using French. The tests were to run for several days, but everything went so smoothly that the organizational representatives present felt that one day was sufficient.[55]

David Cunningham, the MOT civil servant who was chairman of the task force, completed his report on May 11.[56] Cunningham recommended a phased introduction of bilingual service over the next eighteen months. Cunningham's report was passed on to the task force participants for reactions. On May 14, Mike Tonner, CATCA's representative, sent Cunningham a letter criticizing the study, and refused to sign the final report.[57] Tonner felt that the test of increased French use was unrealistic, since it did not examine the impact of increasing the airport's traffic volume by adding a larger number of unilingual French pilots, given existing procedures. Tonner recalled that in planning the test, Cunningham had rejected that suggestion as too dangerous. To Tonner, this rejection proved that bilingual operations at St. Hubert were unsafe. To Cunningham, the test that was actually performed showed that bilingual operations were intrinsically possible, and gave him good reason to believe that procedures could be developed to handle increased traffic levels and more unilingual francophones.

The other participants in the study, such as the Department of National Defence and the local flying schools, accepted the report and willingly signed it.

On May 27, CALPA refused to sign the report. Even though St. Hubert was an almost entirely VFR airport, not serviced by any commercial carriers, Ken Maley was worried about the possibility of unilingual francophone pilots at St. Hubert interfering with flights to Dorval or Mirabel. Criticizing the government for refusing to ask the basic question of whether St. Hubert should be bilingual, he wrote, "the implacability of the government's will in these matters is reminiscent of other totalitarian [sic] regimes."[58] Charitably, one might conclude that Maley resorted to hyperbole to express the frustration the pilots felt over the steps MOT was taking to impose a policy they opposed with growing fervour.

THE FINAL CONTRACT NEGOTIATIONS: DIVIDE AND CONQUER

At 7 p.m. on Friday, May 14, the CATCA national council held a conference call reviewing the situation to that point.[59] MOT had refused to change its final offer of 9.5 percent on wages. More important, the negotiating team considered the terms of reference for the Commission of Inquiry announced by Otto Lang to be much too narrow. Livingston had consulted with Maley, who felt the same way. The national council voted ten to one (Jean-Luc Patenaude being the minority of one) to reject MOT's last offer and call for a strike. Following the vote, Livingston told the council, "IN STRICT CONFIDENCE" the minutes record, that he would be satisfied if Otto Lang made a statement in the House of Commons and issued a press release stating that the commissioner would be authorized to investigate all aspects of the bilingualism issue and that there would be no expansion of bilingualism until he had reported. Livingston also thought that the logical time to set a strike date would be May 31. The CATCA national council had arranged a spring meeting for St. John's from May 26 to 29. The final negotiations could be conducted in St. John's at the same time as the council meeting. Thus, the negotiating team would have the advice of the council during negotiations and its support for the ultimate outcome. Furthermore, St. John's would be a good location because it would inconvenience the MOT negotiators, keeping them at a distance from the ministers who would ultimately have to approve their agreement.

After the meeting, the national council sent to all CATCA locals telegrams which announced the council's recommendation and asked two questions: Are you in favour of rejection of the employer's final offer? Are you in favour of the association proceeding on strike? Since CATCA's constitution requires a period of four days for strike votes, the voting would be completed by Tuesday evening, May 18. The meeting concluded at 7:45, which gave Livingston time to get the telegrams out and issue a press release for the 11 p.m. news.

In his press release, Livingston mentioned the disagreement on salaries, but emphasized that CATCA was "appalled" by Keenan's term of references, and accused the government of not consulting with CATCA.[60]

On Sunday, May 16, Jean-Luc Patenaude gave a press conference of his own. He said that the Keenan Commission was "repetitive and useless," accused his union of "conducting a strike against Quebec, based on ethnic

TABLE 1
CATCA's First Strike Vote—May 18, 1976

Region	Number of Members	First Question: Do You Reject MOT's Final Offer? (percent)			Second Question: Are You in Favour of a Strike? (percent)		
		Yes	No	Abstain	Yes	No	Abstain
Pacific	244	74	18	8	69	21	10
Western	322	89	5	6	89	5	6
Central	286	85	6	9	86	5	9
Ontario	430	78	8	14	78	8	14
Headquarters	103[a] (124 voted)	63	37	0	46	54	0
Quebec	337	26	68	6	20	73	0
Moncton	273	74	11	15	74	11	15
Gander	164	60	21	19	55	24	21
Total	2,159	68.6	21.8	9.6	64.6	25.1	10.3

Source: Public Service Staff Relations Board, *Decision*, exhibit 113.
[a] The vote for headquarters exceeds the total number of members because some members on temporary duty in Ottawa voted there.

racism," and recommended that Quebec members attempt to de-certify CATCA and form a union of their own.[61]

CATCA's internal rift deepened. On Tuesday evening, Jean-Luc Patenaude and Jim Livingston were on the CBC radio program, "As It Happens" debating the issue of bilingualism. The results of the strike vote also became known that night. They are shown in Table 1.

The results show the extent of the split between Quebec francophones and anglophones in the rest of the country. The anglophone controllers were overwhelmingly opposed to bilingualism, with the fiercest opposition expressed by the controllers from the prairies. The relatively weak support for a strike in the Gander region was probably the result of fears that, even if the Gander controllers worked, a strike could lead ICAO to assign control of North Atlantic airspace to another country.

At the same time that CATCA members were voting, Transport Minister Lang was attempting to strike a conciliatory posture. In the House of Commons on Tuesday afternoon he was asked by Donald Munro (PC, Esquimalt-Saanich) if he would broaden the terms of reference of the Keenan Commission to include all aspects of air traffic control and make safety the prime focus of the commission. In his reply he said: "If there is a real desire to have those words broadened to make sure that all aspects of safety are before him, I am certainly willing to consider that."[62] Livingston recognized this overture, and in his press conference announcing the strike vote said, "If it was intended as a message to us, I take it as an encouraging sign."

The next day, Wednesday, May 19, there were more signs of progress. Otto Lang and Jim Livingston met in Ottawa. Lang was willing to broaden the terms of reference, but said that it would be difficult, if not impossible, to delay implementation, since that would be opposed by the Gens de l'Air and by the Quebec caucus. The most Lang could do was to ask for some time, so that he could consult with the Quebec caucus and AGAQ. He asked Livingston to meet him again in two days time, on Friday, May 21.

After the meeting with Livingston, Lang asked McLeish to call Fernand Lalonde to find out if AGAQ would be willing to accept some delay in the implementation of bilingualism. After consultation with AGAQ, Lalonde reported that AGAQ was adamant that the implementation had to go ahead as planned. In order to make his point unmistakably clear, Lalonde, accompanied by Demers and Beaudry, gave a press conference in Quebec City on Thursday, May 20, in which he urged the federal government not to retreat in its implementation program.[63] After hearing Lalonde, Lang realized that there was no point in talking with Livingston on Friday, and cancelled their meeting.

Contract negotiations resumed in earnest in St. John's on Wednesday, May 26. Dawson and his team were there to negotiate the labour-management issues and Walter McLeish to negotiate bilingualism. The two negotiations were separate, because the government side wished to maintain the appearance that it was not bargaining about bilingualism. These talks had a fast-approaching deadline. In order to avert a strike, they would have to conclude sufficiently early in the day on Thursday, May 27, for the CATCA national council to contact the membership by midnight in order to have the four-day voting period before the strike deadline of midnight May 31.

On Wednesday, Livingston and Dawson negotiated, while McLeish waited in the wings. Agreement was reached on a number of issues. In such uncertain times, the contract would be of only one year's duration. On compensation, CATCA decided to push for the maximum salary increase possible, and to concede on other aspects of the compensation package. The negotiating team withdrew proposals for a cost of living allowance and for double overtime. MOT agreed to an 11 percent increase for all controllers, subject to a maximum of $2,400 per person and a minimum increase of $1,000 for trainees. Furthermore, MOT agreed to support CATCA when the contract came to be reviewed by the Anti-Inflation Board.

This left two issues outstanding for discussion on Thursday: bilingualism and vacation for controllers with twenty years or more of service. On the latter, CATCA's demand was that controllers with between twenty and twenty-five years of service receive five rather than four weeks of paid vacation. Livingston's stated rationale for this demand was that it was a way of providing something additional for the more senior members of his union, whose pay increases were restricted to $2,400 by the Anti-Inflation Board. Furthermore, he argued that this would not cost MOT very much because there were very few people involved. In earlier negotiations, Livingston had surmised that the resistance to his position came, not from MOT, but from the Treasury Board. No other group in the civil service received five weeks of paid vacation after twenty years' service. If the controllers got it, other unions would ask for it. Thus, Livingston's tactic was to divide the government side by refusing to settle the vacation issue until that concerning bilingualism was settled. If the government refused, he could threaten a legal strike.

On Thursday afternoon, the CATCA negotiators met with McLeish to discuss bilingualism. This time Dawson was the silent spectator. McLeish recognized that the controllers were serious about striking, and that they had the support of the pilots and much of the English Canadian public. He agreed to broaden the terms of inquiry of the commission to consider the establishment of bilingual VFR service at St. Hubert, Dorval, Mirabel, and in the Montreal TRSA and to commit MOT to table the report in Parliament. He also agreed to delay any further implementation, other than bilingual communications among controllers on the ground, until after the commission reported.

After McLeish's concession, Livingston went back to bargain with Dawson about increased vacations for controllers with twenty years of service. Dawson called Ottawa to confirm that the Treasury Board would not yield an inch. His real objective achieved, Livingston withdrew his demand for increased vacations and the negotiations were completed.

The CATCA national council met at 9:30 Thursday night, and recommended unanimously that the union approve the settlement. The council then sent out telegrams to the branches that night, so that the membership would have the full four-day period in which to vote. Livingston also planned a press conference for 10:30 a.m. Newfoundland time (9:00 a.m. eastern time) the next morning to announce the settlement.

The CATCA council spent Friday dealing with a number of aspects of the bilingualism dispute.[64] The council discussed J. D. Monin's abortive visit to Canada, voted to censure him, and call for his immediate resignation as president of IFATCA. Livingston said that he would meet soon with MOT to discuss CATCA's participation in the simulation exercises. Finally the council passed a resolution concerning the relocation of Montreal controllers. In order to protect opportunities for promotion for controllers within the regions to which Montreal controllers transferred, the council asked MOT to create new positions for the transferring Montreal controllers (i.e., overstaffing) rather than having them fill existing vacancies. However, the controllers knew that MOT had control over staffing and had already indicated that the Montreal controllers would fill vacancies, so this resolution was simply "for the record."

Before he left, McLeish asked Livingston to tread lightly in announcing the settlement and say nothing that might inflame the situation. McLeish needed time to get back to Montreal and convince the Gens de l'Air to accept the settlement. Livingston urged his members to ratify the settlement. Since bilingualism was of great concern, he had to emphasize it. The press release said that

> the main catalyst in reaching the proposed settlement was the amendment of the terms of reference to allow the commissioner to inquire into all aspects of the effect on aviation safety of the introduction of bilingual air traffic control service. In addition, we have received adequate assurance from MOT that there will be no expansion of bilingual air / ground communications beyond that presently in effect until the Commissioner has submitted his full report and it has been made public.[65]

In CATCA's terms, perhaps this was a moderate statement, but how would Quebec controllers perceive it?

While Livingston was speaking to the press, Walter McLeish was flying back to Montreal. As soon as he landed, he called Fernand Lalonde who told him that the agreement was unacceptable to AGAQ, and that there was nothing more he could do to mediate between MOT and AGAQ. At the same moment, Jean-Luc Patenaude gave a press conference in Quebec City in which he denounced the agreement, said that AGAQ did not recognize the mandate of John Keenan, and vowed that the francophone controllers immediately would begin proceedings to disaffiliate from CATCA.[66]

Michel Roy's editorial in *Le Devoir* the following day is an example of a moderate Québécois response to the situation.[67] Roy was not terribly upset by the collective agreement because it had only delayed the implementation of bilingual air traffic control. Nor was he troubled by the broadened scope of the Commission of Inquiry because "if the cause of bilingualism is valid, an inquiry cannot contradict it." However, he was concerned about the appointment of Keenan, who, he said "personally directed the offensive against French in aerial communications." He suggested the appointment of one or two additional commissioners in order to guarantee the impartiality of the operation.

In order to re-enlist AGAQ's support for the inquiry, Sylvain Cloutier hastily arranged a meeting with its executive on the morning of Monday, May 31, at a Quebec City hotel. He decided to bring his staff involved in implementing bilingual air traffic control (McLeish, Lyon, and Bell) along with him. All the leaders of AGAQ were there, as well as Clément Richard, their lawyer, and MPs Pierre De Bané (Liberal, Matane) and Claude Duclos (Liberal, Montmorency).

Roger Demers began the meeting, which was conducted entirely in French, by presenting a set of AGAQ's demands. Despite their objection to the choice of John Keenan as commissioner, they would cooperate with him if a co-commissioner, of equal status and power, were appointed. In order to counteract Keenan's bias, they recommended Benoit Ste.-Marie, director-general of the Quebec Government Aviation Service. They made a number of demands for continuing the implementation program, of which the most difficult to meet would be implementing bilingual IFR air traffic control in some parts of the province before year-end.

Cloutier and McLeish attempted to strike a conciliatory position without making concessions. Cloutier was not opposed to the nomination of a second commissioner, but only Otto Lang could make that decision. McLeish, recalling his discussions with Bell, told the francophones in his imperfect French that the simulations were only a "marketing" operation designed to gain the acceptance of bilingual air traffic control by the anglophones. However, the leaders of AGAQ responded that the simulations were simply a trick and that French would never be used in air traffic control. Ste.-Marie emotionally warned that the English victory on the Plains of Abraham, just a few blocks away, would not be repeated. Ultimately, the meeting descended into shouting and mutual recriminations, and no agreement was reached. Lyon and Bell—both unilingual—relied on a Quebec reporter to tell them what was being said.

After the meeting, Sylvain Cloutier, realizing that unilingual anglophones like Bell and Skinner would never gain the trust of AGAQ, decided that the simulations should be conducted by a bilingual francophone, and asked McLeish to find the man for that job. On his return, Cloutier spoke to Lang about appointing an additional one or two commissioners. However, Lang replied that MOT always used one-man commissions, and he felt that Keenan could expose himself to a sufficiently wide variety of viewpoints through the staff and consultants he hired. Lang was also worried that adding commissioners, especially people with a pro-bilingualism bias like Ste.-Marie, might jeopardize the hard-won agreement with CATCA. He decided to support John Keenan and tough out the criticism.

CATCA announced the results of the ratification vote on Tuesday, June 1. Of the controllers voting, 70 percent voted to ratify the contract. As expected, controllers in Quebec voted by an opposite margin not to ratify.

On Wednesday, June 2, Roger Demers and Pierre Beaudry held a press conference in Quebec City in which they announced the demands they made at the meeting the previous Monday.[68] They also drew the media's attention to McLeish's statement that the simulation studies were merely a "marketing" exercise.

On Friday, June 4, Otto Lang had another meeting with the leaders of AGAQ, this time in Ottawa. The meeting went on for two hours and ended in disagreement. Lang again stood firm with the choice of Keenan as the sole commissioner and asked AGAQ to cooperate with Keenan. Lang and Cloutier presented their response to AGAQ's demands for more rapid implementation of bilingual air traffic control. They promised to do the best they could to meet AGAQ's timetable for matters under MOT's control, such as the implementation of bilingual communications among controllers. However, bilingualism for VFR operations at St. Hubert, Dorval, and Mirabel and IFR operations throughout Quebec could come about before the Commission of Inquiry reported, only if there was unanimous agreement of all parties, which would be most unlikely. In order to make sure that his position was clearly understood by CALPA and CATCA (whose leaders were quite concerned about Lang's frequent meetings with AGAQ), Lang released the text of his letter responding to AGAQ's demands.[69]

Roger Demers and Pierre Beaudry held a press conference of their own. They demanded the removal of John Keenan as commissioner, threatened not to cooperate with him if he remained, and then released copies of his damning memo.[70] This added impetus to a wave of opposition to Keenan's appointment that had been building up throughout Quebec. The linguistic nationalists in the Quebec liberal caucus (Joyal, De Bané, Duclos) were now calling for his resignation and Serge Joyal announced that he would seek a court order to have Keenan removed.

That weekend, June 5 and 6, the Quebec Liberal caucus met at Mont Gabriel in the Laurentians. The younger and more nationalistic members of caucus urged that Keenan be replaced. Others pointed to the possibility of a strike if Keenan resigned and argued that the memo was not indicative of Keenan's own feelings on the issue. A third group in caucus felt that, even if Keenan was unbiased, he did not give that appearance. They thought the commission would not work if Keenan were the sole commissioner and Lang would have to find some alternative. Marc Lalonde, the leader of the caucus, took the third view. Given the divergence of views within the caucus and the necessity of maintaining some appearance of unity, when the meeting adjourned the caucus issued a statement in broad terms, simply stating that it roundly endorsed the government's bilingualism policy.[71]

John Keenan was also pondering his fate that weekend. He had spoken with many legal colleagues, some of whom suggested he resign. A few days previously, he had asked Keith Spicer to arrange a meeting with the Gens de l'Air: a few hours later Spicer called back with word that they would not meet him. This news was a crushing blow: if one of the major parties would not deal with him, how could he mediate? During the weekend, he heard rumours of the dissatisfaction with his appointment expressed in the Quebec caucus meeting: that was the last straw, and he decided to resign immediately.

At 8:00 a.m. on Monday, June 7, Keenan called Cloutier to inform him that he was resigning. Cloutier asked him to wait until he contacted Otto Lang. Keenan said that it was pointless and he was resigning in any event. By 10 a.m. Cloutier reached Lang, who simply accepted the resignation stoically. MOT released Keenan's letter of resignation that afternoon. In the letter, he subtly shifted the blame back to Lang by reminding him, "As I mentioned to you, I realized that my former professional representation of CALPA would be questioned. It was felt, however, that I was the man to accomplish this mandate.... [However,] it now appears that my appointment has become a central issue and that instead of being instrumental in finding a solution, I may be hampered by this controversy."[72]

AGAQ reacted to the resignation with hardly any feeling of vindication. They still felt that the commission was unnecessary and strongly objected to Lang's willingness to give CATCA and CALPA a veto over the implementation of bilingualism.

The reaction in CATCA and CALPA was one of anger. Both organizations expressed publicly their belief that political pressure had forced Keenan out. Some people in CATCA even theorized that they had been duped by the government. They felt that Lang had appointed Keenan because he knew Keenan would be acceptable to CATCA and unacceptable to AGAQ. The Keenan appointment would be used to induce CATCA to settle the contract. Thereafter, because of AGAQ's opposition, the government would force Keenan to resign, and replace him with another commissioner, more favourably disposed to AGAQ's position. CATCA would be able to do nothing, because it had already accepted the contract. This historical reconstruction, which might strike the reader as somewhat paranoid, is however, indicative of the distrust CATCA harboured towards Otto Lang.

Walter McLeish called Jim Livingston, who was in Edmonton at the time, to tell him of Keenan's resignation and to ask for any suggestions he might have for a replacement. Livingston felt that if he did not give a name, then and there, he would not be consulted again, because McLeish would say that he had been consulted and had made no recommendations. In order to satisfy his Edmonton members and to anger McLeish (and Otto Lang), Livingston recommended Calgary lawyer and former provincial Conservative party leader Milton Harradence. Not only did Harradence have the wrong political credentials, he had already established himself as a thorn in MOT's side. A skilled pilot, several years previously Harradence had brought an F-86 Sabre fighter (the major fighter Canada used in the early 1950s) and badgered MOT until he was given a licence to fly it.

On Monday evening, the CATCA national council held another conference call.[73] They took the position that the appointment of John Keenan was one of the conditions of settlement and it had now been breached by MOT. Since they had not formally signed a contract (that being planned for June 23 in Ottawa), they felt they were still in a legal strike position. Members of CATCA throughout the country were upset, and Jim Kouk, director of the central region (Winnipeg) urged a strike within forty-eight hours. However, cooler heads prevailed, and the council reached the consensus that another strike vote would be required. Jim Livingston suggested giving Otto Lang a deadline of midnight June 11 for reaching an agreement with CATCA about the choice of a new commissioner. If no agreement was reached by the deadline, they would hold a strike vote. The resignation of John Keenan put the responsibility back in the hands of Lang, Cloutier, and McLeish. They would have to find some formula for establishing a commission of inquiry that was sufficiently acceptable to anglophone controllers so that CATCA would not strike and to francophone controllers so that they would cooperate.

Chapter Seven

The Strike against Bilingualism

...you and I ought not now to pull on the ends of the rope in which you
have tied the knot of war, because the more the two of us pull, the tighter
the knot will be tied. And a moment may come when that knot will be tied
so tight that even he who tied it will not have the strength to untie it and
then it will be necessary to cut that knot, and what that would mean is not
for me to explain to you, because you yourself understand perfectly.

Nikita Khrushchev, letter to John F. Kennedy, during the Cuban Missile
Crisis, October 26, 1962 (quoted in G. T. Allison, *Essence of Decision:
Explaining the Cuban Missile Crisis*)

This chapter discusses the events following John Keenan's resignation
through to the resolution of the pilots' and controllers' strike against
bilingualism on June 28. Because the strike is an important event in the
history of French-English relations, the narrative goes into some detail
to reconstruct the motivations, strategies, and activities of the major participants. For a week or two, this strike was at centre stage in Canadian
political life: as a result, new players, from the prime minister to everyday citizens, became more deeply involved. In this chapter, the three
strands into which the story branched in the previous six months are
now reintegrated into one. The one major question—the strike—became
the focus of attention. The chapter is divided into two parts: the first
deals with events from June 7 to the initiation of the strike by pilots and
controllers on Sunday June 20, and the second with the strike itself,
until its resolution on June 28. Finally, the word "strike" is used somewhat as a shorthand for referring to the disruption of air service, even
though it was more properly a job action, work stoppage, or wildcat
strike.

ON COLLISION COURSE: JUNE 7–JUNE 20

There was a great difference in the degree of urgency with which CATCA and MOT approached the new state of affairs following John Keenan's resignation. The anglophone members of CATCA were extremely agitated and, throughout the country, they were talking of possible wildcat strikes. Jim Livingston was visiting CATCA locals in Alberta when Keenan resigned. He stayed there for the rest of the week, and was impressed by the way CATCA's leaders had succeeded in mobilizing the membership on the bilingual issue: now Livingston saw his problem as how to channel this militancy into constructive action so as to achieve CATCA's goal of slowing, or even halting, the implementation of bilingualism.

The feeling in the government was very different. The Quebec caucus breathed a great sigh of relief over Keenan's resignation and a number of federal Cabinet ministers began to rethink the wisdom of the appointment. Otto Lang now realized that he had miscalculated by overlooking the possibility that criticism in Quebec would force Keenan's resignation. Others felt that the mistake lay in Lang and Cloutier moving too quickly to name a commissioner, and their insufficient consultation with Cabinet and the caucus. Therefore, it was decided that there would be no undue haste in naming a replacement. Furthermore, it was felt that there should be two commissioners, an anglophone and a francophone (both preferably bilingual), to provide balance. Finally, they would not only be unbiased, but, unlike Keenan, would have to give the appearance of being unbiased. A prime place to look for such commissioners would therefore be the judiciary. The Cabinet and caucus would be more deeply involved in the search; the Quebeckers would concentrate on finding the francophone and Lang on finding the anglophone.

Jim Livingston, facing a great deal of pressure from his membership, called Lang to impress on him the sense of urgency and to ask whether he would appoint a new commissioner by CATCA's deadline of midnight June 11. Lang, not wishing to discuss the changed plans for choosing a commissioner, simply told him that he would make no commitment to meet CATCA's deadline or even to consult further with CATCA.[1]

Otto Lang had other priorities for the coming two weeks. He had long been planning a trip to western Europe to handle a number of matters: signing an air agreement with France, attending a conference of European transport ministers, and viewing European transportation facilities. Because the bilingualism issue had grown in significance, he decided it would be useful to pay a visit to the air traffic control centre at Charles de Gaulle Airport to see bilingual control in operation. He would be in Europe between Sunday, June 13, and Sunday, June 27. In addition to his executive assistants, Sylvain Cloutier would accompany him. In order to send a clear message to CATCA, he publicly announced his plans for the trip on Thursday June 10.[2]

Up to this point, the only ministers who had taken strong public positions on bilingual air traffic control were Otto Lang and the Quebec ministers. English-Canadian ministers, sensing that the pilots and controllers had overwhelming public support in English Canada, maintained a very low profile. On Wednesday, June 9, for the first time, an English-Canadian minister came to Lang's aid, albeit in a speech to a Quebec audience. Finance Minister Donald Macdonald, addressing the Liberal Association in Sherbrooke, denounced the "entirely indefensible" position of CATCA, claimed that "the question of security is a false question," and finally threw down the gauntlet: "I hope we will not see a strike over such a fundamental issue, but we are ready to face an eventual crisis."[3] Macdonald's statement shook CATCA. Previously, its leaders had assumed that English-Canadian opinion could force the Cabinet to back down: Macdonald's speech indicated that the Cabinet might stand behind Lang.

The CATCA national council held another conference call on Sunday June 13.[4] The members felt that MOT's actions were a deliberate provocation and wanted to prepare for a strike. Livingston expressed the view that it would be impossible to control the membership beyond Friday, June 18. While some council members favoured an immediate strike, Livingston was much more cautious, proposing that another strike vote would be held. His concern was that the previous strike mandate had been given in response to MOT's position on several issues: in this instance, he wanted a mandate to strike on the sole issue of bilingualism, thus making it clear that the satisfactory settlement of the other issues was not in dispute. Aware of the questionable legality of wildcat walkouts over bilingualism, Livingston also felt that a strike vote would give CATCA a stronger legal position. Livingston informed the council that Walter McLeish would be willing to meet them in Ottawa to discuss the situation further. Dissuaded from taking strike action precipitously, the council decided to reconvene in Ottawa the following day, meet with McLeish, and then decide on a course of action.

On Monday, June 14, the CATCA national council assembled in Ottawa for yet another stormy meeting with Walter McLeish.[5] Livingston began by accusing the federal government of having pressured Keenan to resign: McLeish countered that he and Lang had made every possible effort to have Keenan stay, and he was tired of having his credibility questioned by both CATCA and AGAQ. Livingston and vice-presidents Tonner and Robertson objected to McLeish's consultations with AGAQ, because CATCA was the only organization authorized to bargain collectively for all controllers: McLeish pointed out that a democratic government must consult with interest groups, and argued that AGAQ had been formed because francophones lacked adequate representation in CATCA, especially since CATCA would not even sign a contract in French.

McLeish, again attempting to act as arbitrator, tried to reach an agreement with CATCA. He dwelt on the breadth of the new terms of reference, and once again promised that no steps would be taken to implement bilingual air traffic control until after the commission reported. Indicating a difference with Lang, he said he personally favoured consultation with CATCA on the choice of a commissioner. He urged CATCA to wait as long as possible before going on strike, and said that Lang could be recalled from Europe if that would help prevent a strike. He concluded by asking the council to stand up to the pressure from the membership and convince them that MOT was acting in good faith. To the last request, one council member retorted that ministers should be discouraged from making inflammatory public statements.

After McLeish left the meeting, the council sat down to consider the mechanics of preparing for a strike. In addition to Jean-Luc Patenaude, one other regional director, J. G. Grant of Moncton, sided with McLeish and urged that CATCA not encourage militancy but wait a few weeks to consult on the choice of a replacement for Keenan. Livingston disagreed, arguing that there would be unauthorized walkouts if no action was taken, and that even consultation over the choice of the commissioner was not a guarantee of the right of prior approval, which Livingston thought necessary. Livingston's argument carried the day and the council decided to declare the previous ratification vote invalid and recommend to the members that they refuse to accept MOT's proposed settlement of their demands in the area of bilingualism. They decided to send out a ballot to members asking for a strike mandate. The four-day balloting period would start on Tuesday, June 15, and the results would therefore be known on the afternoon of Saturday, June 19. John Nelligan, CATCA's legal counsel, advised that MOT would probably seek a court injunction against a strike; therefore, he would prepare CATCA's defence.

On the morning of Tuesday, June 15, Jim Livingston issued a press release informing the media that the CATCA executive had recommended against ratifying the "proposed settlement of the language issue as amended by Mr. Keenan's resignation."[6] The press release claimed that "we find it difficult to believe that any future commissioner could conduct an independent investigation if the government cannot guarantee freedom from political intimidation such as that experienced by Mr. Keenan." The press release drew attention to Lang's absence and to Donald Macdonald's speech which "declared publicly that the safety factor in bilingual air-ground communications is a phony issue, thereby indicating to us the true attitude of Cabinet to the investigation of our concerns.'' Livingston mentioned that CATCA's proposal for a replacement for Keenan (Milton Harradence, who was not named) was not accepted. He also said that he favoured only one commissioner, because if the government had two or three commissioners, it would simply choose the position which suited it best.

THE PMO BECOMES INVOLVED

Up to this point, although the Prime Minister's Office had monitored the bilingual air traffic control problem, it had taken no action of its own. This was for two reasons. First, Otto Lang was a strong minister who preferred to handle problems himself, and neither sought nor welcomed the help of either his Cabinet colleagues or the central agencies. Second, the PMO had other priorities at the time. Michael Kirby, the assistant principal secretary to the prime minister in charge of planning, had commissioned many secret public opinion polls to monitor the nation's political pulse.[7] The polls indicated public concern with economic issues (energy, food prices, inflation) and security issues (gun control, capital punishment). Little concern was being expressed over bilingualism.

In response to Kirby's polls, as well as to its other sources of advice, the government had decided to launch major initiatives in the areas singled out as of greatest concern: the anti-inflation program and the peace-and-security package had been prepared. The latter included gun control legislation and a free House of Commons vote on capital punishment. The free vote was set for Tuesday, June 22, and the PMO was exerting pressure to make sure the abolitionists won.

However, with the threat of a strike and in the absence of Otto Lang, the PMO was finally moved to intervene on the bilingual issue. As fate would have it, this was a difficult week for taking action. The offices were being moved from the Gothic style East Block across the street to the newly renovated Second Empire style Langevin Block. Files were in crates, rooms were being assigned and reassigned, and telephones were not working.

In this chaotic atmosphere, Jim Coutts, the prime minister's principal secretary, and Michael Kirby decided to assign one of their staff members to meet with MOT and investigate the problem. The task went to Jim MacDonald, who was working in Kirby's policy secretariat. MacDonald's expertise was mainly in the area of social policy. However, he was bilingual and deemed to be sensitive to political factors.

The briefings Jim MacDonald received from staff at MOT (Finley, Lyon, Arpin, and others) were disconcerting. The civil servants could explain the technical issues well enough, but they had no idea what to do in the event of a strike. MacDonald was struck by the predominantly anglophone composition of the group. Following the first briefing, he had further meetings and made some phone calls. He often found it difficult to reach people at MOT after 3:30 p.m., and was troubled by the absence of an air of crisis there. He felt that there was more going on than could be accounted for by the defensiveness officials in a line agency normally show towards the PMO. The bureaucrats at MOT appeared to be implementing the policy without any personal conviction or enthusiasm. Mac-Donald, in his earlier work as an executive assistant to Solicitor General Warren Allmand, had come to expect bureaucrats, during similar crises, to support departmental policies and act with much greater energy and enthusiasm than he was now witnessing.

After a day or two, MacDonald wrote a memo to Prime Minister Trudeau in which he concluded that the real problem was that the bureaucracy was unenthusiastic about supporting its minister. He expected that a full-fledged crisis would break almost imminently, and recommended that Lang and Cloutier be recalled from Europe, but that in the meanwhile the Privy Council Office get involved in order to stabilize the situation.

Trudeau took MacDonald's advice and called upon Michael Pitfield, clerk of the privy council, to devise a strategy. Pitfield and his staff quickly realized that legislation outlawing a strike would not be an acceptable solution, since the Conservatives, who had been supporting CATCA and CALPA, would oppose it and delay passage. Furthermore, such legislation might not even have the support of all English-Canadian Liberals. Finally, the House of Commons' agenda was already full, and the debate over capital punishment was a particularly important item. Thus, the strategy they chose was the use of the courts to get injunctions forcing the controllers and, if necessary, the pilots to remain at work. This would avoid the difficulty of a parliamentary debate. They felt certain that they could convince the courts that both the controllers and the pilots would be striking illegally. If the controllers and pilots did go on strike illegally, the issue could be shifted from bilingualism to respect for the legal process, which would put the government on stronger ground. They decided that Treasury Board President Jean Chrétien would be the logical minister to handle the issue. Chrétien would make public statements and the Department of Justice would prepare the government's legal case. On Tuesday, June 15, Jean Chrétien announced that the government considered any strike by air traffic controllers to be illegal, and would therefore take legal action to keep the controllers at work.[8]

Otto Lang spent some time that day in Paris, watching bilingual air traffic control in action at Charles de Gaulle Airport. He reported that he was "favourably impressed" by the operation and by the "delightfully calm atmosphere despite all the hovering around."[9] It is unlikely that

Lang's statement changed many minds. For those who opposed bilingual control, the fact that he had waited so long to visit a bilingual facility was proof that he was ignorant of the issue and politically motivated. Interviewed on "As It Happens" on CBC Radio, Jim Livingston responded to Lang's visit to Paris with scorn:

> If he had taken the trouble to go about thirty miles south of Montreal, there is a control tower down there which my members control and have been controlling now since June of last year bilingually, which has some 2000 more operations a month than Charles de Gaulle has and I am sure they do it just as smoothly and just as comfortably bilingually as the French controllers that he watched in Paris. We have never had objections to bilingual air traffic control in Quebec until the Minister made a commitment to introduce it into airports which are three and four times as busy as Charles de Gaulle and at that point we believe that it is unsafe and controllers cannot handle bilingually that kind of a traffic load safely.[10]

A few days later, the *Globe and Mail* published three letters from pilots, arguing that the standard of air traffic control in Paris is poor and, they felt, unsafe.[11]

On Thursday, June 17, Jim Livingston issued a press statement that, if CATCA's membership voted to strike, the union would begin a nation-wide strike at 3 a.m. on Sunday June 20. The results of the strike vote would be available late Saturday afternoon. Livingston stated that the national council was "confident that their request for a strike mandate will be supported by an overwhelming majority of the 2200 members."[12]

The Department of Justice responded to CATCA's threat by applying for a court injunction to prohibit the strike, and a hearing was set for the Federal Court of Canada, on Friday afternoon.

The impending strike was the main topic in Question Period in the House of Commons on Friday morning. Prime Minister Trudeau, striking a theme he would elaborate a few days later, said: "We are quite disturbed that any group or union in Canada would want to strike against the principle of bilingualism. This in our mind is what is happening now."[13] The New Democratic Party entered the debate for the first time. The NDP had great difficulty in formulating a position on bilingual air traffic control. On the one hand, the party had always supported the principle of bilingualism. On the other hand, it was reluctant to criticize a labour union. Furthermore, Peter Sadlier-Brown, CATCA's representative on the conciliation board, was arguing CATCA's case to his fellow advisers in the party office. Finally, since all the NDP's representation is in English Canada, and especially in the west, the party was reluctant to oppose its constituents. The conflicting pressures were reflected in the two middle-of-the-road questions asked by John Gilbert (NDP, Broadview): whether MOT officials had been meeting with CATCA to avert a strike, and whether the government was taking steps to replace obsolete radar (by installing JETS radar with its alphanumeric display) so as to increase the safety factor in air traffic control.[14]

On Friday afternoon, André Garneau of the Justice Department, representing the government, and John Nelligan, representing CATCA, argued before Federal Court Justice Georges Addy about whether or not an injunction should be granted to prevent CATCA from striking. Addy spent the night pondering the arguments and delivered his judgment at 10 a.m. on Saturday morning, June 19. He decided to grant a temporary injunction against any strike by CATCA for ten days. The injunction also restrained CATCA leaders from in any way counselling their members to strike.

In reaching his decision, Addy's finding was that CATCA and the Treasury Board had entered into a duly-executed agreement on May 27 and that the agreement had been ratified by the members and was in force immediately after the ratification vote was announced on May 31. Furthermore, neither the existence of the Commission of Inquiry nor the appointment of John Keenan as commissioner had been made a condition of agreement for the ratification vote. Therefore, Keenan's resignation could not invalidate either the agreement or the ratification vote. In terms of the public policy issues involved, Addy felt that because of the government's commitment to delay implementation until after the commission had reported, there was no reason to believe that the status quo for air traffic control language would be changed before the collective agreement between MOT and CATCA expired at the end of the year. He therefore rejected the safety argument as a justification for the controllers' action and concluded that: "It is evident that a much more logical and cogent motive would be the fear of loss of opportunities for advancement for unilingual controllers."[15]

The CATCA national council held a conference call at 4 p.m.[16] The results of the strike vote were compiled and found to be quite similar to those of May 19, except that this time the francophone controllers expressed their opposition by refusing to vote. All members of the council were available for the call except for Vice-President Bill Robertson, who did not participate in any council meetings during the next nine days. The council decided to respect the injunction, postpone the strike, and advise all CATCA members to go to work. As well, it passed a resolution that CATCA did not anticipate any circumstances in which it would provide legal or monetary assistance to any member who disobeyed the court injunction. Livingston advised the council of the possibility of another conference call in the event that CALPA took action. The council then sent telegrams to all branches informing them of the injunction and urging all members to respect the court order. Livingston issued a press statement expressing the hope that the controllers, despite their frustrations, would stay on the job.

Now the ball was in CALPA's court. Individual pilots were already concerned that the quality of air traffic service had been deteriorating seriously in the previous few weeks. The week before, an Air Canada DC-8 and a CP Air 727 had come very close to colliding when their flight paths intersected 37,000 feet over North Bay. Ten days before that an Air Canada L-1011 and a CP Air 747 had had a near miss as they approached each other, flying at the same altitude, over Thunder Bay. MOT was also worried by these near-misses.[17] On June 16, H. A. Merritt, the director of air traffic services issued a memo calling the attention of controllers to nine losses of separation which had occurred in the six-week period from the beginning of May to mid-June, three of which were critical (that is, near-misses). By contrast, only five losses of separation had occurred between January 1 and May 1. The losses of separation were not occurring in Quebec, but entirely in English Canada, indicating that the problem was the stress that English-Canadian air traffic controllers were feeling as a result of the bilingual air traffic control issue.[18]

The CALPA directors held a conference call Saturday morning to discuss the situation. They first considered briefing pilots at the airports. The feeling of the board, in light of the controllers' situation, was that this was not enough. One board member said, "This is crazy—why are we flying?" The consensus that emerged was that the time for action had arrived. However, they decided to await another sounding of the controllers' situation. Maley spoke with Livingston again, who told him that the controllers were at work, but were very angry, which Maley reported to his Board of Directors. The CALPA board had a second conference call, and decided unanimously to advise their pilots to stop flying at 3 a.m. on Sunday, June 20. Maley issued a statement, justifying the strike on the grounds that CALPA could no longer "guarantee the safety of the travelling public and flight crew personnel." He announced: "There will be no return to work by pilots until the Government takes clear and effective action to clear up a situation which may at any time result in a catastrophe of major proportions." Maley felt that the situation in air traffic control had deteriorated rapidly, and described the system as being "in a state of siege."[19] The CALPA directors then decided to have local council executives go to the various airports to urge the pilots not to fly.

While CALPA pilots were deciding whether or not to fly, Otto Lang and Sylvain Cloutier, now in England, were also deciding whether or not to fly—back to Canada. On Saturday afternoon (Greenwich time), David

Cuthbertson, Lang's executive assistant, called to tell them about Justice Addy's injunction and to inform Lang that the MP with whom he was to be paired in the free vote on capital punishment (a Liberal who favoured retention of the death penalty) had reneged. While Lang did not wish to return solely because of the strike threat, the expected closeness of the vote on capital punishment almost certainly made his presence in Ottawa mandatory. Lang and Cloutier had all but decided to return when, during dinner, Cuthbertson called again with another piece of news. Otto Lang's father, who had long been suffering from cancer, had died the previous night. Lang and Cloutier then arranged to take Sunday morning's British Airways flight to Mirabel, where Lang would be met by a government aircraft which would take him to Saskatoon for the funeral.

THE STRIKE AGAINST BILINGUALISM

SUNDAY, JUNE 21

Nothing in his experience had prepared Ken Maley for the events he was sure he would encounter in the coming days. He turned to Ron Young, CALPA's director of industrial relations, and said, "You're staying at my side, every step of the way, until this thing is settled." Young, a native of Indiana, had worked as a negotiator for the Air Line Pilots Association in the United States between 1966 and 1970. In 1970, at the age of twenty-eight, he was loaned to CALPA as acting director of industrial relations: he impressed the Canadian pilots, and stayed on in that position in a permanent capacity. Young was recognized to be very quick-witted and articulate, as well as a tough and experienced negotiator. He is the sort of person who can see the bargaining aspect of any human relationship. Maley and Young set up shop at CALPA headquaters, then located near Dorval airport, and were there until 1 a.m. Sunday taking calls, advising pilots, and attempting to ascertain whether the controllers were working.

By Sunday morning the Canadian aviation system was shutting down. The pilots recognized that it was important to justify their action to the inconvenienced public, and therefore lost no time in feeding to the press the file of stories of near-misses and panic felt by unilingual anglophone pilots operating in a bilingual environment. Numerous articles based on this file began to appear. CALPA directors also made themselves available to speak to the press about the near-misses.

Late Sunday afternoon, sixteen controllers in Winnipeg, where support for the strike had been strongest, walked off work because of "tension on the job." Jean Chrétien responded by calling a press conference that evening in which he threatened their prosecution. This threat, as well as the persuasion of the CATCA executive, was sufficient to convince the controllers to return to work a few hours later.[20]

As soon as the pilots stopped flying, the airlines acted to force them to return to work. Air Canada, CP Air, and Eastern Provincial jointly applied for an injunction. The case was heard at an extraordinary Sunday night session of the Federal Court, before Associate Chief Justice Thurlow.[21] Maley and Young rushed to Ottawa for the hearing. John Keenan, once again CALPA's regular counsel, was on vacation, recuperating from his harrowing three weeks as commissioner. He was replaced by Aubrey Golden, a Toronto trial and labour lawyer hastily brought into the case. The argument went on until 2:20 a.m., in a courtroom packed with pilots, stewardesses, and newsmen. Golden argued that, under the Aeronautics Act, pilots have the discretion to take any measures necessary to ensure the safety of their passengers, and were simply doing this in the prevailing uncertain situation. The airlines' lawyer, Brian Crane, did not question the pilots' authority: however, he drew the court's attention to the fact that this was a case of concerted action, taken by all pilots across the country, and organized by CALPA. It was by definition an illegal strike. He used as evidence Maley's statement of the previous Saturday advising pilots not to fly until further notice, as well as the detailed instructions that had been issued to Air Canada pilots as to which flights should be operated. In addition, Crane argued that monetary losses to the airlines were substantial, over $3 million daily to Air Canada alone. Golden tried to counter that the pilots' action was not really a strike, but rather a political protest. At the hearing, Ken Maley volunteered that "The Canadian Air Line Pilots Association is prepared to undertake that it will neither direct nor order its members not to conduct flights. We can give no assurance, however, that flight operations will be resumed under prevailing circumstances."[22] Thurlow felt that the undertaking did not go nearly far enough because there was no offer to cancel the original order of a strike. He therefore granted a temporary injunction against CALPA's action until 2:30 p.m. Thursday, June 24, at which time a second hearing would be held.

MONDAY, JUNE 21

On Monday it became clear that the pilots and controllers had overwhelming support in English Canada—as demonstrated by letters to the editor, calls on talk shows, and man-in-the-street interviews.[23] Passengers stranded at airports, when asked who was to blame for their inconvenience, all pointed an accusing finger at the government. For a substantial segment of the English-Canadian population, the controllers and pilots were heroes, the first group to stand up and oppose the government's hated bilingualism policy. The CATCA and CALPA switchboards were deluged with calls from well-wishers and offers of support.

As predicted by Livingston, it was not possible to restrain the controllers. There were walkouts or sickouts in Vancouver, Edmonton, Calgary, Ottawa, Halifax, Gander, and Toronto. The CALPA office, which kept calling CATCA to find out what was happening next, noticed a strange pattern: CATCA could never predict where the next disruption would occur, but CALPA would first hear rumours of a disruption, and then the CATCA office would call minutes later to confirm them. Some MOT managers were told by controllers in their jurisdictions that they were taking orders from a mysterious CATCA "command centre," which was apparently located in an upper-storey suite in the Ottawa Holiday Inn that looked directly out onto Otto Lang's departmental office in the Place de Ville office complex. If there was such a centre, its existence alone would not fully explain the behaviour of the controllers: clearly, the men were sufficiently angry to go along with action which could subject them to prosecution. Furthermore, these wildcat walkouts served the pilots' interest by providing a justification for their refusal to fly. Jim Livingston, when asked about his activities by the press, replied, "I have been up to my ass in alligators all day ... trying to get [the controllers] to go back."[24]

The government was also trying to get the controllers to go back. The Justice Department began contempt of court proceedings against the sixteen Winnipeg controllers who had walked off the job on Sunday. Jean Chrétien called a noon-hour press conference in which he declared "I don't buy that crazy jazz that they suddenly get sick on Monday morning when they had a court injunction. They had better have a medical certificate. Everyone who is out will be prosecuted."[25]

One place the controllers remained relatively calm was the Montreal centre. J. D. Lyon and his team monitored the centre very closely. The francophones all reported for work in order to express their disapproval of the strike. Lyon relieved some of the anglophones of duty in order to reduce friction.

Walter McLeish called Jim Livingston, to inform him that MOT was now thinking of appointing two commissioners, both from the judiciary. Livingston realized that he would shortly be entering negotiations with McLeish, so he decided to start by taking a hard line. He told McLeish that CATCA was no longer interested in commissions or commissioners and that the only thing that would be acceptable to his enraged membership would be a promise not to expand bilingual air traffic control any further.

While driving from Ottawa back to Montreal, Maley and Young discussed CALPA's next move. They felt that Maley must formally order the pilots to return to work, while at the same time advising them to use their professional judgment. Upon his return, he arranged a conference call with his Board of Directors, who agreed with his plan. The controllers' walkouts convinced pilots not to fly: none were willing to risk the possibility that controllers might walk out while their planes were in the air. Robert Crossley, a CALPA director based in Vancouver, put it very graphically, "A federal judge can tell me to fly till hell freezes over, but I am not going to kill myself. [Without controllers] the airways are unsafe."[26]

No sooner had the conference call ended than Maley received a call from the Progressive Conservative caucus in Ottawa, asking him to address them. It was a fine, sunny, summer day: the CALPA office found a willing pilot, and Maley and Young were flown, VFR, back to Ottawa. For Maley, the politically naive knight of the holy grail of aviation safety, the meeting was a most disillusioning experience. It was chaired by Jack Horner (PC, Crowfoot), the transportation critic.[27] Party leader Joe Clark was absent, but many MPs who had been interested in the issue were there. Maley presented his standard technical arguments against bilingual air traffic control, emphasizing the importance of the listening watch. A number of MPs, though not all, claimed they supported CALPA and sympathized with the pilots. That said, Jack Horner then made it clear that, despite their sympathy, the Tories could not simply come out in support of the pilots. The MPs recognized that the pilots now had the support of all the anglophone rednecks who were coming out of the woodwork. The Conservatives, who wanted to look respectable as they were "preparing to govern" could not afford to identify any more closely with the pilots than they already had. Besides, Horner suggested, by keeping a low profile, the Conservatives would win the support of English Canadians who would see the strike as one more piece of evidence of Liberal incompetence. Young spoke up bitterly. In the United States, where he had grown up, if politicians believed that what a group was saying was right, then they supported the group publicly. Why was the Canadian situation different? Horner just laughed. Unable to convince the Conservatives to support them publicly, Maley and Young left angrily to return to Montreal.

After arriving in Montreal, Maley began discussions with CALPA's second lawyer of the week, Frederick Von Veh, a Toronto labour relations lawyer, partner in the establishment firm of Stikeman, Elliott and secretary-treasurer of the Canadian Bar Association. Maley had been dissatisfied with Aubrey Golden, who seemed too radical, in both his demeanour and his arguments, for an organization which thought of itself as a professional association rather than a union.

On the francophone side, Serge Joyal appeared in Quebec Superior Court with a group of francophone mechanics working for Air Canada, to launch a suit against the airline to end discrimination against the use of

French in maintenance operations at Dorval. The suit asked the court to force the airline to declare French of equal status to English, to permit the workers to use French, and to translate English manuals.[28] Quebec Solicitor General Fernand Lalonde took issue with Jim Livingston's claim that the density of traffic in Montreal is much heavier than in France. He noted that Orly Airport in Paris has 150,000 movements a year, which is the same level as Quebec City. It appeared that no one in the federal government had attempted to present these facts.[29]

Finally, Otto Lang was in Saskatoon for his father's funeral.

TUESDAY, JUNE 22

The air traffic control situation was better, but still not completely normal, with walkouts continuing in Calgary and Moncton. The pilots were still refusing to fly: Bruce Yake, CALPA vice-president, now said that pilots would carry on exercising their prerogative not to fly until the government took "clear and effective action" to resolve the dispute. Air Canada planned to resume service at 2 p.m., but could not do so when its pilots failed to report for work.[30] CP Air was also unable to resume service. The only airlines which had any success in maintaining service were Nordair and Quebecair, which had a greater proportion of francophone pilots than the others. Many francophone pilots working for the other airlines were attempting to organize full crews and find aircraft in order to break the strike. At one point, fifty-one francophone Air Canada pilots sent a telegram to Air Canada President Claude Taylor, indicating their willingness to work. Roger Demers accused Air Canada's middle management, many of whom were members of CALPA, of dragging their feet on logistical arrangements, thereby making it impossible for the airline to keep Quebec operations going.[31]

CALPA was able to enlist the support of sympathetic foreign pilots' associations, and the pilots of British Airways, KLM, and SAS (airlines of countries which use English only for IFR air traffic control) refused to fly to Canada. Late in the evening, both Air Canada and CP Air suspended operations, and began to lay off large numbers of personnel.[32]

The airlines continued the legal fight. Air Canada, CP Air, and Eastern Provincial filed a joint civil suit claiming at least $7 million in damages against CALPA. In addition, they petitioned the Federal Court to require CALPA officers to show why they were not in contempt of the previous day's court injunction. Mr. Justice Georges Addy, who had heard the government's case against CATCA, accepted the airlines' petition and set trial dates in July for Ken Maley and two other CALPA leaders.[33]

One response of MOT to the strike was to activate its situation room, in which a task force of government pilots, flight inspectors, and personnel relations staff monitored where controllers were working and all aircraft that were flying over Canadian airspace. Apart from this, it was business as usual at the bureaucratic level. Many of the pilots and controllers working at headquarters openly supported CATCA and CALPA and proudly wore their "English is the international language of aviation" buttons. They were glad to see someone standing up to what they felt was the imposition of bilingualism for political reasons, without regard to aviation safety or proper procedures. An experienced *Globe and Mail* reporter interviewed three middle-level managers who expressed strong support for the pilots and controllers: never in his memory had he heard civil servants so totally at odds with their political masters.[34]

Tuesday brought news that threatened to compound the governments's problems. The union representing government pilots and flight inspectors, which had been in a legal strike position since January, had been awarded a substantial pay increase by Emmett Hall, the former Supreme Court justice, who served as arbitrator. However, the Anti-Inflation Board announced that it would not allow Hall's settlement to stand.[35]

During Question Period in the House of Commons, the Conservatives were cautious while the NDP were growing more outspoken in their support for CATCA and CALPA. Don Mazankowski (PC, Vegreville) asked Lang if he had consulted CATCA on the choice of a commissioner. Lang responded that CATCA's one suggestion was not helpful and that CATCA no longer seemed interested in a commission of inquiry, but wanted bilingual air traffic control stopped.[36] NDP leader Ed Broadbent asked Jean Chrétien "why the Government's immediate response to the Winnipeg walkout was to apply the full and literal force of the law to the people involved, instead of sending an emissary to negotiate a speedy resolution of the conflict?"[37] Les Benjamin (NDP, Regina-Lake Centre) gave a speech accusing Otto Lang of evading his ministerial responsibility by not consulting with the controllers and pilots after Keenan's resignation, by making an unnecessary trip to see bilingual air traffic control in Paris, and by instituting terms of reference for the Commission of Inquiry which were too narrow.[38] It is clear at this point that western, anglophone, and labour union loyalties within the NDP caucus had prevailed.

Late in the afternoon, Lang and Walter McLeish held a press conference. Lang's objective was to get across certain basic facts which he felt were being ignored by the public and by the media: that bilingual air traffic control would not be implemented anywhere other than Quebec, that the implementation program was not immediate but would take a number of years, and that "if a high powered commission found that there was not adequate safety, that there was a jeopardizing of safety, it would be a practical impossibility for a government to proceed with its implementation." Going still further, Lang said that if one of the two commissioners felt bilingual air traffic control was unsafe, it would not be implemented. He was asked to respond to Keith Spicer's latest suggestion, which was that there be an informal meeting among Lang, CATCA, CALPA, and AGAQ for two, three, four days, or however long was necessary, to reach an agreement. He simply replied that the suggestion was not very helpful, that Walter McLeish was in contact with CATCA and CALPA, and that he himself would be available if his participation was deemed useful.[39]

By Tuesday night, the co-commissioners had been chosen, approved by Cabinet, and had agreed to serve. They were Julien Chouinard, former Quebec Cabinet secretary and a justice of the Quebec Court of Appeal and W. R. Sinclair, of the Supreme Court of Alberta. Sinclair was the anglophone whose mastery of French had drawn praise in Keith Spicer's 1975 Annual Report, and whom Spicer had suggested to Lang in his call from the symposium. Near midnight, Lang called Livingston to inform him privately of the choice of the two commissioners: Livingston was non-committal. Lang tried to reach Maley in Montreal, but he was not there.

Maley and Young were spending Tuesday night in Toronto. Maley had been urged to consult an advertising agency for suggestions as to how best to communicate his message to the public, and a meeting was arranged in Toronto for Tuesday evening. Maley and Young arrived in Toronto, courtesy of another private pilot flying VFR. The advertising agency listened to Maley's account of CALPA's activities up to that point, and concluded that CALPA had done so brilliant a job that they could add nothing. Maley asked them to put that in writing, so he could show it to the board of directors. The agency agreed, after charging $2,000 for the evening's services.

Finally, Tuesday night was an important moment in Canadian history. In a free vote, the House of Commons abolished capital punishment.

WEDNESDAY, JUNE 23

The CALPA pilots were still refusing to fly, so air traffic remained at a virtual standstill. Perhaps because of this, the controllers' walkouts, having achieved their purpose, ended.

The union of government pilots and flight inspectors announced that it would be going on strike on Thursday. Walter McLeish both angrily and apprehensively called Tom Hinton, the president of the union: he wanted to know whether his membership was striking to express support for CATCA and CALPA and how the situation room would be staffed. Tom Hinton had joined MOT after a number of years as a fighter pilot. During that time, he had been chosen as one of the nine elite members of the Golden Centenaires aerobatic team: he had what Tom Wolfe called "the Right Stuff."[40] When compared to the seven fighter pilots who became the first American astronauts, Hinton resembled the dedicated yet personable John Glenn much more than the macho fighter jocks who were the majority of the group. With his moustache, wire-rimmed glasses, and thinning hair, Hinton looked more like an aging folk-singer than a fighter pilot.

Hinton quickly calmed McLeish's fears. He had realized that the anglophone majority in his union supported CATCA and CALPA, while the francophone minority supported AGAQ. He convinced both groups that the only way the union could stay united, and therefore achieve its collective bargaining objectives, was to take a strictly neutral position on the dispute between CATCA, CALPA, and MOT. Also, the pilots and inspectors in the situation room had been designated, and would remain on the job. For McLeish, this was good news.

Otto Lang appeared on the CTV program "Canada A.M.," attempting once again to articulate his basic message:

> We have done what we consider to be every reasonable thing to
> assure the safety of the system. We have given them guarantees.
> They said to us that they were not sure we trust you. What about a
> commission? So we said fine. We will appoint an independent com-
> mission to further assure that safety is assured.... [The strike will go
> on] until we can persuade the pilots that if there is anything more we
> can do to assure safety, tell us and we will do it.[41]

At 11:30 a.m., Lang reached Ken Maley, who was meeting in Toronto with CALPA's new lawyer, Frederick Von Veh. Lang informed Maley of the choice of the two commissioners from the judiciary. Maley urged Lang to delay the announcement so there could be some consultation beforehand, but Lang refused. However, Lang agreed to set up a meeting with Maley and Livingston that evening to discuss the strike.

At mid-day, Lang announced the names of the two commissioners. After the appointments were made public, Keith Spicer called Livingston to advise him that he himself had recommended these two judges. He asked Livingston not to object to them as individuals, but rather, if he wished to object, to attack the principle of the commission of inquiry. Livingston consented to do this.[42] He also knew that continued objections to individual commissioners, especially those whose role is to examine disputes without bias, would make it impossible for any commission to function. Livingston realized that a solution would have to be reached, and that a commission would have to be part of it.

Prime Minister Trudeau was sufficiently worried about the support English Canadians were giving the pilots and controllers that he felt the bilingualism policy, his major political achievement and his solution to the

national unity problem, was in danger. Trudeau decided to make a televised address to the nation on Wednesday night, although his English-
speaking advisers, Jim Coutts and Michael Kirby, tried to dissuade him.
They felt that Trudeau was in a no-win position; anglophones were not
interested in or were negative to bilingualism and Trudeau's support in
Quebec was so strong that the speech could not increase it. For Trudeau,
the electoral calculus was irrelevant, while the message was crucial.

The speech was drafted by Kirby's staff and revised by Trudeau. One
can read two strains in it. Trudeau was enunciating his vision of Canada:
his advisers were attempting to calm the fears of the English-Canadian
public. From Trudeau's viewpoint, the core of the speech was this:

> But why provide [bilingual air service] even in Quebec, you may
> ask? Why not require all French-speaking pilots to become fluent in
> English? That question, my friends, goes to the very root of what
> Canada is all about. It goes to the very roots of the bilingualism
> policy which the government adopted with the support of all parties
> in the House of Commons. Parliament in the name of all Canadians,
> has decided that both English and French-speaking citizens of this
> country have the right to be served in their own language.[43]

For Pierre Trudeau, reason must always prevail over passion. The speech
ended with a fascinating *reductio ad absurdum* by which he attempted to
prove, as though proving a mathematical theorem, that the pilots and
controllers opposing bilingual air traffic control were being irrational. It
was almost as if he felt this would be sufficient to change his opponents'
minds, or at least those of the public.

> The fact is that those pilots and controllers who have put a stop to
> air travel in Canada cannot be protesting against the actual extention
> of bilingual control services to Montreal airports, because no such
> extension has taken place. They cannot be protesting against any
> government decision to provide such a service at Montreal because
> no such decision has been made, and no such decision will be made
> until we know for sure that bilingual procedures will be fully consis-
> tent with air safety in the Montreal region. They cannot reasonably
> be protesting against bilingual air traffic control in principle, because
> it has been working safely in many countries for many years.... What
> they seem to be protesting, therefore, is the very idea of even look-
> ing at the possibility of having safe bilingual control procedures pro-
> vided at Montreal. That seems to me to be an untenable position for
> reasonable people to take.[44]

Examples of the Coutts-Kirby parts of the speech are:

> the federal government places the highest priority on the safety and security of passengers, crew members and the general public. No other goal of public policy has ever or will ever take precedence over the goal of preserving and improving public safety in the air.... If it could be shown that the use of both French and English in conversations between air traffic controllers and pilots in Quebec air space is or could be a safety hazard, the federal government would insist that only the English language be used. Common sense would prohibit any other course of action.... Bilingual air traffic control is not needed outside of the province of Quebec, except possibly in the national capital region, so there is no intention on the part of the government to provide such a bilingual service all across the country. We have no desire to spend your money on expensive public services which are not needed.[45]

Trudeau's speech had little effect on the pilots and controllers. Refusing his assurances, they denied his conclusion that they were behaving irrationally.

At 10 p.m., shortly after Trudeau finished speaking, Otto Lang, Jim Livingston, Ken Maley, Walter McLeish, and Air Canada President Claude Taylor gathered in Lang's office in Ottawa. The meeting was an opportunity to state initial positions and begin communications with a view to ending the impasse. Otto Lang began by asking Maley what would be necessary to convince the pilots that it was safe to resume flying. Maley replied that it would depend on his receiving assurances from Livingston that the air traffic control system was operating safely and that the controllers would stay on the job. Livingston responded that he could not give such assurances unless he had the full support of his council and his membership. The only solution which would win the complete support of the membership was a permanent undertaking by the government that bilingual air traffic control would not be expanded any further. Lang made it very clear he would not give such an undertaking. Two points on which he would not make concessions were that there would be a commission of inquiry and that, if the commission found that bilingual air traffic control was safe, it would be implemented. The charges against the controllers in Winnipeg were also discussed. Lang reiterated that they would not be withdrawn, though he intimated that there was a possibility that penalties could be reduced if work were resumed. At that point, both sides were at an impasse. Maley suggested that the deadlock might be broken if Lang understood the pilots' concerns, and felt this could be done if the

CALPA board were to come to Ottawa to meet with him. Lang was amenable, and invited the CATCA national council to Ottawa as well. Livingston demurred, in order to consult the council before making such a decision. At that point, the meeting concluded.

After the meeting, Walter McLeish and the staff in the situation room spent several hours making arrangements to bring the CALPA and CATCA boards to Ottawa. He chartered a CP Air 737 to pick up the western members.

Jim Livingston held a midnight conference call with his national council.[46] After reporting on the meeting with Lang, he began to survey the feelings of the council and the membership. The council had little trust in the Commission of Inquiry and wanted no more than one commissioner. They put little faith in the statements by either Lang or Trudeau. The council members reported that throughout English Canada morale was high, and there was good public support in eastern Canada and overwhelming support in the west. They felt that the situation was sufficiently stable that they could leave their regions and rely on the men to stay on the job, as ordered. They then decided, with only Jean-Luc Patenaude dissenting, to reconvene in Ottawa as soon as MOT could get them there. At 2 a.m., Jim Livingston called Otto Lang to arrange a meeting with the CATCA council for Thursday evening.

THURSDAY, JUNE 24
For the second consecutive day, controllers were at work throughout the country. Pilots for the major airlines, Air Canada and CP Air, were not. About seven hundred pilots held a rally in Toronto, at which Robert Mac-William, the CALPA regional director, expressing the mood of the meeting, told the press that the pilots still refused to believe the government's assurances, including those of the prime minister, and would continue the strike until the government provided a safe aviation environment.[47]

American pilots, like their European confrères, came to CALPA's aid. Captain J. J. O'Donnell, the president of the United States Air Line Pilots Association (who had asserted at the symposium that it was self-evident that air traffic control was safer in one language than two), announced at a press conference in Washington that all flights to Canada by major American carriers would be suspended at midnight.[48] Ontario Transportation Minister James Snow, himself a private pilot, also entered the fray, declaring that he was "one hundred percent in agreement" with CATCA and CALPA.[49]

The airlines (Air Canada, CP Air, Eastern Provincial) obtained an extension of their court injunction against CALPA to Wednesday, July 1. Pilots who did not return to work by then could be held in contempt of court. By extending the injunction, the airlines were taking a neutral position and allowing the pilots and the government several more days' time in which to resolve their disagreement.

As June 24 was St. Jean-Baptiste Day, Quebec's national holiday, the House of Commons did not meet. However, due to opposition criticism of Prime Minister Trudeau's use of national television to speak about the crisis, the CBC decided, at the last moment, to make time available to Joe Clark and Ed Broadbent to state their parties' positions. Joe Clark began by affirming Conservative support for bilingualism, which he said was not at issue. He then criticized the Liberal government for having mismanaged the implementation so badly that "essentially a technical issue was allowed to become . . . a political issue." He went into specifics, castigating the Liberal party for pressuring John Keenan to resign, Otto Lang for flying to Paris and making inflammatory statements instead of consulting with pilots and controllers, and Prime Minister Trudeau for misrepresenting the views of the pilots and controllers. However, as he would not condone disobedience of the courts, he urged the pilots and controllers to resume flying and to start discussions with the Commission of Inquiry.[50] In short, Clark used the issue in precisely the way Horner had told Maley the Conservatives would use it. Broadbent's speech, which followed, was basically an echo of Clark's.

The chartered plane carrying the CALPA and CATCA directors, dubbed CALPA-ONE by its passengers, made its way slowly to Ottawa. It was delayed in Winnipeg because CALPA Vice-President Bruce Yake demanded that Eastern Provincial Airlines and Nordair pilots be forced to stop flying before the CALPA and CATCA executives met with Lang. Though David Cuthbertson, Lang's executive assistant, denounced the demand as unreasonable, the two airlines apparently agreed to it. While at Winnipeg airport, the CALPA and CATCA directors were given heroes' welcomes by a local flying club. CALPA-ONE landed in Ottawa late Thursday night. Jim Livingston wanted to meet his national council before they met with Otto Lang, so he rescheduled the meeting for noon on Friday.

The pilots checked into the Inn of the Provinces, were quickly briefed by Maley and Young, and then walked across the street to Transport Canada headquarters to confront Lang, Cloutier, and McLeish. The meeting took place in the board room. Ken Maley asked each of his board members to state what he thought the problem was. Many replied that the real problem was Lang's incompetence and the deceitfulness of MOT. Lang listened impassively to the criticism, only responding angrily when one of the pilots called him a liar. One of the participants remembers the setting as though it were an amphitheatre, with the pilots sitting above, hurling questions at Lang, Cloutier, and McLeish in the pit below. Despite the accusations and the focus on the aviation safety question, some of the pilots were aware of the broader political context. One pilot called on the group to be patriotic, and not to let their disagreement shatter national unity. Walter McLeish, sounding more like a politician than did his minister, spoke about bilingual air traffic control as a logical consequence of the Quiet Revolution and above the need to implement bilingual air traffic control in order to keep Quebec in Confederation. The discussion continued on a number of levels for some time. Finally, Glen McRae, a pilot from Transair, made a speech that provided an opening for constructive discussion. He argued that the real issue was trust, and that if the pilots could be convinced that safety was truly MOT's major concern, then a resolution could be found. Almost immediately, Sylvain Cloutier called for a recess, during which he suggested to Lang that this was an opportunity for bargaining with the pilots about concrete things the government could do to show it was serious about aviation safety. Of course, this meeting was not the proper forum for bargaining: that would have to follow later. After the recess, Lang spoke, saying that they had made considerable progress in understanding one another, but, due to the late hour, it would be necessary to continue meetings on Friday.

For the next three days, the CALPA and CATCA leaders stayed at the Inn of the Provinces, a stone's throw from Otto Lang's office in the Transport Canada building. Throngs of reporters gathered in the lobbies at all hours of the day and night to observe the comings and goings of the pilots and controllers between their own suites and the Transport Canada offices, attempting from these movements and overheard comments to deduce the course of events. For the pilots and controllers, the mixture of media attention, incessant phone calls, strategy sessions at all hours, and waiting produced a strange "high." The men were tense, found it hard to eat, and had difficulty sleeping even when they had the time. To cope with the situation, both the pilots and the controllers imposed some discipline by allocating duties and designating press spokesmen (Livingston for the controllers, and Maley and CALPA Publicity Director Roger Burgess-Webb for the pilots). In addition, CATCA secretly booked a board room in the Holiday Inn, so its council could meet without interference.

Across the street at MOT, the atmosphere was also one of crisis. While Lang, Cloutier, and McLeish had more experience coping with crises and with the media, the long hours and countless meetings, added to their normal responsibilities, produced strain and fatigue.

FRIDAY, JUNE 25
This was the morning the rednecks very visibly came out of the woodwork. A group calling itself the "Voice of Canada League" took out a full-page ad in the Toronto *Globe and Mail*.[51] The ad, headed "OUR

GOVERNMENT: RACIST AND ARROGANT" began by asking "What is more important: the cultural rights of 330 French-speaking Quebec air traffic controllers or the safety of the lives of millions of Canadians and foreign visitors who speak many languages and fly in Canadian skies?" The ad concluded with a reference to the decision on capital punishment earlier in the week: "Why should the government be so anxious to spare the lives of murderers—even the murderers of the men who stand between society and chaos—when they are so ready to sacrifice the lives of innocent Canadians in pursuit of a cultural fantasy?" MOT also had an ad in major Canadian papers that day.[52] A quarter of a page in size, it was a very low-key reiteration of the reasons for the bilingual air traffic control policy, its geographical limitation to Quebec, and the promise that current safety standards would not be jeopardized.

Prime Minister Trudeau responded with passion to the Voice of Canada ad by saying "I think the existence of this ad indicates that this country is in very great danger of being divided on as basic an issue as has ever divided the country in 34 years.... the issue in this regard is national unity and no other issue.... we can't force Quebeckers to learn English, and if they don't want to within their own province they will say, 'Well this is basically the separatist issue. If we can't operate even within our own province in our own language, then what the hell are we doing in this country?' Do you know the answer to that? I can't answer the separatists."[53] Opposition Leader Joe Clark, speaking in Question Period, began by denouncing the Voice of Canada League advertisement as "reprehensible," but quickly shifted his attack to the government's low-key ad. Continuing the line of criticism of the previous evening, he asked, "Will the Minister [Otto Lang] not recognize that the kind of advertisement run this morning, coupled with the tone of some of the remarks unfortunately made by the Prime Minister in his speech on the matter, has served to inflame the situation. Would he not agree? I make this plea to him as one whose interest is in trying to achieve a resolution of this question and avoid any inflammation of questions related to bilingualism. Bilingualism is not the issue."[54] Ed Broadbent restated the NDP's support for CALPA and CATCA, asking Lang whether the government would take action to prevent the unauthorized use of French for air traffic control in Quebec.[55]

The CATCA national council assembled in the morning to prepare for the mid-day meeting with Otto Lang.[56] The council divided into roughly three groups: the radical minority, the moderate majority, and Jean-Luc Patenaude. The radicals were so buoyed by their public support that they were certain that if they continued to hold out, they could "bring the government down." Livingston reminded them that they were in Ottawa not to overthrow a government, but to end the impasse. The radicals also argued that their men were opposed to and deeply suspicious of any commission of inquiry, and felt that CATCA should have the right to veto anything the commission ultimately recommended. The more moderate controllers realized it was unlikely that they could extract so total a reversal from Lang. The council pondered the dilemma in which it found itself. The government had not consulted CATCA about the choice of the commissioners and the membership was suspicious that the commission was rigged. Therefore, the council had to force the government to make some concession so that they could say publicly to the membership that they had, in some sense, won. The difficulty was that, to this point, Lang had only indicated concessions he would not make, rather than hinting at those he would.

Jean-Luc Patenaude was present at the meeting because he felt it was important to represent the controllers of the Quebec region. He was closely watched by his colleagues, who feared that he would again inform AGAQ of their secret deliberations. Patenaude decided to say very little and simply listen. Both he and some of the anglophone council members agree that if he had pressed the francophone position too vigorously, he would have found himself in a fistfight, or worse.

Before going to the meeting, Livingston once again reminded his men to stick to the question of bilingual air traffic control, narrowly defined. He urged them to represent the feelings of the membership by speaking frankly, but to refrain from personal attacks.

By all accounts, the meeting was a very nasty affair. To begin with, a number of the controllers objected to Sylvain Cloutier's presence. They had seen him talking, in French, with Patenaude, an hour or so before and some of the controllers were therefore suspicious of this reputedly very powerful francophone. Cloutier agreed to leave the room: he was not terribly concerned about missing the meeting, since he had many other things to do. The council members then got down to business: unconstrained by Cloutier's presence, they began by hurling invective at Lang and McLeish. The reason for the council's anger was their feeling that Lang and McLeish were deliberately undercutting CATCA through their direct dealings with AGAQ and the Committee of Eight and through decisions, such as naming the commissioners, taken without consulting CATCA. Otto Lang listened impassively, as he had done the night before. Walter McLeish gave yet another defence of his decisions and another sociological-historical explanation of the need for bilingual air traffic control. He sounded like Pierre Trudeau on the importance of bilingualism to Canada. Warned by Livingston to consider bilingualism only in its aviation context, the council members paid no heed to McLeish's words. Otto Lang was in no mood to strike any bargains with such a group. He merely reiterated the government's proposed solution: a two-man commission of inquiry, with the terms of reference presented in Parliament on Wednesday. The meeting continued until the controllers had vented their frustrations.

Lang, a law school dean prior to his entry into politics in the late sixties, regarded the CATCA board as somewhat comparable to a gang of uncouth student radicals. Walter McLeish came away from the meeting thinking of the CATCA council as a group of young men who could not see beyond their immediate situation: he had far more respect for the CALPA Board of Directors. David Cuthbertson, Lang's executive assistant, dismissed the CATCA council as a group "without breeding."

The CATCA national council reconvened in their secret boardroom following the meeting.[57] They decided to reject the two-man commission as it then stood, as well as Lang's assurances of the breadth of its terms of reference. Livingston, informing the council that he would then meet Lang as soon as possible to tell him of their decision, asked for counterproposals he could present him. Two suggested by the council were the addition of a third commissioner who would have to be approved by CATCA and a requirement that the government would not recommend bilingual air traffic control unless it was supported unanimously by the commission. Livingston then telephoned Lang to arrange a negotiation session for that evening. Also in attendance would be David Cuthbertson, Sylvain Cloutier, Walter McLeish, CATCA Vice-President Mike Tonner, and Ken Maley and Ron Young from CALPA. The location was Lang's office on the twenty-fifth floor of the Transport Canada building.

Originally, Prime Minister Trudeau had planned a special Cabinet meeting that evening to discuss the crisis: however, as there was nothing yet to discuss, the meeting was postponed until 10 a.m. Saturday morning. This also caused the prime minister to postpone his plans to leave for the second Economic Summit Conference in Puerto Rico until the conclusion of the Saturday Cabinet meeting. After Canada's exclusion from the first such conference—held in France—Trudeau had lobbied hard for its inclusion in the second. Nevertheless, he did not want to leave until he could see a solution to the crisis.

Otto Lang's approach to these negotiations, like his approach to most negotiations, was simple and direct. He quickly stated his bottom line, the position beyond which he would not be pushed. In this instance the bottom line was that the commission would not be disbanded, that the government would attempt to convince the commission that bilingual air traffic control was safe and, if successful, go ahead with its implementation. Finally, he would not interfere with the legal process in which the controllers and pilots were becoming embroiled. Within these limitations, Lang would do whatever he could to convince the controllers and pilots that the government was acting in good faith. He would not introduce bilingual air traffic control into English Canada and would not rig the commission or ignore its results. Lang then asked the controllers and pilots what hostages he had to give them to prove his sincerity and good faith.

Because the pilots' public position had been that they would return to work when the controllers' demands were met, Lang first put his question to Livingston. He, in response, pointed to the fact that the commission had been chosen without consultation with CATCA and expressed the fear that the government would use a split decision to justify doing what it wanted to do. Otto Lang asserted that, by that point, some things were irreversible. Besides the existence of the commission itself, the two commissioners already chosen would have to stay, despite the fact that they had been chosen without consultation. The logical solution would be to involve CATCA in the choice of a third commissioner. However, Livingston was not willing to settle for an empty opportunity for consultation, such as CATCA had been given on many other occasions. Conversely, Lang was not willing to allow CATCA simply to name a third commissioner. As a compromise, they agreed that Lang would choose the third commissioner from a list of five members of the judiciary acceptable to and submitted by CATCA.

Lang had stated on many occasions that a split commission would be a veritable veto on the implementation of bilingualism. Livingston asked him to be more explicit, stating publicly that a prerequisite to the government expanding bilingual air traffic control would be unanimity among the commissioners. Lang consented.

Lang then asked what else the government could do to reassure the controllers that the commission process would be fair and honest and that their concern for safety would be taken into account. At this point, Livingston deferred to Ken Maley. Lang and his associates now realized that the pilots were not simply the controllers' spear-carriers, but that they had demands of their own. Maley and Young talked about various aspects of the commission process, in particular, finding ways to ensure that the commission examined all aspects of the issue, required MOT to do a thorough job of simulating bilingual IFR air traffic control, and took all of CATCA's and CALPA's arguments into account. In addition, they wanted a commitment that bilingual air traffic control would not be implemented without overwhelming support at the political level. The pilots were also concerned that the unauthorized use of French in IFR operations would make bilingual IFR air traffic control a *fait accompli* before the commission decided whether or not it was safe. They began to discuss what MOT could do to prevent that from happening, given that it had been unable to do anything about it in the past. At this point, the two sides were finally negotiating. Ron Young now felt some optimism: it appeared that a way out of the impasse was possible. However, all negotiators know that they can never push their discussions too far without getting the approval of the groups in whose name they speak. Therefore, Young and Maley suggested a recess and, on that hot and humid night, returned to the Inn of the Provinces to meet with their Board of Directors.

Young and Maley began by telling their board that Lang was willing to do anything within reason to ensure that the commission would take the safety issue seriously and would not implement bilingualism unilaterally. The board members responded by criticizing Young, the negotiator, for treating safety, which was an absolute, like wages, a regular bargainable item. Young countered that Lang was responding to their question of Thursday night by doing what he could to gain the pilots' confidence: he then turned the question back on the pilots, asking them what Lang could do to earn their trust. The pilots had no answer, and did not want to look for an answer. Young finally got angry. He told the board that he would be negotiating in bad faith if the pilots did not want a resolution of the crisis. Furthermore, if the crisis were not resolved, the government could fall. He told the board that he would not be a party to bringing down a government, and that, if this was what they wanted, then they could do it without his assistance. He would not go back across the street to bargain with Otto Lang in these circumstances.

Young's threat had a sobering effect on the CALPA directors. They began to forget about the glare of publicity and the hundreds of telegrams of support they were receiving. They began to think instead about why they had lost a week's salary and why they had placed their careers in jeopardy. Glen McRae said that if the only way that CALPA could "win" was for the government to fall, he wasn't interested. The other pilots recalled that their avowed reason for coming to Ottawa was to make the air traffic control system as safe as possible. The pilots' sense of professionalism finally won out, and the board gave Young and Maley a vote of confidence. They decided not to ask Lang to meet with the full board again, thereby delegating such meetings to Maley and Young.

While the CALPA board was meeting, Lang and his associates also were meeting. They began to sketch out the broad outlines of an agreement which Lang would take to Cabinet on Saturday morning for its approval. By the time Maley and Young were ready for another round of negotiations with Lang it was much too late at night, and they all agreed to meet again on Saturday.

SATURDAY, JUNE 26

The emergency Cabinet meeting was held at the prime minister's residence, 24 Sussex Drive. Only ten members, less than a third of the Cabinet, were available, but the group at the meeting did include Trudeau, Lang, Allan MacEachen, and Chrétien. Lang presented the outlines of the agreement he had been in the process of reaching with the controllers and pilots on Friday night. He mentioned the expansion of the Commission of Inquiry to three judges, with consultation on the third; the guarantees to CATCA and CALPA that their concerns over safety would be fully considered by the Commission of Inquiry; the limitation on the unauthorized use of French; and some kind of agreement whereby bilingual air traffic control would proceed only if it had the support of an overwhelming majority of Parliament. Lang assured his colleagues that these terms would be acceptable enough to CATCA and CALPA to get the planes flying again, and would not sell out AGAQ. In reaching its decision, the Cabinet was clearly aware of the political factors involved. It was important to end the strike because of the damage it was doing to the government's entire bilingualism policy, as well as to relations between English and French Canadians. Furthermore, the loss of air service was creating substantial public inconvenience. With the Montreal Olympics but two weeks away, it was essential that a prolonged pilots' strike not become the crowning fiasco in the disastrous story of Canada's preparation for the Olympics.

If the strike went on any longer, the government's low standing in the polls might sink still further. Given the difficult situation they were in, the Cabinet members felt that Lang's outline of his agreement with the pilots and controllers brought peace with honour, so they again trusted him to work out the details. However, there was an expectation of some consultation with various Cabinet ministers as the agreement was being hammered out. The Cabinet meeting concluded, Prime Minister Trudeau hurried to the airport for his trip to Puerto Rico.

During the day, the CATCA and CALPA leaders and their legal advisers worked to formulate a list of five candidates for the position of third commissioner. The list included former Supreme Court Justice Emmett Hall, Ontario Supreme Court Chief Justice William Estey, Federal Court Justice and former Saskatchewan Attorney-General Darrel Heald, Ontario Court of Appeals Justice Charles Dubin, and Nova Scotia Supreme Court Justice Arthur Cooper.

Saturday evening, another muggy one, was the final bargaining session. Having a Cabinet mandate, Lang and Cloutier were now in a position to make the necessary concessions to get the planes flying. Lang kept asking Maley and Livingston what he could do to show that he was acting in good faith and that the government was taking the issue of safety seriously. Besides the addition of a third commissioner, Livingston asked that MOT agree not to expand bilingual air traffic control unless the commissioners agreed unanimously that it was consistent with current safety standards. Maley demanded that Lang immediately formulate, disseminate, and enforce an Air Navigation Order limiting the use of French to the agreed-upon VFR airports and aeradio stations. Advancing a suggestion made by some of the CALPA board members, Maley asked Lang to commit the government to submitting the Commission of Inquiry's recommendations to a free vote in the House of Commons. The free vote on capital punishment held earlier in the week probably prompted the pilots to consider asking for one on bilingual air traffic control.

During these discussions, Otto Lang reemphasized that the government was acting in good faith and again asked how he could give clear evidence of this. Young came up with the obvious answer: "Put it in a formal written agreement." Young detected some nervousness in Cloutier and Cuthbertson: as an experienced bargainer he read this as a signal that, while the MOT side would have preferred something less formal, they could not, given Lang's remarks which had led to his answer, refuse to prepare such an agreement, if pressed. He pressed, and it was agreed. Overwhelmed at their good fortune, Young and Maley looked incredulously at each other, and then called for a recess. The CATCA and CALPA negotiators' bottom line on this issue was that they would have accepted a speech by Lang to the House of Commons announcing the terms of agreement, provided they were able to agree to the text in advance. However, a written agreement was much better. Young said they were now in "fat city" and that he could get Lang to put almost anything he asked for into the agreement. In addition to agreement about the four terms discussed previously (the third commissioner, unanimity within the commission, the Air Navigation Order, the free vote) they would ask Lang to change the earlier terms of reference for the Commission of Inquiry by putting a very heavy burden of proof on MOT to show that bilingual air traffic control would be safe.

In the rewriting session that followed, CATCA and CALPA worked as a team. They asked Lang to add to the terms of reference a statement that bilingual air traffic control would not be demonstrated to be safe unless the commissioners could justify "beyond a reasonable doubt" why CATCA's and CALPA's contrary views should not prevail and to agree to append to the commission's reports any statements from CATCA or CALPA. They changed the wording of the terms of reference so that, in a number of places where the commission was previously permitted ("may") to undertake some procedure it would now be required ("shall") to do it. Maley and Livingston, wishing to avoid a replay of the J. D. Monin fiasco, demanded that MOT and CATCA *jointly* submit a list of controllers who would serve as technical advisers to the commission for the simulation exercises.

Lang and Cloutier agreed to all these changes without much hesitation. For them, two things were important: first, they were re-establishing trust with the controllers and the pilots, which would be essential for the simulations and the work of the commission, and second, they were preserving the commission's integrity. Lang, Cloutier, and McLeish were convinced, beyond any doubt, that bilingual air traffic control could be implemented safely, and they were confident that a commission of intelligent judges, as well as a majority of the House of Commons, could also be convinced. The discussions concluded around midnight. Lang and Cloutier would draft the agreement and show it to Livingston and Maley early Sunday evening. In order to make sure that they remembered everything that had been agreed upon, Lang and Cloutier stayed behind until 2:00 a.m. writing up the terms.

SUNDAY, JUNE 27

One might think that Sunday was spent by the major actors on matters of minor significance, merely putting the finishing touches on the agreement. This did not turn out to be the case.

On Friday, Jean-Luc Patenaude had been in touch with Roger Demers and Pierre Beaudry in Quebec City. Patenaude told them about the meeting between Lang and the CATCA national council, and mentioned that the council had succeeded in excluding Cloutier. Patenaude suggested that Demers, Beaudry, and Michel Charlebois, the head of the air traffic controllers' section in AGAQ, drive down to Ottawa to be present while the final negotiations were going on. The AGAQ leaders had no idea of what was going on in the negotiations Friday or Saturday night, since the other CATCA national council members had ostracized Patenaude. They therefore demanded a meeting with Lang early Sunday morning to find out what had been happening. The meeting began at 9:00 a.m., with Lang assuring the francophone controllers that he was protecting their interests. However, he would not say what the precise terms of the agreement were. This reticence, coupled with what Patenaude had observed on Friday, made the leaders of AGAQ very suspicious that they were being sold out. They angrily told Lang not to count on their participation in the simulation experiments. After the meeting, Patenaude met members of the English press, who were waiting in the lobby of the Transport Canada building, and made it clear to them how AGAQ had been excluded from the negotiations, and repeated the threat of non-participation.[58]

Otto Lang spent Sunday afternoon deciding on the third commissioner and consulting his Cabinet colleagues about the agreement. Lang chose Mr. Justice Heald, whom he knew from Saskatchewan. Even though Heald had been associated with the rival Thatcher faction in Saskatchewan politics, he had nonetheless supported increased French-language instruction at the University of Saskatchewan, which was a hopeful sign of his basic sympathies.

Lang's political consultations with other ministers were probably typified by the same reticence that characterized McLeish's consultation with

Fernand Lalonde about John Keenan. Lang emphasized the choice of Justice Heald and the consistency of the agreement with the parameters set forth in the Cabinet meeting. The impact the agreement would have on public opinion, especially in Quebec, was passed over much more briefly. If things went wrong, Lang could still claim that he had consulted the Cabinet, while the ministers whom Lang consulted could claim that the negotiations were Lang's responsibility. Based on these consultations, Jean Marchand accepted the result. When called for news of the negotiations by Serge Joyal, he told him, "C'est pas si pire" (It's not so bad).

Walter McLeish spent the afternoon responding to the pilots' concerns. He drafted an Air Navigation Order restricting the use of French to show to the pilots. As part of the previous evening's discussion, Maley had asked that McLeish explain to a number of his board members how the simulation exercises would be carried out, so that prior to the signing of the agreement they could determine whether they were technically acceptable. McLeish met late in the afternoon and over dinner with Central Region Director Robert MacWilliam and Captain Ron Daley, the chairman of CALPA's air traffic control committee. The pilots listened to McLeish's presentation, and, while somewhat skeptical, pronounced his plans acceptable. David Cuthbertson and Ralph Goodale, Lang's parliamentary secretary, spent the afternoon getting the agreement typed up and copied.

The negotiating group reconvened Sunday night. Livingston looked at the text of the agreement, and thought that, by putting it so clearly in writing, Lang was committing political suicide. Lang, Cloutier, McLeish, and Cuthbertson, all wearied by the week's events, felt that they had "saved the country." After a few minor changes, the terms were declared acceptable to the CALPA and CATCA negotiators. Lang proposed a meeting to sign the agreement at 9:00 a.m., and a 10:00 a.m. press conference to announce it. It now remained for Maley and Livingston to get the acquiescence of their boards.

The CALPA Board of Directors was quite satisfied with the agreement because it clearly responded to their concerns about safety. The pilots who had asked for a free vote in the House of Commons were pleasantly surprised because they had never really expected to get it. However, detracting from their pleasure at the agreement was a growing awareness of the high cost they felt they had paid. They, and all CALPA members, had lost a week's wages. There was also the possibility of contempt-of-court charges against individual pilots. Finally, they had become more deeply embroiled than they had wished in a political process they did not completely comprehend. Many of the board members looked at the agreement, pronounced it acceptable, and then started making plans to leave

Ottawa so that they would be able to draw their normal salaries beginning Monday.

Jim Livingston and John Nelligan, CATCA's lawyer, had to exercise all their persuasive talents to convince the national council to approve the settlement.[59] Livingston recounted the process by which the third commissioner was chosen and showed the council members the draft Air Navigation Order. Nelligan reminded the council that the free vote in the House of Commons gave them a second chance in the event the Commission of Inquiry ruled in favour of bilingual air traffic control. His legal opinion was that the phrase "beyond a reasonable doubt" saddled the government with a burden of proof comparable to that faced by the Crown in a criminal case. Discussing the legal situation, Livingston felt it was unlikely that any controllers other than the Winnipeg sixteen would be prosecuted, and the sixteen might well receive suspended sentences.

Livingston then told the council that he had not expected to do as well as he had, and suggested that the only alternative to the agreement would be a public relations contest between CATCA / CALPA and the government "which could lead to the destruction of one side or the other." Nelligan supported him, saying that he was surprised by Lang's magnanimity, and recommended that, if CATCA accepted the agreement, they should do it in such a way as not to cause the government unnecessary loss of face. At this point, Nelligan departed so as to leave the ultimate decision to the council. Bill Robertson, who had been mysteriously absent from all council meetings that week, reappeared at midnight. Shortly after that, CALPA President Ken Maley came to announce that the CALPA board had accepted the agreement and that the pilots were anxious to return to work. He asked for some assurance that the controllers would provide safe service, and said that a verbal commitment from the national council, then and there, would suffice. Maley also felt that a prompt return to work might avoid the litigation being considered against CALPA. Livingston reminded his men that all pilots had lost eight days of pay, while only a few controllers here and there had lost a few hours' worth. The pilots were being threatened with numerous contempt-of-court charges and $7 million in lawsuits, while only sixteen CATCA members had been charged with contempt. Maley advised the CATCA council that if the controllers were to stage a walkout of their own, it would not be completely supported by CALPA.

Recognizing CALPA's position, and acknowledging that they had obtained more than they had realistically expected, the CATCA board voted to submit the collective agreement, as modified by the memorandum of understanding, to the membership and recommend ratification. This step was important, since their action had been conducted in the name of the membership, and their legal contention had been that Keenan's resignation invalidated the previous ratification vote. The final matter dealt with was Jean-Luc Patenaude's behaviour during the previous months. Formal notice was served that he would be charged with conduct detrimental to the union, and the charges would be heard at a special council meeting in Ottawa on July 12.

MONDAY, JUNE 28

Livingston, Maley, Lang, Cloutier, and McLeish assembled in Lang's office at 9:00 a.m. to sign the agreement and discuss the comments they would be making at the press conference. Livingston and Maley did not want to appear together with Lang, but would speak after he finished. Cloutier was apprehensive about the reception the agreement would have in Quebec and tried to minimize the damage it might cause. He asked Livingston and Maley both to say that the agreement did no more than put into writing commitments the government for several months had been making to ensure that the implementation process was done carefully and thoroughly. Both Livingston and Maley declined: they did not want to help the government save face if it meant so radical a downplaying of the concessions which they had won and now intended to demonstrate to their membership. Cloutier also wanted them to say that they would live with the results of the commission report, but both were noncommittal on that request.

At the 10:00 a.m. press conference, Lang announced the key elements of the agreement and argued that it did not in any way represent a retreat by the government on its bilingualism policy.[60] Livingston emphasized that his membership would be asked to ratify the collective agreement, as amended by the memorandum of understanding. Maley reiterated his belief that air traffic control is safer in one language than in two. After their initial announcements, both Livingston and Maley were asked what would happen if the commission came up with a unanimous finding that bilingual air traffic control was safe. Livingston answered in a very low-key way, emphasizing his support for the Commission of Inquiry, and admitting that, if the commission found that there were no valid safety reasons for objecting to bilingual air traffic control, it would be very difficult for CATCA to fight it. Ken Maley's response was very different. He interpreted CALPA's agreement with Lang as only an agreement to participate in the commission process, without necessarily accepting the result. It was for the membership, not for him, to decide whether they would accept a unanimous recommendation supporting bilingual control. This led to further questions about whether the dispute had merely been postponed, rather than settled, and Maley replied "I would hope not, but it could be."[61] Maley's answer made headlines. It also made the exercise look rather futile if one of the parties to the negotiations did not feel bound by the outcome of the study.

Even before the agreement was signed, pilots had begun reporting for work. The airlines resumed partial operations on Monday, and by Tuesday, they were returning to normal.

While airline operations were returning to normal, the political atmosphere in Quebec for the remainder of the week and beyond was anything but normal. The Lang-CATCA-CALPA agreement, viewed in cold print and coupled with Maley's interpretation, led to a reaction of astonishment and then outrage by the entire French-Canadian people.

Chapter Eight

The Turning Point: July 1976 to January 1977

"Day and Night," woodcut by M. C. Escher, 1938

INTRODUCTION

At the moment the Lang-CALPA-CATCA agreement was signed, it appeared that CATCA and CALPA, with overwhelming popular support in English Canada, were close to winning their struggle against bilingual air traffic control. The two groups had recognized the previous December that they had to "play catch-up ball" against MOT, and by July had succeeded brilliantly. However, the agreement really represented the high water mark in their fortunes. By January 1977, the situation had been completely reversed. CATCA and CALPA were fighting battles that taxed their resources and had lost their support in English Canada. On the other hand, AGAQ was boasting of a new-found maturity. Some commentators were even claiming that AGAQ had already won the war. This chapter will describe the months that represent the turning point.

The Escher woodcut, which introduces this chapter, epitomizes the concept of a turning point on which the chapter is based. The momentum in a struggle does not shift instantly; rather, it occurs gradually. At the beginning of the transition period, one can see antecedents, small hints to show that at some time in the future the losing side may emerge triumphant. Conversely, even at the end of the transition period, the side which ultimately will be defeated, nevertheless wins the occasional battle. Thus, victory emerges from defeat and defeat emerges from victory, just as the white birds emerge from the black and the black emerge from the white. This chapter will also show that the common interpretation that the election of the Parti Québécois on November 15, 1976, was solely responsible for turning the issue around is quite incorrect, because the momentum had clearly shifted before then.

THE POLITICAL REACTION IN QUEBEC

French Canadians were bitter about the Lang-CATCA-CALPA agreement because they felt its terms precluded the possibility of their using French for communication between pilots and controllers. This was a humiliating defeat, calling into question a right for which they had long been struggling, and one that had appeared to be on the verge of recognition, namely, their right to speak French to one another, particularly at work, in Quebec. To many French Canadians, it gave the lie to the hope that the federal government would defend their linguistic rights. René Lévesque, calling it "the sad outcome of 109 years of federalism and eight years of French power," concluded that only an independent government could protect the French language in Quebec.[1] Many life-long federalists began to think that Lévesque might be correct. Premier Bourassa, who had previously been silent, was finally compelled to react publicly. In a speech, he presented his own view of the political implications of the crisis, stating that "If the federal government is incapable of respecting something as essential, fundamental, and normal as the use of French in Quebec—incapable perhaps because of its indebtedness to the anglophone majority—then we must modify the constitution."[2]

The federal Cabinet ministers from Quebec were torn between their anger at the agreement Lang had negotiated and their realization of the political necessity of making the best of a bad situation. Communications Minister Jeanne Sauvé expressed their anger when, in a telephone interview, she said "It certainly is a painful thing when any government has to kneel down to a bunch of fanatics."[3] Prime Minister Trudeau and Quebec leader Marc Lalonde reacted somewhat differently. Lalonde did not hear about the agreement over the weekend, as he was at his cottage in the country. However, when he phoned Lang early Monday morning and heard the terms, he was deeply dismayed, and asked Lang to postpone the press conference so that he could consult Prime Minister Trudeau, who was still in Puerto Rico. Lang replied that a postponement was impossible, whereupon Lalonde called Trudeau to inform him of the terms: both men were troubled by the agreement, but realized that the government would have to live with it. When interviewed on the flight back to Canada, Trudeau enigmatically told reporters that the agreement was "as total a victory on paper as was needed." When asked whose victory he was referring to, he replied, "not a victory of the government over anyone else but a victory of Canada in reaching a settlement."[4] Perhaps, in his ironic mind, Trudeau meant that it was as total a paper victory for the pilots and controllers as was needed to induce them to return to work. Lalonde, with his deep loyalty to Trudeau, rushed to his defence by making the strongest possible justification of the agreement at a press conference and on two television interviews on Tuesday.[5] He reiterated the government's intention to do everything possible to convince the Commission of Inquiry that bilingual air traffic control was safe and suggested that Quebeckers could express their feelings constructively by supporting AGAQ financially.

Keith Spicer was deeply troubled by the agreement, which he considered an immense blow to the dignity of the French-Canadian people. He even contemplated resigning as commissioner of official languages, because the government's handling of the affair had made it almost impossible for him to defend the Official Languages Act to Quebeckers. Spicer called Trudeau on the evening of Wednesday, June 30, to tell him that the only reason he was not resigning was that it would set the cause back still further. Spicer said that he would stay on, but only so as to attack the agreement: his words to Trudeau were, "I regret having to kick you in the teeth, but there must be at least one English tongue taking the franco-phone side on the news tonight!" Spicer criticized the agreement on Quebec television and in a column which appeared in *Le Devoir* on July 2.[6] His message to English Canadians was different: he told them that no longer could any intelligent person claim that the government had put its language policy ahead of safety, and once again argued the virtues of toler-ance and French education.[7] Spicer hoped that his comments would defuse the emotionalism and restore perspective among both language groups, conditions he felt essential to the success of both the Commission of Inquiry and, ultimately, of Canada's language policy.

Jean Marchand, who had been given the Cabinet portfolio of minister of the environment the previous December, was deeply troubled when he saw the text of the agreement. As an experienced negotiator, he felt that Lang had made unnecessary concessions. On Wednesday, June 30, he went to a meeting of the Priorities and Planning Committee of Cabinet, where he bitterly criticized Lang. However, the committee decided that, given the possibility of another strike if any attempt were made to disown the agreement, it would have to stand. Marchand met with Trudeau a little later and decided to resign, feeling that one French-Canadian resignation from Cabinet was necessary to show that they all did not unhesitatingly accept the agreement. Beset with personal difficulties, Marchand had already considered resigning, and now felt that by taking this protest action, he would permit those whose political careers still lay ahead of them a chance to remain in Cabinet. Marchand announced his resignation to a meeting of the Quebec caucus that evening.[8] The speech provoked an emotional catharsis: some members were in tears and others were urging him to reconsider. However, his decision was firm. Later that night, he met with Sylvain Cloutier, who broke into tears of frustration. On Thursday, July 1, there were numerous informal meetings of the Quebec caucus. The members assessed the situation and emerged with a new commitment to work for French language rights. In this context, Marchand's resignation can be seen as an act which transcended both the common reactions of simple outrage and soldierly loyalty, and led to their synthesis in a renewed commitment by the caucus.

Otto Lang and Sylvain Cloutier, both physically exhausted and emotionally drained by the previous weekend's negotiation, were bitterly disappointed by the lack of support by French-Canadian ministers. Lang felt that the protest could have been blunted if these ministers had argued that the agreement actually represented a victory over CATCA and CALPA, because it assured the accomplishment of bilingual air traffic control at the conclusion of the commission's work. For Lang, Madame Sauvé's criticism was almost the last straw: he informed Trudeau that if there was any more public criticism of him by the Cabinet, he would resign. None of Lang's critics had any interest in taking his place and his threat made the caucus aware of the dangers of a continuing public display of disunity. By Friday, a measure of commitment and solidarity had returned to the Liberal caucus, replacing the spirit of bitterness and dissension with which the week had begun.

Bilingual air traffic control also created disharmony within the Conservative ranks. Joe Clark spent Sunday, July 4, at a Conservative party meeting in Ste. Marguerite, a small town north of Montreal. There he was asked to support a resolution urging that MOT treat AGAQ as an autonomous organization of equal status with CATCA and CALPA. Clark, realizing that his nationally televised speech on bilingual air traffic had won him no support in Quebec, decided to move his party's position to something more acceptable to Quebeckers. Not only did he support the resolution, but he also expressed interest in meeting with AGAQ. Quickly, arrangements were made for him to meet AGAQ leaders on Monday afternoon in Montreal.[9]

When Ken Maley saw stories about Clark's Ste. Marguerite speech in the Monday morning papers, he was outraged: all his work in winning the support of the Conservative caucus had been undermined in a single day. He called the Conservative Research Office to find out what had happened. Apparently, Maley was not alone in his alarm, for he soon learned that quite a few caucus members had also been disturbed by Clark's new policy initiative. Clark back-pedalled furiously. At 10:00 a.m. on Monday, he announced that he was too busy to meet with AGAQ.[10] The episode was an embarrassing one for Joe Clark, showing that his caucus gave him less than unquestioning loyalty, and indicating how hard he would have to work to bring them to support his more progressive approach to Quebec.

While the politicians were coming to terms with the Lang-CATCA-CALPA agreement, the world's attention shifted elsewhere. On Saturday night, July 3, the Israelis conducted their daring rescue of the hostages held at Entebbe. Sunday, July 4, was the bicentennial of the American Declaration of Independence.

The last word on political reaction belongs to Prime Minister Trudeau. After his initial comments on the plane back from Puerto Rico, he kept silent until everyone else had spoken. Then, on Friday, July 9, he was interviewed on radio and television by journalists Michel Roy of *Le Devoir*, Claude Beauchamp of *Le Soleil*, and Laurent Laplante of *Le Jour*.[11] In response to vigorous questioning, he stoutly defended his government's handling of the strike. While admitting that a different person might have negotiated a different (and, from the government's viewpoint, more favourable) agreement, he praised Otto Lang as "one of the most solid and courageous defenders of bilingualism among all the anglophone ministers," and maintained that the agreement with CATCA and CALPA had not given up "the essentials." For example, the commitment that bilingual air traffic control would not be implemented without unanimity among the judges was inconsequential, because it would have been politically impossible for the government to change the status quo if the judges were not unanimous. He suggested that the free vote was "a tactic which will obligate the Opposition, I think, to show its true colours." He urged AGAQ to do as he himself had done years earlier, namely, to come to Ottawa and win its case for the rights of francophones. On the other hand, if AGAQ would not cooperate with the Commission of Inquiry, the government would go to France, if necessary, to find bilingual controllers and pilots for the simulation exercises. This interview was a dramatic contrast to his address to the nation on June 23. That speech was constrained by its format, hedged by the disclaimers written in by his English-Canadian advisers and trivialized by the ineffectual attempt to demonstrate the irrationality of CATCA's and CALPA's positions. The interview showed Trudeau at his combative best, expressing his deep commitment to bilingualism in powerful arguments thrown back to a jury of tough questioners.

ACROSS TWO SOLITUDES: THE RESPONSE OF THE ENGLISH PRESS

When the bilingual air traffic control controversy gave rise to the pilots' strike, it drew the attention of the best reporters in English Canada, the influential columnists, and the editorialists. Their articles show an evolution in their thinking, as they watched the struggle unfold, and particularly as they watched the reaction within Quebec. The first reporter in English Canada to understand the issue as it was seen in Quebec was William Johnson, then a political reporter in Ottawa for the *Globe and Mail*. Johnson grew up in a mixed English-French household, and is fluent in both languages and sensitive to both cultures. During the strike, he reacted as a Quebecker and was therefore incensed at the way the overwhelmingly anglophone staff of the *Globe and Mail* was treating the issue. The *Globe*'s editorial of June 21, entitled "Because of Ottawa's Haste," put the blame for the strike entirely on the shoulders of the government and absolved the pilots and controllers. On June 22, a front-page article by Arnold Bruner repeated, in rather spectacular form, the tales of near-misses and confusion over the skies of Quebec, which CALPA had been disseminating.[12] The last straw for Johnson was hearing a prominent economics reporter discussing the issue declare, "You really have to sympathize with the controllers and the pilots. After all, they put their lives on the line every day!" Johnson responded by turning out a series of investigative articles that brought out aspects of the issue of which English Canadians were unaware. On Friday, June 25, he refuted Bruner's article with a story revealing, for the first time in the English-Canadian press, the details of the Keenan memorandum, along with an admission from CALPA as to its authenticity.[13] Late the next night, he interviewed Ken Maley, catching him clad in a towel, emerging from the shower. The article based on this interview, which was published on Saturday, June 26, began "Kenneth Maley, leading his 2800 pilots in a battle against bilingualism, routinely flies into bilingual European airports and finds them safe. But Mr. Maley, president of CALPA, says that CALPA will never accept bilingualism for instrument flights in Canada."[14] Johnson continued his reporting, with articles about the loyalty problem in MOT and about the many racist letters Otto Lang was receiving from English-Canadian bigots.[15]

English-Canadian columnists gradually began to recognize the bigotry that was being stirred up in English Canada during the strike. Douglas Fisher wrote that "there is a deep residual resistance to bilingualism in English Canada, below the surface of piety put on by the leaders of the major political parties" and John Gray echoed that "We're back to the basic question of being able to speak French in Quebec."[16] Richard Gwyn carried these observations a pessimistic step further and wrote a column which concluded: "Most English-Canadians no longer care whether Quebec separates. A small minority wish Quebec would go; a much larger number are just fed-up with paying Danegeld: a majority consider separation inevitable and are concerned mainly that the break be clean and painless."[17] A few days later, with the strike settled, Gwyn became more hopeful, saying "somehow English Canada has to be put back... into a mood of sympathy and understanding. If this doesn't happen, Canada as we know it just isn't going to last."[18] Similarly, Geoffrey Stevens, columnist for the *Globe and Mail*, concluded "This dispute drew English Canadians, those who cannot bring themselves to accept the French fact in Canada, out of the woodwork in droves.... I'd feel much happier if English Canadians who do believe in the French fact and in bilingualism would venture out of the woodwork, too."[19]

By the time the pilots' strike had gone on for a week, the English-Canadian editorialists were beginning to support the Commission of Inquiry and call for an end to the strike and cooperation with the commission.[20] After the strike ended, the English press became much more interested in the issue and, instead of simply accepting the CATCA-CALPA version of the story, began publishing a wide range of opinions. While supporters of unilingualism were often heard, there were many more articles presenting AGAQ's point of view than had been published before the strike. The *Globe and Mail* is an interesting example: despite the tone of its editorials, the reporters were given free rein. In addition to Johnson's articles, there were commentaries on the anti-French backlash the strike had generated in English Canada and excerpts from Roger Demers' speech to the symposium on the language of air traffic control were also published.[21] The *Ottawa Citizen* published a series of articles in its "Forum," including a call for understanding by former Deputy Minister of Transport and Air Canada President John Baldwin and the case for bilingual air traffic control, as argued by Jean LeMenach, a francophone pilot.[22] In addition, a number of newspapers and magazines began their own investigation of the problem. Frank Howard, writing in the *Ottawa Citizen*, checked the traffic levels at Montreal and Paris airports and found them quite similar, thereby refuting the controller workload argument against bilingual control.[23] Finally, late in August, the *Montreal Star* published two long background articles about bilingual air traffic control and the

Toronto Star several about bilingualism.[24] Thus, the English media began to make the other side of the issue available to their readers. Opinions in English Canada were changing.

THE STRUGGLE FOR BILINGUALISM: NEW INITIATIVES

In the days and weeks following the signing of the agreement, the supporters of bilingual air traffic control, the government, and neutral parties such as the judiciary took a number of initiatives which together began to shift the momentum back to AGAQ's side.

The leaders of the Gens de l'Air returned from Ottawa to Quebec City on Monday June 28, before the text of the Lang-CALPA-CATCA agreement had been made public. When they heard the terms in Quebec City, they were outraged. MP Pierre De Bané arranged a meeting with ministers and MPs in Ottawa for that evening, and an MOT Viscount brought Patenaude, Beaudry, Demers, Charlebois, Charette, lawyer Clément Richard, and Laval University political scientist Léon Dion, who was acting as their adviser, back to Ottawa to meet with Otto Lang, Marc Lalonde, Serge Joyal, and Jean Chrétien. AGAQ presented several demands: it wanted the government to support the attempt to disaffiliate from CATCA, to promise not to institute an Air Navigation Order forbidding the use of French for IFR communications in Quebec, and to agree to implement bilingual air traffic control as soon as the simulator studies confirmed that it could be done safely.[25] At one point, Jean-Luc Patenaude argued that the draft Air Navigation Order was the first federal regulation since Confederation which forbade the use of French, and which could therefore become a dangerous precedent. Chrétien and Lalonde looked at the draft, concluded that Patenaude was correct, and undertook that the text could be changed to refer to those situations in which it was permitted to use French. Other than this specific literary change, there was little the ministers could do to satisfy AGAQ: they were unwilling to abrogate Lang's previous agreement, Lang argued that the agreement did not give up the essentials, and the ministers all urged AGAQ to cooperate with the Commission of Inquiry. The meeting ended inconclusively. The AGAQ group returned to the waiting government Viscount, which took them to Quebec City. By 3:00 a.m., when they reached Quebec City, it was too foggy to land. The pilot proposed that they return to Ottawa, but Clément Richard vetoed that suggestion and demanded that they return to French-speaking Montreal for the night.

After considering the government's words, on Friday, July 2, AGAQ held a press conference. Beaudry and Demers announced that AGAQ would not participate in the simulations nor cooperate with the Commission of Inquiry. In fact, they threatened legal action against the commission.[26] Also, the Quebec City controllers decided to begin using French for IFR air traffic control with cooperating pilots.

When the terms of the agreement became public, the legal community began to raise serious questions as to whether the Commission of Inquiry could function as an impartial judicial body.[27] Justices Heald, Chouinard, and Sinclair met immediately and decided it was essential to re-establish their legitimacy. They drafted a letter to Otto Lang which discussed the implications of the agreement for their terms of reference and concluded that the agreement dealt with how the government would handle the commission's report, but imposed no constraints on the way in which the commission would do its work.[28] The letter was released to the press by Otto Lang on July 6 and set to rest the doubts of the previous week.

The government began to respond to the situation on a number of levels. The Prime Minister's Office and the Privy Council Office formed an ad hoc committee to consider changes in the content, implementation, and public presentation of its bilingualism policy so as to make it more effective, particularly within English Canada. Anglophone members of the prime minister's staff thought this was a useful development because, in the past, the intensity of the commitment by Trudeau and his closest francophone supporters had precluded any serious discussion of this problem. A number of francophone ministers and MPs informed their anglophone colleagues that in the present climate of opinion, only anglophones could sell bilingualism to English Canada. Some anglophone ministers and backbenchers who had previously kept a low profile on bilingualism responded with speeches in this vein.[29]

The Cabinet decided not to drop contempt-of-court charges against the sixteen Winnipeg controllers. Their hearing was set for early August, and on July 20 the Department of Justice laid charges against another 155 controllers in numerous locations who had refused to work or claimed they were sick during the first days of the strike.

Walter McLeish continued to push ahead with the aspects of the implementation program which were under his control. Two weeks before the strike, he had found a francophone to direct the simulator studies. Pierre (Pete) Proulx, was a completely bilingual francophone who, after fifteen years as an operational controller in Quebec City and Montreal, had become regional manager of air traffic services in Moncton. Proulx had also been involved in the air traffic control implementation team which studied the Lisson report, and had advocated serious study of how bilingual air traffic control could be implemented, rather that dismissing it as impossible. When first offered the job, Proulx demurred: he did not want the hassles and, besides, he was dubious about using two languages for control of IFR traffic. McLeish listened to Proulx, then shook his hand, and welcomed him aboard anyway. Proulx accepted. By mid-July, he had moved to Ottawa, was briefed by Ron Bell on the work that had been done to that point, and began reading everything he could find on bilingual air traffic control.

The first major challenge Proulx faced during the summer was negotiating agreements with CATCA, CALPA, and AGAQ for their participation in the simulation exercises. A formal agreement was not reached with CALPA, but the organization decided to send Bob MacWilliam, director for the central region, as a permanent observer to the exercises. MOT agreed to pay the expenses of other pilots who participated. By early August, Proulx had worked out an agreement with CATCA.[30] MOT agreed to include in the simulation exercises all the difficult situations which CATCA was certain would prove unilingual air traffic control was better than bilingual control. MOT accepted CATCA's choice of two controllers (Don Redden and Mike Tonner, both of whom had been members of the negotiating team) to be members of the simulation team, as well as a number of bilingual controllers who would participate in the simulation exercises. CATCA filled these latter positions with bilingual controllers who opposed bilingual air traffic control.[31] Finally, MOT agreed to pay the salaries and expenses of all CATCA participants.

Proulx met with AGAQ for the first time in August. While he spoke their language, he could not convince them to participate. AGAQ presented him with all their grievances, and its lawyer, Clément Richard, put the presentation in the context of francophones' long-standing grievances against Ottawa and the anglophones. Proulx, a calm and politically astute individual, just listened: when AGAQ was finished, he said that he could not correct the injustices of the past, but could only deal with the present problem. He requested another meeting and asked them to present a list of specific demands for changes they wanted made in the design of the simulation experiments, which would serve as the basis for their next round of negotiations.

Another problem, on which McLeish resumed work, was the implementation of bilingual air traffic control at St. Hubert. By summer, French was being used so frequently at St. Hubert that the airport was, de facto, bilingual. David Cunningham, who had headed the St. Hubert Task Force, began work on the next phase of the St. Hubert study, which would deal with formal procedures for bilingual operations.

Finally, there was a personnel change at MOT which was at least partially related to bilingual air traffic control. William Huck, the air administrator, had planned to retire on December 31. He decided to advance his retirement to August and remain as a consultant for the rest of the year. He felt awkward because the bilingual air traffic control problem, which was the air administration's major concern at that time, was being handled by Cloutier, who dealt directly with McLeish. By stepping aside for

McLeish, who by then was the heir-apparent, he would strengthen McLeish's hand. A Public Service Commission Board considered Huck's replacement, and Walter McLeish, not surprisingly, was named. He took over officially on August 21.

CATCA AND CALPA: WINNING VICTORIES, BUT LOSING THE WAR

CATCA and CALPA's struggle intensified during the summer. The tide was turning against them, especially on the legal front. Nevertheless, they won a number of victories, which were well reported by the French press, and resulted in a strengthening of AGAQ's resolve and an increase in its public support throughout the province. On July 12, the CATCA national council reassembled in Ottawa to try Jean-Luc Patenaude on charges of action detrimental to CATCA.[32] In formulating the charges against him, many council members wished to include the "crime" of advocating bilingual air traffic control. Jim Livingston, thinking one step ahead, realized that the francophone controllers would almost certainly be planning to form their own union and disaffiliate from CATCA. To counter this, CATCA's action would have to be defensible in any future disaffiliation hearing. Livingston told the council that it was no offence to support bilingual air traffic control, and that the association should be open-minded enough to have members on either side of the controversy. What he felt was reprehensible was Patenaude's urging francophone controllers to form their own union and disaffiliate from CATCA: therefore, the council decided to concentrate on Patenaude's urging of disaffiliation. At the hearing, Patenaude was accompanied by Clément Richard and MPs Joyal and De Bané. Jim Livingston pointed out that CATCA's rules permitted him only one adviser, who was not allowed to speak. When Clément Richard attempted to speak, Vice-President Robertson objected, and Livingston ordered the room cleared. Shortly thereafter, Patenaude and Richard returned: Richard informed the CATCA council that he and Patenaude were no longer interested in remaining for a "Rhodesian trial," and therefore left.

The CATCA council unanimously found Patenaude guilty. However, rather than expel him from the union, it suspended him as Quebec director for a six-month period, ending December 31, 1976. In addition to headlines and stories about this affair, a number of Quebec newspapers printed a rather unflattering picture of Livingston, who was smiling self-confidently, as if he were gloating over the suspension of Patenaude.

On July 9, Jim Livingston announced the results of the ratification vote on the contract, as amended by the memorandum of understanding. The anglophones were overwhelmingly in favour: the francophones voted with their feet, ignoring the ballot completely.

The CATCA national council would not consider the contract to be in force until MOT prepared an acceptable Air Navigation Order (ANO) restricting the use of French. By mid-July, MOT had prepared two drafts of the ANO, but neither had been published in the *Canada Gazette*. Sympathetic civil servants kept Livingston informed of all changes. Livingston and Maley, becoming impatient, met with Lang on July 19 (which was the third day of the Olympics) to demand the immediate issuance of the ANO. Livingston warned that his members were upset and advised that he would be unable to prevent another round of wildcat walkouts if the ANO were not issued.[33] On July 26, the government issued an ANO which permitted the use of French for VFR services at the small Quebec airports, in VFR communications with aeradio stations in Quebec, and for emergencies. In all other circumstances, English alone was to be used. *Le Jour* greeted the issuance of the ANO with the banner headline "Air Regulations: It is CATCA that has imposed its will!" and *Le Devoir*'s banner headlines read "Ottawa decrees aviation unilingualism."[34] The CATCA national council decided that day that the ANO was acceptable and authorized Livingston to sign the contract. The council stuck to the position it had taken in 1974 that signing the contract in both languages was acceptable if the Treasury Board would stipulate that, in the event of a disagreement between the English and French versions, the English version would prevail.

The legal battle over the contempt-of-court charges began in July. CATCA decided to pay the legal fees and possible fines for the 155 additional controllers who were cited for contempt and hired a lawyer in each location where its members were charged.[35] Livingston responded to these charges by claiming that "the government is trying to bleed us to death." He estimated that court costs and legal fees could amount to $750,000 and appealed for donations. The *Toronto Sun* printed a postal box number with the title "Air Safety" to which donations could be sent.[36] At a July 26 meeting of the national council, Livingston reported that the article in the *Toronto Sun*, as well as two radio interviews, had brought in $1,100 in donations within a week.[37] He wanted to start a full-scale national publicity campaign to raise more money. However, one major problem was that all the prominent people whom he had asked to associate their names with his campaign refused to do so. Livingston attributed it to their fear of retaliation by the government. The council finally authorized $5,000 for advertising for the publicity campaign.

The case against the sixteen Winnipeg controllers was heard by Mr. Justice Bastin of the Federal Court in Winnipeg on August 6. Unlike his colleague Mr. Justice Addy who, in granting the original injunction, saw ulterior motives in CATCA's actions, Bastin took their actions at face value. He delivered a one-paragraph judgment which read, in part:

...with respect to the public it can be assumed that every passenger would prefer to survive through the use of English than be killed by a misunderstanding caused by the imprudent use of French. ... In view of the nature of the issue I have decided that I should let bygones-be-bygones. I find you guilty of contempt but I impose no penalty.

Le Devoir's headline for its story about the Bastin decision read: "The reward for blackmail: Let bygones-be-bygones!"[38] All the lawyers CATCA had hired met in Winnipeg to attend the hearing and to plan their strategy. The transportation and legal fees for that day alone came to $10,000. Furthermore, the Department of Justice announced its intention to appeal Bastin's ruling. After the ruling, Livingston decided not to spend the $5,000 on an advertising campaign, and also began to think about some way of settling the remaining cases without further litigation. On September 21, he reported to his national council that the "word of mouth" appeal for funds which had begun in July had brought in a total of only $2,400.[39]

As the situation was growing bleaker and bleaker for CATCA and CALPA, they received an item of terribly perverse good news.[40] On September 10, there was a mid-air collision at high altitude between British and Yugoslavian jets over Yugoslavia, killing the 176 passengers aboard both airplanes. It was soon learned that, at about the time of the collision, the Yugoslav pilot was using Serbo-Croat to converse with air traffic control, while the British pilot was using English. Perhaps if the pilots had been using the same language, either one might have corrected a controller error or taken evasive action, and the accident would not have occurred. From CATCA's and CALPA's viewpoint, the preliminary reports suggested this was the perfect accident! However, in the changed climate of opinion, both organizations took a cautious attitude toward the crash, making no statements in the weeks after it happened, preferring to await a full accident report before commenting.

AGAQ: The Struggle Intensifies

During the summer, the Gens de l'Air formulated a coherent strategy for the coming month's struggle. They had two inter-related objectives: to open up the aviation industry in Quebec to francophone participation and to bring about the introduction of bilingual air traffic control as soon as possible. In order to achieve these goals, they began action on a number of fronts. To nullify CATCA's claim to be a national union, the controllers in Quebec began preparing an application to the Public Service

Staff Relations Board to form their own bargaining unit. Because the members of AGAQ were suspicious of the ability of the Commission of Inquiry, as constrained by the Lang-CATCA-CALPA agreement, to undertake the objective inquiry which they were certain would favour bilingual air traffic control, they refused, for the time being, to cooperate with the commission or to participate in the simulation exercises. While the francophones were, seemingly, sitting on their hands, they were actually taking steps to make the terms of reference of the commission and the procedures of the simulation exercises more favourable to their cause. These steps included behind-the-scenes negotiations with MOT and a legal challenge of the legitimacy of the Commission of Inquiry. In addition, the courts could be used to achieve other goals, such as overturning the Air Navigation Order and Air Canada's Rule 14A, both of which placed limits on the use of French by francophone aviators. Legal challenges are costly: therefore, AGAQ planned a fund-raising campaign. However, the campaign had another purpose besides raising money for legal battles. By this point, the leaders of AGAQ had drawn the conclusion that political power, rather than objective validity, is the key to determining whether a policy will be accepted by the government. As they saw it, AGAQ's arguments were technically correct but, hitherto, CALPA and CATCA had a monopoly on political power. By building public support in Quebec, AGAQ would be breaking up the CATCA-CALPA monopoly.

The first initiative, the campaign to disaffiliate Quebec controllers from CATCA, began at an all-night meeting at Dorval on August 17–18. The forty-four controllers present formed the Syndicat des Contrôleurs Aériens du Québec (SCAQ) and elected an executive. They decided to begin recruiting as many controllers throughout Quebec as possible. They began to prepare a case for disaffiliation which they would present to the Public Service Staff Relations Board.[41] They had to act quickly, because PSSRB regulations require that disaffiliation requests be presented before the end of the current contract which, in their case, was December 31.

Throughout the fall, the controllers worked on their project. By mid-December, SCAQ had recruited 185 members, or 55 percent of the 333 controllers in Quebec. On December 15, they held a meeting in Montreal at which a constitution and by-laws were formally adopted. On December 29, they filed an application with the Public Service Staff Relations Board for independent certification. The application was accompanied by four volumes of supporting evidence. The board set March 22 as the date for a hearing on the request.

AGAQ began its legal struggle in August. Serge Joyal and forty-one Air Canada pilots petitioned the Quebec Superior Court to invalidate Air

Canada's Rule 14A which restricted the use of French on the flight deck, to require Air Canada to translate its flight operations manual into French and to permit the use of French on its own radio frequency, and finally, to require MOT to permit bilingual air / ground communications throughout Quebec. Hearings began before Chief Justice Jules Deschênes on August 10. The discussion of translation of operations manuals put both MOT and Air Canada on very weak ground. Pierre Arpin, called as a witness, admitted that he was unaware that the Secretary of State's Department had produced a French-English lexicon for aviation language as early as December 1974. Air Canada argued that translation of the manuals would be too long and too costly. Deschênes asked precisely how long and how costly. Air Canada's counsel did not have an immediate answer: two days later, he returned with the reply that, with a crash program, it could be done in two years. Air Canada witnesses also admitted that the airline had never asked Air France for its manuals, which might have been of help in any translation.[42]

On September 7, Mr. Justice Deschênes handed down his ruling, which was a near-total victory for AGAQ. He struck down Air Canada's Rule 14A, required the airline to permit its pilots to speak French among themselves, and ordered the airline to produce a translation of the flight operations manual as soon as possible. However, he let stand the Air Navigation Order restricting the use of French in air-ground communications because he felt it would more properly be considered in the Federal Court.[43] Air Canada immediately appealed. A three-judge panel heard the appeal, and on September 22 announced that it rejected it by a vote of two to one.[44] At that point, Air Canada, pressured behind the scenes by the Prime Minister's Office, the Privy Council Office, and Keith Spicer, decided to accept the Appeal Court judgment: President Claude Taylor announced that the airline would comply as rapidly as possible.[45] Despite the government's protestations of its good faith, AGAQ still refused to participate in the simulation exercises.[46] This refusal began to draw criticism within Quebec. For example, Léon Dion, who had served as an informal adviser to AGAQ throughout the summer, also wrote a column, which concluded with a dramatic peroration:

> AGAQ finds itself placed at a crucial juncture in Canadian history. One does not choose whether or not to make history: circumstances impose it. If AGAQ decides to limit its actions to the judicial level, it is working only for itself. If it decides, on the other hand, to participate in the simulation exercises, to obligate Parliament and the Government to show either their good will or their opposition, it could write a page in history which would be of signal importance for both Canadians and Quebeckers.[47]

The only consequence of Dion's rhetoric was that the AGAQ leadership severed their ties with him. The legal strategy continued and, on September 13, Serge Joyal presented a motion before the Quebec branch of the Federal Court of Canada, requesting that the Air Navigation Order be nullified.

In order to provide financial backing for its ongoing legal battles as well as to gain political clout, AGAQ launched its fund-raising appeal late in August. A support committee, which included as members Marc Lalonde, Serge Joyal, Robert Burns, a Parti Québécois MNA, Jean Cournoyer, Quebec minister of natural resources, René Matte, Créditiste leader, and Fernand Daoust, the secretary general of the Quebec Federation of Labour. The committee set as its objective the raising of $100,000 in donations. A membership drive was launched and the committee began selling buttons bearing AGAQ's slogan "Il y a du francais dans l'air" (There is French in the air).[48] By September 24, AGAQ had collected $35,000 in donations and 20,000 badges were in circulation. By the end of its fund-raising campaign in May 1977, it had collected $147,000 in individual donations, while incurring $28,000 in expenses.[49]

The politicians who joined the support committee did so in order to benefit from an association with the controllers and pilots, who were now heroes among almost all francophone Quebeckers. On September 8, Cultural Affairs Minister Jean-Paul l'Allier announced that the government would make available the services of Marcel Deschamps, a civil servant and a pilot, who would serve as AGAQ's permanent secretary general, a task which was becoming too big for Beaudry to handle on a part-time basis.[50] The next day, Solicitor General Fernand Lalonde announced a grant of $25,000 to pay AGAQ's administrative costs.[51] Lalonde also let it quietly be known that if AGAQ were willing to replace Clément Richard with a lawyer recommended by the Liberal party, the grant would be increased to $100,000 and the government would pay all of AGAQ's legal bills.[52] The leaders of AGAQ refused the offer. They were satisfied with Richard, they felt that they could raise as much money themselves as the government offered, and, most important, they wanted to maintain their independence.

At the same time that the fund-raising campaign was getting underway, AGAQ was negotiating with Pierre Proulx about participation in the simulation exercises. In September, AGAQ presented Proulx with seventeen demands which MOT would have to meet before the Quebec controllers would participate in the exercises. The seventeenth demand, that Proulx replace Professor Stager, the unilingual anglophone consultant, was rejected out-of-hand. On September 27, Demers and Beaudry sent a formal letter to Marc Lalonde and Otto Lang, outlining their demands, which dealt with the following six areas: MOT must reduce the duration of, and increase the francophone participation in, the simulation exercises; MOT must agree not to prosecute violations of the Air Navigation Order while it was being challenged in court; the government must take a neutral stance towards the Quebec controllers' attempt to disaffiliate from CATCA; the government must recognize AGAQ's status as equal to that of the other aviation organizations; MOT must shift control of airspace over eastern Quebec to the Montreal centre; and the government must permit the immediate use of French for VFR operations throughout the province.[53] Proulx spent all of October working closely with Sylvain Cloutier preparing a response to the demands, which was sent to AGAQ on November 2.[54] The package that Proulx and Cloutier put together met most of AGAQ's demands in the first five areas. The one demand it was not possible for MOT to implement was immediate bilingual VFR air traffic control. Proulx and Cloutier could only promise to complete their studies by the end of the year and begin consultation with all the organizations. If, as was most likely, there was not unanimous approval, the studies would have to be reviewed by the Commission of Inquiry. Only when the commission indicated its agreement could implementation begin.

Proulx met with AGAQ early in November to discuss the response. Demers' initial reaction was positive. However, after several hours of discussion with the other leaders of AGAQ, as well as with its political supporters, Demers informed Proulx that MOT had not gone far enough and that AGAQ members would not participate in the simulation exercises. Proulx interpreted AGAQ's refusal to participate as a political calculation. By early November, when the negotiations were taking place, it was becoming apparent to all that the Parti Québécois had a significant chance of forming the government in the November 15 elections. By that point, the leaders of AGAQ may have felt that they would be able to extract more concessions from the federal government in the political environment which would follow the elections. On November 10, Roger Demers held a press conference to announce that AGAQ would not participate in the simulation exercises.[55] MOT and AGAQ were at a stalemate. MOT, bound by its agreement, would not implement unilaterally any increase in bilingual air traffic control. AGAQ would not participate in the simulation exercises: while the exercises were ready, they could not begin without bilingual controllers, almost all of whom were members of AGAQ.

Meanwhile, AGAQ continued its legal battle to have the Air Navigation Order overturned. The case was heard on December 20 and 21 in the Federal Court in Quebec City, before Mr. Justice Louis Marceau. AGAQ was now represented by Guy Bertrand, replacing his law partner Clément Richard, who had been elected to the National Assembly as a Parti

Québécois MNA, and appointed Speaker. Bertrand emphasized the unseemly origins of the ANO, and argued that it was in violation of both the Official Languages Act and Quebec's language law (Bill 22). The federal government's argument was that it had the right to issue air navigation orders under the powers of the Aeronautics Act. On January 12, Marceau announced his decision, in which he upheld the ANO.[56] His reasoning was that it did not contravene the spirit or the letter of the Official Languages Act and that Bill 22 did not apply to aviation, which was clearly under federal jurisdiction. Marceau interpreted the Official Languages Act as committing the federal government to the goal of providing services in both languages where possible, but not obliging it to provide total bilingual service everywhere and immediately. He found the ANO to be neither in bad faith nor an abuse of power: he concluded that Otto Lang had done what he felt was necessary to end the pilots' and controllers' strike.

Many commentators were disappointed with Marceau's decision, especially in the light of the Deschênes ruling on Air Canada. Claude Ryan, editor of *Le Devoir*, saw this as an honest difference of opinion between two judges: "One [Deschênes] gives Section 2 of the Official Languages Act a very extended power; the other [Marceau] considers it an introduction to other more specific provisions which give it its true meaning, measured in terms of the possible rather than in the light of a norm of absolute equality immediately and universally applicable."[57]

Ryan hoped that AGAQ would appeal so that the higher courts, and possibly Parliament, would choose between the two conflicting interpretations. Many people of all political persuasions argued that AGAQ had a responsibility to all Quebeckers to appeal in order to clarify uncertainties about the use of French in other areas besides aviation. Premier Lévesque announced that the provincial government would provide financial aid to pay for AGAQ's appeal. The leaders of AGAQ argued long and hard over the matter. Many felt that the appeal would simply deflect energy from their original objective of increasing the use of French in the aviation sector. Finally, their sense of public duty (supported by government grants) prevailed and, on January 20, AGAQ announced that it would appeal Marceau's decision.

This decision was good news for MOT. The militant Quebec City controllers defiantly noted every occasion that French was used for an IFR operation in violation of the ANO. By this time, the Quebec City controllers had accumulated several thousand violations. MOT took the position that it would not prosecute such violations while the ANO was before the courts. AGAQ's appeal kept the ANO before the courts and enabled MOT to avoid the difficulties which would have resulted from prosecuting the Quebec City controllers.

Pierre Proulx spent December sitting uncomfortably on his hands, with the simulations ready, but without any bilingual controllers. Mike Tonner, one of CATCA's participants on the simulation team, had already moved to Ottawa from his home base in Gander. Without anything else to do, Tonner began taking French classes! Finally, Cloutier and Lang decided to try to break the deadlock by persuading individual controllers to participate in the simulations, regardless of AGAQ's position. On January 3, McLeish, Maurice Pitre, the regional manager of air traffic services for Quebec, and Pierre Proulx held a press conference in Montreal. They explained the justification for and nature of the tests, and the need for controllers to participate. They tried to stress that the simulation exercises were not to determine whether or not to have bilingual air traffic control, but how to do it.

After the press conference, Proulx and Pitre went to the VIP lounge at Dorval and waited for the controllers to come. They spent four anxious hours from 10:00 a.m. until 2:00 p.m. before anyone arrived. The first visitors were anglophone controllers who came to complain about the situation in the Montreal centre and to argue that the system should be unilingual. After a while, some francophone controllers arrived. Proulx and Pitre told them that, because the Montreal centre was seriously short-staffed, the controllers would be paid on an overtime basis. They warned them that, one way or another, MOT would hold the simulation exercises, possibly by using the bilingual controllers supplied by CATCA, who were known to be opponents of bilingual air traffic control. Proulx and Pitre asked the francophones whether they were willing to see the issue decided on the evidence produced by CATCA's participants and whether they were willing to lose the war because they refused to join the most crucial battle.

By January 7, twelve controllers—seven francophones and five anglophones—agreed to participate. In the next weeks, despite AGAQ's public opposition, more and more francophone controllers broke ranks and agreed to participate. By February 15, forty controllers had presented themselves—a sufficient number to get the tests underway.[58]

Enter the Commission of Inquiry

During the fall, the Commission of Inquiry began its work in earnest. The justices set up their offices in Ottawa and began to hire staff. They felt it essential to be impartial and to be seen as impartial: this objective was reflected in every last detail of their actions. They hired two lawyers, Yves Fortier, a bilingual francophone from Montreal, who had served as counsel to a number of royal commissions, and William Graham, a bilingual anglophone from Toronto. The justices wanted to learn about the air traffic control system first hand. Rather than studying Canadian facilities, where they would be unable to ignore the views of the staff, they visited air traffic control facilities in Washington and New York. Again to maintain neutrality, they hired as consultants the American aviation planning firm of R. Dixon Speas Associates. The justices asked the consultants to undertake two major background studies: first, to determine which languages were used for air traffic control throughout the rest of the world, and, second, to investigate the causes of as many aircraft accidents as possible, to see how many could be traced to the use of two languages.[59]

The commission lawyers were also set to work examining the files at MOT, so as to understand the evolution of the policy up to that point, and to find major documents which would illustrate that process at the hearings.

By early November, after they had launched all of these studies, the commissioners were waiting for the simulation exercises to begin and pondering their next step. They were then presented with MOT's study recommending the implementation of bilingual air traffic control at St. Hubert. After reading it, the justices began to feel that they should hold a first set of hearings that would deal only with bilingualism in VFR operations at St. Hubert, Mirabel, and the Montreal TRSA. They checked this with the consultants, who felt that such an approach would be valid. The hearings were scheduled to begin on January 17, 1977.

CATCA AND CALPA ON THE DEFENSIVE

By September, it was becoming clear to Jim Livingston that the many battles over bilingualism would absorb inordinate amounts of the association's resources and energies. Furthermore, lacking public support, both would have to be generated internally. Therefore, Livingston looked for inexpensive ways to end the minor battles. On October 5, John Nelligan proposed to the Department of Justice that the 155 other controllers who were charged with contempt of court would be willing to write letters of apology if the charges against them were dismissed. On November 10, the Justice Department accepted the proposal.[60] On December 2, at the Justice Department's recommendation, Federal Court Justice Thurlow dismissed the charges.

Jim Livingston succeeded in persuading the CATCA council to moderate its position vis-à-vis its francophone members. He did this by proposing that CATCA deal with the bilingualism problem by dividing it into two parts. CATCA would increase its internal bilingualism so as to alleviate the conditions which gave rise to the francophones' disaffiliation request. On the other hand, the question of the language of air traffic control should be resolved by the Commission of Inquiry: there CATCA would reiterate its technical arguments for the superior safety provided by unilingual air traffic control. The council modified its position on the translation of the contract slightly, offering to sign it in both languages if it contained a clause that, in the event of discrepancies between the two versions, the one most beneficial to the employee would prevail.[61] However, the Treasury Board would not accept this proposal, arguing that translation errors could result in a situation where an employee could claim greater benefits than had been the intention of either the Treasury Board or the union.[62] Once more there was an impasse, and the 1976 contract was finally signed in English only.

By November, the acting Quebec regional director of CATCA who replaced Jean-Luc Patenaude had himself resigned. Livingston decided to ask Patenaude to resume his position as director before the end of his suspension.[63] Livingston's rationale was that Patenaude had indicated that he was willing to work with CATCA, and that he had made no more public statements critical of CATCA since his suspension. Indeed Patenaude had not been part of the group organizing SCAQ: by July, he had tired of political activity, and decided to "drop out" for a while, giving his time to apolitical pursuits, such as bicycling and a girlfriend. One reason Patenaude returned to the CATCA board was that he was not certain that disaffiliation would occur: if it did not, he felt that the controllers in the Quebec region deserved to have their cause advanced within the union to which, by default, they would belong.

CATCA held a council meeting from November 16 to 19.[64] Patenaude, who returned to the council at the meeting, brought along a bottle of champagne, which he offered to the council to congratulate them for the important role they had played in electing the Parti Québécois government the day before the meetings began. The controllers, accepting the validity of Patenaude's claim, felt they deserved an entire case of champagne.

The council agreed to continue its new policy of bilingual services to its members, which had already resulted in translation costs of $17,500 in the previous six months. The council also began to plan for the upcoming hearings of the Commission of Inquiry. A brief would be prepared to argue against the extension of bilingual service at St. Hubert. The association budgeted $10,000 to cover its costs of participating in the commission hearings, and hired Colin Gravenor, a bilingual Montreal lawyer at a per diem of $600, as counsel.

Throughout the summer and fall CALPA was having some of the same troubles as CATCA was experiencing. After the strike ended and public opinion began to change, the pilots found that the campaign they had undertaken for what they felt were the purest of motives was now perceived as an expression of English-Canadian racism. Furthermore, they still had to contend with the residue of antagonism between anglophone and francophone pilots, as well as with the litigation that had begun during the strike.

One way that CALPA tried to counter the change in the climate of opinions was to publish a number of papers, outlining its position on the bilingual air traffic control question, the history of the dispute, and the ICAO position.[65] However, this time CALPA had the displeasure of seeing its press releases ignored and unreported.

CALPA held its biennial convention in Montreal, on November 23–25, at which Ken Maley was re-elected president. Nevertheless, some delegates were critical of the bad publicity CALPA had received as a result of Maley's occasionally impetuous statements on the issue of bilingualism.[66] The delegates passed several resolutions at the convention which suggest more moderate positions on the language question. They resolved to support the use of French in air traffic control "when safety is not being compromised" and they amended the CALPA instruction manual to say that French could be used for flight deck conversation if there were procedures prepared for doing so.

The bilingualism dispute had also hurt CALPA financially. Its members had lost $2.5 million in salaries, and the legal and other costs of the strike by then totalled $300,000. There was worse to come. The airlines' contempt-of-court action against CALPA was heard by Mr. Justice Cattanach in the Federal Court in January. Throughout the case, it became clear that Cattanach did not dispute the right of a pilot not to fly if he felt the situation was unsafe. What was at issue was how unsafe the situation actually was, and whether CALPA officers had made a sufficient effort to convince the pilots to return to work. Mr. Justice Cattanach announced his decision on February 18. He found CALPA guilty because its leaders had not taken "prompt, effective, and affirmative steps" to ensure compliance with the court order. He fined CALPA $5,000.[67]

Perhaps the clearest indication of the way the bilingual air traffic control issue had turned around during the summer can be seen by comparing the editorials in *Canadian Aviation*, the major publication of the anglophone aviation community, in June and August. In June, editor Hugh Whittington, in an editorial entitled "Will Some One Cry 'Enough'?" concluded: "Finally, we challenge someone in authority in Ottawa to summon up enough intestinal fortitude to face across the river and cry 'Enough!'"[68] The editorial in August, entitled "A Time for Co-operation" acknowledged that the bilingual air traffic control issue had by then "become another confrontation between English and French speaking Canadians that threatens to rip this country apart" and exhorted CATCA and CALPA to "cease trying to prove that bilingualism is unsafe and concentrate their considerable expertise and experience seeing if it can be made safe."[69]

173

The change in climate which the controllers and pilots noticed during the summer became more evident after the election of the Parti Québécois on November 15. Prime Minister Trudeau's popularity increased dramatically and "national unity" became a major political issue once again.[70] English Canadians appeared to feel some need to atone for their sins which had led Quebeckers to vote for a separatist government. Public support for CATCA and CALPA dropped still further.

Prime Minister Trudeau recognized the shift in the English-Canadian mood. Addressing a crowd of several thousand at a citizenship ceremony in Toronto he departed from his prepared text: "And if [French Canadians] don't intend to learn English we don't intend to force them to learn English. And if they want to fly their airplanes over their province by speaking French they can fly their airplanes over their province speaking French."[71]

Trudeau wondered how the crowd would react to these words which, a few months previously, would have brought hoots of derision and shouts of outrage. Now he was greeted with a loud burst of applause. It was in this new climate of opinion that the hearings of the Commission of Inquiry began.

Chapter Nine

Towards a Solution: The Commission's Initial Hearings and Interim Report

One point is certain, that truth is one and immutable; until all the jurors agree they cannot all be right.

Washington Irving, *The Widow's Ordeal*

INTRODUCTION

By early 1977, the focus of the bilingual air traffic control dispute had shifted to the hearings of the Commission of Inquiry, held in Montreal, and the simulation exercises that were getting underway in Hull. Both of these processes had two objectives: the determination of public policy, and the resolution of the many conflicts within the aviation community which the bilingual air traffic control issue had generated. Yves Fortier, who served as counsel to this commission of inquiry as well as a number of others, was well aware of the latter function, when he described commissions of inquiry as "an educational process, a way of clearing the air, a way of letting it all hang out, the dirty linen and the clean. A way of demystifying the whole issue."[1] This chapter will show both how public policy was clarified and the various conflicts resolved by the initial hearings and interim report. Other relevant activities within the aviation community, such as SCAQ's attempt to become certified as the sole bargaining agent for Quebec controllers, CATCA's continuing collective bargaining impasse with MOT, and a split within the ranks of AGAQ, are also followed up.

THE INITIAL HEARINGS OF THE COMMISSION OF INQUIRY

The hearings were held between January and March in a setting described most eloquently and ironically by Sandra Gwyn:

The mise en scène, for an Ionesco touch, is that apotheosis of
Anglo-Scottish ascendancy, the ballroom of the Windsor Hotel in
Montreal. Seedy and extremely drafty splendour. Prisms missing
from the crystal chandeliers. Grime settling into the frieze with
Grecian urns. Gold leaf peeling off the walls. It is, however, the
Commission's executive director assures me, cheap.[2]

The major participants in the hearings were MOT, CATCA, CALPA,
and the Quebec controllers. While AGAQ did not officially attend,
because it continued to deny the legitimacy of the commission, there
were two representatives of the Quebec controllers. Since St. Hubert was
one of the topics being discussed at the hearings, the local controllers
prepared a brief expressing their support for bilingual operations at their
own airport, and were represented by one of their number, Richard
Lemay. In the fall, Jean-Luc Patenaude had split with the leaders of
AGAQ because he felt their confrontational posture was not advancing
the cause of bilingual air traffic control. He decided to attend the hearings,
however, acting in his capacity as Quebec regional director of CATCA
and as a representative of Quebec controllers. As he put it:

I'm responsible for 220 guys whose dues helped pay for CATCA's
lawyer and for CATCA's brief opposing bilingual air traffic control.
I'm damn well going to make sure that they get their two cents'
worth in. I belong to AGAQ and I believe in what they are trying to
do. But I also believe in technical solutions to technical problems.
What happens if Quebec doesn't separate? Will we still be able to
use our own language in our own airspace?[3]

Lemay himself appeared as a witness, and both Patenaude and he
cross-examined witnesses called by the other participants. Patenaude was
particularly active in the hearings: because he was not a lawyer, the commissioners made allowances and the counsel for other groups advised him
as to how to formulate effective questions. Both Lemay and Patenaude
were given leave with full salary by MOT, which made it financially possible for them to participate. In addition, CATCA covered Patenaude's
expenses.[4]

CATCA was represented by Colin Gravenor, as well as by Vice-
President Bill Robertson, who helped plan strategy and also appeared as a
witness. CALPA was represented by John Lenahan, the lawyer for the
American Air Line Pilots Association, as well as by three pilots. Finally,
MOT was represented by Bernard Deschênes, Q.C., an experienced and
fluently bilingual Montreal lawyer who had performed a good deal of work
previously for MOT.

The hearings began with a number of witnesses, primarily civil servants at MOT, who were called by the commission in order to explain the basic facts of air traffic control, the evolution of MOT's policy on bilingual air traffic control, and MOT's recommendations on language use in the areas under examination by the commission: VFR operations at St. Hubert, Mirabel, and in the Montreal TRSA. Yves Fortier, who did most of the examination of the commission's witnesses, soon established himself as a dominant presence at the hearings. Sandra Gwyn, rather journalistically, explained why:

> Consider, first, Yves Fortier, the Commission's counsel. The way to think of him is as master of ceremonies. The right tension-diminishing joke at the right time; a crisp put-down when things get out of hand. A brilliantly successful Montreal lawyer in his early forties, with a squash player's stride and a dazzling array of three-piece suits, who specializes in complex inquiries. Watching Fortier perform, switching from English to French and back again without missing a beat, in the middle of examining a witness, it occurs to me that he epitomizes the Canadian style at its most elegant: the kind of dual-culture Canadian that, if English and French Canada go their separate ways, will soon cease to exist.[5]

Most of the first five days of the hearings were given over to the examination by commission counsel Fortier and Graham of Archie Novakowski, the chief of airspace and procedures in the Air Traffic Services Branch at MOT. Novakowski, an operational controller in Edmonton and air traffic control instructor before moving to MOT headquarters, gave a thorough, precise, and rather dry recitation of Canadian airspace organization and air traffic control procedure.

The large number of reporters who were present at the first few sessions of the hearings were disappointed by Novakowski's highly technical presentation: where was the confrontation they were waiting for? It finally came when Fortier finished his examination. CATCA and CALPA had been waiting for days to attack the MOT position, and they chose to put to Novakowski some difficult questions which would reveal MOT's weakness. John Lenahan, representing CALPA, very quickly asked Novakowski about the listening watch: "You would agree, would you not, that the pilot, to the extent that he is able to do so safely, listens to the radio and monitors communications that come over that radio from other aircraft that are in his vicinity?"[6]

Novakowski was in a most difficult position. As a procedures expert, he felt that it was inappropriate to have bilingual air traffic control until the proper procedures were introduced. However, until procedures were developed, he was unwilling to say whether two languages were as safe as one. He was distinctly uncomfortable being asked questions that were designed to lead him to make statements that lawyers would use as evidence on one side of the dispute or another. Thus, his answer to Lenahan was very guarded: "I would say yes that the aspect of monitoring and listening to air traffic control would, to some extent, provide [the pilot] with additional information which may or may not be pertinent to that particular flight."[7]

Lenahan went on to ask about the effect of two languages on controller workload, saying: "You would agree that bilingual control adds another factor to the calculus, another burden that he must bear in controlling traffic?" Novakowski replied guardedly again: "I don't know whether it would be considered a burden. It's something they get used to. It's their environment, it's the environment in which they work."[8]

For Lenahan and Gravenor, Novakowski was a warm-up for the main act, Walter McLeish, who spent his first three days on the stand telling Fortier and Graham how the bilingual air traffic control policy had evolved. Then Lenahan and Gravenor began their cross-examination. They tried to show that McLeish had originally supported unilingual air traffic control, that most of his subordinates continued to do so, and that the decisions to implement bilingual control were politically motivated and technically unsound. McLeish steadfastly held his ground in the face of Lenahan's and Gravenor's grilling. His strategy was simple: he was quite open in admitting that, yes, he had changed his mind and that, yes, some of his subordinates had been opposed to bilingual air traffic control and that, yes, there had been political interest in air traffic control language. However, he would not concede the fundamental point CATCA and CALPA were trying to prove: he felt that the decisions taken to implement bilingual air traffic control had and would continue to have a solid technical justification. The following exchanges epitomize McLeish's defence of his position.

McLeish: I originally had difficulty in understanding how we could go about providing bilingual service in IFR operations.... as I became more and more familiar with the problem and approached it from purely a professional point of view, I began to see and the more I understood it, the more I recognized that it was possible, until I became convinced that it can be done.

Lenahan: Are you saying without reserve that to your knowledge all those people and those subalterns to those persons who work under your jurisdiction that have expert knowledge on the subject of air traffic control are in accord with what you say?

McLeish: [They] are in accord with the objectives of MOT in pursuing those procedures to enable us to further implement the use of the French language assuming that these procedures are all certifiable, that they are not in degradation of the current level of safety...[9]

Gravenor pressed McLeish on the original 1974 decision to permit the use of French for VFR operations at five Quebec airports.

Gravenor: Would you be prepared to admit at this stage of the questions on this report that the purpose for the exercise of the Peters Study was a result of a political decision or a policy directed to your department to regulate an illegal situation which already existed in Quebec airspace?
McLeish: No, that is not correct.... Mr. Marchand indicated that he had received a brief from AQCNA urging the use of French and he asked what activity we had under way with respect to the recognition of the fact that the French language was being used at Quebec airports. We had in fact discussed this on a couple of previous occasions and I indicated to him that we were thinking very seriously that we should have a safety investigation done on the situation at Quebec City, and he said, "fine" and "carry on, let me know what the results are." Marchand's intervention was a significant reason for the study.

Gravenor: Did you ever receive any memoranda from Mr. Marchand relating to the constitution of the Peters team?
McLeish: I did not.[10]

On the last day of his cross-examination of McLeish, Colin Gravenor attempted to ask him about the Zagreb, Yugoslavia, crash. Yves Fortier objected to the question on the grounds that no official investigation had been completed, that the crash had happened in an IFR, rather than a VFR environment, and that discussing the crash would be "lend[ing] the offices of counsel to this Commission to any scare tactics, to any sensationalism, to any smokescreen of catastrophes, crashes, or incidents which unfortunately have been known to be used by some of those appearing before this Commission."[11] The Commission upheld Fortier's objection.

Midway through the cross-examination, Gravenor passed McLeish in the foyer during a lunch break, and muttered to him, in a joking way that was more than half-serious, "I'll get you yet, you..." However, the steadfast faith in the correctness of his actions which McLeish had developed made him an excellent witness. By the end of his time on the stand, he was able to stand down with his credibility unscathed. McLeish's testimony marked a crucial turning point in the hearings: the department's integrity had not been destroyed.

The hearings then moved on to the question of bilingual operations at St. Hubert. For five days, David Cunningham, the head of the St. Hubert task force, recounted the group's activities the previous spring in response to questioning by Fortier and Graham. The airline pilots present realized that language use at St. Hubert was not a major priority for them, since they neither used nor would use that airport. Furthermore, they wanted to establish an image of reasonableness and objectivity for the discussions of bilingual IFR control at the next set of hearings, which would be of importance to them.[12] Therefore, at the outset of the hearing on Monday, February 15, Captain G. D. Richardson, representing CALPA, rose to address the Commission:

Although the evidence clearly shows that no in-depth safety studies which could lend themselves to statistically provable conclusions were carried out, it does indicate that bilingual VFR control is presently a fact at St. Hubert.

Given the nature of the traffic at St. Hubert and the role which this airport plays in aviation in Quebec, we are faced with an existing reality; though the possible risk factor in a two-language system at that airport has not been scientifically assessed, the circumstances there indicate the risk is probably acceptable.[13]

CALPA's statement was followed by Richard Lemay, who discussed the effect of de facto bilingual VFR operations at St. Hubert on controller workload and stress. He testified:

[With two languages] there is a much better understanding and that avoids our having to repeat the same directions two, three, or four times, as was previously the case. ... So, for our part, we feel much safer in the exercise of our control. We have a better confirmation of the fact that the pilot has received and properly understood our directive. There is not that concern or that anxiety to know whether the pilot understood or not.[14]

By February 28, all the commission's witnesses had testified. The commission then heard testimony from CATCA and CALPA's witnesses. Both organizations had approached numerous MOT bureaucrats, particularly regional air administrators in English Canada, who a few months before had been so forthright (in private) in their opposition to bilingual air traffic control. When asked to testify, these individuals, fearing for their careers, all refused. One person who was willing to testify was Desmond Peters, author of the initial 1974 report recommending the use of French in air traffic control for VFR operations at Quebec. Peters recounted the incident in April 1974 which led him to recommend against the use of French for normal operations: when asked by Gravenor to explain the contradiction between the memo based on the incident and the report, he said: "In the first place, I was involved in an incident that could have proven dangerous. The second case which is the report of May 2, it was written as a result of an objective study and a logical conclusion." While Peters was quite frank that he was distressed by what he felt were pressure tactics on the part of the francophone controllers to have bilingualism recognized for VFR operations, his conclusion did not give Gravenor much comfort: "In the VFR situation, the safety process has evolved to one that is relatively safe now, in fact, really safe." Finally, Peters expressed his own opinion about air traffic control language use:

If you are asking me if one language should be used, I would say: yes, one language should be used. I know it is the policy of the government and of the Ministry that two languages be used if at all feasible, and presumably if at all feasible, it will be used.... I honestly believe also that this will not come about in our system until such time as it has been proven safe by the Ministry.[15]

While Peters' testimony was at variance with MOT policy, his assertion that policy would not be changed until new policies had been proven safe, provided support for the ambience of professionalism that McLeish exuded and that Gravenor had not been able to destroy.

Bernard Deschênes and Jean-Luc Patenaude worked hard to weaken the credibility of the witnesses who followed. John Dreher, a psycholinguist from the University of Southern California, made theoretical arguments that one language would create less stress for controllers than two. Bernard Deschênes' cross-examination showed that he was not at all conversant with the Canadian situation, and had no data to show that air traffic control is safer in countries using only one language.[16] CATCA even called an official from the Canadian Transport Commission, who testified that train conductors also use a listening watch. Jean-Luc Patenaude, who by then was exercising his newly developed legal skills with growing confidence, broke down the analogy by asking how much amateur railroading there is in Canada.[17]

CATCA's final witness was Vice-President Bill Robertson. When asked by Yves Fortier to comment on Lemay's assertion that the controllers at

St. Hubert felt reduced stress because of the use of two languages, he could only summon up personal experience:

> I would like to relate sort of perhaps a personal experience which leads me to believe that switching languages back and forth can be a problem and that is in a social situation, not in the pressure of high density airports, but in my own family, my father's tongue is Dutch, and there have been occasions when he has had to translate for members of the family with people who don't speak English. And invariably within about five minutes the confusion will arise, and he will address the English-speaking person in Dutch and the Dutch-speaking person in English.... I have never scientifically tested it out, but it leads me to believe that in a high density pressure situation, this could also apply but, of course, the results could be a bit different than sitting in a livingroom having a conversation.[18]

The final witness was Charles Miller, a noted American aviation consultant. Miller gave equivocal answers rather than the condemnation of Canadian policies that CATCA had hoped for. When asked if a reduction in the capability of the listening watch would diminish safety in an air traffic control system, he answered, "Well, it certainly has the potential to do that, but I find it hard to speak in terms of safety of a system based on any one parameter.... All other things being equal, yes, it is going to make it less safe. But very rarely do things come into existence like this, everything else being equal."[19] Finally, when asked by Fortier whether a two-language system, possibly with reduced traffic, might retain or enhance safety, he responded: "Mr. Fortier, I am the eternal optimist in aviation. I think you can do anything in aviation, if you are willing to take the time and put the effort into it."[20]

The hearing concluded on March 25, with summary statements given by Bernard Deschênes, Colin Gravenor, and Captain Richardson. Deschênes was very cool and rational. He suggested that the commissioners consider four options: a totally English air traffic control system, total and immediate bilingualism, partial bilingualism and (the preferred option), the gradual introduction of bilingualism. Only in rejecting the first option did a note of passion creep into his argument when he said: "If one is not to consider unilingual francophone Quebeckers as second class citizens and refuse them access to aviation, one must reject the solution of anglophone unilingualism." He then outlined nine possible arguments against bilingual air traffic control and attacked each, using statements made by CATCA and CALPA witnesses, where possible. In order to refute the controller workload argument, he quoted Richard Lemay's testimony that having two languages decreased stress and advised the commissioners to go to St. Hubert themselves and see "controllers operating in such an effective and smooth manner that they certainly cannot be traumatized to the slightest degree due to the use of two languages." In response to the criticism of MOT's studies, he replied:

> The great majority of these studies were carried out in the real-life environment of the airports concerned... the great majority of the participants were of anglophone origin and not biased in favour of the introduction of bilingualism, as we have clearly seen in the case of Mr. Peters, but they convinced themselves about the necessary safety aspects of improving such a system by the introduction of a second language and then reported to their superiors.[21]

Deschênes then attacked MOT's critics, saying: "we have had a clear demonstration that none of them have carried out studies in the various briefs submitted which insist on studies but offer none." He made sure to remind the commissioners that CATCA had endorsed the use of French at Quebec City without having undertaken any detailed study, even before the Peters report had been completed.

Captain Richardson of CALPA was really addressing the next set of hearings on IFR bilingualism and therefore put great emphasis on the listening watch argument. He began his remarks by wrapping himself in the mantle of professionalism: "I have heard laymen discuss our profession and our job. It never fails to amaze me the depth of misunderstanding and the lack of knowledge they exude." He then went on:

> Twenty-five years ago, as an ab initio pilot, I was lectured ad nauseum on the value of the listening watch to the safety of myself and my aircraft. In twenty-five years of flying I have seen no reason to change. Yet [now] I am being told that the listening watch does not matter any more. Gentlemen, that is just not true. I doubt that there is a professional pilot who can truthfully look back and deny that a listening watch has saved him from an incident or a major disaster. I would be remiss if I did not point out to you that this has been my experience many times, not just once in a while. I am such a believer in the listening watch that if bilingual control is implemented, I will learn the lexicon of the other language, and I hope the francophone does too, for both our sakes.[22]

Colin Gravenor's concluding speech very clearly reflected the anger that his clients felt towards MOT.[23] He attacked Richard Lemay's claim that bilingual air traffic control reduced stress on controllers by making a questionable analogy: "No one ever asks an impaired driver on a Canadian highway to tell us whether he is or is not impaired... with all respect to the very polite, good faith and honest presentation Mr. Lemay gave to this commission, he is not the proper judge." Gravenor's major argument was that MOT's studies were technically inadequate and produced merely to justify political decisions. He claimed that "many MOT witnesses that have been in the box are career-wise, psychological-wise or dollar-wise under the gun." He reminded the commissioners of the fable of the emperor's new clothes, suggesting that McLeish was the emperor and his subordinates the tailors, as McLeish told his subordinates to "go out and tell me what procedures I should introduce to have bilingual air traffic control" rather than "go out and tell me if the air traffic control system is safe and, if it is, how I maintain it."

THE COMMISSION'S INTERIM REPORT

The commissioners retired behind closed doors to consider both the testimony at the hearings and the data that had been gathered by their consultants. The commission's major recommendations constituted an almost complete victory for MOT. The commission unanimously recommended that bilingual air traffic control be provided for VFR flights at St. Hubert, for VFR flights through the Montreal TRSA, and for those traversing, but not landing or taking off at, Mirabel. Mr. Justice Chouinard wanted to allow VFR flights to land and take off using both languages at Mirabel, but the majority (Sinclair and Heald) felt that the question of mixing small aircraft and large jets in a bilingual environment could best be considered in the context of both Dorval and Mirabel together. On the other hand, all three judges observed that unilingual francophone pilots were too frequently crossing the Mirabel positive control zone without permission and felt that this safety risk could be alleviated by introducing bilingual control for these VFR aircraft. Finally, the commissioners recommended that the necessary support services (maps, recorded weather information) be provided in both languages.[24]

The report began with a short history of the bilingual air traffic control problem. Their reading of the history led the commissioners to conclude "at the very outset it will be well to lay to rest any suggestion that some actions taken by officials of the Department were motivated by political considerations. The Commission is of the opinion that such suggestions were unfounded, and that nothing more need be said about them."[25] CATCA's major contention, the cornerstone of Gravenor's argument, was thereby rejected.

The report discussed the results of the research undertaken by the consultants. It was found that eighty-three countries use more than one language in air traffic control, as compared with forty-five which use English alone. While acknowledging that the use of multiple languages in a country does not mean that multiple languages are used at every airport, the report did state that "the analysis clearly establishes that air traffic control services are made available at airports throughout the world in a substantial number of languages."[26] Some patterns are clearly apparent in the data. Countries using English alone are mainly those which are anglophone or which were colonized by the United Kingdom (e.g., the Bahamas, Barbados, Burma, Cyprus, Ghana, Pakistan). In the economically developed countries, which is Canada's reference group, all non-anglophone countries except the Netherlands use two or more languages for air traffic control.

The study of aircraft accidents done by R. Dixon Speas Associates examined over 17,000 reports of accidents involving aircraft over 12,500 lb. in weight which had occurred in the previous twenty years.[27] It was based on the British air registration board's world airline accident summary, which was the best source the consultants could find. Though the limitation of the data to aircraft over 12,500 lb. excluded many reports of accidents involving small aircraft flying VFR, the commissioners felt that it was important evidence bearing on the overall safety of bilingual air traffic control.

The study was looking for accidents influenced by the use of more than one language for air traffic control (the sort that supporters of unilingual air traffic control would fear in a bilingual context) and accidents involving imperfect communication because one or more of the parties were using a language they did not perfectly understand (the sort that supporters of bilingual air traffic control would fear in a unilingual context). Thirty-three accidents were found to be language related, but data were available at the time for only twenty-two. Of these, seventeen involved language difficulties which were irrelevant to the commission's study, such as misunderstandings in a language in which all parties were fluent. Five were of interest to the commission. Of these, one had insufficient data to draw a conclusion. Three involved language difficulties where either the pilot or the controller was using a language other than his mother tongue—the situation that AGAQ felt necessitated bilingual air traffic control in Quebec. Only one, a mid-air collision in 1960 over Rio de Janeiro between a United States aircraft being controlled in English and a Brazilian aircraft being controlled in Portuguese, was the type of accident which CATCA and CALPA could claim might have been prevented through the use of one language only. Not surprisingly, the opponents of bilingual air traffic control had been publicizing the Rio de Janeiro accident for several months. The commission was aware of the 1976 Zagreb accident but, in the absence of an official accident report, drew no firm conclusion about it. The commission was very much impressed by the results of the consultants' study. The Rio de Janeiro incident, which CALPA had been publicizing so widely, was not one of many accidents in bilingual environments that unilingual control could have averted; rather, it stood alone. The commissioners drew the following conclusion:

> If one stops to think of the number of flights that must have been made, and of the miles flown, and the passengers carried, during the past 20 years in 83 countries throughout the world where air traffic control services are provided in two or more languages, one is left with an abiding conviction that there is nothing inherently dangerous in bilingual air traffic control.[28]

In addition to discussing the consultants' study, the report went through all of the arguments advanced against bilingual VFR air traffic control. The commission did not accept the argument that MOT's studies were of poor quality; rather, it accepted McLeish's assertion, in cross-examination by Lenahan, that MOT had used all reasonable and feasible means to evaluate bilingual air traffic control for VFR flights.[29] It had been claimed that there was expertise in other countries which MOT had not consulted. Basing its conclusions in part on Charles Miller's testimony, the commission found that no one could refer in a concrete way to such expertise or how it might have been brought to bear on the problem in Quebec. This was due to the way in which air traffic control had developed. Those countries with bilingual systems had been bilingual from the outset: thus, the development of bilingual control was synonymous with the development of air traffic control. Bilingualism was taken for granted as one of the characteristics of the system, and no great attention was paid to it. Similarly, all unilingual systems developed as unilingual. As no country had ever thought of converting from one system to another, no one had ever studied carefully such questions as whether one system is safer than the other, or how to implement a conversion from one system to another. So international expertise did not provide the answers to MOT's questions.

The commission cast doubt on the argument of the hypothetical stray unilingual francophone pilot for several reasons: none of the 17,000 accidents examined were due to stray pilots; CALPA did not express any worry about the problem; and finally, improved documentation and service for francophone pilots would make the problem less likely to occur.[30] The controller workload argument was answered by Lemay's evidence.[31] The commission recognized the importance of the listening watch argument and admitted that this provided the most serious objection to bilingual VFR service.[32] However, the report demonstrated how often VFR pilots change frequencies, which makes it difficult, if not impossible, for them to draw a complete mental map of the sky based on overheard radio messages. Finally, the commission considered the key virtue of bilingual air traffic control to be the increased comfort and safety for francophone pilots, who would be able to use their mother tongue.

Finally, the report dealt with St. Hubert, the Montreal TRSA, and Mirabel separately.[33] In the case of St. Hubert, substantial weight was put on CALPA's statement that it termed the risk there "probably acceptable." The discussion of the TRSA argued that the goal of keeping VFR aircraft well separated from commercial IFR aircraft would be furthered if controllers used both English and French. The report also noted that the provision of bilingual service for the Montreal TRSA would make it easier to keep St. Hubert pilots from straying through the TRSA into the Dorval control zone, which was a serious hazard. The report concluded by noting that VFR service in French would not impair operational efficiency or create implementation costs.[34]

Transport Minister Lang tabled the commission report in the House of Commons on July 8, asserting: "I am pleased with the recommendations contained in this report, which have the full support of the government."[35] The opposition parties then responded. Conservative leader Joe Clark announced that "We are certainly prepared to support the unanimous recommendations." The NDP completely reversed its position of the previous year and Ed Broadbent, with his characteristic exuberance, proclaimed: "I am delighted with the recommendations, and we look forward to their speedy implementation." With such support, there was no need to hold a free vote on the Interim Report.

CALPA issued no public statement. However, the headquarters *Newsletter* of July 12 discussed the report.[36] While the report, which dealt primarily with VFR operations "is of limited interest to us," CALPA was pleased that the commission recognized the importance of the listening watch. The newsletter concluded that this was an "encouraging indication that the Commission of Inquiry and the IFR simulation studies have the potential to allow a more objective look at the whole issue."

CATCA had much less to rejoice about. Salvaging what it could, the national council expressed gratitude that no decision was to be made on the use of French for VFR services at Dorval or for VFR landings and takeoffs at Mirabel until the IFR simulations were completed. The council, while stating that it was "unconvinced that MOT has done sufficient study on the question of bilingual air traffic control at St. Hubert or that it has developed adequate safety procedures there," nevertheless supported the recommendations. At the press conference where he announced CATCA's reaction, Jim Livingston was asked what his response would be if the next phase of the commission supported bilingual IFR air traffic control, and he replied, "I would recommend...however reluctantly... that we've had our say, our day in court, and that we should accept the findings of the Commission of Inquiry."[37]

One might speculate that CATCA's position was influenced by several factors, such as the awareness of a changed climate of public opinion within English Canada and the need to maintain cohesiveness within the union. The latter was particularly compelling, because at that time the Public Service Staff Relations Board was still deliberating on SCAQ's request for certification as the bargaining agent for Quebec controllers and because CATCA was preparing for a strike, this time over financial issues.

The only group which opposed the recommendations was COPA. President Russell Beach called the report "incredible" and once again called for the use of English only.[38] Finally, public reaction was very tranquil. French Canadians saw it as simple justice. The change of opinion in English Canada led to easy acceptance there. Bilingual air traffic control was now no longer a front-page issue: once again, it had become a technical question.

IN THE AVIATION COMMUNITY

Throughout the winter and spring, a battle was being waged within the executive of the Gens de l'Air between Pierre Beaudry and Roger Demers. Beaudry was growing dissatisfied with the direction that the organization was taking under the stewardship of Demers and Secretary-General Marcel Deschamps. Beaudry also felt AGAQ was falling victim to the iron law of oligarchy, as Deschamps and Demers were making too many decisions without consulting the membership. Finally, he was growing impatient with the delays the controllers were encountering in their legal struggle and felt that some direct action was required.

This conflict came out in the open at AGAQ's first annual conference, held in Quebec City on the weekend of May 21 and 22. Attendance was low at the meeting, with only seventy-five of the organization's 1,700 members present. The opening session was attended by representatives of all the political parties, who lauded AGAQ, emphasized the importance of its struggle, and pledged continuing support. After the politicians left, the power struggle began. In his opening speech, Roger Demers emphasized the tenaciousness of anglophone opposition, but stated that "the emotional phase of our struggle has passed and we must now pursue the defence of French in the ongoing legal proceedings." Pierre Beaudry proposed that pilots, controllers, and other aviation workers in Quebec speak only French for one 24-hour period in order to dramatize their objective. After that proposal was defeated, Beaudry proposed that the directors of AGAQ meet once a month and that AGAQ pay their expenses and wages for these meetings. Also, Beaudry proposed that the Quebec government give AGAQ a grant to cover Deschamps' salary, rather than pay Deschamps directly, which would make it possible for AGAQ to replace Deschamps if they wished. These proposals were also rejected. Having been defeated, Beaudry, and several supporters walked out of the meeting, resigning in protest.[39]

As these events transpired, CATCA had to deal with the certification request by SCAQ. As part of the process, CATCA was required to turn over all its records of the past few years to see if the evidence supported the allegation that there was systematic discrimination against francophones. The case was heard before the Public Service Staff Relations Board in March and April. Jim Livingston was cross-examined for several days. He maintained that he did not in any way discriminate against francophone members and that CATCA at all times provided typical union services, such as representation in grievances. He also claimed that CATCA's position on bilingualism was always decided democratically and francophone members were never prevented from expressing their views or from using AGAQ to advance those views. He pointed out that CATCA's position on bilingualism had, over time, evolved towards a greater acceptance of the use of French in air traffic control and within his organization. Livingston justified the disciplinary action of Jean-Luc Patenaude as something that any union would do in response to an executive who publicly advocated disaffiliation. Livingston's foresight during the previous year in recognizing that CATCA's record had to be clean gave him a strong defence.

The CATCA executive knew that the major weakness in their case was their refusal to sign contracts in French. On the last day of the hearings, John Nelligan, CATCA's attorney, informed the PSSRB that in the future CATCA would sign its collective agreements in both languages.[40] After the hearing was completed, the board began a long process of deliberations in this most unprecedented case involving an intra-union fight over cultural and linguistic rights. Furthermore, the board was well aware that, if SCAQ was allowed to separate, this could be a significant precedent for francophone groups within other public service unions.

While the board was deliberating, CATCA was preparing for another strike. This time the major issues were financial.[41] The government was prepared to offer an 8 percent salary increase, the maximum allowed by the anti-inflation regulations. CATCA and MOT had been working for several years on a reclassification of controllers' jobs: CATCA's reclassification proposal would have resulted in an increase of 4.6 percent in controllers' total compensation, while the government's proposal would have resulted in an increase of less than 1 percent. As part of the reclassification proposal, CATCA argued that IFR controllers in Toronto be put in a special category because the traffic volume there was higher than anywhere else in the country: this was unacceptable to MOT.

After no settlement was reached through conciliation, and despite government warnings that the controllers would be legislated back to work, CATCA struck on Sunday August 7.[42] The strike brought Canadian air travel, with the exception of some international flights operated through American border cities, to a halt. Parliament was recalled on Tuesday August 9 and, with the support of the Conservatives and the opposition of the NDP, legislation was passed to end the strike and settle the disagreement on the government's terms.[43] Even though he knew the strike would hurt CATCA's image, Livingston felt it was important for his membership to take some kind of militant action to indicate how serious they were about the reclassification package, because negotiations for the 1978 contract were to begin soon afterwards.

The legislated end to the strike did not satisfy the controllers, particularly those in Toronto who were demanding a higher classification. The Toronto controllers manifested their feelings through a work-to-rule campaign in which they enforced separation standards as strictly as possible, thus creating substantial delays during the busy travel period of late August and early September. The work-to-rule campaign brought no public support. The Toronto *Globe and Mail*, one of the strongest supporters of the controllers on the bilingualism issue, was now one of its strongest opponents. In one of its editorials, the *Globe* wrote: "Canadians know what is wrong with controllers. They are recalcitrant employees, paid good salaries, who are sulking because the government would not agree to give them larger pay increases than the anti-inflation guidelines allow to the rest of us. Yielding to them in any way, shape, or form, would be yielding to blackmail."[44]

The pilots were also angered by the slowdown but, trapped by their own ideology, they remained publicly silent. What the controllers were doing was perfectly safe, though inefficient. As CALPA's public positions were based only on consideration of safety, nothing could be said. The work-to-rule campaign was brought to an end later in the fall when MOT agreed to recognize and begin discussions with a "Committee of Eight" Toronto controllers.

Chapter Ten

Tying Threads Together:
The Problem Resolved

Science is the search for truth—it is not a game in which one tries to beat his opponent or do harm to others.

Linus Pauling, *No More Wars*

INTRODUCTION

In order for full bilingual air traffic control to be implemented in Quebec, there were two necessary conditions: its acceptance by the English-Canadian public and acquiescence of the aviation community. The two previous chapters have shown how the attitudes of the former changed so substantially that the *Interim Report* of the Commission of Inquiry was received without any controversy. Based on its acceptance of the *Interim Report*, one could have predicted that the English-Canadian public would have been equally willing to accept a final report recommending full bilingual air traffic control in Quebec whenever the Commission of Inquiry issued it. However, it took over two years for the final report to emerge. In those two years, out of public view, a very important process of reconciliation and change was going on within the aviation community, involving both the policies of organizations and the behaviour of individuals. The simulation exercises, and the commission's hearings to evaluate them, were a key element in this process.

THE SIMULATION EXERCISES

The simulation exercises attempted to examine the differences between bilingual and unilingual IFR air traffic control under the most realistic representation possible of the actual world. MOT's objective was to develop procedures that would maintain existing safety standards in a

191

bilingual system, something which Walter McLeish believed to be eminently possible. CATCA and CALPA wanted to prove that it would be impossible, given any procedures, to develop as safe a system using two languages as with one. This difference in objectives and beliefs provided a constant source of tension underlying the exercises.

These simulations were the first major project to use MOT's new simulation centre in Hull.[1] The centre's control room provided four controller positions, each with its own radar screen. Thus, any given IFR sector (such as the Montreal terminal) could be represented. In an adjacent room sat a number of clerks, trained to copy the behaviour of real-world pilots. The clerks sat at computer consoles, conversing with air traffic control and entering information which would cause the computer to generate radar images of the imaginary aircraft they were piloting. In some exercises, real pilots handled the communications and the clerks entered the data. Each clerk could handle up to five aircraft, and up to eighty aircraft could be shown on the system at a given time. The system was augmented by linking up to the simulation centre a number of aircraft simulators (physically located in Ottawa and Montreal and operated by real pilots). The aircraft simulators would appear on the controllers' radar, and the controllers could converse with the pilots flying them. The simulation centre also had an observation room in which one could unobtrusively watch the controllers and listen in on their conversations with the pilots.

The simulation exercises were conducted for three day periods.[2] On the first day, the controller subjects were oriented and performed some practice runs. On the second day they performed a set of exercises handling unilingual traffic; on the third day, similar exercises were performed under bilingual conditions, that is, with a substantial percentage of the pilots speaking French. Sometimes the second day's exercises would be bilingual and the third day's exercises unilingual. Each controller worked a number of different positions (such as arrivals or departures) on both days. At the end of each day of exercises, there was a debriefing session to ascertain the controllers' and simulator pilots' responses to the exercises, as well as to hear their suggestions as to how their simulation could be made more realistic.

There were two groups of controllers involved in the exercises, regular Montreal centre controllers who had volunteered and CATCA's designated subjects. All those who participated had taken the French lexicon course and were certified to use both languages for communications with pilots and with other controllers. However, they did not have substantial experience at controlling in both languages (in comparison to, say, controllers in France).

The radar in the simulation centre did not use the alphanumeric display that would be available with the JETS system, thereby forcing the controllers to remember language use on bilingual days, as well as all the relevant flight information. Controllers kept track of language use by designating with a yellow marking pen the flight progress strip of aircraft whose pilots used French.

Data were gathered during the second and third days on communications characteristics, communications errors, and losses of separation. Communications characteristics included the duration of controller messages and latency—that is, the time required by controllers to respond to messages. Communications errors included those which occurred on both bilingual and unilingual days, such as a controller failing to correct a pilot's error in reading back a clearance, and those which occurred only on bilingual days, such as a controller addressing a message to a pilot in the wrong language.

The exercises were designed to compare the performance of individuals in bilingual and unilingual air traffic control systems. By using a number of controllers and having each handle a number of control positions, it was possible to perform statistical analyses (known as analyses of variance) that would indicate whether differences in outcomes were a result of differences in individuals, differences in the air traffic control positions, or difference between the bilingual and unilingual systems, or some combination of all these factors.

The simulation exercises were officially known as the bilingual IFR communications simulation studies, or BICSS. The key people involved in running the exercises were Pierre Proulx, Deputy Director Brian Walsh, an experienced electrical engineer who was in charge of technical matters, Vic Dupéré, a Montreal centre manager in charge of coordination with the Montreal controllers, and Professor Paul Stager, who was in charge of the research design and data analysis. A number of MOT staff were also seconded to the team on a full-time basis. In choosing his people, Proulx did not restrict himself to those who professed themselves to be supporters of bilingual air traffic control. Rather, he chose individuals whom he felt could be scientific and objective and who would be willing to modify their views in the light of new evidence. In addition to the MOT staff, there were three organizational representatives: First Officer Bob MacWilliam, representing CALPA, COPA, and the airlines; and Mike Tonner and Don Redden, representing CATCA. Proulx treated them as full team members, involved them in all phases of the study, and elicited their suggestions as to how to improve the studies. He did not want to have them sit on the sidelines and then, when everything was finished, criticize the team for its errors. The Commission of Inquiry was represented by staff members of R. Dixon Speas Associates, its consultants, who quietly watched the process unfold. Their observations would be used by the commissioners in their assessment of the simulations.

The first phase of the simulation exercises dealt with en route air traffic control, simulating two sectors of the Montreal centre's airspace: Granby-Sherbrooke (southeast of Montreal) and James Bay—north and northwest of Montreal. In each exercise, actual traffic data were used to formulate a two-hour exercise. The traffic flow was substantially higher (42 percent higher for James Bay and 19 percent higher for Granby-Sherbrooke) than the actual average flow, in order to make the exercises challenging. On bilingual days, 25–35 percent of the traffic used French, which was higher than actually occurred or would be expected to occur even if bilingual air traffic control was implemented. The simulation exercises were to begin with the first orientation session on March 16. As a late winter snowstorm raged outside the centre, Proulx waited nervously for the Montreal controllers to arrive. They showed up at 8:45, and the exercises were finally under way! This first set ran for eleven weeks, from March 16 to June 1, 1977. The first eight weeks used Montreal controllers who had volunteered the previous January: the last three weeks used test subjects provided by CATCA.

Organizationally, the first simulations were rough going. The early debriefing sessions were quite argumentative, with debates over first principles about the validity of bilingual air traffic control. Proulx, a generally calm person, exercised tight control over the meetings and kept the discussions pragmatic and technical. He simply refused to talk about politics and ruled out of order discussions about such matters as MOT's bad relations with CATCA or CATCA's mistreatment of francophones. He continually forced the participants to put their prejudices aside and analyse what happened on that particular day. Professor Stager approached the discussions in his own calm and knowledgeable way. He was dealing with a group of people who had little, if any, acquaintance with experimental research, and he often had to explain his research design. On a number of occasions when a pilot or controller had a "bad" day, the other participants were inclined to scrap the day's data. Stager, aware of the law of large numbers, argued that this was unnecessary: these episodes were simply noise in the data, and if the sample was large enough, the signal would come through over the noise.

Though the data were not being analysed thoroughly as they were being gathered, it was becoming clear to all participants that the performance of the controllers was roughly similar on both bilingual and unilingual days. This was a minor battle won for bilingualism. Redden, Tonner, and Mac-William simply shrugged it off, saying that everyone knows that en route control is not very difficult nor the traffic level very high. The real test would come with the more complicated and busier terminal environment.

At that point, Proulx needed someone familiar with the Montreal terminal to spend the summer working with Professor Stager to design the Montreal terminal exercises. He chose Tom Fudakowski, a fluently bilingual Montreal controller who had sided with the anglophones and had been a member of the Committee of Eight. Though Fudakowski had grave doubts about the safety and efficiency of bilingual control, he was willing to be objective and open-minded.

Fudakowski and Stager worked together to design an exercise which embodied all the complexity of the Montreal terminal environment, including the wide variety of aircraft flying in the area, the use of two airports, and the frequent shifts in runway use. On bilingual days, 30 percent of the traffic used French, a much higher percentage than had ever been experienced or ever was anticipated in the future. Don Redden, who worked at the Toronto centre, argued for as heavy a volume of traffic as possible. He maintained that the only real test of the viability of bilingual control would come under the most difficult conditions imaginable. As a result, the traffic level planned for the exercises was about sixty aircraft movements per hour, which was substantially higher than the average of forty-seven actually experienced during peak hours in May and June 1977. Furthermore, this traffic level was even slightly higher than that on the busiest day during the 1976 Olympics, when there was more air traffic in Montreal than ever before or since.

During the summer, the project team was hard at work designing a way to test the listening watch.[3] The initial methodology was to give a map to pilots flying the simulator aircraft: after they had been listening to a radio frequency for a while, they would be asked to indicate the locations of the other aircraft on the map. This was tried in the test runs, and it was found that pilots were too busy to locate accurately other aircraft. The maps were taken away and the pilots were given cassette recorders and asked to note if there were any flights of vital interest to them and whether they had overheard any transmission errors.[4]

A third study, led by Tom Fudakowski, was also begun during the summer to determine whether it was possible to simulate a mix of VFR and IFR traffic.[5] By December, the team had concluded that it was impossible to perform such a simulation. Furthermore, after reviewing procedures at major Canadian airports, the team concluded that IFR and VFR aircraft used different frequencies almost all the time, so that the listening watch would be of little, if any, assistance in maintaining separation between them.

At the same time that his staff was preparing the terminal exercises, Pierre Proulx was trying to convince the francophones to participate. He approached the Montreal terminal unit controllers, many of whom had resigned from AGAQ, along with Pierre Beaudry. The controllers were now more favourably disposed towards participating because of the satisfactory outcome of the commission's *Interim Report* and because of the endorsement of the en route controllers who had participated in the previous set of exercises. Also, the terminal controllers themselves began to feel that the exercises would provide practice for controlling in a bilingual environment.

Proulx also approached the leaders of the Gens de l'Air to urge their organization's full participation in the simulation exercises. He argued that there would probably be enough controllers among those who had resigned from AGAQ, who were willing to participate so that the simulation exercises could be held. If AGAQ participated, its full membership, particularly pilots, would have some influence on the nature of the bilingual air traffic control system which would ultimately emerge.

On November 15, Proulx was finally able to get AGAQ to accept an agreement with MOT, which was then signed by Walter McLeish and Roger Demers on November 28.[6] AGAQ agreed to encourage its members, both pilots and controllers, to take part in the exercises, as both simulation participants and observers. MOT agreed to defray the costs and acknowledged that AGAQ's participation in the exercises was not to be considered an endorsement of the Commission of Inquiry.

The terminal simulation exercises started on November 16. The first group of controllers were so upset by the high traffic level they encountered on the practice day that they threatened to quit. Proulx and Fudakowski held a tense evening meeting with them. Fudakowski felt that it was essential to convince the controllers who distrusted him for his role in the Committee of Eight that this was not his way of getting revenge. The controllers argued that the exercises had arrivals coming into the Montreal area at such a rapid rate that, in real life, they would handle it by telling controllers in other centres not to let planes take off and by forcing those already in the air to enter holding patterns. Proulx and Fudakowski agreed to rearrange the arrivals pattern, and lowered the overall traffic level slightly to fifty-seven departing or arriving aircraft per hour, which was still 21 percent higher than the average peak-hour traffic level in May and June 1977.[7]

By the second week of the exercise the general pattern was becoming clear. The controllers were handling traffic in two languages just as effectively as in one. They switched easily from one language to the other. Communications errors appeared to be no more frequent on bilingual days. One of the controllers reminded Fudakowski that in 1976, on a television program, Fudakowski had said that bilingualism would probably slow down a 55-minute flight from Toronto to Montreal to 60 to 65 minutes. Fudakowski admitted that he had been wrong. Proulx, Stager, Walsh, and Fudakowski now had the satisfaction of sensing for the first time that they had found a solution. The terminal simulations were completed on January 20, 1978, and provided six weeks of data based on the participation of regular Montreal controllers and two weeks of CATCA members.

At this point, Tonner, Redden, and MacWilliam were receiving unpleasant surprises. The bilingual system was working even in a difficult terminal environment with a very high traffic level. MacWilliam was disappointed by the listening watch study as most of the pilots were turning in blank tapes, or were simply naming the flights they overheard on their frequency or making comments on the operation of their own flights.

All three now set their sights on the third phase of the exercises, which were simulations of the terminal operation in exceptional situations. Redden and Tonner believed that under some situations, involving either bad weather or complicated holding patterns, the bilingual system would break down, while the unilingual system would still function. MacWilliam was pushing for a more serious test of the listening watch. In response, Tom Fudakowski came up with the idea of forcing the controllers to make errors to see if the real pilots flying aircraft simulators could catch them.

Phase three ran from April 1 to April 11. The exercises consisted of three 1¼-hour sessions, with a different situation in each. The first session began with poor weather, very close to the minimum for IFR operations. After fifteen minutes, a total electrical failure at Dorval required that aircraft go into a holding pattern, which was maintained for fifteen minutes until the electrical system was repaired. In the second session, a rapidly moving cold front accompanied by thunderstorms closed Mirabel, thus shifting all operations to Dorval. Controllers had to redirect traffic to avoid the storms. In addition, the winds shifted, necessitating a change in the runways in use at Dorval. In the third session, after the storm had passed through Montreal, the winds shifted again and all takeoffs and departures were confined to one runway at Dorval. In these exercises the traffic level was reduced to an average of forty-one operations per hour, rather than the fifty-seven used in the previous terminal simulations. The reason for this is that in the real world, if conditions were so adverse, controllers would not accept a higher rate of traffic into the terminal area, and would simply request the en route controllers to hold traffic. Even so, the project team felt that the forty-one operations per hour was higher than controllers would actually accept. At the same time all this was occurring, the new listening watch tests were being conducted. Tom Fudakowski stood in the control room and at opportune moments instructed individual controllers to make mistakes so as to create losses of separation which pilots keeping a listening watch could detect.

Once again, the results of the exceptional situations study confirmed the previous two studies. There was little difference between the performance of the controllers on bilingual and unilingual days. As for the listening watch, the results were equivocal. Some controller errors were detected, but many were not. The listening watch did not appear to be foolproof. In order to gather more data, the members of the BICSS team studying the listening watch commissioned a search through the files of MOT, CATCA, and CALPA to find instances where pilots detected errors or where they had sufficient information to detect errors, but did not.

Altogether, the simulations provided 346 hours of controller data for MOT runs and eighty hours of CATCA runs. The simulations also provided information on simulator flights by 150 pilots, of whom 100 were commercial airline pilots and the rest members of COPA and AGAQ and MOT employees.

Following the completion of the simulator studies, the MOT members of the team went to work cleaning up the data and writing the reports. Throughout the study there had been some disagreements as to what should be counted as communications errors, and a number of team members had done samples and come up with different totals. Proulx and Fudakowski decided to do a final, official count. The convention they followed was to deny controllers the benefit of the doubt, and to count everything that might possibly be considered an error. Finally, Professor Stager went off to his cottage to do the statistical analysis of the data and write the final report.

The reader should not think that the results of the study convinced Tonner, Redden, and MacWilliam that bilingual air traffic control was as safe as unilingual control. They would only admit that they had failed to beat MOT at its own game. However, if CATCA and CALPA were to oppose bilingual air traffic control in the next set of hearings before the Commission of Inquiry, they would have to prove to the commission that MOT's game was unfair, a biased representation of the real world, and something that could not be taken seriously.

RECONCILIATION WITHIN THE AVIATION COMMUNITY

While the simulation exercises were being conducted, many other aspects of the conflict were being resolved by the aviation community. By the fall of 1977, it was clear that something needed to be done to improve relations between MOT and CATCA. The first step was taken when McLeish and his staff invited CATCA leaders to a weekend retreat outside Ottawa. In an informal setting, some progress was made in breaking down personal animosities and increasing understanding. Shortly after that, bargaining began anew for the next contract, which would cover the period beginning January 1, 1978. On January 27, a new contract was signed, in which the controllers received a 6 percent increase in total compensation, which was within the anti-inflation regulations.[8] However, MOT finally accepted CATCA's reclassification proposal, which increased salaries by an average of 4.6 percent. The two parties were able to reach an agreement without recourse to conciliation for the first time in CATCA's history.

One unfortunate residue of the pilots' strike was bitterness and mis-understanding between English and French members of the aviation community. A story told during the hearings before Justice Deschênes on Air Canada's Rule 14A exemplifies the depth of misunderstanding among pilots. A francophone Air Canada pilot was leaving Montreal on a flight to Montego Bay, and, after finishing his normal air / ground com-munications, he said farewell to the Montreal controller in the language of Molière, which angered his anglophone co-pilot. The francophone tried to discuss this with the anglophone, who would hear none of it and said he did not support bilingualism. Several hours later, over Cuba, the anglo-phone spoke English with air traffic control, but at the end of the conver-sation, said "adios," as it is the normal practice of pilots to bid farewell to controllers in their native tongue. The francophone pilot tried to tell the anglophone that it is no worse to salute a Cuban in Spanish than a Que-becker in French. The anglophone was not convinced: in fact, except for exchanges of information necessary to flying the aircraft, he refused to speak to his co-pilot for the rest of the month that they were together as crew.[9]

Sometime during 1977 and 1978 these hypersensitive attitudes began to change. CBC television luminary Patrick Watson described the aviation community as going to the edge of the chasm, even peering into it, and taking a step backward towards sanity and reason. The anglophone pilots, especially after the election of the Parti Québécois and the *Interim Report* of the Commission of Inquiry, began grudgingly to accept that the introduction of bilingual IFR communications was inevitable. The pilots were not convinced that bilingual air traffic control would ever be as safe as single-language control. However, the time and effort being put into the simulation studies instilled some confidence that the procedures developed to implement bilingualism would be thoughtful and compre-hensive, rather than unthinking and hasty, as they had feared when, in December 1975, Otto Lang first announced his intention to implement bilingual IFR air traffic control. Anglophone pilots began to realize that bilingualism was something they would have to learn to live with, in much the same way that they had learned to live with airport approach and runway utilization patterns dictated by noise abatement policies rather than by aeronautical efficiency.

Upon realizing this, anglophone pilots began once again to treat francophone controllers as professionals, and they, to respond in kind. Courtesy
began to reappear: anglophone pilots flying in Quebec now began their
transmissions with "Bonjour" and ended with "Salut," even though the
rest of the transmission was in English. One pilot described the practice as
a way of signalling to controllers "I'm okay, you're okay; I accept what
you are if you accept what I am."

Perhaps the final indication of the regained feelings of collegiality was
that the anglophones put away their "English is the international language
of aviation" and francophones their "il y a du francais dans l'air" buttons,
which were by then symbols of an era through which they had finally
passed.

In 1978, AGAQ's legal struggle drew to a close. On June 27, 1978, a
panel of three judges of the Court of Appeals rejected AGAQ's appeal
against Federal Court Judge Louis Marceau's decision upholding the con-
stitutionality of the Air Navigation Order restricting the use of French.[10]
The panel, consisting of Justices Louis Pratte, Gerald Le Dain, and G. M.
Hyde, was unanimous.

On July 24, AGAQ announced that it would not appeal this decision to
the Supreme Court. It was felt that the two judgments had proven the
ineffectiveness of the existing Official Languages Act in protecting their
rights, and it was now up to the politicians to amend the act. Furthermore,
AGAQ's objective was to have French introduced into aviation communications in Quebec. Since the simulation exercises by then had shown
that French could be used safely in air traffic control, it would be the
responsibility of MOT to see that the expected favourable recommendations of the Commission of Inquiry were implemented.[11] AGAQ's decision not to appeal could have created difficulties for MOT, because MOT
could no longer avoid prosecuting violations of the ANO on the grounds
that it was being contested before the courts. However, MOT took the
position that it did not wish to prosecute violations because such prosecu-
tions could be lengthy and would be made moot by the expected decision
of the Commission of Inquiry validating bilingual air traffic control.[12]
Meanwhile, the Quebec City controllers continued using French for IFR
operations: by midsummer, the number of instances recorded there had
passed 10,000.

After the Court of Appeals judgment, the francophone controllers
suffered one more setback. The Public Service Staff Relations Board, after
agonizing over SCAQ's certification request for fifteen months, announced
on September 26, 1978, that it would not certify SCAQ. The judgment
was not based on the "hidden agenda" issue of national unity, but dealt
more narrowly with the claims of CATCA and SCAQ.[13] The ruling upheld
CATCA's claims that it provided its Quebec members with typical union

representation, that its decisions were reached democratically, and that it had evolved over time towards a greater acceptance of the use of French on the job and within the union. However, the board denounced CATCA's refusal to sign its contracts in French as "a deplorable lack of sensitivity to the feelings of its francophone members many of whom, rightly or wrongly, perceived this as a policy designed to humiliate them."

Though CATCA won the case, it emerged from the process of the hearings a changed union. Jim Livingston and the other leaders of CATCA took the disaffiliation request sufficiently seriously that, not only did they prepare a thorough defence, but they modified their behaviour in some degree in order to influence the outcome. Though AGAQ issued the expected denunciation of the decision, the francophone controllers reacted calmly. Now that they were winning the battle for bilingualism within CATCA and in the simulation exercises, the certification request had lost its urgency.

The leadership of CATCA and CALPA changed during this period. Both Ken Maley and Jim Livingston, exhausted by the strike and the continuing battles over bilingualism, announced that they would not run again. Maley was succeeded by Captain Roland Cook as president of CALPA in November 1978 and Livingston by Bill Robertson as president of CATCA in June 1979.

THE BICSS REPORTS

On October 23, 1978, Proulx presented drafts of all the BICSS reports to the representatives of the interested organizations. A meeting was planned for November 6 and 7 to discuss suggested revisions, which would then serve as a basis for the final report. CATCA and CALPA felt that the results were unacceptable and that they would let the reports stand as MOT's position and present detailed critiques to the Commission of Inquiry. Proulx then obtained Otto Lang's authorization to make public the entire corpus of the report. In early January 1979, MOT released materials and working documents.[14]

The simulation exercises compared communications characteristics, communications errors, and losses of separation on unilingual and bilingual days. The analysis of communications characteristics determined that variations in the number and length of controller transmissions were largely determined by individual differences among controllers and very little by the difference between bilingual or unilingual conditions. Average controller transmissions were found to be slightly longer in French than in English in both the en route and terminal exercises. For example, in the terminal exercises, the controllers handling arrivals took an average of 3.1 seconds for a message in French and 2.9 seconds in English. This

TABLE 2
INCIDENCE AND NATURE OF CONTROLLER ERRORS

	Unilingual		Bilingual	
Type of Error	Errors	Rate[a]	Errors	Rate[a]
En route				
Errors excluding language	278	5.09	241	4.45
Language errors[c]				
False starts	0	0	32	0.59
Language change	1	0	11	0.20
Total errors	279	5.11	284	5.24
Number of transmissions	5,462		5,421	
Terminal				
Errors excluding language	1,009	5.01	982	4.95
Language errors[c]				
False starts	0	0	75	0.38
Language change	0	0	46	0.23
Total errors	1,009	5.01[b]	1,103	5.56
Number of transmissions	20,147		19,847	
En route and Terminal				
Errors excluding language	1,287	5.03	1,223	4.84
Language errors[c]				
False starts	0	0	107	0.42
Language change	1	0	57	0.23
Total errors	1,288	5.03[b]	1,387	5.49
Number of transmissions	25,609		25,268	

SOURCE: Transport Canada. *Report of the Bilingual IFR Communications Simulation Studies*, volume 1, *Summary Report and Recommendations* (Ottawa: Supply and Services Canada, 1979), pp. 149–51.

[a] Error rate is in errors per 100 transmissions.

[b] Differences statistically significant at 5 percent or better. (That is, we would expect the error rates to be lower in 95 out of 100 samples.)

[c] In a false start, the controller realizes before completing his transmission that he has been using the incorrect language. In a language change, he completes the transmission and realizes he has been using the incorrect language because the pilot does not respond.

was not of sufficient magnitude to affect the efficiency with which operations would be conducted.[15] In order to examine the impact of bilingualism on the efficiency of the overall system, the project team took photographs of the radar scopes at the end of the exercises and analysed departure and arrival times. The results showed a great similarity between bilingual and unilingual days, indicating that bilingualism caused no loss in system efficiency.[16]

Using data from phases I and II, analysis of controller errors identified a total of 1,387 errors, or 5.49 per 100 transmissions on the bilingual days. This was 8 percent higher than the 1,287 total errors (5.03 per 100 transmissions) found on unilingual days, a statistically significant difference. Of the 1,387 errors on bilingual days, 164 were traced to language use. Of those, 107 were false starts, in which a controller begins a transmission in the wrong language, and corrects himself before he has finished.[17] The other fifty-seven were language changes, a more serious error in which a controller completes a transmission in the incorrect language and, hearing no reply, must begin again in the correct language. A language change error occurred once per 430 transmissions. The findings are set out in Table 2.

These results seem to contradict CATCA's assumption that the increased workload due to bilingual communications would dramatically increase controllers' errors of all kinds. Furthermore, most of the language errors were false starts, which were less serious than incorrect language transmissions. The BICSS team felt that the relatively infrequent errors due to the use of two languages would be reduced when controllers gained experience working in a bilingual environment and when the JETS system provided an alphanumeric display that would distinguish French-speaking and English-speaking pilots.

Participants in the simulations, especially the pilots, were surprised and concerned by the high error rates in the exercises. In order to determine whether these were representative of the real world, the project team compared samples of several hours of unilingual control tower tapes and of unilingual simulation exercise tapes and found that the incidence of controller and pilot errors was indeed comparable.

The BICSS team also reviewed losses of separation, which were defined as instances when aircraft came closer to one another than the prescribed standard. The team identified fourteen losses of separation in the en route exercises of which seven occurred on unilingual days and seven on bilingual days. There were eighty-five losses of separation in the terminal exercises, forty on unilingual days and forty-five on bilingual days. In neither case was there a statistically significant difference in the rate at which losses of separation occurred. Ten were identified as more serious than the others: of these, four were on bilingual days and six on unilingual days. The BICSS team concluded that "from an operational viewpoint, language was not found to be the cause of any separation loss, and there was no evidence that language had influenced any particular operating irregularity."[18]

The BICSS team also reported on its listening watch study.[19] There were two major sources of data: pilot responses to the controller errors that Tom Fudakowski introduced into the simulation exercises and MOT and

CALPA records of losses of separation and incident reports. From the latter, the team compiled a list of seventy-two incidents which occurred between 1974 and 1978, where pilots either detected errors through the listening watch or failed to do so, even though they had sufficient information. The team recognized that the list was not exhaustive, because controllers and pilots are often reluctant to report errors, and because some go undetected.

Of a total of ninety-seven errors, thirty-two, or one-third, were detected by pilots. It was also found that the listening watch was more effective in the en route environment than in the terminal area because there is less traffic in the former and pilots are tuned in to each radio frequency for long periods of time. The study concluded that "the listening watch has some value in the existing system but technological innovations in progress and proposed (such as automated air-ground data interchange)... will in certain areas progressively limit the amount of information available to pilots from which to detect errors."[20]

The BICSS report followed the analysis with recommendations for changes in air traffic control procedures designed to minimize language errors and to compensate for the reduced effectiveness of the listening watch. Some of these were: having controllers provide traffic information for aircraft in holding patterns, encouraging pilots to use only one language in the course of a flight, and encouraging pilots to avoid confusion between English and French pronunciations of letters of the alphabet by using the ICAO phonetic alphabet (Alpha for A, Bravo for B, etc.).[21]

An unexpected benefit of the study was that some problems in nonlanguage aspects of control procedures came to light. For example, it was discovered that many controllers paid insufficient attention to pilots' readbacks of clearances and infrequently caught pilot errors. A number of changes in the air traffic controllers' Manual of Operations resulted from these findings.[22]

The final part of the BICSS package was an implementation plan. The critical factor affecting implementation was the shortage of controllers. At that time, there were seventy controllers at the Montreal centre, which had a required complement of ninety-two. Furthermore, the transfer of airspace from Moncton and the expansion of air traffic control services into northern Quebec would bring the required complement up to 155. The capacity of the Quebec region to train and absorb new controllers was limited to twelve per year. Therefore, the report did not envisage the completion of implementation until 1986. The cost of instituting the bilingual system was estimated at a net present value of $12,000,000, most of which would be for navigational aids, and expansion of the Montreal centre to handle all Quebec airspace.[23]

Though Proulx and the team members were confident that they had done a thorough and professional job in these studies, they were nevertheless apprehensive about having given their opponents such a large target to shoot at. They wondered whether CATCA and CALPA would be able to pick the studies apart, or whether they would flounder in the morass of the data.

THE COMMISSION'S SECOND SET OF HEARINGS: FEBRUARY AND MARCH 1979

The second set of hearings of the Commission of Inquiry was a far more restrained affair than the first. The topic was much narrower: did the case put forward by MOT in the BICSS documents for bilingual IFR air traffic control make sense? These hearings aroused much less interest in the press and the general public. After the change in English-Canadian opinion and the publication of the *Interim Report*, most observers took the outcome of these hearings to be a foregone conclusion: the press is never interested in foregone conclusions.

Many of the cast of characters did not change: the commissioners themselves, Commission Counsel Fortier and Graham, MOT Counsel Deschênes, and Jean-Luc Patenaude representing Quebec controllers. CALPA was represented by Bob MacWilliam because of his knowledge as a participant in all aspects of the simulation exercises. CATCA replaced the aggressive Colin Gravenor with Catherine MacLean, a junior partner in John Nelligan's law firm. MacLean had handled CATCA work previously, but the Commission of Inquiry was to be her first experience with expert witnesses and the minutiae of air traffic control procedure. The other aviation organizations were not represented for most of the hearings.

The hearings began on February 5 with Walter McLeish's general outline of the approach taken in the simulation exercises. Unlike his dramatic cross-examination at the previous hearings, this time he referred many of the questions to the more knowledgeable MOT witnesses who were to follow him.[24]

On February 6, MOT unveiled its four-headed witness: Pierre Proulx, Brian Walsh, Paul Stager, and Tom Fudakowski took the stand together to testify about the simulation exercises. For the next seven days of the hearings, this group was examined by Fortier and Graham about the methodology and results of the exercises and the recommendations. Then followed six days of cross-examination by Catherine MacLean and Bob MacWilliam. In the cross-examination, MacLean and MacWilliam both tried to establish the major points of their argument—that the simulations were unrealistic, that the listening watch is an important way of avoiding accidents, and that the study failed to test the listening watch adequately. The four witnesses coolly responded to their attackers. One advantage the four had was that if one of the group got into trouble, there was always someone else who could answer the question. However, they seldom got into trouble. MacWilliam and MacLean were rarely, if ever, able to get them to contradict one another: each, when asked, stood behind the others' testimony. The two inquisitors had a great deal of difficulty in assimilating all the materials in the BICSS reports, especially the statistical analysis, with which both were completely unfamiliar, and thus their questions were often more tentative and exploratory than cutting and revealing. (Presumably, both CALPA and CATCA could have hired their own experimental psychologists to analyse the data, but they probably felt that the small likelihood of this affecting the commission's final conclusions did not justify the expenditure.) Of the four, Professor Stager was the most difficult to cross-examine. He responded with long, complicated answers, bristling with professional terminology, which rarely gave Mac-William or MacLean an opportunity for difficult follow-up questions.

The MOT witnesses were then followed by a number of witnesses from the various organizations. The most interesting aspect of Bob Mac-William's testimony, elicited in examination by Yves Fortier, was that, as a result of the simulation exercises, he had modified his understanding of the listening watch.

> I might have even said before these tests and before we looked at the real world stuff, I might have even said that to a certain degree, you know, that this mental picture was an important thing, that you really kept track of everybody at all times, and to a certain extent in some airspaces I think you still do that. Not the total traffic but you certainly can keep track of two or three in a non-radar environment when there is only two or three airplanes. . . . it seems what [the pilot] does is constantly sift this information that he hears and almost subconsciously tries to bring those ones forward that he thinks might affect him and it is not involved with sort of geographically keeping track of the airplanes or anything of that nature, I think now, in my own opinion anyway, that that is how it is done rather than in this total big mental picture.[25]

Pierre Beaudry, still refusing to recognize the legitimacy of the commission, was forced by subpoena to testify. He argued that there were a number of francophone IFR pilots, himself included, who felt more at ease, and would therefore be safer, using French.

A key witness was Eric St. Denis, one of the CATCA subjects in the simulation exercises. Some of his testimony supported CATCA's position: he observed that pilots use the listening watch to learn about weather or traffic conditions and he personally decided to leave Montreal because he was uncomfortable with bilingual air traffic control. On the other hand, his statements about the realism of the exercises and the effectiveness of the listening watch provided strong confirmation of MOT's position. On the simulations, he said: "When in the terminal exercise the runway change came about, I found that we became quite intense about what we were doing. As a matter of fact, you almost felt like you were in a real pressure environment. Okay. It was really busy."[26] And on the listening watch, he said: "In the years that I have been [a controller] I have never that I can recall, had a pilot correct a mistake, or correct a transmission, or a read-back that may have been erroneous."[27] Walter McLeish and a number of the francophone controllers were present for the latter statement, and as soon as the hearing recessed, they gathered together, and with smiles and handshakes, anticipated imminent victory.

The two final witnesses were consultants to the commission whose task it was to review different aspects of the simulation exercises. Jean-Yves Frigon, a psychology professor at the University of Montreal, watched the simulation exercises and reviewed Stager's research design and results, and concluded that the work had been done very competently, with no important biases. John Keitz, an aviation consultant for R. Dixon Speas Associates, had been an observer at the simulation exercises. He concluded that the exercises were "conducted in a professional manner at all times."[28] Furthermore, "the air traffic control simulator at Hull is probably as good as or better than any other air traffic control simulator in the world."[29]

The final days of the hearings saw two controversial pieces of evidence entered into the record. CALPA wanted to enter a large number of reports of fact-finding boards investigating losses of separation which, it felt, illustrated the importance of the listening watch. CATCA objected because the reports, which mentioned individual controllers by name, were normally kept confidential. MOT objected because the use of the reports would implicitly involve throwing out the conclusions of the fact-finding boards and launching another investigation of each incident. The commissioners decided to accept the reports as evidence on which it would receive written submissions, but not to conduct public hearings on them.

In May 1978, Mr. R. Dixon Speas, the founder of the firm which served as consultant to the commission, submitted a personal brief expressing his opposition to bilingual IFR air traffic control in Quebec. At about the time he wrote the brief, Speas retired from the firm: furthermore, the firm, because its commission assignments, then still in progress, required complete neutrality, publicly dissociated itself from Speas' views. In his brief, Speas argued that, given present technology, he did not feel that bilingual IFR operations would be safe or efficient at Montreal because of the heavy traffic flow, the extended periods of bad weather, and the fatigue suffered by pilots arriving on international flights. To implement bilingual control would mean that airlines and pilots would be "dragged kicking and screaming against their will and best judgment into bilingual IFR operations [and] the emotional upheaval would represent a safety hazard."[30] This situation would lead to bad publicity for Canada within the aviation community.

The commission then heard the closing arguments of the major protagonists. Catherine MacLean, representing CATCA, presented two days of oral argument, while MOT, CALPA, and AGAQ produced long written submissions.

MacLean's argument, unlike Colin Gravenor's presentation at the first set of hearings, concentrated on the substance of the government's position, and dispensed with attacks on its motives. She began by advancing the controller workload argument, contending that "had the traffic levels been high enough and had the traffic been more complex this would have very probably resulted in a difference [between bilingual and unilingual systems] showing up in losses of separation."[31] She also criticized the exercises for undertaking no direct physical comparison of the stress controllers felt in the unilingual and bilingual contexts. Her argument contained a critique of the commission's study of the causes of accident: bilingual air traffic control could increase stress, which would result in controller errors leading to accidents, but which would not be attributed directly to bilingual air traffic control in accident reports. She also argued that there was no demand for bilingual IFR service because there were few, if any, unilingual francophones with IFR licences—as contrasted with the many unilingual francophones with VFR licences.

CALPA's written argument criticized shortcomings in the simulation exercises, argued that the BICSS team underestimated the importance of the listening watch, and criticized the procedures the team had developed to compensate for the loss of the listening watch.[32] For example, CALPA claimed that because the aircraft flight profiles were generated by computer and several aircraft were represented by the same clerk "pilot," the equivalent of real-world variation in voice communications and styles of flying had not been achieved in the tests. Because all the clerk "pilots" were sitting in the same room and could see each other, they would not interrupt each other. In the real world, with bilingual communications, interruptions could become more frequent because unilingual pilots would not realize when messages in the other language were completed.

The brief also argued that the actual data on the listening watch underestimated its effectiveness because they did not include instances where pilots did not report errors they corrected, while undetected errors almost invariably lead to losses of separation and were therefore included. Furthermore, the brief asked whether, if all the incidents entered into the evidence had occurred in a bilingual setting, the procedures would have been unfailingly applied and, even if they were, whether they would have been sufficient to avert disaster in every case. The brief then argued that the simulation exercises revealed a shocking frequency of errors and losses of separation, which raised doubts about the safety of the present IFR system. Introducing French would make it still more unsafe. CALPA's argument concluded by asking whether MOT had proven, beyond a reasonable doubt, that bilingual IFR control would not degrade safety. The pilots were sure it had not.

A written submission on behalf of the Quebec controllers was prepared by Patenaude, Beaudry, Louis Doucet, and Robert Fleury (a Montreal IFR controller), all of whom were given several days of paid leave for that purpose by the Quebec region of MOT. Their major contribution was to deal exhaustively with the problem of stray unilingual francophone pilots. They examined every possible situation in which it could occur, and outlined procedures to deal with each.

In the MOT written submission, Bernard Deschênes and Pierre Proulx attempted to defend the BICSS studies by refuting the CATCA-CALPA arguments and drawing upon the testimony of various witnesses to support its position.[33]

The realism of the simulations was defended in several ways. They showed that latencies (that is, delays in responding to messages) were close to equal for both the actual pilots flying aircraft simulators and the clerks acting as pilots. In response to the argument that the francophone controllers were motivated to perform better on bilingual days, Deschênes and Proulx reminded the commission that they had the offsetting handicap of inexperience with bilingual air traffic control.

Deschênes and Proulx responded to the listening watch argument by recalling Bob MacWilliam's testimony which "consistently used words such as perhaps, probably, very likely, you hear, little bits of information, speculate, you might hear, which indicates that he is admitting that a pilot does not have all the information required and he must speculate on the activities in his environment based on information overheard and partially understood."[34] Eric St. Denis' statement that he could not recall any instances of pilots correcting errors was also cited prominently. They responded to the fact-finding board reports by re-examining each of them and showing how the use of one or two languages would not have affected whether or not the pilot discovered controller errors through the listening watch. In one case, in which two 747s were approaching Mirabel for landing and one pilot responded erroneously to instructions to the other aircraft, they concluded that if the two pilots were using different languages this confusion would not have happened in the first place![35]

As for the difference in error rates between the bilingual and unilingual days, Proulx and Deschênes argued that the most important errors—losses of separation—occurred at the same rate. The difference in the rate of controller errors would be remedied because language errors would be compensated for by improved procedures and greater familiarity with bilingual control. Finally, they reminded the commission that the error rate for the simulations was similar to that for actual air traffic control tapes they reviewed. If CALPA thought that the existing system was unsafe, why were pilots not refusing to fly?

Finally, Proulx and Deschênes responded to the argument that the testimony had not proven that a demand existed for IFR service in French. The only real test of the claim would be to offer such service (thereby breaking the vicious circle of "pas de demande, pas de service, pas de demande") and see if the demand materialized. If CATCA and CALPA were correct, then there would be no demand and "in practice, we would be left with the present unilingual system."[36]

THE FINAL REPORT OF THE COMMISSION OF INQUIRY

The commissioners considered the evidence presented and on August 10 submitted their *Final Report* to Don Mazankowski, the minister of transport in the Conservative government, which was elected in May 1979. The report was a unanimous endorsement of the bilingual air traffic control program presented by MOT.

The commission concluded that the simulations were a valid comparison of bilingual and unilingual air traffic control.[37] The commissioners appear to have been impressed with St. Denis' testimony about the realism of the methodology and Frigon and Keitz's approval of the research design and results. The commission felt that the traffic in the simulations was sufficiently demanding to constitute a valid test and accepted Proulx's argument that making the traffic level any more demanding would have led controllers to reject the exercise. The commissioners noted that the similarity in latencies for real pilots and clerks simulating pilots indicated the exercises provided an accurate representation of pilot behaviour. The commission rejected CATCA's contention that controller stress was not tested directly, as it accepted Stager's argument that performance measures were the best indirect tests of stress. The judges also cited Beaudry's evidence (as well as Lemay's in the previous hearings) that the use of French put francophone pilots at ease, and therefore reduced stress for controllers. The commission's consultants monitored tapes at Geneva and Mexico City airports, both of which are bilingual and similar to Montreal in the level and types of traffic and found that the rates of false starts and language changes were lower than in the simulations or actually observed at Quebec City. This gave the commissioners confidence that more experience and better procedures would be able to reduce language errors at Montreal and Quebec City.

The commission expanded its review of aviation accidents by bringing its data up to date as of March 1979. Other than the Rio de Janeiro accident of 1960, no accidents were found where it could be concluded that "the use of two languages could have had anything to do with the accident."[38] It should be noted that a final report still had not been prepared on the Zagreb, Yugoslavia, accident by that time.

The commission then went on to consider three major arguments against bilingual air traffic control: the listening watch, the stray francophone pilot, and the complications of combining VFR and IFR traffic in a bilingual context.

The commission agreed with everyone else in the aviation community that the listening watch is important and that steps which diminish its effectiveness should be resisted unless they are required in the overall interest of safety.[39] However, the commission was impressed by the measures MOT would take to compensate for any diminution in the effectiveness of the listening watch due to bilingualism. The commission implied that CALPA's opposition to bilingual IFR control on the grounds of the listening watch argument was less than sincere because CALPA had not opposed the imposition of alphanumeric radar displays, even though this was projected to reduce voice communications by 30 to 50 percent, and therefore also reduce effectiveness of the listening watch. The commission side-stepped detailed comment on the incidents discussed in the listening watch study and the CALPA and MOT briefs. It agreed with Frigon's testimony that an empirical comparison of accident rates in bilingual and unilingual countries would be a more effective way to test the listening watch argument than through laboratory simulation exercises. The report then remarked that the accident study had done just that, and concluded that bilingual air traffic control was safe.[40]

The commission rejected the stray unilingual francophone pilot argument because there was little evidence that such pilots, either by design or inadvertently, strayed into airspace in which they would not be linguistically competent, either in Quebec or the rest of the world, and because it felt that procedures suggested by AGAQ to handle the problem could be implemented. At the very worst, the problem could be handled as a total communications failure, for which procedures had also been developed.[41]

The commission felt that the strongest evidence that it was possible to mix IFR and VFR operations safely in two languages at a major airport was that this was being done quite effectively—without accidents and without special procedures—at Geneva and Mexico City, two airports with similar traffic levels and mixes to Dorval.[42]

The commission finally considered R. Dixon Speas' personal brief against bilingual air traffic control.[43] His argument that it would not work in Montreal was rejected by noting that Mexico City, Geneva, and Orly (Paris) are three airports which are similar to Montreal in almost every relevant criterion (traffic load, VFR/IFR mix, language mix, level of international traffic, extent of bad weather) and where bilingual air traffic control is working. Speas' argument about emotional upheavals and bad publicity were something the commissioners had heard before: in fact, the commission's existence itself was the response, and, it was hoped, the solution, to those problems.

With all the arguments cleared out of the way, the rest of the report was devoted to detailed recommendations about the implementation of bilingualism in general and at specific airports. By and large, the recommendations followed those made in the BICSS studies.

The commissioners had spoken: how would the politicians respond?

THE CABINET DECISION AND INDUSTRY AND PUBLIC REACTION

From the time Joe Clark and his Conservative government took office, bilingual air traffic control was a concern. Clark felt it was essential for his government to establish credibility in Quebec: his handling of this issue would be the first real test of his ability to respond to Quebec's demands. He was very much concerned about how the right wing of his party, in particular the backbenchers who had been so vocal in their support of CATCA and CALPA, would respond to the report of the Commission of Inquiry.

Transport Minister Don Mazankowski was also concerned. While he knew that the party's official position of accepting whatever the commission recommended was quite tenable, he was worried about how to avoid any dispute with CATCA and CALPA. Shortly after he became transport minister, Mazankowski approached both Roland Cook, the new president of CALPA, and Bill Robertson, the new president of CATCA, to introduce himself. One of the topics which came up in these initial discussions was, of course, bilingual air traffic control. Mazankowski told both men that he would make no decision until he received the report of the Commission of Inquiry and that he would consult them as soon as he received it.

Mazankowski and Clark both received copies of the *Final Report* of the Commission of Inquiry on Monday, August 13. They read it carefully, and were heartened because it was clear, unequivocal, and, most important of all, unanimous in its support for bilingual air traffic control. Mazankowski personally contacted the leaders of CATCA, CALPA, and COPA, and had Pierre Proulx contact AGAQ. Mazankowski told them the general tenor of the report and reiterated his government's policy of accepting and implementing a unanimous report. He told them he would be making an announcement soon to that effect. In these conversations, Mazankowski, Cook, and Robertson all expressed their own political concerns. Both Cook and Robertson, recognizing that they had had their day in court and lost, wanted to save face. In addition, they wanted to be involved in the implementation process. Mazankowski, for his part, wanted to avoid any political controversy. Furthermore, he was troubled by the promise of a free vote which Otto Lang had made three years before. It was not clear whether he was legally bound by Lang's promise. However, a decision to have the vote would keep the issue alive until Parliament met in October and could embarrass the government if some Conservative backbenchers chose to vote against bilingual air traffic control. Mazankowski told Cook and Robertson that he would prefer not to have the free vote, but that he would have it if they so demanded. Cook and Robertson both responded that the issue was not very important to them personally, but that they could not commit their organizations to releasing Mazankowski from Lang's agreement. Their response would ultimately depend on the reactions of their members, as well as that of the general public, to the report. No deals were made in these discussions. However, the mutual understanding of priorities made it possible for both the government and the aviation organizations to act in such a way as to avoid the free vote.

On Thursday, August 16, an event occurred which was both a personal loss and a political opportunity for Clark and Mazankowski. John Diefenbaker died in Ottawa: his elaborate funerary rites in the following days captured national attention and pushed bilingual air traffic control off the front pages.

Following his consultation with the aviation organizations, Mazankowski had his officials prepare a short memorandum to Cabinet, recommending acceptance of the report of the Commission of Inquiry, and proposing that the announcement be made as soon as possible. The free vote was to be ignored at that time.

On Sunday afternoon, following Diefenbaker's funeral, Mazankowski met with Cloutier and McLeish to prepare a press release announcing the decision. For Cloutier and McLeish, this was a victory, and their draft release reflected this perception. Mazankowski's concern was that the statement be as low-key as possible, and he toned down their draft.

The Cabinet document, with the press release appended, was presented to the Inner Cabinet on Monday, August 20, and was accepted with little debate. Clark made clear the government's policy, as well as its political priorities. Mazankowski made it clear that he would handle the announce-ment and any resulting political flak.

On Monday, the Gens de l'Air, wishing to ensure that the government went along with the Commission of Inquiry report without any further delay, informed the Quebec press of its contents. *Le Devoir* and *Le Soleil* both carried reports on the commission's conclusions on Tuesday.[44] Mon-day evening Prime Minister Clark had his first meeting with Premier Lévesque, and told him what the Cabinet had decided.

On Tuesday, Transport Minister Mazankowski made the formal an-nouncement of the Cabinet's acceptance of the *Final Report*. The announcement was low-key, as the aviation organizations wished. Mazankowski thanked the commissioners for their efforts, and praised their report as "most comprehensive" and "painstaking in detail." Finally, he announced the formation of an implementation team and pro-mised that it would work "in close consultation with the interested avia-tion associations."[45]

CATCA and CALPA took their cue from Mazankowski and responded in an equally low-key fashion. Both organizations admitted that they had had a fair hearing and therefore accepted the commission's conclusions. They also stated their intention of continuing their involvement in the implementation process.[46]

AGAQ's reaction, expressed by Roger Demers, in a press conference on August 22, was a mixture of satisfaction at the result, disdain at the time and difficulty required to prove something which it considered self-evident, and pressure to make sure that the implementation, in particular the transfer of airspace to the Quebec region, would be followed up promptly. Finally, Demers hoped that the improvement in relations between anglophone and francophone pilots and controllers would facili-tate the implementation process.[47]

The airlines were calm about the decision. Air Canada announced that its few all-francophone crews would be allowed to use French in commu-nications with air traffic control as soon as the report was implemented. All the foreign carriers quietly accepted the change.[48]

At the political level, there was also widespread approval. Former Prime Minister Trudeau congratulated the Conservatives on their deci-sion. He also suggested that the government conduct the free vote because "a unanimous vote could help to dispel any concerns about a backlash to the report."[49] One wonders if Trudeau did not prefer a free vote for precisely the same reason Mazankowski wished to avoid it.

The Quebec government did its best to be critical of the decision. Louis O'Neill, communications minister, while admitting it was a good deci-sion, said "It's ridiculous that in Canada it takes three years to decide this while in other places they've been using two languages in air communications for years.''[50] Transport Minister Lucien Lessard was more expansive. He called the decision insignificant ("They've given birth to a mouse") and feared that there would be "interminable delays" in implementation. Keith Spicer aptly dismissed Lessard's criticism as "dog-without-a-bone-sniping" and asked "Why do Lessard and his PQ colleagues hate this end to aviation insanity? Because it denies them a pre-referendum replay of the English-French holy war they so brilliantly exploited to fly into power."[51]

The English-Canadian backlash which Mazankowski feared did not occur. Twenty-five major English newspapers throughout the country wrote editorials on the government's decision. Of these, only one expressed complete opposition (*Toronto Sun*), and five (*London Free Press, Vancouver Province, Victoria Times, Winnipeg Tribune, St. John's Telegram*) qualified their approval. Syndicated columnists were overwhelming in their approval. Very few citizens wrote letters to newspapers or to Mazankowski. Indeed, in the public mind, the dispute had been settled long ago, and the government's decision came almost as a dénouement.

IMPLEMENTATION AND KEY ACTORS' RETROSPECTIONS

The implementation process has moved along quite smoothly. Bilingual VFR operations were authorized on January 3, 1980, at Mirabel and April 1, 1980, at Dorval: thus VFR service in French is now available at all Quebec airports. Bilingual IFR operations were authorized beginning May 30, 1980. The Air Navigation Order was changed accordingly. No controllers were prosecuted for using French without authorization.

The use of French for VFR operations has grown quite dramatically in recent years. One major reason is that a significant constraint on the use of French was loosened when in November 1978, the Department of Communications amended the rules for aeronautical radio operators' licences to allow unilingual francophones to qualify without any knowledge of English, provided they fly only in areas where bilingual air traffic control is available. As a result, 80 percent of the VFR operations at the original five airports designated bilingual in 1974 now use French. French usage at St. Hubert has also grown to the point that 30 percent of its operations are now in French.

Only 3 to 5 percent of all IFR operations throughout the province are in French. One factor holding this percentage down is that there are very few all-francophone crews flying for the major carriers. This percentage is expected to increase as more francophones take jobs as pilots. Pierre Proulx, who is now director of air traffic services, predicts that the maximum level to which French use could increase is 20 percent of IFR operations.

The new JETS radar displays were installed in Montreal in November 1980. In order to help controllers avoid errors, English-speaking pilots' aircraft are represented with circles and those of French-speakers with triangles. Controllers also use a yellow marker on flight progress strips for French-speaking pilots.

The relocation program ultimately gave rise to an important legal decision. Don Kelso, the controller who refused to give up his incumbent's rights, appealed his transfer to Cornwall in the Federal Court, but lost. He then appealed to the Supreme Court, which overturned the Federal Court. The Supreme Court ruling means that unilingual public servants cannot be forced to surrender their incumbents' rights, and could be a significant precedent.[52]

A few words remain to be said about the major protagonists. Otto Lang, following his defeat in the 1979 election, became an executive of a major grain company. He admits that his oversight in the Keenan affair was in failing to anticipate that political pressure would force Keenan to resign.[53] However, he feels vindicated by the eventual outcome, and believes that the infamous agreement was successful in clearing the way for it. Others on the government side share this sense of vindication. Walter McLeish, who retired as air administrator in September 1982, recounts his feelings this way:

> I feel totally comfortable with the result. I once stood alone in the department, and inched my way, with no support here at MOT and with the premeditated impatience of AGAQ and the programmed negativism of CATCA and CALPA. I feel I provided leadership to steer a course that will be positive for air traffic services and for the country as a whole.[54]

Sylvain Cloutier, remembering bilingual air traffic control as one of the most complicated issues he has ever encountered, also takes pleasure in the outcome and in the "unity of thought and action [that characterized] how closely the Lang, Cloutier, McLeish trio had operated throughout that period."[55] Similarly, Proulx, Fudakowski, Walsh, and Stager all derived a great deal of satisfaction from the simulation exercises, which they feel were competently and thoroughly done, despite the great organizational difficulties.

On the other side of the controversy, Ken Maley has returned to Canadian Pacific as a pilot, and Jim Livingston, overcoming his six-year absence from operational controlling, checked out as an IFR controller in the Halifax terminal unit. Livingston emerged from his six years as president with a great sense of relief that he had held his union together in a very difficult period. As CATCA past-president, he continues to be involved in association activities, including some liaison with the Mont-real controllers. That he has been able to do this is, he feels, evidence of the francophones' respect for his sense of fairness.

The original leaders of AGAQ have also moved on to other things. Roger Demers returned to his job as a pilot for the Quebec Government Aviation Service: the new president of AGAQ is Michel Doyon, a Quebec City lawyer and private pilot. Pierre Beaudry completed his studies in law and business administration at Laval University, with scholarship support from Transport Canada. He is at present an executive assistant to the president of Quebecair. Jean-Luc Patenaude is a supervisor in the Quebec City control tower. Patenaude sees the strike and hearings as the high-water mark of his career, in comparison to which his present work lacks excitement. Ever the challenger of practices he thinks unjustified, he recently submitted a grievance demanding that smoking be forbidden in the control tower. His argument was that the lateral smoke inhaled by non-smoking controllers had deleterious health effects which might lead them to fail the annual medical examinations required to maintain their licences.[56] Unfortunately for the non-smokers' cause, MOT did not accept Patenaude's grievance.

On the part of all the major protagonists (Lang, Cloutier, McLeish, Livingston, and Maley) there is a very strong sense of regret at mistakes that were made and at the intensity of the conflict and the depth of the personal antipathies that resulted. Furthermore, there are francophone controllers who, while feeling vindicated, still share some anger that the process took so long. Also, many of the controllers who left Montreal resent what they feel was unjust treatment. While the aviation community has collectively survived this quarrel, there are individuals who bear scars that time does not easily heal.

THE FUTURE OF BILINGUAL AIR TRAFFIC CONTROL

It is clear that the air traffic control system finally has been able to accom-modate the demands of francophone pilots and controllers to use French in Quebec, and has moved to a new state of equilibrium. The reader might wonder whether this new linguistic equilibrium is stable, or whether there are factors which could upset it once again. Clearly, the major factor which could cause disruption is an attempt by francophone pilots to com-municate with air traffic controllers in French outside the province of Quebec. If this were widespread, MOT would be faced with the unenvi-able choice of disciplining these pilots and retaining a unilingual system or providing bilingual controllers throughout much of Canada. The former action would be seen as a failure by the government to implement the Official Languages Act and continued evidence of the second-class status of French. The latter course would create great conflict with CATCA, which would fight to preserve the jobs of unilingual anglophone controllers, and would also be very difficult to implement, because a large number of bilingual controllers would have to be trained. At present, there is a shortage of bilingual controllers even for the Quebec region, which is not expected to be alleviated until 1986.

Is this a likely scenario in the near future? Probably not. Let us consider the likely behaviour of francophone VFR and IFR pilots. VFR pilots generally do not fly very far from their home base: thus, unilingual francophone VFR pilots will not create a demand for bilingual air traffic control far outside the borders of Quebec. They can probably be handled through the provision of bilingual VFR service in northern New Brunswick, the national capital region, northern Ontario, and possibly eastern Ontario, the most likely destinations to which they would fly. In fact, at the present time, there is already some French used informally for VFR communications in northern New Brunswick. Providing bilingual air traffic control in these areas, if done gradually, would involve a relatively small number of positions, so that a peaceful accommodation could be reached with CATCA. This prediction also assumes that pilots belonging to francophone minorities outside Quebec who use French at home and English at work will accept the use of English when conversing with air traffic control, which seems likely.

Francophones who wish to use French for IFR, with their greater mobility, could create a demand for bilingual service far beyond the borders of Quebec. However, if, as in the past, holders of IFR licences tend to be those of higher socio-economic status, it is likely that they will be sufficiently bilingual that they can use English outside Quebec. Furthermore, since English continues to be the language of international aviation, francophones with IFR licences have a strong incentive to develop their knowledge of aviation English so as to be able to fly in the United States and other countries. Nevertheless, there is still the problem that francophones with IFR licences who fly in French in Quebec may run into difficulty outside Quebec because of stress or because they overestimated their skill in English. It is conceivable that MOT could respond to this problem by going beyond the "stray unilingual francophone pilot" procedures to ensure that there are one or two bilingual controllers available at the various centres outside Quebec for such emergencies. If the number of controllers required is small, this could be done without jeopardizing the jobs of unilingual anglophones and antagonizing CATCA.

Another factor upon which the stability of the present system depends is the high level of bilingualism of Quebec controllers. The present generation of Quebec controllers (people like Patenaude, Beaudry, and Doucet) acquired their English-language skills before joining MOT and refined them through instruction in English and experience in the years when the Montreal and Quebec centres were English-only environments. The new generation of Quebec controllers will have less experience with English, for several reasons. More of their training is in French. Because teamwork is essential in air traffic control and because francophones, regardless of how bilingual they are, prefer to speak French with one another, French is used almost exclusively for conversations among controllers in the Montreal and Quebec centres. Thus, they will be using English mainly to converse with English-speaking pilots flying in Quebec. However, there is no reason to believe that their English-language skills will not be sufficient to handle that traffic. Their language patterns will simply be closer to those of the bilingual controllers in Switzerland and France, whose performance was examined by the Commission of Inquiry and found to be safe and efficient. The new francophone controllers will be comparable to many members of the managerial and professional classes of Quebec francophones, who are now working mainly in French, but who retain sufficient skill in English to be able to communicate with the English-speaking North American milieu.[57]

All told, the new status quo in air traffic control language is reflective of the linguistic status quo in Canada, in which there is not perfect equality between the two official languages, but in which the use of French (especially at the elite level) in Quebec has increased dramatically and in which there is greater, though far from perfect, availability of French services outside Quebec. The struggle of the Gens de l'Air brought the air traffic control system from complete English dominance to something comparable to other sectors of Quebec society. Whether francophones will want to bring the air traffic control system to a state of complete equality between the two languages and whether English Canadians would accept it remains to be seen, just as it remains to be seen in other sectors of society. There is considerable ambivalence on the part of francophones, as reflected in the common nationalist sentiment, that strengthening the use of French in Quebec is much more important than increasing its availability across the country.[58] The sentiment may make the status quo in air traffic control language a durable one. However, if francophones demand the increased availability of French for air traffic control across the country, one hopes its provision can be accomplished with less conflict than in the past. The Commission of Inquiry has already resolved the safety issue, which was the source of so much emotionalism in the past, so that future questions of the language of air traffic control may be dealt with on the more practical level of economic interests. Finally, the precedent of the struggle itself might serve as a lesson to pilots, controllers, and MOT bureaucrats to temper extremism and induce compromise.

Chapter Eleven

Conclusions and Implications

If men could learn from history, what lessons it might teach us. But passion and party blind our eyes, and the light which experience gives us is a lantern on the stern, which shines only on the waves behind us.

Samuel Taylor Coleridge

Though mindful of Coleridge's melancholy dictum, this chapter discusses the major themes of the story, relating them to the relevant academic literature and drawing out their implications for future research on and our understanding of similar situations.

THE NATURE OF LINGUISTIC CONFLICT

Both analysts and policy makers have viewed the conflict between English and French Canadians as a struggle for organizational power, namely the ability to determine the linguistic and cultural characteristics of key institutions.[1] Such policies as the francization programs of both Liberal and Parti Québécois governments in Quebec and the federal government's attempt to increase bilingualism within the public service have had as a major goal the increasing of the organizational power of French Canadians relative to English Canadians. Both policies have achieved real success: the representation of French Canadians within the Quebec commercial elite and within the upper echelons of the federal civil service has increased dramatically.[2] Furthermore, this transformation of Canadian society has come about relatively peacefully. The bilingual air traffic control controversy was exceptional, in that it involved the sharpest confrontation in the workplace between the two groups that has been witnessed in recent years. This section attempts to show why this was the case. Two

220

episodes in the controversy are examined, the conflict at the Montreal control centre and the pilots' strike.

Other writers have interpreted both events as being motivated by the narrowest definition of economic self-interest, that is, the preservation of one's job, on the anglophone side, and, on the francophone side, self-advancement by taking an anglophone's job.[3] My analysis demonstrates that the discord in both instances was motivated by a broader struggle for organizational power and by conflicting notions of professional ethics, as expressed by the safety issue.

Finally, the discussion of the situation at the Montreal control centre has implications for determining the conditions under which it is possible for any bilingual organization to be stable, in the sense that it does not become unilingual, in either French or English.

THE MONTREAL CONTROL CENTRE CONFLICT

Consider, first, the motivations of the Quebec City controllers who began the struggle for bilingual air traffic control. The two major spurs to action were the belief that aviation safety would be increased by providing service in French to unilingual francophone pilots flying VFR, and the feeling that, by exercising their right to work in their mother tongue, they were asserting their human dignity. They were not struggling for jobs as controllers, since they already had them. The fact that, by 1974, almost everyone in the Quebec tower and centre was francophone, or at least bilingual, meant that French was the common language of communication. This made the use of French for transmissions to pilots the logical next step. The controllers considered the problem in terms of their professional ethic of safety, and, as Jean-Luc Patenaude so eloquently pointed out, concluded that they could live with their consciences more readily if they used French.

The drive by francophone controllers in the Montreal centre to use French had both similarities with and differences from that in Quebec City. They, too, were not fighting for prestigious jobs as controllers, because they also had them. Safety was a concern to them, though perhaps less so than to the Quebec City controllers, because they did not think that the use of French for IFR operations in Montreal would increase safety (as was the case for VFR operations in Quebec City) but rather that bilingual IFR operations could be just as safe as unilingual IFR operations. More relevant was their right to use French as their language of work. Why, however, was it necessary for them, literally, to fight for this right?

The presence of approximately sixty unilingual English-speaking controllers at the centre made it impossible for French to be used at all.

Teamwork is important in IFR air traffic control and any overheard conversations must be understood. With this large group of unilingual anglophones, there would always be at least one or two on a shift, so the only way that the requisite teamwork could be provided was if everyone spoke English. Not only did the francophone controllers, like the overwhelming majority of all bilingual francophones, prefer to speak French with one another, but they came to view the denial of this right by a unilingual anglophone minority as a grave insult.

Analysed as an organizational pyramid, the Montreal centre was francophone at the top (since the regional administrator and his senior staff were all francophone), francophone at the bottom, but with a layer of unilingual anglophones in the middle, primarily in the senior operational and supervisory IFR positions. This is a sharp contrast with what Breton and Grant have pointed out is the pattern in many businesses in Quebec: there, the senior management are unilingual anglophones, the workers at the bottom are unilingual francophones, and there is a "belt" of bilingual francophones in the middle who, both figuratively and literally, translate communications between top and bottom. Over time, as francophones have advanced within the organizations, the bilingual belt has moved higher up the pyramid.[4] This pattern is consistent with peaceful and gradual change, because most francophones in the organization are able to use their own language and because, over time, francophones come to occupy higher and higher positions. On the other hand, the pattern in the Montreal centre led to revolutionary change. Because the francophones were frustrated in their desire to use French under any circumstances by the anglophone "irreductibles" (an apt term of reference, indeed), they chose to speak French in order to make the anglophones either conform to their practice or leave the centre.

The francophone revolution at the Montreal centre succeeded, and the unilingual anglophones (as well as a number of bilingual controllers) left. Now French alone is used for conversations among controllers within the centre and for conversations between controllers and management, while both languages are used for conversations with pilots.

An interpretation of this struggle based on narrow economic self-interest would argue that the francophone operational controllers pushed the anglophones out in order to take over the supervisory positions. However, this conflicts with the fact that operational controllers hold their supervisors, who often can no longer check out on the radar, in low esteem. A collectivist interpretation would respond that the francophone operational controllers did not want to become supervisors themselves: they wanted to have francophone supervisors. A second difficulty with the narrow economic interpretation is that there were some bilingual francophone controllers who sided with the unilingual anglophones because they believed that unilingual IFR control was safer.

The situation at the Montreal centre has some interesting implications for organizational language use. Organizational bilingualism often derives from the requirement to provide service to the public in both languages, which can be called external bilingualism. In many instances this is easy to achieve, in that very few people in the organization need to deal with the public and the communications are sufficiently restricted in scope that a high level of second language knowledge is not required.

On the other hand, internal bilingualism could be much more problematic. In jobs requiring teamwork, there will be a strong preference on the part of bilinguals to use their mother tongue because implicit to teamwork is the understanding of overheard conversations. Anyone who speaks a second language less than perfectly knows that he is more effective when speaking directly to the other party, when there is no background noise, or more generally, when the ratio of signal to noise is high. What distinguishes our mother tongue is that we can function more effectively in it at very low signal-to-noise ratios. Furthermore, since research has shown that bilinguals strongly prefer to use their mother tongue when talking to bilinguals of the same mother tongue, we can conclude that if a feature of an organization is a need for teamwork and there is a preponderance of bilinguals of one mother tongue (rather than a balance of both), the organization will tend over time to become unilingual, even though all its members are bilingual.[5] Furthermore, the bilinguals whose mother tongue is unused may tend to leave the organization.

On the other hand, the sort of organization that could maintain a true bilingualism is one that is segmentable, in the sense that individuals do a great deal of their work alone or in small units where many conversations involve small groups working face-to-face, in which it is possible for people to feel relatively comfortable using their second language. Such a structure could even tolerate the presence of a substantial proportion of unilinguals, as long as unilinguals of different languages need not converse directly with one another, or can find a bilingual to act as translator. In this type of organization, as well, one would expect that having roughly equal proportions of individuals of both mother tongues would contribute to stable organizational bilingualism.

The line of research suggested by these considerations is the quantitative exploration, probably by means of simulation modelling, of the stability of language use in organizations. This research would be somewhat similar in spirit to Schelling's work on neighbourhood stability.[6] Schelling presents neighbourhoods consisting of two groups, each of whose members is assumed to be unwilling to be in the immediate vicinity of more than a given percentage of individuals of the other group. In some cases, the only outcome that satisfies all individual preferences is total segregation. A linguistic analogue to Schelling's model would be much more complicated, since it would deal with four groups (anglophones and francophones, bilingual and unilingual) as well as individual preferences for language use and considerations of efficiency (such as the need for teamwork). The findings of such models could be of interest to students of language policy by providing information about how to set up groups within organizations that would be viably bilingual, rather than gravitating towards a unilingual equilibrium.[7] For instance, one might discover that representation of francophones in proportion to their share of the total population (27 percent) is insufficient to sustain an internally bilingual organization under a wide range of assumptions.

THE PILOTS' STRIKE

The organizations involved in these events displayed a wide variety of motives, which went beyond narrow economic self-interest. Consider CATCA first. In mid-1975, CATCA irrevocably lost its struggle to prevent the designation of the Quebec region IFR jobs as bilingual, when Jean Chrétien upheld his staff's designation. This meant that all future IFR controllers in Quebec would have to become bilingual. Moreover, a few months later, as a result of the conflict at the Montreal centre, CATCA admitted that it could no longer preserve these jobs for their anglophone incumbents. Bill Robertson's memo of December 18, 1975, which concluded that the unilingual anglophones should be moved out of the centre as quickly as possible, is compelling evidence of that admission.[8] Finally, the CATCA council gave its formal recognition of the change at the Montreal centre at its meeting in early March 1976, at which it accepted bilingualism among Quebec controllers.[9] All told, the evidence makes it clear that from early 1976 onward, CATCA was no longer fighting to save the jobs of unilingual anglophone controllers in Montreal. The anglophones in Montreal themselves were aware of this and used their own organization (the Committee of Eight) rather than CATCA to protect their own interests.

Even though CATCA, by 1976, was no longer fighting for the jobs of the Montreal anglophones, there is evidence that the controllers were fighting perceived future threats to their material interests. This concern took two forms: first, a realization that the controllers who were transferring out of Montreal, by filling vacant positions in the receiving regions, were diminishing opportunities for controllers already there (such as a Montreal IFR controller stepping into an IFR job at Toronto centre to which Toronto tower controllers aspired), and second, the fear that the bilingualism policy would spread beyond Quebec, thereby requiring controllers in other parts of the country to be bilingual. The controllers' first worry was quite well founded: MOT refused to agree to CATCA's request that controllers leaving Montreal overstaff positions in the receiving regions in order to preserve promotional opportunities for the controllers already there. As for the second factor, one can make a strong case that the spread of French-speaking air traffic control far beyond Quebec was most unlikely. Otto Lang and Walter McLeish had said many times that they had no intention of expanding it to any place outside of Quebec other than Ottawa and possibly Moncton. The controllers had realized by the spring of 1976 the difficulties MOT was encountering in filling the newly bilingual positions in Quebec. How rapidly, therefore, could bilingual positions in the rest of Canada be filled? Furthermore, how attractive would it be to francophone controllers to work in parts of English Canada where their families would face the threat of assimilation? However, these arguments only show that the spread of bilingual air traffic control beyond Quebec was unlikely, though not impossible. If the anglophone controllers sincerely believed that the government was determined to spread bilingual air traffic control as far as possible, albeit in the long-run, and that francophone pilots would create a demand for the use of French outside of Quebec, then one might see how they could fear that the loss of their jobs was possible.

In this situation, the nature of the controllers' fears depended heavily on the signals received from MOT. As will be discussed in the next section, the fact that Otto Lang and Walter McLeish often appeared to act as partisans on the francophone side gave them cause for concern. Furthermore, the role of the Quebec Liberal caucus in supporting the Montreal controllers who wanted to use French and in contributing to the pressure which led John Keenan to resign, weakened the controllers' faith that Lang or McLeish could serve as effective mediators and stand up to the pressure from Quebec.

The safety issue was also of great concern to the controllers. The Clarke Institute of Psychiatry conducted an occupational health study of controllers in the Ontario region, sending out questionnaires in June and October 1976 and April 1977. The responses indicated a much higher level of stress in the first mailing, at the time of the strike, and the major cause given by the controllers was the bilingualism dispute.[10] Quite likely, this increased level of stress was responsible for the abnormally high rate at which losses of separation were occurring in the skies over English Canada in May and June 1976. In their responses to the Clarke Institute questionnaire, the controllers based their opposition to bilingualism both on material factors (the threat to job security and their resentment of the controllers relocating from Montreal), and the safety argument, rather than on one or the other.

225

In what way did these controllers think bilingual air traffic control was unsafe? They had generally not witnessed it in operation, and therefore could not imagine how anyone could control as efficiently or safely in two languages as in one. Though they conceded that bilingual control could be conducted in a VFR environment with little traffic, they were certain it would be impossible in a busy IFR environment. The listening watch argument, while mentioned, was less central to their view than it was to the pilots', since the controllers believed that pilots rarely caught their errors.

For the controllers the safety argument was also related to their perception that MOT was unable to put technical priorities ahead of political considerations. The controllers had been taught detailed procedures and had been indoctrinated in their importance: they knew that the claim that they had followed procedures was the best defence at a fact-finding board investigation of a loss of separation. They felt that the informal use of French before proper procedures were developed was unsafe, although, because of political pressure, MOT would accept it as a fait accompli. In his discussions with CATCA, Walter McLeish always said that the flow of traffic would be reduced, if necessary, to maintain safety standards. However, the controllers did not believe him. They felt that the airlines and the passengers would exert pressure on MOT, which McLeish would be unable to resist, to increase the traffic flow, even at the expense of safety.

A final factor that might be considered to have motivated the anglophone controllers was simply bigotry. Indeed, actions by some of CATCA's anglophone members, such as the circulation of stickers showing a beaver aviator strangling a frog aviator, were clearly racist.[11] This behaviour might be explained sociologically. The controllers generally have a moderate level of formal education. Sociological studies have shown that English Canadians' tolerance for the aspirations of French Canadians is positively correlated with formal education.[12] Why this occurs is not clear: the educational curriculum might inculcate a value of tolerance towards French Canadians or the individuals who receive higher education might, because of their socio-economic backgrounds, be more inclined to tolerance of French Canadians. At any rate, the result is that we can expect the controllers to show a lower "background" level of sympathy for French Canadians to moderate the expression of their material and professional interests than would a group with a higher level of educational attainment.

Perhaps the best indication of the feelings of the anglophone controllers was the widespread support for a strike, particularly in the west, indicated in two strike votes. If the major factors motivating them were simply concern over the reduced opportunities caused by relocating Montreal controllers and fear that units would imminently be identified as bilingual, we would expect to have seen the strongest support for the strike in Ontario and the Atlantic region, since they were receiving the greatest number of relocating controllers, and Moncton, Ottawa, and northern Ontario were in the greatest danger of becoming bilingual in the near future. The very high level of solidarity indicates that the anglophones were motivated by a number of other factors, such as the fear of bilingual air traffic control spreading from sea to sea, the professional concerns embodied in the safety argument, and their overall mistrust of MOT.

It is unlikely that the anglophone pilots belonging to CALPA were acting to protect their own jobs because bilingual air traffic control requires the controller, and not the pilot, to be bilingual. The pilots were sufficiently well informed to realize that MOT's proposals would not diminish the availability of English for air traffic control in Quebec. Furthermore, the major Canadian airlines, such as Air Canada and CP Air, would always require their pilots to be completely comfortable flying in English because most of their operations are in parts of the world where French would never be available for air traffic control. Simple economic efficiency dictates that pilots be capable of flying as many as possible of their airline's routes.

The pilots' opposition to bilingual air traffic control arose primarily from their professional ethic, which gave rise to the belief that bilingual air traffic control would diminish safety. This argument actually has a number of themes, which emerge from the articles pilots wrote, their incident reports to CALPA, and my own interviews. First of all, anglophone pilots became apprehensive when overhearing controllers speaking a language they did not understand because they felt this created an additional source of uncertainty in their environment. Numerous pilots said that they did not feel as safe when they flew in countries using two languages as in those using only English. Ken Maley, in his interviews with Patrick Watson and William Johnson, said that he did not feel that countries with bilingual air traffic control were unsafe, in the sense that their air traffic control systems did not measure up to an absolute standard of safety below which pilots would refuse to fly, but he did feel that bilingual systems were less safe than unilingual ones.[13] The listening watch argument was also given as a reason why bilingual air traffic control would reduce safety. My interviews suggest that this argument was advanced most seriously by the older pilots, who began their careers in an era when it was easier to use the listening watch. In contrast, the younger pilots, who grew up in the era of sectorized airspace and digital display radar, gave the listening watch somewhat less importance.

Second, the pilots did not see any benefits to be gained by implementing bilingual IFR air traffic control in Quebec because they felt that everyone who presently had or in the future would obtain an IFR licence would be fluent in English. They did not see how a unilingual francophone would want to invest the time and money for an IFR licence if he were only to use it to fly in Quebec. Thus, the pilots opposed a change which they felt would provide no benefits, but would reduce safety. It should be noted that there were a large number of bilingual francophone pilots who shared this view. Two vocal members of this group were Captain Charbonneau, who wrote the famous letter to the newspaper proclaiming his preference for using English for flying and French for making love, and Captain Desmarais, the writer for *Canadian Aviation*. This view was also supported by foreign pilots, even those based in countries which provided bilingual air traffic control. The foreign pilots (as exemplified by Captain Vermeulen of the Netherlands, who spoke at the International Air Safety Symposium) were disappointed that a country which had been in the forefront of the move to international standardization, was now taking a retrograde step.

Third, the pilots' position can also be seen as an expression of discontent because their professional interests had in recent years frequently been frustrated by government decisions taken on the basis of factors other than aviation safety or efficiency. These feelings were explained very perceptively by Captain Peter Cranston, a pilot flying for MOT, in a brief to the Task Force on Canadian Unity:

> ... you [that is, the pilot] complained to high heaven when they laid the footings for the new high-rise on the approach to runway 31. Two years later, the tenants are complaining about the noise and you are asked to make what you consider to be a dangerous turn just after take-off to avoid them.... Many senior pilots never quite got over this "erosion of command authority" caused by the various changes. A common complaint of professionals everywhere.... Then a senior pilot comes into the airport traffic pattern and perhaps finds in front of him George the salesman who likes to use his own aircraft on business trips.... George, not a professional, occasionally gets confused by the rapid-fire chatter of the tower controller, asks for repeats, hesitates in his response, and senior captain grits his teeth, wishing all amateurs could be sent down to the Gaspé or somewhere. Then he hears that in response to demand, and the Official Languages Act, the government is planning to allow VFR control in French. IN FRENCH! Good God? No way! Enough is enough!
>
> In an inherently hostile environment, a certain caution is developed. The greater your experience, the more ways you can see for things to go wrong. In a milieu where technology changes rapidly,

pilots must be adaptable. At the same time, they believe that "where change is not necessary, it is necessary not to change." Professional instrument-rated pilots are a small tight group. . . . within that group, even the francophone members were unable to see any benefit in French IFR control.[14]

Thus, for the anglophone pilots in CALPA, and for some of the francophones as well, opposition to bilingual air traffic control became something of a holy war in defence of their professional commitment to safety and in opposition to this last, worst example of political meddling in the business of flying large passenger aircraft.

The francophone airline pilots who supported bilingual air traffic control also did so primarily on the basis of their professional concern — interpreted differently, however. First of all, they were generally younger than the francophone pilots opposing bilingual control, which suggests that they were not as concerned about the listening watch and that they had the usual tendency of younger people to accept change more readily. Furthermore, because they were bilingual, they did not have the same feelings of uncertainty when flying in countries using two languages. Finally, many of them went from initial feelings of indifference about language to support for bilingual air traffic control because they were convinced by the francophone controllers whom they met in AGAQ that a bilingual system could operate as safely and efficiently as a unilingual system and that the use of French for air traffic control in Quebec was an affirmation of their rights. Finally, AGAQ also received support from a number of partially bilingual francophone pilots who worked as bush pilots, flying instructors, or pilots for local carriers. These pilots did have a direct material interest in the use of French for IFR services, because it might open up some positions for them at Quebecair and the Quebec Government Aviation Service, both of which operate almost entirely in Quebec.

This discussion has shown the complexity of the motives of aviation professionals on both sides of the dispute, including concern for one's present job, concern for one's job in the distant future, concern for one's own life and limb (on the part of pilots), concern for the lives of people for whom one feels morally responsible (on the part of controllers), and the influence of one's professional beliefs about how a job should be performed. It was as a result of all these factors that this became such an emotional dispute: had it merely been a struggle for jobs, a more peaceful accommodation could have been reached. Being aware of the way in which diverse motivations can combine to influence behaviour should be important to both the researcher attempting to explain events and the practitioner attempting to influence them.

CHAPTER ELEVEN

THE AMBIVALENT ROLE OF GOVERNMENT

Government can play two different roles in society. In the pluralist view, government acts as the referee and scorekeeper in the ongoing struggle between interest groups for social advantage. Opposing views see government in a more active role, serving either as an expression of the interests of certain classes or as a vehicle for the ideas of political leaders, and attempting to shape the society's evolution in certain definite directions.[15] Governments often play these roles simultaneously with respect to different issues in the political agenda. For instance, a government might act as a partisan on the basis of its ideology, priorities, or platform. However, no ideology or statement of priorities is so all-encompassing as to specify a definite position on all issues. As a result, there are many issues on which political leaders take a pragmatic position, making their decisions on the basis of the merits of the case. Given that governments generally have the objective of retaining power, this means making decisions that will maximize its likelihood. Such a course may therefore imply conferring benefits on marginal or "swing" voters, rather than on those most or least likely to vote for the government, regardless of the policies it follows.[16] If the issue involves conflict between several social groups, governments may attempt to set up a structure in which the groups can resolve their differences themselves, and the government can take public credit for the solution.

What is fascinating about the bilingual air traffic control controversy is that government played both the roles of partisan and mediator simultaneously. This situation arose in part because people at different levels played different roles, and in part because individuals' feelings were, in fact, ambivalent, and the ambivalence was reflected in their behaviour. The next section discusses the role played by government, first at the leadership level and then at the bureaucratic level. Finally, the Commission of Inquiry is discussed in order to show how it ended the ambivalence, and defined roles clearly.

THE LEADERSHIP LEVEL

This section is entitled the leadership level, rather than the political level, because two of the key players, Cloutier and McLeish, are public servants. However, they became so closely identified with Otto Lang in the management of the issue that the three must be considered together.

Initially, the government's approach to the bilingual air traffic control problem was very clearly that of a mediator. Up until late 1975, the government's efforts involved finding ways to bring the aviation organizations together so that they could solve the problem themselves. Examples of this are the decision not to implement any sections of the BILCOM

230

report without consultation with the aviation community, and the establishment of the Finley Committee in which MOT, in the person of Hart Finley, attempted to play the role of mediator. Furthermore, the minister of transport, Jean Marchand, generally took a mediator's role. While he did add some impetus to the study of bilingual VFR operations in Quebec City, he left it to his officials to reach a decision. He also took no clear position on whether IFR operations should be bilingual.[17] The francophone controllers pressed both Jean Marchand and Prime Minister Trudeau's staff to apply the Official Languages Act to air traffic control. Even though the bilingualism policy was one to which the Trudeau government had a clear ideological commitment, its response to the controllers initially was to advise them patiently to resolve their problems within the aviation community.

The federal government's position acquired a partisan element when Otto Lang spoke to the controllers at the Montreal centre in December 1975, and put forth his plans to proceed with the implementation of full bilingual air traffic control in Quebec, in stages, as it was proven safe. This came about partially as a result of the pressure of the Quebec Liberal caucus and partially as a result of the conflict in the centre. Lang himself continues to believe that his statement did not represent a change from his previous policy, because he was completely confident that bilingual air traffic control could be made safe.[18] However, the tone and the dramatic context of his remarks, as well as his listing of the steps that would soon be taken led the partisans, on both sides, to conclude that the government had itself become a partisan. Hence, Livingston's immediate meeting with Lang and the decision by both CATCA and CALPA to fight bilingual air traffic control with all available weapons. Conversely, the champagne toast that Patenaude, Demers, and Louis Doucet drank when they arrived in Quebec City after the speech is a clear statement of their reaction.

This partisan tone was in evidence throughout the following winter and spring. Lang, Cloutier, and McLeish made it clear on many occasions that they believed, with almost religious faith, that bilingual air traffic control could be implemented safely and that they planned to do so. Lang communicated this position clearly in his speech to the air safety symposium. Furthermore, Lang saw no need to go along with Keith Spicer's suggestion, made at the time of the symposium, that the problem be handled by a commission of inquiry. Even when forced to have a commission of inquiry, Lang, Cloutier, and McLeish tried to limit its terms so as not to delay the implementation program. Walter McLeish's numerous speeches to CATCA and CALPA about the need for bilingual air traffic control as a response to historical grievances of francophones and his comment that the simulation exercises were simply a "marketing exercise" made clear his role as partisan as well.

Despite all these signals of partisanship, there were other signals that the government had some sympathy for the anglophone side and was sometimes behaving as mediator. When it became clear that a commission of inquiry would be established, McLeish and Cloutier attempted something resembling shuttle diplomacy to get both sides to agree to the commission's composition and mandate. McLeish himself, while certain that bilingual air traffic control could be made as safe as unilingual control, felt it would lower operational efficiency, and was frank in telling CATCA that the question of operational efficiency legitimately could be raised as a factor influencing public policy. Partly as a result of these statements and partly because McLeish, as recently as mid-1975, had been opposed to bilingual IFR air traffic control, the leaders of CATCA and CALPA concluded that McLeish was really on their side, but was being forced to support bilingual air traffic control by his superiors. On one occasion, McLeish told the leaders of CATCA that he not only supported bilingual control but had to appear to support it. From this, they concluded that he did not really support it, but was being compelled by the politicians to appear to do so. One rather candid bureaucrat recalls that though McLeish often met with CATCA and reiterated his position in support of bilingual air traffic control, the CATCA executives smirked and said to one another sotto voce, "Sure, Walter..." As will be discussed in the section of this chapter dealing with personality, there was some psychological validity in the controllers' perception of McLeish. He was feeling some ambivalence about bilingual air traffic control, and it showed in his behaviour.

The government's ambivalent role had a number of implications. Relations with the two sides of the aviation community were made more difficult. The francophones took Lang's statement at the Montreal centre as a promise, and therefore felt that any steps the government took in the direction of a mediating role, such as the establishment of the Commission of Inquiry, were a betrayal. The anglophones, while recognizing that Lang and Cloutier were partisans opposed to them, believed that McLeish was secretly on their side. This, coupled with the support they had from most of McLeish's subordinates, convinced them that the government's position was based entirely on politics, without any reference to aviation technology. This strengthened their resolve to fight. The ambivalence of the government's role was reflected in the decision not to wage a publicity campaign in support of bilingual air traffic control, because it was considered to be inappropriate. This simply made it easier for the pilots and controllers to win over anglophone opinion. On the other hand, the choice of John Keenan as commissioner is reflective of the partisan face of the government's position. Lang, Cloutier, and McLeish were so convinced that bilingual air traffic control could be proven safe that they were willing to appoint as commissioner someone who had been associated with the partisan side they opposed. Had they taken a mediating role, they would have appointed a commissioner who was both impartial and had the appearance of impartiality so as to make the commission more politically effective.

The situation that Lang, Cloutier, and McLeish faced was one that called for a basic strategic choice of whether to be partisans or mediators, and then the orchestration of all their tactics to reinforce the strategy that was chosen. The implication that seems to emerge from this experience is that government arouses great suspicion on the part of interest groups when it attempts to play the roles of both partisan and mediator simultaneously, because they call for such different behaviour.[19]

THE BUREAUCRACY

A great deal of the literature on bureaucracy has emphasized situations of conflict between the bureaucracy and its political masters. The context in which this has most often been examined is the relationship between ministers and mandarins, especially experienced mandarins and inexperienced ministers.[20] Since the mandarins are acting in their role as advisers, the tactics involve slanting their advice by presenting the minister with only one realistic option and using the pressure of deadlines to force him to accept their advice. This story deals with a different phenomenon, namely, the opposition by civil servants of lower rank to the clearly expressed policy preferences of both an experienced minister and equally experienced mandarins.[21] Because bureaucracy is hierarchical and because norms of obedience to superiors are sufficiently strong to justify dismissal for their violation, this opposition is covert. It takes the form of foot-dragging, leaking, and non-anticipation. Uncooperative bureaucrats find other priorities that make it difficult for them to carry out orders with which they disagree. They quietly send brown envelopes of documents (without a return address) either to sympathetic journalists or, in this case, to known opponents of the government's policy. They either refuse to think in advance about the problems their policy may encounter or, if they think about them, they keep their thoughts to themselves. The covert nature of this opposition was made most clear by the deafening silence that greeted CATCA when it asked the numerous opponents of bilingual air traffic control in MOT to testify publicly at the first set of hearings of the Commission of Inquiry.

The covert bureaucratic opposition clearly hurt Lang, Cloutier, and McLeish. The leaked documents enabled CATCA and CALPA to anticipate many of MOT's actions. The response of Lang, Cloutier, and McLeish was to become more secretive, thus making documents available and confining meetings only to those known to be within the small circle of loyalty. One bureaucrat in that circle observed that the cost of such a tactic was the impairment of the upward flow of information. Furthermore, the bureaucracy's lack of zeal meant that it would have been difficult for MOT to mount a full partisan strategy (including a public relations campaign) because there would be no loyal staff work to support it. These effects therefore confirm what authors such as Allison and Halperin have pointed out in the context of the fragmented United States government and Lipset and Schultz have noted in the context of Canada's more cohesive parliamentary government, namely, that even the lower levels of the bureaucracy have the power to thwart their political masters.[22]

How can politicians overcome this bureaucratic resistance to their policies? There are a number of possible tactics. One usually is not the dismissal of the disloyal. Civil service norms make it impossible to dismiss individuals without strong evidence of malfeasance: by its nature, covert opposition leaves no such evidence. One alternative is to reassign the necessary support work to either a unit in the bureaucracy or to external consultants who will perform it with the required vigour and loyalty. If that is not possible, a second alternative for the politician, or perhaps his executive assistant, is to monitor the bureaucracy closely. This takes time, but will improve performance. Finally, the politician must often meet his civil servants half way. In many instances, bureaucratic opposition to political initiatives is due as much to the way they are to be undertaken as to their content. From a bureaucrat's viewpoint, concern for procedure is quite rational. The bureaucracy will remain long after the politician moves on, and initiatives undertaken today which do not follow standard procedures could be precedents which create difficulties in the future. This appears to have been the case, at least partially, with the MOT bureaucrats' opposition to bilingual air traffic control because one of their major concerns was that it was being implemented with insufficient attention as to how it would mesh with existing procedures. The work of the simulation exercises seems to have neutralized the opposition of a good number of MOT bureaucrats by convincing them that adequate procedures could be developed. Furthermore, a francophone who worked on bilingual air traffic control at MOT headquarters recalls that his anglophone colleagues began to accept it when they came to think of it as a purely technical question of how to build additional redundancy into a bilingual system.

A sharp contrast with the MOT bureaucracy's handling of bilingual air traffic control is the Federal Aviation Administration's handling of the August 1981 strike by the Professional Air Traffic Controllers' Organization. The FAA began preparing for such a strike as early as the spring of 1980. By the time the strike began, the FAA had developed a computer-based plan that would allow 75 percent of commercial aircraft flights to operate even with a loss of two-thirds of the country's controllers, had updated supervisors' qualifications so they could serve as operational controllers, and had secretly stored operating plans for the new system at all major control centres.[23] This strong staff support made possible the success of President Reagan's policy of firing the striking controllers and refusing to negotiate.

THE COMMISSION OF INQUIRY
Commissions of inquiry, like royal commissions, have generally been regarded by students of public administration as a policy instrument which is minimally coercive and minimally effective. For example, Doern puts them together with ministerial speeches, conferences, information, advisory bodies, and research as forms of exhortation.[24] More coercive policy instruments include budgetary and tax expenditures, regulation, and public ownership. In this view, commissions of inquiry are usually established because the government wants to indicate that it is concerned about a problem, without committing itself to any particular course of action. Commissions may also be established to do research on policy issues about which the government is simply uninformed. The Commission of Inquiry into Bilingual Air Traffic Services in Quebec departed quite sharply from this model.

The most important role the commission had to play was to establish itself as the mediator in the bilingual air traffic control dispute, so that the Ministry of Transport could then adopt what was by then its appropriate posture, namely, that of a partisan. We should recall that the commission's role as mediator was called into question at its outset by the terms of the Lang-CATCA-CALPA agreement. The commission clarified its role by its letter interpreting the agreement, and by its insistence on being above the appearance of bias in the choice of its staff, the procedures it followed, and its research methodology. Furthermore, Pierre Proulx, the head of the simulation exercises took the commission's lead, and also operated in a mediating mode, by choosing as his staff for the simulation exercises people who were open-minded, and by refusing to get involved in historical disputes in order to focus on the purely technical problem of comparing bilingual and unilingual air traffic control systems. Ultimately, Proulx became a partisan, in arguing that the results of the simulation study supported the government position. However, he did not become a partisan until after the study was completed and he had confidence in its results.

This commission of inquiry had the good fortune to be investigating a narrowly defined problem, for which it was possible to find concrete answers. It did not have to cope with the vague mandates characterizing many other commissions. Thus, the commission supervised three major pieces of policy analysis (the study of language usage at foreign airports, the study of accidents, and the simulation exercises) which all pointed to the same conclusion, and put it on a much sounder footing than if it had to make its recommendations on the basis only of conflicting testimony. The Commission of Inquiry also had its rules of evidence established for it beforehand, in terms of the unanimity requirement and other aspects of the Lang-CATCA-CALPA agreement designed to put the burden of proof on the government. When the data satisfied its rules of evidence and burden of proof, its conclusion was clear.

This commission also differed from many others because it had the power to oversee the implementation process. By forcing MOT to present its implementation plans for public scrutiny, this allayed the fears of the anglophones that bilingual air traffic control would be implemented in a haphazard manner. In addition, the commission also explored the consequences of change with many groups who would be affected by it. For example, commission counsel or consultants visited all the airlines flying into Montreal. In one case, the president of a major American carrier was shocked to hear that Montreal air traffic control could become bilingual. He vowed that his airline would never fly into a city with bilingual control. "What about Mexico City?" asked the counsel. "Of course that's English," replied the president. When the counsel showed the president that Mexico City was bilingual, he had a convert.

The commission performed another important function by reducing the emotionalism of the problem, which is something we would expect a good mediator to do. This came about in several ways. The hearings allowed CATCA to air publicly all its accusations against MOT. The commission bought time, which allowed tempers in the aviation community to cool. Finally, the simulation exercises allowed a number of the pilots and controllers to take part in the process of change.

Finally, this commission suggests another area, not considered by previous scholars, where commissions of inquiry may be useful, namely as part of the collective bargaining process in the public service. To begin with, the process itself makes it impossible for the government to adopt the role of mediator, since, as employer, it has a partisan position. Secondly, though the Public Service Staff Relations Act (or comparable provincial legislation) restricts the range of negotiable issues, public service unions will continue to bargain about public policy issues which have an impact on the conditions of their employment. They will do this by convincing the public that it has an interest in the issue, thereby opening up public debate. We can expect the police unions to attempt to negotiate about safety (for example, the use of body armour or two-man car patrols) and about the powers of civilian review boards. Similarly, teachers' unions may demand to negotiate about such policy issues as student discipline, student/teacher ratios, and curriculum content.

There are two problems in leaving the resolution of these issues to bilateral negotiations between the government and the union. First, it gives the public no direct input into their resolution, despite the fact that its interests are involved. Secondly, it is inadvisable to settle such disputes by means of traditional labour arbitration or conciliation boards because the arbitrators' experience in labour relations does not equip them to understand the issues in sufficient depth to make a wise decision.[25]

Commissions of inquiry about public policy issues arising from the collective bargaining process will be dealing with problems that are concrete, which should facilitate the finding of answers. Finally, the fact that these issues arise as part of the ongoing relationship between labour and management means that some settlement must be reached, so that the commission cannot simply be ignored. Thus, the highly successful experience of this commission of inquiry might serve as a model for future commissions of this kind, which is a use of this policy instrument that previous authors have overlooked.

THE ROLE OF PERSONALITY

One major theme of this study is that the personalities of key players, and the interactions among them, can have a substantial impact on policy decisions. This also implies that if other individuals (such as, for instance, other members of Trudeau's Cabinet) had held these positions, the results might have been quite different.

Let us review the places in this story where personality appears to have made a difference. The five key actors in this story were Lang, Cloutier, McLeish, Maley, and Livingston. To some extent, Lang, Cloutier, and McLeish made up a unit, because they worked so closely together and because they seemed to share some important traits. They were all extremely self-assured individuals, possessed of great confidence in their own judgment. Once they came to a conclusion as to what the right policy was, they were most unwilling to back down or reverse their course. They all displayed a deep commitment, bordering at times on religious belief, that bilingual air traffic control was the right thing, both in aviation and as politics. Furthermore, Otto Lang's approach was that government's task was to implement policies that were the right solutions to problems, rather than to mediate between diverse and conflicting interests.

The trio developed their strong belief in bilingual air traffic control partially as a psychological reaction to an external force. Under substantial pressure from the Quebec Liberal caucus, they were forced in December

1975 to move from a position as mediator to what the entire aviation community perceived as a partisan position on the francophone side. They coped with the psychological strain this created by becoming firm believers that bilingual air traffic control could be implemented safely. In Otto Lang's case, his firm belief led him to deny that his policy had shifted substantially: thus, he could continue to feel that he was in control of events. One piece of evidence as to how accustomed to his new role Lang became was that he scorned Keith Spicer's suggestion, made in March 1976, of setting up a commission of inquiry. Not only did Lang want his own department to solve the problem, but he was quite indignant over Spicer's professed uncertainty as to whether bilingual air traffic control could be made as safe as unilingual control.

In Walter McLeish's case, there was substantially more inner conflict. Unlike Lang and Cloutier, who had no aviation background, McLeish's background and training led him initially to oppose bilingual air traffic control. He was in the process of changing his mind as the events leading up to the strike unfolded. Clearly, such a change creates cognitive dissonance. It appears that McLeish dealt with the psychological conflict in two ways. On the one hand, he openly expressed his doubts about bilingual air traffic control, not in terms of the aviation profession's primary goal of safety, but in terms of the secondary goal of operational efficiency. On the other hand, he often covered up his inner doubt with outer self-confidence, arguing about the virtues of bilingual air traffic control with all the confidence and self-assurance that Cloutier and Lang showed.

The choice of John Keenan can only be explained as a result of the collective sense of certainty that Lang, Cloutier, and McLeish developed. McLeish, who initially recommended Keenan, felt that if he himself could change his mind about bilingual air traffic control, then any open-minded member of the aviation community would do likewise. Lang and Cloutier were not worried about whether, if Keenan came to the conclusion that bilingual control were unsafe, such a conclusion would be accepted in Quebec, simply because they felt that was an impossibility. They were also not worried about the response to Keenan's appointment in Quebec, feeling that francophones would be just as confident as they were that he would come up with the right answer. Their confidence led them to overlook the traditional francophone insecurity about the ability of the federal government to protect their linguistic rights. Finally, they did not imagine that Keenan would resign in response to the criticism, because they expected that he would do what they were sure they would have done in his position, simply "tough out" the criticism. Clearly, other individuals in their shoes would have looked for someone other than John Keenan. Some more inclined by personality to a mediator's role would have looked for a commissioner who gave all appearances of being unbiased, such as the judges who ultimately were chosen.

The Lang-Cloutier-McLeish approach was strikingly evident in the negotiations with Maley and Livingston. The trio was backed into a corner, forced to make some concessions so that Livingston and Maley could show their supporters a victory and get the planes flying again. The three were so certain that their approach would be proven correct by the Commission of Inquiry that they were willing to accept the guarantees demanded by CATCA and CALPA with little difficulty. Furthermore, the minutes of the CATCA national council meetings, as well as my own interviews, indicate that they gave more than they had to. From an intellectual point of view, history has shown that their conclusion that they did not give in on the essentials was correct. However, from a political point of view, what they failed to anticipate was how adverse the reaction in Quebec would be. They approached these negotiations, not as negotiators, but as problem solvers. Almost naively, Lang kept asking what was necessary to solve the problem and get the planes flying again.

The personal style of Lang, Cloutier, and McLeish was evident in their approach to crisis management during the strike. Lang had established a reputation as a person who believed strongly in his own competence, and who therefore resented offers of help he thought were unnecessary. Thus, he, Cloutier, and McLeish handled the crisis by themselves, not seeking, and not being offered, very much assistance or consultation from the rest of the government. This is in striking contrast to the approach followed by CATCA and CALPA in gathering their decision-making groups together in Ottawa, while at the same time maintaining continuous contact with pilots and controllers throughout the country, as well as making numerous calls to outside supporters and advisers in order to assess public support.

There is a growing literature on crisis management: the most notable recent study is Michael Brecher's *Decisions in Crisis*, which is an exhaustive analysis of the major decisions made by the Israeli Cabinet before and during the 1967 and 1973 wars.[26] Brecher's most interesting conclusion was that, contrary to what the previous literature on crisis management suggested would happen, the Israeli government coped with the spectre of likely war by intensifying its search for information, considering more alternatives, consulting widely, and expanding the decision-making group.[27] In this way, the Israelis overcame the inherent stress of the situation and made decisions which proved successful. Clearly, the crisis management behaviour of CATCA and CALPA more closely approximated that of Brecher's Israeli model than did that of MOT. While some of the reasons for this are structural (namely, the strike did not represent as great a threat to Canada's security as the wars did to Israel's, precluding the focusing of undivided attention on the strike) nevertheless, a different minister of transport might have consulted more widely in formulating his strategy.

Lang's approach to crisis management has particular implications for a system of parliamentary government, in which the cabinet has collective responsibility. When a minister, with little or no consultation with his colleagues, makes a decision which, by force of circumstances is irreversible, his colleagues must support the decision publicly—or resign (as Jean Marchand did, in this case). When ministers make decisions unilaterally, they therefore run the risk of demoralizing the Cabinet and ultimately reducing their own prestige within it, which happened to Lang as a result of his handling of the pilots' strike.

Let us look at Ken Maley and Jim Livingston, the men who sat across the table from Lang, Cloutier, and McLeish in that final weekend of negotiations. Maley's strength was his sensitivity to the feelings of his membership and his willingness to serve as their spokesman. However, a failing that he displayed was an inability to translate the strongly felt beliefs of the membership into pragmatic bargaining positions. For example, in August 1975, Maley and his board, despite the advice of Keenan and Young, took such an uncompromising stance that Maley's hands were virtually tied during the meetings of the Finley committee, which is one factor that contributed to its failure. During the strike, it was Young whose threat to stop representing CALPA in the negotiations with Lang started the CALPA board thinking about how to negotiate an end to the strike.

One of the roles of a leader is to be an organization's public spokesman. In this instance, one of Maley's attractive personal characteristics—his candour and openness—became a serious flaw on a number of occasions when clever interviewers induced him to make ill-advised and inflammatory statements which both undercut the image CALPA was trying to project and aroused opposition. Three instances of this are his statement that pilots unanimously supported the August 1975 position on bilingual air traffic control, which aroused the opposition of francophone pilots, his statement that "this bilingualism and biculturalism thing has gone too far," which almost nullified the professional image the pilots were trying to project, and his statement at the press conference announcing the memorandum of understanding that CALPA would not commit itself in advance to accept the results of the Commission of Inquiry, which contributed to the great outpouring of support for AGAQ in Quebec immediately after the strike. Another leader might have handled these situations very differently, and thereby reduced tensions.

Jim Livingston was praised by nearly everyone I interviewed as being a tough and effective negotiator. His CATCA colleagues appreciated his ability to consider all sides of an issue and to think about long-term strategy. Livingston took a stronger leadership position on his board than did Maley on his. Livingston also had a clearer understanding that his task went beyond speaking for the membership: he realized that, while they would be satisfied with rhetoric, ultimately he would have to act pragmatically in his negotiations with MOT. In many instances, especially during the strike, Livingston acted as a moderating influence with CATCA, by attempting to apply its policies in a fair way to its francophone members and by arguing that CATCA policy on bilingualism had to be based on professional concerns rather than on bigotry. Even as the rift between anglophone and francophone in CATCA widened, Livingston realized the need to reunify the union in the future. He therefore did his best to ensure that CATCA's record would stand up to the scrutiny of the Public Service Staff Relations Board.

Despite these virtues, Livingston displayed a key failing. He was, on occasion, excessively zealous as a bargainer, with the result that he sometimes approached issues in what was a narrow, legalistic, and ultimately ungenerous manner. What he lacked was magnanimity. Probably the best example of this was his refusal to sign the 1974 contract in French. Coming very early in his term as president, this sent a very strong signal to the Quebec membership that he was not on their side. Ultimately, it was not in his union's own interest, because it contributed to the disaffection in Quebec which split CATCA.

Thus, we can see how these various character traits—the steadfast faith in their position that Lang, Cloutier, and McLeish showed, Maley's inability to avoid inflammatory answers to reporters' questions, and Livingston's occasional lack of magnanimity – all combined to intensify hostility and thus influence the ultimate outcome. It is quite likely that, with other people in those positions, many aspects of the story would have been different.

This study has substantial implications for our understanding of the role of personality in affecting public policy outcomes. First of all, previous public policy studies have emphasized that personality is important, but have then dealt with it in a wholly inadequate manner. For example, Graham Allison stated that personality was at the core of his Model III, or bureaucratic politics paradigm:

For players are also people; men's metabolisms differ. The hard core of the bureaucratic politics mix is personality. How each man manages to stand the heat in his kitchen, each player's basic operating style, and the complementarity or contradiction among personalities and styles in the inner circles are irreducible pieces of the policy blend.[28]

However, in Allison's Model III description of the Cuban missile crisis, there was little that revealed the unique personality traits of the various actors.[29] The description of the Excom, Kennedy's ad hoc committee of advisers, differentiated the various members only on the basis of ideology: some were hard-liners and others were moderates. It happened that the latter were ideologically and personally closer to Kennedy, and he therefore accepted their advice. It is hard to see how the personalities, in the commonly accepted sense of the term, of any of the participants affected the outcome.

A more sophisticated study of the effects of personality would start with several hypotheses. First, personality traits of the adults in positions of authority are relatively stable, certainly over short periods of time. Second, we cannot often say that their traits, a priori, are good or bad: rather, a given trait in two different situations may lead to completely different outcomes, success in one and failure in the other. A very clear example of this is former United States President Carter. Three of his notable personality traits were that he had a high energy level, that he was pragmatic rather than ideological, and that he needed to acquire a great deal of information before making decisions. As a result, he spent incredible numbers of hours studying problems in great detail. His veritable absence of a clear ideology meant that he could not find a quick answer by applying a belief system or find trusted subordinates who could apply his ideology. The result was that he wasted much of his time, failed to project a positive image to the public, and ultimately was defeated.[30] However, on one instance these same personality traits probably contributed to the major achievement of his presidency, the Camp David agreement. In this case, the degree of mutual trust between the Israeli and Egyptian governments was small, making it impossible for the heads of state to reach a broad agreement in principle and leave it to their subordinates to iron out the details. Rather, it was necessary to consider all details at the highest level. By immersing himself in the minutiae and by his willingness to work until a solution was reached, Carter was probably, in large measure, personally responsible for the agreement. Furthermore, under a different president it might not have happened.

If we hypothesize that personality makes a difference, the next step would be to suggest categories within which information about personality can be organized. Three possible approaches would be cultural / ideological, managerial, and psychohistorical. The first, which Allison illustrated in *Essence of Decision*, would concentrate on individuals' role conceptions, life philosophies, and personal values. The managerial approach would concern itself with an individual's willingness to take risks, his ability to delegate authority, and his negotiating skills. This book has focused on the managerial approach. In addition, a number of authors have attempted to classify personality types on managerial lines. Examples are Downs' typology of climbers, zealots, conservers, advocates, and statesmen and Maccoby's gamesmen, jungle fighters, and craftsmen.[31] The psychohistorical approach uses psychoanalytic categories to explain the personality development and behaviour of extraordinary individuals. Examples of this are Erikson's study of Gandhi and the Georges' study of Woodrow Wilson.[32] The latter very skilfully pointed out how Wilson's personality structure led to his failure to win Senate ratification of the Treaty of Paris.

Of these three approaches, the virtue of the third is that it explains personality, rather than simply taking it as given. Its problem is that it is sufficiently taxing that a complete study almost always focuses on a single individual. Ideally, a study which explores the interaction of a set of individuals would wish to provide some psychohistorical background about all of them. Of course, I have not done so in this book. However, I feel that my emphasis on the managerial aspects of the five key personalities in the story has added a level of interpretation which goes beyond the cultural / ideological approach. Ultimately, historians and students of public policy will come to understand the influence of personality on history and policy only if they increase the sophistication of their understanding of personality.[33] In this regard, we have hardly scratched the surface.

Finally, there may be some practical applications resulting from such an understanding. This knowledge might be of use in the matching of individuals to leadership positions. For instance, when a first minister chooses his cabinet, how much thought does he give to the interaction of the personalities with the problems likely to arise in the various positions? How much thought does he give to the nature of the personal interactions between individuals whose organizational roles demand constant cooperation? While some attention undoubtedly is devoted to these questions, a more rigorous approach could have substantial benefits.

THE PUBLIC, THE ELITE, AND THE VIABILITY OF CANADA

The central theme of this book has been conflict and compromise between English and French Canadians. Implicitly, it has explored the conditions which are necessary for both linguistic groups to coexist within the political framework of a single state. In recent years, this theme has been examined analytically by the literature on consociational democracy. The basic notion of consociational democracy, as expounded by the Dutch political scientist, Arend Lijphart, is that countries whose populations are composed of subgroups which hold mutually antagonistic ideologies and which have little face-to-face contact with one another may nevertheless remain both democratic and united. This can occur, he argues, if the following two conditions hold: first, the political system must be deferential, so that the antagonistic masses trust the elites to resolve political problems, and second, the members of the elite must be committed to the maintenance of the society and able to transcend their subcultural differences so as to reach agreements that accommodate all groups.[34]

This model is applicable to Canada as a description of the process of accommodation that has frequently occurred between francophone and anglophone elites.[35] For example, Richard Simeon, in *Federal-Provincial Diplomacy*, described how, after a federal-provincial conference on pension plans in April 1964 ended in disagreement, ministers and officials of the federal and Quebec governments held secret negotiations which resulted in an agreement two weeks later.[36] Another example was the behind-the-scenes negotiations among all parties which led to a unanimous parliamentary resolution on language policy within the civil service in June 1973.[37] By that time, the implementation of bilingualism in the civil service had created substantial resentment on the part of unilingual anglophone civil servants. The negotiators found a way of responding to the anglophones' discontent without stimulating what many MPs and senators felt would have been an antagonistic public controversy between English and French.

However, the situation described in this book was one where, certainly before the pilots' strike, and even to a great degree thereafter, the pattern of elite bargaining and compromise did not work. The key reason is that the elites (that is, the leaders of the aviation organizations) mobilized antagonistic public opinion to create support for their causes. The internal dynamics of the situation led to public mobilization. Because the francophones were a small group, with little legitimacy, not taken very seriously until 1975 by either the government or their anglophone colleagues, public pressure was the best way they could gain legitimacy. On the other hand, the only way the anglophone controllers could slow the implementation of bilingualism was to introduce it into collective bargaining. As was shown in chapters 6 and 7, the best way a union can win in public sector collective bargaining is to have strong public support.

This issue became so divisive because anglophones and francophones were so strongly opposed in their feelings towards the government's language policy. For Quebec francophones, the issue at stake was whether francophone controllers and pilots, like their compatriots, had the right to speak French with one another in the workplace. On the other hand, anglophone resentment towards the government's bilingualism policy had been building up for several years before the strike. They felt that bilingualism was being given priority over many other values, and often expressed it in the complaint that too much money was being spent on bilingualism. Through the bilingualism policy, the government had increased opportunities for francophones and restricted opportunities for anglophones. Also, there were some English Canadians who resented the change in Canada's self-definition to that of a bilingual country and the consequent change in its symbolism and imagery. Finally, anglophone resentment was probably so bitter because the consociational consensus of elite opinion suppressed public debate over bilingualism. The controllers and pilots were able to strike this chord of anglophone anger so effectively because they linked the safety argument with opposition to bilingualism, thus calling upon the ultimate value to set in opposition to bilingualism: the value of human life. Those English Canadians who did not want to admit publicly that they did not want to share power with French Canadians or that they could not accept symbols with which French Canadians could identify found in this argument a position that was publicly legitimate and defensible.

The media also played an important role in the mobilization of public opinion on this issue.[38] In general, the media tends to react to problems, rather than anticipate them, and to treat them superficially, rather than in depth. Canada has the additional problem that, like their compatriots, correspondents for the English and French media have very little contact with one another.[39] During the CATCA-CALPA publicity campaign, the English media generally repeated their arguments, with little critical investigation. Reporters and editorialists often approach a difficult technical issue, such as bilingual air traffic control, not on its own merits, but in terms of its context.[40] Thus, the English media saw it in the context of the government's unpopular bilingualism policy and of the political difficulties suffered by the Trudeau government. They ignored opportunities to learn about the other side of the story from Jean-Luc Patenaude, Lang, and Cloutier, or from francophone writers. They only became interested in the specifics of the issue after its context changed to that of the angry Quebec reaction to the Lang-CATCA-CALPA agreement. The francophone media treated the issue much more thoroughly, as can be expected, given that one of their main concerns has long been the issue of language in Quebec. Nevertheless, they were less than thorough in showing their readers the reasons underlying the concerns that the anglophone pilots and controllers expressed. Overall, the media were not very effective at interpreting the two solitudes to one another.

The bilingual air traffic control issue illustrates the magnitude of the forces working to divide Canada on linguistic lines. There are strong resentments between the two language groups. It is simply a fact of life that interest group leaders mobilize public opinion behind their causes and draw on the hostility between the two groups. It is equally a fact of life that the media often emphasize the sensational and avoid in-depth analysis. The optimistic consociational view appears not to come to terms with these facts, as it assumes that all that is needed for a country like Canada to remain united is good will on the part of its elites. The bilingual air traffic control dispute occurred, not because the interest groups and political leaders were men of ill will, but rather because their very human failings exacerbated a situation already made difficult by the hostility of the population at large.[41] Based on this study, I would therefore define conditions for Canada to remain united in a very different way than that suggested by the consociational model.

A Canadian state will survive if its citizens, who harbour strong regional loyalties believe that, in the long run, its national government's policies will meet their expectations in providing a legitimate share of the nation's wealth, status, and power to a greater degree than would be the case in any less cohesive structure. This hypothesis is presented in regional terms so as to be equally applicable to the alienated west as to Quebec. In this view, it is the national leaders who, by their policy decisions, taken under pressure from both provincial and interest group leaders, decide on the regional distribution of wealth, status, and power. Examples of policies which presently affect or in the near future will affect the distribution of wealth, status, and power are bilingualism, the utilization of the Western Canada Development Fund, the price set for Canadian oil, and the allocation of powers under the constitution. Provincial premiers and interest group leaders play a role in defining regional expectations and advancing regional interests. Both the media and intellectuals play a role in articulating definitions of what the various regions legitimately can expect. In addition to raising expectations, they communicate the attitudes of other regions, thereby informing citizens of the expectations of the groups with which they will be bargaining. Also, they interpret past and present policies, so as to determine whether yesterday's expectations are now being satisfied.

The Gens de l'Air provide a good example of an interest group whose leaders were forced to confront the dilemma of whether the existing federal system was an appropriate framework within which to advance their interests. After the Lang-CATCA-CALPA agreement was signed, they wavered between two viewpoints. One, articulated by Clément Richard, was that it would be impossible to achieve change with the existing federal system. Thus, participation in the simulation exercises or the Commission of Inquiry hearings would be futile, because the only way that bilingual air traffic control could come about would be in a sovereign state of Quebec. In the other view, the apparatus of the federal government—the courts, the simulation exercises, and the Commission of Inquiry—was seen as sufficiently effective that controllers were willing to participate. The controllers searched their souls and ultimately decided, though with considerable skepticism, to try once again to advance their cause through the federal government. The most notable individual example of this was Jean-Luc Patenaude's representation of Quebec controllers at the Commission of Inquiry. In addition, the controllers who chose to participate in the simulation exercises were making this same affirmation.

The role of the intellectual in interpreting history in order to define today's expectations can be exemplified by the interpretation of the bilingual air traffic control controversy recently presented by a Concordia University professor, Hubert Guindon, in an article in *Canadian Forum*. The thrust of Guindon's article was a prediction of defeat for the Parti Québécois in the April 1981 election and an argument that a period in opposition would be valuable for the PQ, so that it could purify and rededicate itself to achieving separation.

In his article, Guindon set out to demonstrate that the francophone leaders of the federal Liberal party are "ethnic hybrids," "minority men in a majority setting," and ineffectuals who cannot advance the cause of Quebec. He cited as his proof their behaviour during the pilots' strike. Trudeau was criticized because a few days after his speech to the nation about the strike, "he packs his bags and goes to Bermuda," implying that he went on vacation, rather than to the first International Economic Summit to which Canada was invited. Guindon went on that, after Trudeau left, "Otto Lang, naturally, promptly surrendered to all of the pilots' and controllers' demands." Finally, Guindon asked, "How can Trudeau, who would not meet the challenge of CATCA and CALPA to the official language policy endorsed by all parties in Parliament, be expected to make the substantive changes needed by Quebec's changing political economy?"[42]

Guindon's was a misinterpretation with a purpose: to show that the existing system cannot satisfy expectations in the future, he retells history in such a way as to suggest that it did not satisfy them in the past. If one read only Guindon about bilingual air traffic control, one would probably conclude that English still is the only language used for air traffic control in Montreal. If Guindon's interpretation becomes the new dogma, there will probably be people in Quebec who believe just that. Indeed, an anglophone friend of mine recalls telling a francophone friend of his shortly after the Clark government accepted the *Final Report* of the Commission of Inquiry that it was important to have the Conservatives acknowledge this victory for the francophones. The francophone friend asked, "What victory? The air traffic control issue was a great defeat for us." Clearly, events can be mythologized to suit the ideologies that people hold.

Guindon had his purpose in writing his article, and I had mine in writing this book. I would like to think, however, that the difference is that mine became clear to me after, rather than before, I did the research. On a political level, I wrote to show an instance where francophone expectations, after some resistance, rapidly were met in the context of a federal state. I also wrote to show how professional concerns about the hurried imposition of change were ultimately reflected in the design of a safer air traffic control system. This is a story which might leave the reader with some guarded optimism about the future of the Canadian confederation. At least it will serve as one more item of evidence that must be dealt with in the ongoing debate about our future.

Finally, on a personal level, I wrote this book as an exercise in the historian's art, an attempt to comprehend and retell a fascinating and complex episode in our recent past and to illustrate the interaction of social forces, individual personalities, and sheer randomness that produces history.

Appendixes

Appendix A
Memorandum of Understanding

BETWEEN: THE MINISTER OF TRANSPORT
AND: THE CANADIAN AIR TRAFFIC CONTROL ASSOCIATION
        (CATCA)
AND: THE CANADIAN AIR LINE PILOTS ASSOCIATION (CALPA)

IT IS HEREBY AGREED

1. THAT the public Commission of Inquiry which has been announced be composed of three (3) judicial appointees; the third being acceptable to CATCA before any public announcement of his appointment is made.
2. THAT a prerequisite to the expansion or introduction of any bilingual air traffic service be a unanimous report of the Commission declaring the proposed expansion or introduction to be consistent with the maintenance of current safety standards in Canadian air operations.
3. THAT the terms of reference now contained in Order in Council PC-1976-1576 should include a provision to the effect that "the Commissioners shall append to their reports any statement on the aspects of the inquiry reported upon, received from CATCA or CALPA within a specified period of time designated by the Commission".
4. THAT the terms of reference should include a further provision to the effect that "the Commissioners shall not in any of their reports indicate that safety has been demonstrated unless they can justify beyond a reasonable doubt why any contrary view expressed by CATCA or CALPA should not prevail".
[Articles 5 and 6 revised the original terms of reference to include "implementation costs" in two places and to obligate, by the word "shall," the Commission to undertake various procedures, such as consultation with the industry, rather than permitting it, by the word "may," to undertake such procedures.]
7. With reference to the "specially appointed professional advisers" mentioned in paragraph (c) on page 1 of the terms of reference, Transport Canada and CATCA will submit a joint list of appropriate controller advisers to the Commission.

8. THAT Transport Canada will submit before July 1 a recommendation to the Privy Council which the Government will process expeditiously and publish in the Canada Gazette at the earliest possible date as an air navigation order with regard to the use of language in the air, and Transport Canada undertakes to pursue the enforcement thereof.

9. THAT, following the tabling of the final report of the Commission in Parliament, the Government will present a resolution to the House of Commons seeking concurrence therein in a free vote.

This MEMORANDUM OF UNDERSTANDING was signed at Ottawa, on the 28th day of June, 1976, subject to acceptance by the membership of the Canadian Air Traffic Control Association.

The Honourable Otto Lang,
Minister of Transport

J. M. Livingston, President,
Canadian Air Traffic Control Association

K. A. Maley, President,
Canadian Air Line Pilots Association

Appendix B

Glossary of Aviation Terminology

Aeradio operator—individuals, located in northern Canada, who provide advisory information to pilots by means of two-way radio.

Air navigation order (ANO)—orders issued to pilots by the Ministry of Transport regarding aircraft operations.

Airways—three-dimensional "air highways" located at upper altitudes and used by commercial aircraft.

Area control centre (ACC)—an air traffic control unit which provides en route and terminal control for pilots flying IFR in a given flight information region.

Clearance—instructions given by controllers to pilots under positive control to undertake a given portion of a flight.

En route control—air traffic control for IFR pilots flying en route between their origin and destination.

Flight information region (FIR)—a large area of en route airspace controlled by an area control centre. Canadian airspace is divided into eight flight information regions.

Flight progress (data) strip—small strip of paper containing information about a given flight used by IFR controllers to help keep track of the flight.

Instrument flight rules (IFR)—rules governing flight by pilots who use instruments and air traffic control clearances to navigate. Pilots flying IFR can fly with zero visibility (e.g., in cloud).

Joint en route terminal system (JETS)—a Canadian system providing alphanumeric display radar, which was installed at Canadian area control centres in 1981.

Listening watch—pilots are required to maintain a listening watch on the appropriate radio frequency. In this context, it refers to the "party line" aspect of the listening watch: pilots may overhear transmissions to other aircraft, and detect controller or pilot errors in those transmissions.

Notice to airmen (NOTAM)—temporary instructions to pilots issued by the Ministry of Transport. NOTAM's are of a provisional nature, as compared to ANO's, which are the basic rules of flying.

Positive control—a pilot is said to be flying under positive control when his flight is under the direction of air traffic control.

Positive control zone (PCZ) —airspace in the immediate vicinity of a busy airport, generally a radius of five miles around the airport, up to an altitude of 2,000 feet. All pilots flying in that airspace must be under positive control.

Terminal control unit (TCU) —air traffic control unit which controls pilots flying IFR in a radius of forty miles of a major airport.

Terminal radar service area (TRSA) —airspace within a radius of twenty miles of a busy airport and between the altitudes of 2,000 and 9,500 feet. All aircraft flying through the TRSA must be under positive control. The TRSA is used to facilitate separation between commercial aircraft and small aircraft in the vicinity of busy airports.

Visual flight rules (VFR) —rules governing the operation of aircraft in which pilots maintain separation from other aircraft visually. VFR flying requires good weather.

Appendix C
Organizational Acronyms

AGAQ — Association des Gens de l'Air du Québec: association of francophones in all sectors of the aviation industry, formed in 1975, to increase francophone rights and participation.

AQCNA — Association Québécoise des Contrôleurs de la Navigation Aérienne: association of francophone air traffic controllers, formed in 1974, and a precursor to AGAQ.

BICSS — Bilingual IFR Communications Simulation Study: study conducted by MOT, using the air traffic control simulation centre, to compare the safety of bilingual and unilingual air traffic control.

BILCOM — Bilingual Communications Task Force: task force of MOT civil servants which, from late 1973 to early 1975, studied the bilingual air traffic control problem.

CALPA — Canadian Air Line Pilots Association: union and professional organization representing pilots flying for major Canadian airlines.

CATCA — Canadian Air Traffic Control Association: union and professional organization representing Canadian air traffic controllers.

Committee of Eight — a group of eight Montreal controllers who negotiated a relocation agreement between MOT and the controllers who left Montreal in 1976 and 1977 because of their opposition to bilingual air traffic control.

COPA — Canadian Owners and Pilots Association: organization representing Canadian private pilots.

ICAO — International Civil Aeronautics Organization: international organization which coordinates aviation practices throughout the world.

IFALPA — International Federation of Air Line Pilots Associations.

IFATCA — International Federation of Air Traffic Controllers Associations.

MOT — Ministry of Transport: in this book, used informally to refer to any part of the federal transport ministry. More precisely, most units mentioned are part of the Canadian Air Transportation Administration, which itself is part of MOT.

PSSRB — Public Service Staff Relations Board: the tribunal which oversees collective bargaining between the government and the public service unions.

253

SCAQ—Syndicat des Contrôleurs Aériens du Québec: association formed in 1976 by Quebec air traffic controllers who attempted to disaffiliate from CATCA.

Notes

Notes to Introduction

1. Viv Nelles, "Rewriting History," *Saturday Night*, February 1981, pp. 12, 13, 14, 16.

Notes to Chapter One

1. See Transport Canada, Civil Aeronautics, *Air Regulations and Aeronautics Act* (Ottawa: Supply and Services Canada, 1978), pp. 31–33.

2. The federal transportation ministry was known as the Department of Transport from 1936 until 1970, the Ministry of Transport from 1970 to 1974, and Transport Canada from 1974 until the present. The acronym MOT is employed because that is most commonly used by Transport Canada employees today. The section of MOT responsible for aviation is the Canadian Air Transportation Administration (CATA). This name will not be used because of its similarity to CATCA, the acronym for the Canadian Air Traffic Control Association. The reader should remember that references to the activities of MOT refer more specifically to the activities of the air administration within MOT.

3. The national training school was moved from Ottawa to Cornwall in 1978, as part of the government's policy of decentralization of the federal bureaucracy.

4. A study comparing air traffic controllers with other MOT employees found no significant difference in stress levels. However, the authors cautioned that the demanding selection process for air traffic controllers might mean that controllers are better able to cope with stress than the rest of the population. See A. MacBride et al., "Level of Distress among Canadian Government Employees," paper presented to the annual meeting of the Canadian Psychiatric Association, Winnipeg, September 1981.

5. See A. MacBride, A. Formo, and S. J. Freeman, "Organizational Structure as a Source of Psychosocial Stress among Air Traffic Controllers in Ontario," paper presented at the Department of Psychiatry, University of Toronto, September 8, 1978, p. 5.

6. Ibid., pp. 6–8.

7. Sandra Gwyn, "The Surly Bonds of Bigotry," *Saturday Night*, April 1977, pp. 15–19.

8. Ken Romain, "Traffic controllers plan to seek parity with pilots," *Globe and Mail*, September 10, 1979, p. B1.

9. CALPA, *Constitution and By-Laws*, revised 1977 (Brampton, Ontario: by the author, 1977), pp. 4–6, 9–11, 30–43.

10. CALPA, *Administrative Policy Manual*, revised 1977 (Brampton, Ontario: by the author, 1977), p. 1.

Notes to Chapter Two

1. The ICAO recommendations on air-ground communications can be found in Commission of Inquiry into Bilingual Air Traffic Services in Quebec, *Interim Report* (Ottawa: Supply and Services Canada, 1977), pp. 60–63.

2. Raymond Breton and Daiva Stasiulis, "Linguistic Boundaries and the Cohesion of Canada," in Raymond Breton, Jeffrey Reitz, Victor Valentine, *Cultural Boundaries and the Cohesion of Canada* (Montreal: Institute for Research on Public Policy, 1980), pp. 280–81.

3. R. W. Goodwin, "Use of the French Language in Air Traffic Control," memo to director of air traffic services, Quebec region, MOT, October 2, 1962, p. 1.

4. Ibid., p. 2.

5. Les dossiers du Devoir, numéro 2, *La Langue du ciel: le bilinguisme dans les communications air/sol* (Montreal: Le Devoir, February 1977), p. 11.

6. G. A. Scott, "Use of French Language in Montreal Area Control Centre," memo to Quebec regional director, air services, MOT, July 23, 1969.

7. Official Languages Act, Revised Statutes of Canada, C. 54, s. 1. See sections 9(1), 9(2), 10(1), and 10(3).

8. Bureau of Management Consulting, *Air Traffic Control Occupational Study* (Ottawa: Information Canada, 1970), p. 207.

9. Ibid., p. 206.

10. Ibid., pp. 211–17.

11. J. R. Campbell, "CATCA Policy on Bilingualism," memo to CATCA branch chairmen, August 24, 1971.

12. See Public Services Staff Relations Board, *Decision* between Le Syndicat des Contrôleurs aériens du Québec, applicant, and Her Majesty in right of Canada as represented by the Treasury Board, Employer, and The Canadian Air Traffic Control Association, intervener, and a group of employees, objectors (Ottawa, September 26, 1978), pp. 23–24. Henceforth referred to as PSSRB, *Decision*.

13. Ibid., pp. 24–25.

14. J. R. Campbell, "Bilingualism: Meeting with the Hon. Don Jamieson, Minister of Transport, November 26, 1971: Special Bulletin to CATCA national council and branch chairmen, December 1, 1971."

15. MOT, "Air Traffic Control Implementation Team Report" (Ottawa, July 1972).

16. PSSRB *Decision*, pp. 27–28.

Notes to Chapter Three

1. "Aéroport, 1975," *Time* (Canadian edition), August 25, 1975, p. 9.

Notes to Chapter Four

1. Jean-Luc Patenaude, interview, May 6, 1981.
2. The discussion of why francophone controllers first mobilized in Quebec City is based on Irène Lépine, "The Air Traffic Controllers Dispute: 1976," M.A. thesis, Department of Sociology, McGill University, August 1980, pp. 85–92.
3. Roch Desgagne, "Le Contrôle de la navigation aérienne sera bilingue au Québec," *Le Soleil*, March 13, 1974.
4. Roch Desgagne, "Qu'attend Marchand pour favoriser l'usage du français dans le service aérien?" *Le Soleil*, March 18, 1974.
5. Roch Desgagne, "Les Contrôleurs aériens peuvent parler le français au Québec," *Le Soleil*, April 11, 1974.
6. Association Québécoise des Contrôleurs de la Navigation Aérienne, "Mémoire," April 14, 1974.
7. "Il faut maintenir l'anglais dans les Communications aériennes," *Le Soleil*, April 6, 1974, p. 7.
8. Pierre Guy Charbonneau, letter to the *Montreal Star*, March 27, 1974, p. A-8.
9. CATCA, "Minutes of the Spring Council Meeting, Quebec City, April 29–May 1, 1974," pp. 11–17, 20.
10. Ibid., pp. 18–19.
11. Roch Desgagne, "Entente sur l'usage du français entre les contrôleurs aériens francophones et leur association Canadienne," *Le Soleil*, May 1, 1974, p. 65; Hubert Bauch, "Controllers united for strike after agreeing on use of French," *Globe and Mail*, May 2, 1974, p. 8.
12. Maurice Baribeau, "Use of French in Air/Ground Communications," memorandum to William Huck, January 22, 1974.
13. Desmond J. Peters, "Air Traffic Control—Quebec—Language and Safety Implications," memorandum, April 5, 1974.
14. McLeish's recounting of these conversations can be found in Commission of Inquiry into Bilingual Air Traffic Services in Quebec, *Hearings*, volume 14, February 8, 1977, pp. 1620–27. Under cross-examination, McLeish stated that Marchand did not draft the terms of reference for his study, nor tell him what should be concluded.
15. Ibid., volume 22, March 1, 1977, p. 2913.
16. Even here, he had doubts, later telling the Commission of Inquiry, "In every case without exception—I think this is rather unusual—in every case, the controllers gave us some example that the pilot is overshooting and they tell him: turn left, and he says 'Roger' and continues on. They say 'What is your name?' and he says 'Roger.' It was the same example from each of the controllers which kind of indicates to me that it is a story that was perhaps cooked up." Ibid., p. 2829.

17. Aviation Safety Bureau, "Report: Aviation Safety Investigation, Bilingualism in Air/Ground Operational Communications," May 2, 1974.

18. "Le Québécois a toujours 'pollué' les sphères de l'aviation," *Le Soleil*, October 16, 1976.

19. Aviation Safety Bureau, "Report," appended pp. 2–4.

20. Walter McLeish, letter to Captain J. B. Wright, May 15, 1974.

21. MOT, "NOTAM 12/74: Use of the French Language in Aeronautical Voice Communications," June 19, 1974.

22. PSSRB, "Complaint under Section 20 of the Public Service Staff Relations Act between Jean-Luc Patenaude and Canadian Air Traffic Control Association" (Ottawa: March 12, 1976), pp. 5, 6, 13.

23. MOT, "Project BILCOM: An Assessment of the Demand for the Use of Both Official Languages in Canadian Domestic Air/Ground Communications" (Ottawa: May 25, 1975).

24. Pilots based in English Canada were surveyed, but their responses so overwhelmingly favoured English that the number was not reported.

25. L'Office de la Langue Française is responsible for implementing Quebec's language legislation, in particular by making French the language of work.

26. Jacques Guay, "Le français dans les airs: Bourassa donne son appui aux pilotes," *Le Jour*, April 24, 1975, p. 1.

27. Commissioner of Official Languages, *Fourth Annual Report: 1973–74* (Ottawa: Information Canada, 1975), pp. 300–322 ("Transport—'Promises, Promises'").

28. Roch Desgagne, "Il faut concilier bilinguisme et sécurité (Spicer)," *Le Soleil*, April 23, 1975, p. C19.

29. "Ottawa will speed study on French for air controllers," *Montreal Gazette*, April 25, 1975, p. 2.

30. "French condemned," *Ottawa Citizen*, April 24, 1975, p. 4.

31. MOT, memorandum from special assignment team to director-general, civil aeronautics, re. BILCOM *Minority Report* Recommendations, May 23, 1975.

32. The Davey Task Force on Transportation Policy was set up to respond to the expectations for major transportation policy initiatives stimulated by Prime Minister Trudeau during the 1974 election campaign. The task force reviewed demand and capacity in the national transportation system, and made several recommendations designed to rationalize pricing and investment policies. See Transport Canada, *Transportation Policy: A Framework for Transport in Canada* (Ottawa: Information Canada, June 1975).

Notes to Chapter Five

1. John Keenan, "Meeting Regarding Project BILCOM, Ottawa, June 26, 1975," CALPA memo, reprinted in Les dossiers du Devoir, numéro 2, *La Langue du ciel* (Montreal: Le Devoir, February 1977), p. 40.

2. CALPA, "Headquarters Bulletin," July 2, 1975, p. 1.

3. Ibid.

4. John Keenan, "Meeting Regarding Project BILCOM, Ottawa, June 26, 1975."

5. House of Commons *Debates*, July 29, 1975, p. 8025.

6. Denis Masse, "Les Controleurs aériens francophones: Nous ne cèderons pas au chantage des pilotes," *Le Soleil*, August 9, 1975, p. A2.

7. Quoted in Sandra Gwyn, "The Surly Bonds of Bigotry," *Saturday Night*, April 1977, p. 19.

8. Paul Dalby, "Pilot's lack of English blamed for near-crash at Toronto," *Toronto Star*, August 15, 1975, p. 1.

9. "Aéroport, 1975," *Time* (Canadian edition), August 25, 1975, p. 9.

10. John McManus, "Pilots, Marchand to discuss bilingual air control issue," *Winnipeg Free Press*, August 15, 1975, p. 3.

11. *Montreal Star*, August 27, 1975, p. A2.

12. Ibid.

13. "Pilots' ultimatum," *Victoria Daily Colonist*, August 10, 1975, p. 4; "Heed the Pilots," *Montreal Star*, August 11, 1975, p. 6; "Safety vs Bilingualism," *Winnipeg Free Press*, August 11, 1975, p. 29; "Pilots and patois," *Vancouver Sun*, August 11, 1975, p. 4; "Language Confusion Deadly in Aircraft," *Sudbury Star*, August 11, 1975, p. 4; "Tongue in the clouds," *Globe and Mail*, August 12, 1975, p. 6; "Air safety comes ahead of bilingualism," *Toronto Star*, August 7, 1975, p. B4; "Flight Language," *Edmonton Journal*, August 12, 1975, p. 4.

14. "Breath-taking arrogance: Air traffic threat," *Calgary Herald*, August 30, 1975, p. 6; "Air controllers use Canadians as pawns," *Globe and Mail*, August 29, 1975, p. 6; "Public safety isn't the issue," *Ottawa Citizen*, August 30, 1975, p. 6.

15. "Tongue in the Clouds," *Globe and Mail*, August 12, 1975, p. 6.

16. "Ottawa Pays the Ransom," ibid., September 2, 1975, p. 6.

17. Commissioner of Official Languages, *Fifth Annual Report: 1975* (Ottawa: Information Canada, 1976), p. 143.

18. Advisory Committee—Bilingual Air-Ground Communications, "Minutes of Meeting September 23–24, 1975," Holiday Inn, Ottawa, September 23, p. 2.

19. Ibid., p. 3.

20. CALPA, "CALPA Proposals to the Advisory Committee" and "The Position Taken by the Canadian Air Line Pilots' Association as a Member of the Special Advisory Committee," September 1975.

21. Advisory Committee, "Minutes," September 24, p. 5.

22. Ibid., p. 14.

23. Ibid., September 23, pp. 6, 14.

24. Ibid., p. 16.

25. Ibid., September 24, p. 9.

26. H. R. Finley, "Draft Report—Advisory Committee on Bilingual Air Communications," October 1975, appendix E.

27. Association des Gens de l'Air du Québec, "Bilinguisme dans les communications air-sol, Province de Québec," presented October 9, 1975, pp. 6, 7.

28. Otto Lang, interview with Patrick Watson, "The Watson Report," January 13, 1977.

29. MOT, "Study of Control Procedures, Facilities and Air Traffic Services at Quebec Airport," October 1975.

30. "En guise de protestation contre le francais: Multipliez les incidents, dit la CALPA aux pilotes," *Le Devoir*, October 16, 1975, p. 1.

31. Canadian Press report, filed by Bob Douglas, October 16, 1975.

32. See A. Maslove and E. Swimmer, *Wage Controls in Canada, 1975–78: A Study of Public Decision Making* (Montreal: Institute for Research on Public Policy, 1980).

33. House of Commons *Debates*, October 27, 1975, p. 8598.

34. A. R. Novakowski, "Draft Report on Bilingual Air Traffic Control," November 1975, pp. 2, 4.

35. MOT, "Report of the Committee on Inter and Intra ATS Unit Coordination," January 7, 1976, p. 2.

36. Notice to Airmen (NOTAM), November 12, 1975.

37. William Huck, "Memorandum to the Deputy Minister," November 12, 1975.

38. Roger Demers, telegram to Prime Minister Trudeau, November 16, 1975.

39. Jacques Guay, "Ottawa recule: Tout le système aérien au Québec risque d'être gravement perturbé," *Le Jour*, November 18, 1975; "Ottawa interdit le français sans consulter Québec," ibid., November 19, 1975.

40. House of Commons *Debates*, November 18, 1975, p. 9190.

41. "'Unfair attack' on Lang," *Ottawa Journal*, November 24, 1975.

42. Walter McLeish, interview with Patrick Watson, "The Watson Report," December 4, 1975, p. 9 of transcript.

43. Ibid., p. 6.

44. CALPA, "Headquarters Bulletin," December 12, 1975, p. 1.

45. William Huck, "Language Use in Air Traffic Control," memorandum to Quebec regional administrator, Canadian Air Transportation Administration, August 8, 1975.

46. Patrick Finn, "Bilingualism almost closed Dorval centre," *Montreal Star*, May 5, 1976.

47. Bill Robertson, vice-president, CATCA, "To: National Council, File Note— Bilingualism Situation—Montreal ACC," December 18, 1975, pp. 1, 2.

48. Daniel Marsolais, "Les Contrôleurs continueront à parler français," *La Presse*, December 10, 1975.

49. House of Commons *Debates*, December 9, 1975, p. 9838.

50. Commissioner of Official Languages, *Fifth Annual Report*, pp. 145–46.

51. Michel Roy, "C'est le reglement." *Le Devoir*, December 12, 1975, p. 5.

52. William Johnson, "Language tensions in Dorval control centre threaten safety of passengers, Spicer says," *Globe and Mail*, December 13, 1975.

53. House of Commons *Debates*, December 12, 1975, p. 9962.

54. "Transport Minister Otto Lang Announces Bilingual Air Communications will be Introduced Progressively in Quebec," Transport Canada news release number 153-75, December 13, 1975, pp. 1–5.

55. Ibid., p. 5.

56. CATCA, "memorandum to branches and facilities re. Bilingualism in Air Traffic Control," January 6, 1976.

57. Robertson memorandum, p. 3.
58. House of Commons *Debates*, December 15, 1975, p. 9997.
59. Michel Roy, "Le ciel aussi sera français," *Le Devoir*, December 15, 1975, p. 5; "Attérrir à Victoria," *Montreal Gazette*, December 16, 1975; "Air Language," *Montreal Star*, December 16, 1975; "Safety First," *Ottawa Citizen*, December 17, 1975; "For the Worst of Reasons," *Globe and Mail*, December 15, 1975; "French in the Air," *Winnipeg Free Press*, December 15, 1975.
60. Montreal Ad-Hoc Committee, "Minutes," December 17, 1975; ibid., "Suggested Outline for December 18, 1975 Meeting with W. McLeish and Company," December 17, 1975.
61. Committee of Eight, "Minutes: Committee Meeting," December 18, 1975; Ibid., "Minutes of Meeting between the Controllers' Committee and MOT Officials from Ottawa," December 18, 1975.
62. House of Commons *Debates*, December 9, 1975, p. 9838.
63. Canadian Institute of Public Opinion, "The Gallup Report," June 1975 to March 1976.

Notes to Chapter Six

1. MOT, Committee on Inter and Intra Air Traffic Services Unit Coordination Report, January 7, 1976.
2. MOT, St. Hubert Bilingual Task Force Report, May 1976, pp. 1, 2.
3. CATCA, minutes of national council meeting, February 5, 1976, p. 2.
4. CALPA, memorandum to all members, January 6, 1976.
5. House of Commons *Debates*, February 16, 1976, pp. 10998–99.
6. "Language issue is Safety," *Vancouver Province*, February 20, 1976; Victor Mackie, "Near miss: Pilot MP fears French might have caused crash," *Ottawa Journal*, March 3, 1976; "Language Mixing 'Perilous'," *Ottawa Citizen*, February 17, 1976.
7. House of Commons *Debates*, February 9, 1976, p. 10781.
8. CATCA, minutes of national executive meeting, January 19, 1976, p. 1.
9. Accounts can be found in Pierre Bergeron, "Le bilinguisme dans les communications aériennes: Ottawa entend aller de l'avant," *Le Droit*, March 2, 1976; Patrick Best, "More French for Quebec pilots," *Ottawa Citizen*, March 2, 1976; Denis Lord, "usage du francais fait monter de 40 p.c. le trafic aérien à Québec," *La Presse*, March 2, 1976.
10. Captain J. R. Desmarais, "Safe, Expeditious, Political Control of Air Traffic," *Pilot*, Spring 1976, p. 5.
11. PSSRB *Decision*, p. 80.
12. See Commissioner of Official Languages, *Fifth Annual Report*, pp. 206–8.
13. Desmarais, "Safe, Expeditious, Political Control," pp. 6–7.
14. J. M. Livingston, "Two Languages in Air Traffic Control: A Position of Protest," *Canadian Air Traffic Control Association Journal*, Spring 1976, p. 23.
15. Pierre Beaudry, "Notes for a Speech," March 1976, pp. 5, 16, 17.
16. Captain H. Vermuelen, "Comments," *Canadian Air Traffic Control Association Journal*, March 1976, pp. 16, 25, 28.

17. Desmarais, "Safe, Expeditious, Political Control," p. 10.

18. Gilles Constantineau, "Un expert suisse: Rien ne prouve les dangers du bilinguisme dans le ciel," *Le Devoir*, March 4, 1976; Patricia Poirier, "Américains et anglophones font le procès du français," *Le Droit*, March 3, 1976; Clément Brown, "Symposium sur le bilinguisme: Dialogue de sourds," *Montreal-Matin*, March 3, 1976; "French in the Air," *Winnipeg Free Press*, March 6, 1976; "Flying too high in bilingual skies," *Windsor Star*, March 3, 1976; "Language and Safety," *Montreal Star*, March 5, 1976; "The Language of Safety," *Globe and Mail*, March 18, 1976.

19. See Public Service Staff Relations Act Section 56 (2), Revised Statutes of Canada, Chapter P-35.

20. PSSRB *Decision*, p. 79.

21. On May 31, 1982, the Supreme Court of Canada made an important ruling which will significantly affect the designation process. In 1980, MOT decided to depart from its previous practice and designate almost all operational controllers. CATCA appealed the decision, but the Supreme Court, in a unanimous ruling, upheld MOT. The Court held that the duties referred to in section 79(1) of the Public Service Staff Relations Act are the normal duties of the bargaining unit, rather than some subset of duties to be maintained during a strike. (See The Hon. Mr. Justice Martland, *Reason for Judgment* between the Canadian Air Traffic Control Association and Her Majesty the Queen in right of Canada as represented by the Treasury Board, in the Supreme Court of Canada, May 31, 1982.) Therefore, the PSSRB cannot decide that a lower than normal level of service is acceptable during a strike and designate employees accordingly. The implication of the judgment is that, if the Treasury Board can show the PSSRB the duties of the employees of a bargaining unit are "in the interest of the safety or security of the public" then the PSSRB must designate them. The union, on the other hand, would have the task of proving the opposite, which could well be in opposition to its own long-run interests. It is likely that the Treasury Board will use this case as a precedent in order to designate most of the employees in bargaining units such as doctors, nurses, pilots and aviation inspectors, police and firefighters. This would greatly reduce the effectiveness of strikes by such groups.

22. J. M. Livingston, "File Note—Special Council Meeting, February 29, 1976," February 12, 1976.

23. Guy Deshaies, "Les 'gens de l'air' du Québec ignoreront l'ordre de grève," *Le Devoir*, February 28, 1976; "No bilingualism strike," *Montreal Gazette*, February 28, 1976.

24. CATCA, minutes of national council meeting, February 29–March 3, 1976.

25. P. E. Arpin, letter to J. M. Livingston, March 3, 1976; CATCA, minutes of national executive meeting, March 20, 1976, p. 1.

26. J. Finkelman, "Terms of Reference of the Conciliation Board," PSSRB file number 190-2-48, March 4, 1976.

27. PSSRB, "Complaint under Section 20 of the Public Service Staff Relations Act between Jean-Luc Patenaude and the Canadian Air Traffic Control Association" (Ottawa: March 12, 1976).

28. CATCA, minutes of national executive meeting, March 20, 1976, p. 3.

29. P. E. Arpin, letter to J. M. Livingston, March 26, 1976.

30. Jean Chrétien, letter to M. Charlebois, April 1, 1976.

31. J. M. Livingston, "CALPA Support in Opposition to the Expansion of Bilingual ATC," memorandum to CATCA national council, branches and facilities negotiating team, March 26, 1976.

32. Robert McKenzie, "Plane Language: the pilots mince no words in the fight over using French in air traffic control," *Toronto Star*, January 10, 1976.

33. CALPA, "Headquarters Newsletter," April 30, 1976.

34. Ibid.

35. CATCA, minutes of national executive meeting, March 20, 1976, p. 2.

36. J. M. Livingston, "Controller Relationships—Montreal Centre," memorandum to national council, branches and facilities, March 30, 1976.

37. CATCA, minutes of the spring national council meeting, St. John's, Nfld., May 26–29, 1976, Attachment 7.

38. Otto Lang, "Bilingual Air Traffic Services," memorandum to MPs and senators, April 5, 1976.

39. Canadian Institute of Public Opinion, "The Gallup Report: French-English views differ on emphasis on bilingualism," May 19, 1976.

40. Ibid., "The Gallup Report," April 1976.

41. Order-in-Council P.C., 1976–2143, May 13, 1976.

42. PSSRB, "The Report of the Board of Conciliation established in the matter of the Public Service Relations Act and a dispute affecting the Canadian Air Traffic Control Association and Her Majesty in Right of Canada as represented by the Treasury Board," file number 190-2-48, May 11, 1976.

43. Peter Sadlier-Brown, "Addendum to the Report of the Board of Conciliation established to dealing with the dispute between the Treasury Board and the Canadian Air Traffic Control Association," May 11, 1976.

44. MOT, "Statement by Transport Minister Otto Lang on Bilingual Air Traffic Control in Quebec," May 12, 1976; MOT, "Bilingual Air/Ground Communications Background," May 12, 1976. The list of relevant laws and studies was copied, almost verbatim, from a letter written by Roger Demers, published in *Canadian Aircraft Owner*, February 16, 1976.

45. House of Commons *Debates*, May 14, 1976, pp. 13516–17.

46. Both at the time of Keenan's appointment and in the following weeks, there were rumours in Ottawa that Otto Lang chose Keenan as commissioner because Keenan promised that he would bring down a report validating the implementation of bilingual air traffic control. (See Michel Roy, "Lang entre l'invraisemblable et l'absurde," *Le Devoir*, June 18, 1976.) My research found those rumours to be totally without foundation.

47. CBC Radio, "The World at Six," May 12, 1976; CTV Newsline, May 12, 1976.

48. J. D. Lyon, "Information Bulletin: Special Task Force—Quebec ATS Personnel Problems, 'Air Traffic Control Linguistic Relocation Allowance,'" April 9, 1976.

49. Interview of André Dumas, Quebec regional air administrator, by Herb Luft, "Pulse News," television station CFCF—Montreal, April 30, 1976.

50. Patrick Finn, "Bilingualism almost closed Dorval centre," *Montreal Star*, May 5, 1976, pp. A-1, A-2.

51. CATCA, minutes of the spring national council meeting, St. John's, Nfld., May 26–29, 1976, attachment 8.

52. Guy Deshaies, "Air Canada interdit le français à son personnel navigant," *Le Devoir*, May 10, 1976.

53. Michel Roy, "Le français, on y vient. . . . Pierre Nadeau se dissocie des '14 soleils,'" *Le Devoir*, May 31, 1976.

54. MOT, "Director General Civil Aeronautics Announces Language Usage on Flight Deck Policy," press release 74/76, June 4, 1976.

55. J. F. Falvey, "St. Hubert Control Tower—Use of French Language," memorandum to director of air traffic services, MOT, March 29, 1976; D. J. Douglas, "Aviation Safety Report—St. Hubert Airport, March 30–April 1, 1976," MOT, April 1976; St. Hubert Bilingual Task Force, minutes of meetings of April 28, 1976.

56. MOT, St. Hubert Bilingual Task Force Report, May 1976.

57. J. M. Tonner, letter to D. L. Cunningham, May 14, 1976; CATCA, "Record of Dissent by CATCA to the Report of the St. Hubert Bilingual Task Force," May 14, 1976.

58. K. Maley, letter to D. L. Cunningham, May 27, 1976.

59. CATCA, minutes of special council meeting conference call, May 14, 1976, p. 2.

60. "Air control union calls for strike," Canadian Press report, *Ottawa Citizen*, May 15, 1976.

61. "Quebecers may quit over bilingualism: Split threatens air traffic controllers," Canadian Press report, *Globe and Mail*, May 17, 1976.

62. House of Commons *Debates*, May 18, 1976, p. 13612.

63. Government of Quebec, "Conférence de presse du Solliciteur général du Québec et Ministre responsable de l'application de la Loi sur la langue officielle, Me Fernand Lalonde," May 20, 1976, p. 4.

64. CATCA, minutes of the spring national council meeting, St. John's, Nfld., May 26–29, 1976, p. 16.

65. J. M. Livingston, press release, May 28, 1976.

66. Denis Masse, "Les Contrôleurs du Québec vont demander la désaffiliation lundi," *La Presse*, May 29, 1976.

67. Michel Roy, "La langue du ciel: repli stratégique," *Le Devoir*, May 29, 1976.

68. "Air workers say federal officials concede bilingual traffic inquiry not justifiable," Canadian Press report, *Globe and Mail*, June 3, 1976.

69. Otto Lang, letter to Roger Demers, June 4, 1976; MOT, "Transport Minister Otto Lang Urges l'Association des Gens de l'Air du Québec to Support Keenan Commission," press release 73/76, June 4, 1976.

70. "Quebec controllers against probe head," Canadian Press report, *Ottawa Citizen*, June 5, 1976.

71. "Quebec Liberal MPs tell Ottawa to expand bilingual air control," Canadian Press report, *Globe and Mail*, June 7, 1976.

72. John Keenan, letter to Otto Lang, June 7, 1976.

73. CATCA, minutes of special council meeting conference call, June 7, 1976.

Notes to Chapter Seven

1. CATCA, "Special Council Meeting Conference Call," June 13, 1976, p. 1.

2. "Lang to study foreign systems," Canadian press report, *Ottawa Citizen*, June 11, 1976.

3. Canadian Press report, June 9, 1976.

4. CATCA, "Special Council Meeting Conference Call," June 13, 1976, pp. 1, 2.

5. CATCA, "Minutes of Special Council Meeting," Ottawa, June 14, 1976, pp. 1–7.

6. CATCA, statement by J. M. Livingston, June 15, 1976.

7. Richard D. French, *How Ottawa Decides: Planning and Industrial Policy-Making, 1968–1980* (Toronto: James Lorimer and Company, 1980), pp. 83–84.

8. Gilles Paquin, "Les contrôleurs aériens: Ottawa ne tolérera pas un grève illégale," *Le Droit*, June 16, 1976.

9. Leo Ryan, "Lang impressed by bilingual air traffic control at Paris airport," *Globe and Mail*, June 16, 1976, p. 1.

10. J. M. Livingston, interview on "As it Happens" (CBC Radio), June 17, 1976.

11. See letters by J. R. Buykes, Toby Riley, Larry Roberts, to *Globe and Mail*, June 19, 1976, p. 6.

12. "Government lawyers plan to seek court injunction to head off controllers' strike expected Sunday," Canadian Press report, *Globe and Mail*, June 18, 1976, p. 1.

13. House of Commons *Debates*, June 18, 1976, p. 14654.

14. Ibid., p. 14656.

15. The Queen v. Livingston, *Federal Court Reports*, 1977, pp. 369–79.

16. CATCA, "Special Council Meeting Conference Call," June 19, 1976.

17. "Pilots' group reveals near-miss of two jets," Canadian Press report, *Globe and Mail*, June 19, 1976, p. 8.

18. Interviewed about this, Aviation Safety Branch Director Hart Finely said, "I can't honestly say whether the increased number of near misses has anything to do with air-ground communication. It conceivably could have, in that some controllers may be inattentive to their job. It's just conceivable, and as a result they are not being as professional as they could be." *Edmonton Journal*, June 22, 1976.

19. Loren Lind, "Air Canada, CP seek injunction: Pilots stop work, flights cancelled," *Globe and Mail*, June 21, 1976, p. 1.

20. Ibid.

21. Greg Watson, "Air travel still stalled as injunctions are defied," *Ottawa Citizen*, June 21, 1976, p. 1.

22. A. J. Thurlow, "Reasons for Order: In the Federal Court of Canada, Trial Division, Between Air Canada, Canadian Pacific Airlines, Ltd., Eastern Provincial Airlines (1963) Ltd., Plaintiffs, and Kenneth A. Maley, Robert A. MacKinnon, Canadian Air Line Pilots Association, Defendents," June 21, 1976, p. 3.

23. See "Most side with pilots—but many don't care," *Globe and Mail*, June 26, 1979, p. 1, and William Johnson, "Two solitudes still divide Canada, letters on air dispute show," ibid., July 10, 1976, p. 4.

24. Thomas Claridge and Darryl Dean, "Controllers return but chaos persists," ibid., June 22, 1976, p. 2.
25. Ibid.
26. Ibid.
27. One year later, out of dissatisfaction with Joe Clark's leadership, Jack Horner left the Conservatives and joined the Liberals. He was appointed minister of industry, trade, and commerce.
28. "Joyal, Air Canada workers charge anti-French bias," *Montreal Gazette*, June 22, 1976.
29. "Le 'fanatisme' des contrôleurs," Canadian Press report, *Le Devoir*, June 22, 1976.
30. Andrew Phillips, "Air Canada near full shutdown," *Montreal Gazette*, June 23, 1976.
31. "Telegram sent to carrier: Air Canada could operate in Quebec: pilot," Canadian Press report, *Globe and Mail*, June 28, 1976, p. 4.
32. Peter Whelman, "Airlines closing one by one; foreign pilots back colleagues," *Globe and Mail*, June 23, 1976, p. 1.
33. Ibid.
34. "Lack of consultation caused festering air traffic control situation, pilots' official says," Ottawa Bureau of the *Globe and Mail*, June 26, 1976, p. 2.
35. John King, "334 pilots plan strike, House told," *Globe and Mail*, June 23, 1976.
36. House of Commons *Debates*, June 22, 1976, p. 14744.
37. Ibid., p. 14745.
38. Ibid., p. 14786.
39. Transcript of press conference by Hon. Otto Lang and Walter McLeish, June 22, 1976, pp. 1, 2, 4, 9.
40. See Tom Wolfe, *The Right Stuff* (New York: Farrar, Straus and Giroux, 1979).
41. Otto Lang, interview on Canada A.M. (CTV television), June 23, 1976, pp. 2, 3 of transcript.
42. CATCA, "Special Council Meeting, Conference Call," June 4, 1976, p. 1.
43. Prime Minister Trudeau, "Statement on National Television and Radio on the Disruption of Civil Aviation," June 23, 1976, p. 3.
44. Ibid., pp. 4–5.
45. Ibid., p. 2.
46. CATCA, "Special Council Meeting, Conference Call," June 24, 1976, pp. 1, 2.
47. Dorothy Lipovenko, "Injunction against pilots extended to Wednesday," *Globe and Mail*, June 25, 1976, p. 5.
48. Thomas Claridge, "Pilots from 10 U.S. airlines join walkout in Canada," ibid., June 25, 1976, p. 1.
49. "Sauf au Québec, le trafic paralysé," *Le Devoir*, June 25, 1976.
50. Joe Clark, "Statement on CBC Television and Radio, Thursday, June 24, 1976."
51. Voice of Canada League, "Our Government: Racist and Arrogant," advertisement in *Globe and Mail*, June 25, 1976, p. 9.

52. Otto Lang, "Bilingualism in the air," advertisement, ibid., p. 10.

53. John King, "Air crisis is Canada's worst since conscription, PM says," ibid., June 26, 1976, p. 1.

54. House of Commons *Debates*, June 25, 1976, pp. 14834, 14835.

55. Ibid., p. 14836.

56. CATCA, "Special Council Meeting," Ottawa, June 25–28, 1976, pp. 1,2.

57. Ibid., pp. 2,3.

58. "Lang optimistic on talks but controllers cautious," Canadian Press report, *Globe and Mail*, June 28, 1976, p. 1.

59. CATCA, "Special Council Meeting," Ottawa, June 25–28, 1976, pp. 3–6.

60. John King, "Pilots agree to fly but reserve right to walk out again if commission favors bilingualism," *Globe and Mail*, June 29, 1976, p. 2.

61. Ibid.

Notes to Chapter Eight

1. Hubert Bauch, "All political stripes in Quebec attack federal concessions on airport French," *Globe and Mail*, June 30, 1976, p. 1.

2. Patrick Doyle, "Air crisis basic to repatriation: Premier," *Montreal Gazette*, July 5, 1976.

3. "Minister says Lang gave in," *Ottawa Citizen*, July 3, 1976.

4. "Government stuck to its original terms, didn't back down to pilots, Trudeau says," *Globe and Mail*, Tuesday, June 29, 1976, p. 2.

5. Marc Lalonde, press conference, Quebec, June 29, 1976; Marc Lalonde, interview Radio-Canada, June 29, 1976; Marc Lalonde, interview TVA, June 29, 1976.

6. Keith Spicer, "Des éclaircissements souhaitables dans l'enquête Sinclair-Chouinard-Heald," *Le Devoir*, July 2, 1976.

7. "Ottawa's policy on bilingualism requires selling job, Lang says," *Globe and Mail*, June 30, 1976, p. 2.

8. Louis Tardif, "Sylvain Cloutier pleurait après l'accord CATCA-CALPA," *Le Soleil*, November 8, 1976; Geoffrey Stevens, "It may be a smart move," *Globe and Mail*, July 2, 1976, p. 6; William Johnson, "Marchand quits over air bilingualism: Government members work to patch up party split," *Globe and Mail*, July 1, 1976, pp. 1–2.

9. "Give French group full role, Clark asks," *Ottawa Citizen*, July 5, 1976; "Aujourd'hui: Les Gens de l'air rencontrent Clark," *Le Jour*, July 5, 1976.

10. "L'AGAQ critique violemment Clark," *Le Devoir*, July 7, 1976.

11. "Transcription de l'entrevue accordée par le Premier Ministre sur les ondes de Radio-Canada aux journalistes Laurent Laplante (*Le Jour*), Claude Beauchamp (*Le Soleil*) et Michel Roy (*Le Devoir*), Ottawa, le 9 juillet, 1976."

12. Arnold Bruner, "Those near-misses: Pilots blame the two-language control system," *Globe and Mail*, June 22, 1976, p. 1.

13. William Johnson, "Reports by pilots of near-collisions over Quebec part of a publicity campaign devised last year," ibid., June 25, 1976, pp. 1–2.

14. William Johnson, "Pilots won't budge in bilingual battle: 'Certainly would not accept it in instrument flying,' chief says," ibid., June 26, 1976, p. 1.

15. "Lack of consultation caused festering air traffic control situation, pilots' official says," Ottawa Bureau of the *Globe and Mail*, June 26, 1976, p. 2; William Johnson, "Two solitudes still divide Canada, letters on air dispute show," *Globe and Mail*, July 10, 1976, p. 4.

16. Douglas Fisher, "Bilingualism team misjudged resistance," *Montreal Gazette*, June 23, 1976. John Gray, "PM's problem is still bilingualism," *Ottawa Citizen*, June 25, 1976.

17. Richard Gwyn, "Confederation collapsing: Issue of Quebec in sharp focus," *Ottawa Journal*, June 26, 1976.

18. Richard Gwyn, "Language row: doubts stick," ibid., June 29, 1976.

19. Geoffrey Stevens, "An extended breather?" *Globe and Mail*, June 29, 1976, p. 6.

20. "The new attempt to legitimize bigotry," *Montreal Star*, June 25, 1976, p. A-6; "Bilingualism backlash," *Montreal Gazette*, June 23, 1976; "Aviation language issue," ibid., June 26, 1976; "Order the pilots to fly," *Ottawa Citizen*, June 26, 1976; "Unjustified disruptions," *Ottawa Journal*, June 22, 1976; "Pilots, controllers fog safety issue," *Toronto Star*, June 23, 1976; "Back to the skies," *Vancouver Sun*, June 29, 1976; "Trying to stop shouting," *Globe and Mail*, July 1, 1976, p. 6.

21. Mary Trueman et al., "Anti-French backlash sparked by airport bilingualism issue," ibid., July 5, 1976, pp. 1–9. Roger Demers, "Bilingualism is realistic," ibid., July 8, 1976, p. 7.

22. John Baldwin, "Safe, safer...unsafe? Air Canada's ex-president asks for understanding in air control issue," *Ottawa Citizen*, July 7, 1976; Jean LeMenach, "Bilingual air traffic control is essential," ibid., July 6, 1976.

23. Frank Howard and Kitty McKinsey, "The Bureaucrats," ibid., July 6, 1976, p. 2.

24. Patrick Finn, "Air industry war of words escalates," *Montreal Star*, August 20, 1976; Patrick Finn, "Is bilingualism in the air safe?," ibid., August 21, 1976. Daniel Stoffman, "Bilingualism: The going gets tougher," *Toronto Star*, July 20, 1976; Daniel Stoffman, "Total immersion courses: a success story," ibid., July 21, 1976.

25. William Johnson, "Marchand quits over air bilingualism," *Globe and Mail*, July 1, 1976, pp. 1–2. Lise Bissonnette, "L'Assemblée appuie les Gens de l'air; Dion est pessimiste," *Le Devoir*, July 2, 1976; "Air bilingualism to proceed, Dion says," *Montreal Star*, July 2, 1976.

26. Guy Deshaies, "Les Gens de l'Air dissent NON a Lang," *Le Devoir*, July 3, 1976, pp. 1, 7.

27. Richard Cleroux, "Air inquiry judges face limitation of freedom of thought, Quebec Chief Justice says," *Globe and Mail*, July 1, 1976, p. 4.

28. The Commission of Inquiry into Bilingual Air Traffic Services in Quebec, *Interim Report* (Ottawa: Supply and Services Canada, 1977), pp. 1–3.

29. "Support bilingualism Sharp tells constituents," *Toronto Star*, July 13, 1976; "John Munro se porte à la défense des Gens de l'air," *Le Devoir*, July 12, 1976; Bob Kaplan, "le bilinguisme au Canada," ibid., July 22, 1976; David Collenette, "Une entente dangereuse pour les francophones et dangereuse pour les principes de la démocratie parlementaire," ibid., July 14, 1976.

30. Jim Livingston, "CATCA participation—bilingual IFR simulation," memorandum to CATCA national council, D. J. Redden, E. St. Denis, G. Richard, G. Dion, R. Laviolette, August 20, 1976.

31. For example, Eric St. Denis, one of the test subjects, left the Montreal centre as part of the relocation program. Regarding R. Laviolette, one of the CATCA observers, see Greg Watson, "Francophone air controller rejects French," *Ottawa Citizen*, June 25, 1976.

32. See W. J. Robertson et al., "Resolution under Article 4 of the By-laws, Canadian Air Traffic Control association," June 20, 1976; CATCA, minutes of the special council meeting, Ottawa, July 12–14, 1976.

33. "Use of French in cockpits subject of discussions today," *Globe and Mail*, July 19, 1976; CATCA, "Special Council Meeting: Conference Call," July 19, 1976.

34. "Sauf dans quelques aéroports du Québec: Ottawa décrete l'unilinguisme aérien," *Le Devoir*, July 27, 1976; "Le règlement de l'air: C'est CATCA qui a imposé sa volonté!" *Le Jour*, July 27, 1976.

35. CATCA, "Special Council Meeting: Conference Call," July 20, 1976.

36. Robert MacDonald, "Controllers' Chief: Ottawa 'racist' in court action," *Toronto Sun*, July 22, 1976.

37. CATCA, "Special Council Meeting Conference Call," July 26, 1976.

38. "La récompense du chantage: 'Let bygones be bygones!'" *Le Devoir*, August 13, 1976.

39. CATCA, "National Council Meeting," September 21–23, 1976, p. 7.

40. William Shawcross, "The three errors that killed 176 in air collision," *Times* (London), November 28, 1976; Jonathan Manthorpe, "Canadian pilots awaiting report on Yugoslav crash," *Globe and Mail*, September 21, 1976.

41. PSSRB, *Decision*, pp. 5–10.

42. "La traduction des manuels d'Air Canada au cœur du litige," *Le Devoir*, August 12, 1976; Gerald LeBlanc, "Air Canada pourrait traduire ses manuels d'ici deux ans," ibid., August 13, 1976.

43. "Extraits du jugement Deschênes," *La Presse*, September 14–16, 1976.

44. Leon Levinson, "Air Canada loses court try against French-use order," *Montreal Gazette*, September 23, 1976.

45. Patrick Finn, "Airline speeds up French use," *Montreal Star*, October 15, 1976.

46. "Des précisions qui ne changent rien aux yeux des Gens de l'air," *La Presse*, September 3, 1976.

47. Léon Dion, "Le dilemne des Gens de l'Air du Québec," *Le Devoir*, September 9, 1976.

48. Guy Deshaies, "Création d'un comité d'appui aux gens de l'air," ibid., August 27, 1976.

49. Roch Desgagne, "Les Gens de l'air poursuivent la lutte de plus belle," *Le Soleil*, May 21, 1977.

50. "Quebec aids controllers on language," *Globe and Mail*, September 8, 1976.

51. Gerald LeBlanc, "Québec engage $25,000 dans le combat des Gens de l'air," *Le Devoir*, September 9, 1976.

52. "Lalonde répond à Richard," ibid., September 24, 1976.

53. Roger Demers and Pierre Beaudry, letter to Marc Lalonde (copy to Otto Lang), September 27, 1976.

54. Otto Lang, letter to AGAQ, November 2, 1976.

55. Paul Bennet, "Les francophones passent outre aux directives de Lang," Le Soleil, November 11, 1976.

56. Lise Bissonnette, "Le juge Marceau déboute les Gens de l'Air," Le Devoir, January 13, 1977. Louis Marceau, "Pourquoi j'ai rejeté la requête des Gens de l'air," Le Soleil, January 13, 1977.

57. Claude Ryan, "Le bilinguisme: des jugements discordants," Le Devoir, January 14, 1977.

58. Guy Deshaies, "Les tests de français dans l'air commencent," ibid., February 15, 1977.

59. The Commission of Inquiry into Bilingual Air Traffic Services in Quebec, Interim Report (Ottawa: Supply and Services Canada, 1977), pp. 4–6.

60. André M. Garneau, letter to John P. Nelligan, Q.C., November 10, 1976.

61. CATCA, minutes of national council meeting, September 21–23, 1976.

62. Peter V. Dawson, letter to J. M. Livingston, October 4, 1976.

63. CATCA, "Special Council Meeting, Conference Call," November 5, 1976.

64. Ibid., "Minutes of fall council meeting," November 16–19, 1976.

65. CALPA, "The CALPA position on the use of two languages in air traffic control"; "The settlement of the recent air transportation disruption in Canada"; "A history of events leading to the bilingual air traffic control dispute," August 1976.

66. "Ken Maley réelu à la tête de la CALPA," Le Soleil, November 27, 1976.

67. "La CALPA condamnée pour outrage à la magistrature," ibid., February 18, 1977.

68. Hugh Whittington, "Will someone cry 'enough!'" Canadian Aviation, June 1976.

69. Hugh Whittington, "A time for cooperation," ibid., August 1976.

70. In the February 1977 Gallup poll, the Liberals led the Conservatives 41 percent to 37 percent, and by June 1977 had increased their lead to 51 percent to 27 percent.

71. Globe and Mail, February 17, 1977.

Notes to Chapter Nine

1. Sandra Gwyn, "The Surly Bonds of Bigotry," Saturday Night, April 1977, p. 18.

2. Ibid., p. 18.

3. Ibid.

4. CATCA, "Special Council Meeting—Conference Call," February 8, 1977, pp. 2–4.

5. Gwyn, "Surly Bonds of Bigotry," p. 18.

6. Commission of Inquiry into Bilingual Air Traffic Services in Quebec, transcripts of hearings, January 25, 1977, p. 551.

7. Ibid.

8. Ibid., p. 593.

9. Ibid., February 8, 1977, pp. 1576, 1577, 1581.

10. Ibid., pp. 1622–27.

11. Ann Laughlin, " 'Scare tactics' blocked at air language hearings," *Montreal Gazette*, February 10, 1977.

12. CALPA, "Headquarters Newsletter," February 21, 1977, p. 2.

13. Commission of Inquiry, transcripts, February 15, 1977, pp. 2325–26.

14. Ibid., p. 2326.

15. Ibid., March 1, 1977, pp. 2829, 2866.

16. Ibid., March 10, 1977, pp. 3870–3970.

17. Ibid., March 15, 1977, p. 4172.

18. Ibid., March 16, 1977, p. 4305.

19. Ibid., March 23, 1977, p. 4680.

20. Ibid., p. 4706.

21. Ibid., March 25, 1977, pp. 4752–4818.

22. Ibid., pp. 4820–26.

23. Ibid., pp. 4827–50.

24. Commission of Inquiry into Bilingual Air Traffic Services in Quebec (Ottawa: Supply and Services Canada, 1977), pp. 55–59.

25. Ibid., p. 70.

26. Ibid., pp. 55–59.

27. Ibid., pp. 60–66.

28. Ibid., p. 65.

29. Ibid., p. 70.

30. Ibid., pp. 71–73.

31. Ibid., pp. 73–75.

32. Ibid., pp. 76–80, 82.

33. Ibid., pp. 86–123.

34. Ibid., pp. 126–27.

35. House of Commons *Debates*, July 8, 1977, pp. 7473–75.

36. CALPA, "Headquarters Newsletter," July 12, 1977.

37. "Bilingual air traffic safe, inquiry concludes," *Globe and Mail*, July 9, 1977, p. 1.

38. "Des pilotes amateurs anglophones contre le bilingualisme," *Le Soleil*, July 11, 1977.

39. Roch Desgagne, "Scission au sujet de l'orientation de l'association des gens de l'air," ibid., May 24, 1977.

40. PSSRB, *Decision*, p. 142.

41. Terrance Wills, "Controllers blame politics for threat of air strike," *Vancouver Sun*, July 27, 1977.

42. John Honderich, "Air controllers reject move to avert strike," *Toronto Star*, August 6, 1977, p. 1.

43. House of Commons *Debates*, August 9, 1977, pp. 8153–90.

44. "If the slowdown continues," *Globe and Mail*, August 22, 1977, p. 6.

Notes to Chapter Ten

1. See Transport Canada, *Report of the Bilingual IFR Communications Simulation Studies. Working Document 5: Description of the Simulation and Evaluation Centre* (Ottawa: Supply and Services Canada, 1979). Henceforth reports in this group will be referred to as BICSS.

2. For a thorough description of the exercises, see Transport Canada, *BICSS, Working Document 2. Simulation Design Characteristics*.

3. See Transport Canada, *BICSS*, volume 1, *Summary Report and Recommendations*, pp. 56–59.

4. See ibid., volume 2, *Analyses of Communications Data*, pp. 156–57.

5. See ibid., volume 6, chapter 5, "Report of the Study Team to Examine the Feasibility of Simulating VFR/IRF Mix," pp. 93–144.

6. See Les Gens de l'Air du Québec, "Protocole d'entente entre l'Association des Gens de l'Air du Québec et Transport Canada," Sainte-Foy, Quebec, November 28, 1977.

7. See Commission of Inquiry into Bilingual Air Traffic Services in Quebec, *Final Report* (Ottawa: Supply and Services Canada, 1980), p. 68. Henceforth referred to as Commission of Inquiry, *Final Report*.

8. MOT press release number 13/78, "Air Traffic Controllers Agreement," January 27, 1978.

9. Ingrid Saumart, "La bataille judiciaire commence contre les normes d'Air Canada," *La Presse*, August 10, 1976.

10. "Les Gens de l'Air déboutés en appel," ibid., June 30, 1978. Robert Décary, "Le français dans l'air: judgment décevant," *Le Devoir*, July 4, 1978; Robert Décary, "Le français dans l'air: victoire ou défaite?" ibid., July 5, 1978.

11. Les Gens de l'Air du Québec, "Communiqué," July 24, 1978; Les Gens de l'Air du Québec, "Communiqué: Du français dans l'air sans la Cour Suprême," July 25, 1978.

12. Guy Deshaies, "Ottawa ne paraît pas vouloir intervenir malgré l'ordonnance," *Le Devoir*, July 27, 1978.

13. PSSRB, *Decision*.

14. Discussions of the results can be found in Transport Canada, *BICSS*, volumes 1 and 2; Stager, Proulx, Walsh, and Fudakowski, "Bilingual Air Traffic Control in Canada," *Human Factors* 22 (1980); 655–70; and Stager, Proulx, Walsh, and Fudakowski, "Bilingualism in Canadian Air Traffic Control," *Canadian Journal of Psychology* 34 (1980): 348–60.

15. Stager et al., "Bilingualism in Canadian Air Traffic Control," pp. 354–55.

16. Transport Canada, *BICSS*, volume 1, pp. 96–97.

17. Ibid., pp. 100–102, 150–51.

18. Ibid., pp. 40–44.

19. Ibid., pp. 45–49, 54–63.

20. Ibid., volume 2, p. 152.

21. Ibid., volume 1, pp. 45–49.

22. Ibid., pp. 50–53.

23. Ibid., pp. 113–16.

24. Commission of Inquiry, transcripts, February 5–6, 1979, pp. 4855–5010.
25. Ibid., March 13, 1979, pp. 7687–90.
26. Ibid., March 21, 1979, pp. 8072–73.
27. Ibid., p. 8039.
28. Ibid., March 28, 1979, p. 8489.
29. Ibid., p. 8491.
30. R. Dixon Speas, "Private Observations and Concerns—Bilingual IFR-ATC for Quebec Province," letter to the Commission of Inquiry, May 31, 1978.
31. Commission of Inquiry, transcripts, April 4, 1979, p. 8975.
32. CALPA, "Submission to the Commission of Inquiry into Bilingual Air Traffic Services in Quebec," April 26, 1979.
33. MOT, "Submission to the Commission of Inquiry into Bilingual Air Traffic Services in Quebec," April 5, 1979.
34. Ibid., p. 38.
35. MOT, "Notes Additionnelles du Ministère des Transports," May 9, 1979.
36. MOT, "Submission to the Commission of Inquiry into Bilingual Air Traffic Services in Quebec," April 5, 1979, p. 74.
37. Commission of Inquiry, *Final Report*, pp. 63–93, 104–8.
38. Ibid., p. 117.
39. Ibid., pp. 170–85.
40. Ibid., p. 178.
41. Ibid., pp. 205–11.
42. Ibid., pp. 186–204.
43. Ibid., pp. 217–29.
44. "Du français dans tous les aéroports du Québec," *Le Soleil*, August 21, 1979, pp. 1, 2; Lise Bissonnette, "Le ciel québécois sera bilingue," *Le Devoir*, August 21, 1979, pp. 1, 6.
45. "Ottawa agrees to bilingual air control over Quebec," *Globe and Mail*, August 22, 1979, p. 1.
46. David Blaikie, "Pilots, controllers accept bilingualism without fight," *Toronto Star*, August 23, 1979, p. 1.
47. Bernard Descôteaux, "La langue du ciel: l'AGAQ se réjouit," *Le Devoir*, August 23, 1979, p. 1; Léonce Gaudreault, "Le français dans l'air: de millions de dollars pour découvrir ce qu'on savait déjà (Roger Demers)," *Le Soleil*, August 23, 1979, p. 1.
48. "U.S. airlines will 'learn to live' with Quebec bilingual air control," *Toronto Star*, August 25, 1979.
49. Mary Trueman, "Loto just first Clark giveaway, Trudeau warns," *Globe and Mail*, August 23, 1979, p. 1.
50. "PQ ministers laud Ottawa's air traffic language decision," Canadian Press report, *Port Alberni Valley Times*, August 22, 1979.
51. Keith Spicer, "An end to the holy war in the air," *Vancouver Sun*, August 30, 1979.
52. "Reinstate English controller, court says," *Globe and Mail*, February 4, 1981, p. 10.
53. Otto Lang, letter to the author, May 14, 1981.
54. Walter McLeish, interview, October 17, 1980.

55. Sylvain Cloutier, letter to the author, April 13, 1981.

56. "Le tabac interdit dans les tours de contrôle?" *Le Devoir*, December 30, 1980.

57. Raymond Breton and Gail Grant, *La Langue de travail au Québec* (Montreal: Institute for Research on Public Policy, 1981).

58. For an extended discussion of these issues, see Raymond Breton and Daiva Stasiulis, "Linguistic Boundaries and the Cohesion of Canada," in Raymond Breton, Jeffrey Reitz, and Victor Valentine, *Cultural Boundaries and the Cohesion of Canada* (Montreal: Institute for Research on Public Policy, 1980), pp. 137–328.

Notes to Chapter Eleven

1. See Albert Breton and Raymond Breton, *Why Disunity? An Analysis of Linguistic and Regional Cleavages in Canada* (Montreal: Institute for Research on Public Policy, 1980).

2. Raymond Breton and Daiva Stasiulis, "Linguistic Boundaries and the Cohesion of Canada," in Raymond Breton, Jeffrey Reitz, and Victor Valentine, *Cultural Boundaries and the Cohesion of Canada* (Montreal: Institute for Research on Public Policy, 1980), pp. 147–212.

3. Two examples of this interpretation are Un groupe d'économistes québécois, coordination par Pierre Harvey, "Le bilinguisme dans le ciel: Qui profite de la discrimination?" *Le Jour*, July 10, 1976, and Drummond Burgess, "The Backlash," *Last Post*, October 1976, pp. 18–27.

4. See Raymond Breton and Gail Grant, *La Langue de travail au Québec* (Montreal: Institute for Research on Public Policy, 1981), pp. 55–57.

5. Ibid., p. 70.

6. See Thomas Schelling, "The process of residential segregation: neighbourhood tipping," in A. Pascal, ed., *Racial Discrimination in Economic Life* (Lexington, Mass: Heath Lexington, 1972), pp. 157–82, and Thomas Schelling, "Dynamic models of segregation," *Journal of Mathematical Sociology* 1 (1971): 143–86.

7. Previous research in the area of language choice in Quebec organizations has focused on explaining variations in language use for cross-sections of Quebec organizations at a given point in time. (See Breton and Grant, *La Langue de travail*, pp. 41–86.) This approach concentrates on the internal organizational factors and attempts to explain the dynamics of language use over time. Ultimately, I see the two approaches as complimentary, not contradictory.

8. Bill Robertson, vice-president, CATCA, "To: National Council, File Note — Bilingualism Situation — Montreal ACC," December 18, 1975.

9. CATCA, minutes of national council meeting, February 29–March 3, 1976.

10. See A. MacBride et al., "Psychosocial stress among air traffic controllers during the 1976 contract dispute over bilingualism," paper presented to the annual meeting of the Royal College of Physicians and Surgeons of Canada, Montreal, February 9, 1979, and A. MacBride et al., "The psychosocial impact of a labour dispute," *Journal of Occupational Psychology* 54 (1981): 125–33.

11. J. D. Schmidt, personal letter to J. M. Livingston, October 30, 1976.

12. See M. Ornstein, H. Stevenson, and A. Williams, "Public Opinion and the Canadian Political Crisis," *Canadian Review of Sociology and Anthropology* 15, no. 2 (1978): 158–205, especially 195.

13. Ken Maley, interview with Patrick Watson, "The Watson report," CBC television, December 11, 1975; William Johnson, "Pilots won't budge in bilingual battle," *Globe and Mail*, June 26, 1976, p. 1.

14. Captain Peter K. Cranston, "Brief to the Task Force on Canadian Unity," unpublished, 1978.

15. For similar discussions, see William A. Gamson, *Power and Discontent* (Homewood, Illinois: Dorsey Press, 1968), pp. 1–38, and Raymond Breton, "The Socio-Political Dynamics of the October Events," *Canadian Review of Sociology and Anthropology* 9, no. 1 (1972): 33–56, especially 53–54.

16. Anthony Downs, *An Economic Theory of Democracy* (New York: Harper Bros., 1957).

17. "Controllers may join pilots in walkout over French use," Canadian Press report, *Globe and Mail*, August 9, 1975, p. 3. Marchand is quoted as saying, "At first sight, I don't see how we can make French official in Montreal with all the international and domestic flights it gets."

18. "The reference to a change of policy [in December 1975] is slightly overstating the situation because of our complete confidence that bilingual air traffic control could be made safe. We therefore drew small distinction between the two ways of phrasing our policy." Otto Lang, letter to the author, May 14, 1981, p. 1.

19. Breton drew a similar conclusion in his analysis of the behaviour of the federal government during the October crisis. (See note 15 above.)

20. See Henry Kissinger, *The White House Years* (Boston: Little, Brown, 1979); R. H. S. Crossman, *The Diaries of a Cabinet Minister* (London: H. Hamilton and J. Cape, 1976); Flora MacDonald, "The Minister and the Mandarins," *Options* 1 (September/October 1980): 29–31; R. MacGregor Dawson in *The Conscription Crisis of 1944* (Toronto: University of Toronto Press, 1961), pp. 69–92, details the opposition of the career officers to Defence Minister McNaughton's attempts to avert conscription by increasing enlistment.

21. For a similar discussion of the power of the bureaucracy, see Albert Breton and Ronald Wintrobe, "Bureaucracy and State Intervention: Parkinson's Law?" *Canadian Public Administration* 22, no. 2 (1979): 208–26.

22. See Graham T. Allison, *Essence of Decision: Explaining the Cuban Missile Crisis* (Boston: Little, Brown, 1971); Morton Halperin, *Bureaucratic Politics and Foreign Policy* (Washington: Brookings, 1974); Seymour M. Lipset, *Agrarian Socialism*, rev. ed. (New York: Anchor Doubleday, 1968), pp. 307–31; Richard J. Schultz, *Federalism, Bureaucracy, and Public Policy: The Politics of Highway Transport Regulation* (Montreal: McGill-Queen's University Press and The Institute of Public Administration of Canada, 1980).

23. Robert Lindsey, "Lines and Pilots Find New Setup Working Safely," *New York Times*, August 13, 1981, pp. 1, 13.

24. See G. Bruce Doern, "Rationalizing the Regulatory Decision-Making Process: The Prospects for Reform" (Economic Council of Canada Regulation Reference, September 1979), pp. 12–17; V. S. Wilson, "The Role of Royal Commissions

and Task Forces," in G. Bruce Doern and Peter Aucoin, eds., *The Structures of Policy-Making in Canada* (Toronto: Macmillan, 1971), pp. 113–29.

25. Paul Weiler, *Reconcilable Differences: New Directions in Canadian Labour Law* (Toronto: Carswell, 1980), p. 228.

26. Michael Brecher with Benjamin Geist, *Decisions in Crisis: Israel, 1967 and 1973* (Berkeley: University of California Press, 1980), pp. 341–406.

27. Ole R. Holsti, "Limitations of Cognitive Abilities in the Face of Crisis," in C. F. Smart and W. T. Stanbury, eds., *Studies on Crisis Management* (Montreal: Institute for Research on Public Policy, 1978), pp. 39–55.

28. Allison, *Essence of Decision*, p. 166.

29. Chris Argyris, "Some Limits of Rational Man Organization Theory," *Public Administration Review* (May/June 1973): 253–67, especially 259–61.

30. Colin Campbell, "The President's Advisory System under Jimmy Carter: From Spokes in a Wheel to Wagons in a Circle," paper presented to the annual meeting of the American Political Science Association, Washington, D.C., August 1980.

31. Anthony Downs, *Inside Bureaucracy* (Boston: Little, Brown, 1967); Michael Maccoby, *The Gamesman* (New York: Simon and Schuster, 1976).

32. Two notable studies in psychohistory are Erik H. Erikson, *Gandhi's Truth: On the Origins of Militant Nonviolence* (New York: Norton, 1969), and A. L. and J. L. George, *Woodrow Wilson and Colonel House: A Personality Study* (New York: Dover, 1964).

33. A good approach to the study of the influence of personality is Fred I. Greenstein, *Personality and Politics* (Chicago: Markham, 1969).

34. For an explanation of consociationalism, see R. J. Van Loon and M. S. Whittington, *The Canadian Political System: Environment, Structure, and Process* (Toronto: McGraw-Hill Ryerson, 1976), pp. 58–75. Lijphart's views can be found in A. Lijphart, *The Politics of Accommodation: Pluralism and Democracy in the Netherlands* (Berkeley: University of California Press, 1968); *Democracy in Plural Societies: A Comparative Exploration* (New Haven: Yale University Press, 1977); "Consociational Democracy," *World Politics* 21 (1969): 207–25; and "Cultural Diversity and Theories of Political Integration," *Canadian Journal of Political Science* 4 (1971): 1–12.

35. There has been substantial debate over the applicability of this model to Canada. See K. D. McRae, *Consociational Democracy: Political Accommodation in Segmented Societies* (Toronto: McClelland and Stewart, 1974); Robert Presthus, *Elite Accommodation in Canadian Politics* (Cambridge: Cambridge University Press, 1973); William Irvine, "Cultural Conflict in Canada: The Erosion of Consociational Politics," Ph.D. thesis, Yale University, 1971; S. B. Wolinetz, "The Politics of Non-Accommodation in Canada," paper presented to the annual meeting of the Canadian Political Science Association, London, Ontario, May 1978.

36. Richard Simeon, *Federal-Provincial Diplomacy* (Toronto: University of Toronto Press, 1972), pp. 54–60.

37. V. S. Wilson, "Language Policy," in G. B. Doern and V. S. Wilson, eds., *Issues in Canadian Public Policy* (Toronto: Macmillan, 1974), pp. 235–83.

38. Soderlund et al. studied the press treatment of several issues affecting national unity in 1976 (air traffic control language, the Quebec election, the

Olympic Games, Quebec separatism, patriation of the BNA Act, federal language policy, Quebec language policy, and bilingualism in general) and found that the treatment of bilingual air traffic control in both the English and French papers was the most divisive of all issues discussed, in the sense that editorials tended to support either AGAQ or CATCA-CALPA without qualification, rather than emphasizing the merits of both sides of the dispute and urging compromise. W. C. Soderlund et al., "Prelude to the 'National Unity Crisis': Newspaper Coverage of Issues Affecting Political Integration in Canada during 1976," paper presented to the annual meeting of the Canadian Political Science Association, London, Ontario, May 1978.

39. See Arthur Siegel, "French and English Broadcasting in Canada: A Political Evaluation," paper presented to the annual meeting of the Canadian Political Science Association, London, Ontario, May 1978.

40. For a discussion of the lack of technical expertise among reporters, see Tom Kent et al., *Royal Commission on Newspapers* (Ottawa: Supply and Services Canada, 1981), pp. 168–70.

41. One factor contributing to the difficulty of controlling the situation by means of elite accommodation was the ease with which the controllers and pilots could be mobilized. Both had free access to long-distance telephones and two-way radios. In the case of the controllers, news would be spread along the national network of hotlines (with the exaggeration and misinformation that characterizes repeatedly relayed messages) to controllers in the entire country, in minutes. Thus, the opinions of the membership could be quickly conveyed to the leadership, influencing their action. This phenomenon was noticed many years ago in S. Lipset, M. Trow, and J. Coleman, *Union Democracy: The International Politics of the International Typographical Union* (Garden City, N.J.: Anchor Doubleday, 1965), pp. 206–7, 302–3, 467. They explained the extraordinarily democratic nature of that union at least partially as a result of the relative ease of communications within it.

42. Hubert Guindon, "The Future of the PQ," *Canadian Forum*, March 1981, pp. 20, 21, 39, 40.

Index

31–36; and BILCOM report, 47–48,
50; and Finley committee, 64–66;
and simulation exercises, 69, 82–83,
106–7, 160–61, 191–97, 201–5; at
Montreal centre, 74–75; at St.
Hubert, 108–9; and Commission of
Inquiry, 178–79, 181, 184–86,
207–12; in future 217–19. *See also*
CATCA; CALPA; AGAQ
Bilingual Communications (BILCOM)
study, 44–45, 69, 88, 100–101,
230–31, 253; organization, 38–39,
43; results, 47–48; response of aviation organizations, 48–50, 55–59
Bilingual IFR Communications Simulation Studies (BICSS): research
design, 193–94, 197; research experience, 194, 196–98; analysis of data,
201–5; discussion at Commission of
Inquiry, 206–10
Bilingualism: Official Languages Act,
25–26, 28, 40, 73, 90, 94, 169, 200;
government policy, 135, 139–40,
160; Parliamentary resolution, 29,
78, 244; public opposition in English
Canada, 60, 61, 87–88, 97, 128, 158,
244–45; in organizations, 218–19,
221–24. *See also* CATCA; CALPA;
SCAQ; Commission of Inquiry
Bourassa, Robert, 48, 153
Brecher, Michael, 239–40
British Airways, 127, 131
Broadbent, Ed, 132, 138, 140, 187
Buisson, Roger, 39, 73–74
Bureaucracy: lack of coordination, 40;
covert opposition to government
policy, 233–35. *See also* Ministry of
Transport
Burns, Robert, 167

Campbell, J. R., 17, 28, 29
Canadian Air Line Pilots Association
(CALPA), 32, 41, 45, 71, 77, 106,
108–9, 115, 156, 157, 164, 190, 201,
231; structure and functions, 19,
253; and BILCOM report, 49, 50,
56–57, 58–59, 60–61, 63, 64–65, 66;
publicity campaign, 83–85, 88,
89–90, 96; and Commission of
Inquiry, 101–2, 103–4, 116, 161,
177–78, 180, 183, 185, 186, 187,

193, 206, 208–9, 211, 212–13, 214;
and pilots' strike, 126, 127–28,
129–30, 131–32, 133–34, 137–39,
142–45, 148–49, 150, 172–73, 227,
239, 240
Canadian Air Traffic Control Association (CATCA), 27–28, 29–30, 39,
41–42, 64, 66, 108, 189–90, 218,
233–34, 241; structure and functions, 16–17, 253; and Montreal
control centre, 24–25, 30, 46, 50,
75, 224; and BILCOM report, 57,
63; publicity campaign, 83, 85,
95–97; collective bargaining, 1976
contract, 76, 90–95, 97–100, 104,
109–13, 119, 120–22, 124; and
Commission of Inquiry, 106–7,
116–17, 161, 176, 178–80, 181–82,
183–84, 187–88, 198, 206–7, 208,
210, 212–13; and pilots' strike, 129,
137, 138, 139, 140–43, 145–47,
149–50, 226–27, 231–32; internal
bilingualism, 38, 42, 162, 171–72;
litigation, 125, 163–64, 171; disaffiliation hearing, 189, 200–201
Canadian Owners and Pilots Association (COPA), 63, 66, 85, 106, 108,
193, 198, 213; function, 57, 253;
attitude towards bilingual air traffic
control, 57, 64, 188
Carter, President James, 242
Cattanach, Justice, 173
Charbonneau, Guy, 41, 228
Charette, Guy, 39–40, 41, 44, 159
Charlebois, Michel, 147, 159
Charles DeGaulle Airport, 119–20,
123–24
Chouinard, Julien, 133, 160, 184
Chrétien, Jean, 50, 76, 92, 95, 123,
127, 132, 144, 159, 224
Circuit, 7–8, 10
Clark, Joe, 130, 138, 140, 155–56, 187,
212–14, 247
Clearance, 9, 193, 204, 251
Cloutier, Sylvain, 59, 217; background
and personality, 50, 51, 237–39;
deputy minister of transport, 67–70,
73–76, 85, 89, 97, 99–100, 105,
114–17, 155, 168, 170, 213, 216,
230–33; activity during pilots' strike,
119, 126, 138–39, 141, 146–47, 150

Nadeau, Pierre, 107
Nielsen, Erik, 84
Nelligan, John, 125, 149, 171, 189
New Democratic Party (NDP), 125,
   132, 187, 190
Notice to airmen (NOTAM), 45, 58,
   65, 69–70, 71, 104
Novakowski, Archie, 69, 177–78

O'Connor, Tom, 92, 98–100, 102–3
O'Donnell, John J., 60, 87, 137
O'Grady, Captain, 89
Office de la Langue Française, 48,
   107, 258n25
O'Neill, Louis, 214
Osbaldeston, Gordon, 46

Parti Québécois, 4, 88, 99, 153, 168,
   172, 174, 199, 220, 247
Patenaude, Jean-Luc, 217, 221; personality and background, 37, 53, 62;
   AGAQ publicity director, 61–62, 75,
   94, 113, 147, 159, 231, 245; and
   CATCA, 39, 42, 46–47, 75, 109–10,
   121, 137, 141, 150, 162, 172; and
   Commission of Inquiry, 176, 181,
   205, 209, 247
Pelletier, Gerard, 28
Peppler, William, 64
Personality: influence of, on public
   policy, 3, 237–43
Peters, Desmond: Quebec City airport
   incident, 43–44; Quebec City airport
   safety study, 44–45, 64, 100; Commission of Inquiry testimony, 181,
   183, 257n16
Pitfield, Michael, 123
Pitre, Maurice, 72, 170
Positive control, 19
Positive control zones (PCZ), 10–11,
   22–23, 184
Pratte, Justice Louis, 200
Proulx, Pierre: background and personality, 28–29, 160, 194; and air traffic
   control implementation study, 28–
   29; director of simulation exercises,
   160–61, 167–68, 170, 193–98, 201,
   235; Commission of Inquiry testimony, 205–6, 209–10; director of air
   traffic services, 215

Public opinion: regarding bilingualism,
   97, 128; regarding Liberals' popularity, 79, 99, 145, 174
Public Service Staff Relations Board
   (PSSRB), 92, 94, 189, 200–201, 262

Quebecair, 48, 131, 229
Quebec City airport, 23, 43, 44, 45, 68,
   86, 102, 221
Quebec Government Air Service. See
   Quebec Government Aviation
   Service
Quebec Government Aviation Service,
   40, 48, 56, 61, 63, 65, 217, 229

Radar, 9, 12, 13, 16. See also JETS;
   IFR
Redden, Don, 193–95, 197, 198
Richard, Clément, 88, 114, 159, 161,
   162, 167, 168–69, 246
Richardson, G. D., 180, 182–83
Robertson, Bill: president of CATCA,
   16–17, 201, 212–13; disappearance
   during pilots' strike, 125, 149; vice-
   president of CATCA, 76, 91, 97,
   120, 162, 176, 224; testimony to
   Commission of Inquiry, 181–82
Roy, Michel, 73, 113–14, 263n46
Ryan, Claude, 169

Sadlier-Brown, Peter, 92, 98–100,
   102–3, 124
Ste.-Marie, Benoit, 56, 114
Saunders, Paul, 43
Sauvé, Jeanne, 153, 155
Scott, G. A., 25
Simard, Gilles, 56
Simeon, Richard, 244
Sinclair, Justice W. R., 87, 133, 160,
   184
Skinner, George, 82, 114
Snow, James, 137
Speas, R. Dixon, 207–8, 212
Spicer, Keith: commissioner of official
   languages, 49, 62–63, 86–87, 88,
   166; and Finley Committee, 63–64,
   66–67; visit to Montreal control
   centre, 73; response to pilots' strike,
   154; and Commission of Inquiry,
   87, 115, 133–34, 215, 231, 238

DATE

LOWE-MARTIN No. 1137